# NEW CENTURY BIBLE
# COMMENTARY

*General Editors*

RONALD E. CLEMENTS
(Old Testament)

MATTHEW BLACK
(New Testament)

# EZRA, NEHEMIAH, ESTHER

# THE NEW CENTURY BIBLE COMMENTARIES

EXODUS (J. P. Hyatt)
DEUTERONOMY (A. D. H. Mayes)
JOSHUA, JUDGES, RUTH (John Gray)
1 and 2 CHRONICLES (H. G. M. Williamson)
EZRA, NEHEMIAH, ESTHER (D. J. A. Clines)
JOB (H. H. Rowley)
PSALMS Volumes 1 and 2 (A. A. Anderson)
ISAIAH 1–39 (R. E. Clements)
ISAIAH 40–66 (R. N. Whybray)
EZEKIEL (John W. Wevers)
THE GOSPEL OF MATTHEW (David Hill)
THE GOSPEL OF MARK (Hugh Anderson)
THE GOSPEL OF LUKE (E. Earle Ellis)
THE GOSPEL OF JOHN (Barnabas Lindars)
THE ACTS OF THE APOSTLES (William Neil)
ROMANS (Matthew Black)
1 and 2 CORINTHIANS (F. F. Bruce)
GALATIANS (Donald Guthrie)
EPHESIANS (C. Leslie Mitton)
PHILIPPIANS (Ralph P. Martin)
COLOSSIANS AND PHILEMON (Ralph P. Martin)
1 and 2 THESSALONIANS (I. Howard Marshall)
THE PASTORAL EPISTLES (A. T. Hanson)
1 PETER (Ernest Best)
JAMES, JUDE, 2 PETER (E. M. Sidebottom)
THE JOHANNINE EPISTLES (K. Grayston)
THE BOOK OF REVELATION (G. R. Beasley-Murray)

*Other titles are in preparation.*

# NEW CENTURY BIBLE COMMENTARY

*Based on the Revised Standard Version*

# EZRA, NEHEMIAH, ESTHER

D. J. A. CLINES

WM. B. EERDMANS PUBL. CO., GRAND RAPIDS

MARSHALL, MORGAN & SCOTT PUBL. LTD., LONDON

*For Miriam*

Copyright © Marshall Morgan & Scott (Publications) 1984
All rights reserved
Printed in the United States of America
for
Wm. B. Eerdmans Publishing Company
255 Jefferson Ave. S.E., Grand Rapids, MI 49503
and
Marshall Morgan & Scott
3 Beggarwood Lane
Basingstoke, Hants, U.K.

ISBN: 0 551 01118 1


Library of Congress Cataloging in Publication Data

Clines, David J. A.
Ezra, Nehemiah, Esther.

(New century Bible commentary)
Bibliography: p. xv
Includes index.
1. Bible. O.T. Ezra — Commentaries. 2. Bible.
O.T. Nehemiah — Commentaries. 3. Bible. O.T.
Esther — Commentaries. I. Title. II. Series.
BS1355.3.C55   1984      222      84-18883

ISBN 0-8028-0017-3

# CONTENTS

PREFACE      vii

ABBREVIATIONS      ix

SELECT BIBLIOGRAPHY      xv

## INTRODUCTION TO EZRA-NEHEMIAH      1

I   The Canonical Books of Ezra-Nehemiah and their
relation to extra-canonical literature      2
II   Sources of Ezra-Nehemiah      4
III   Composition of Ezra-Nehemiah      9
   1  *Method of composition*      9
   2  *Date of composition*      12
IV   Historical background and problems      14
   *The date of Ezra's coming to Jerusalem*      16
V   Purpose and theology of the Chronicler      25
VI   Analysis of Ezra-Nehemiah      31

## COMMENTARY ON EZRA      33

## COMMENTARY ON NEHEMIAH      135

## INTRODUCTION TO ESTHER      251

I   Contents of the Book of Esther      252
II   Canonicity      254
III   Historicity      256
IV   The function of the Book of Esther      261
V   The Book of Esther and the Festival of Purim      263
VI   Literary influences on the Book of Esther      266
VII   Theology of the Book of Esther      268
VIII   Date of Composition      271
IX   Analysis of the Book of Esther      272

## COMMENTARY ON ESTHER      273

INDEX OF AUTHORS      335

GENERAL INDEX      340

033272

# PREFACE

On the one hand, it seems perfectly natural to have a commentary on Ezra, Nehemiah, and Esther in the one volume. Three 'historical' books, from the Persian period, grouped together in our English Bibles. On the other hand, the gulf between Ezra-Nehemiah and Esther is enormous. In Ezra-Nehemiah what one is struck by is the massive actuality of names, lists, records, edicts, autobiography, memoir – somewhat battered in transmission, to be sure, and linked with stretches of 'continuity' that is nothing if not tendentious. In Esther, by contrast, it is the story, not facts, that is sacred: dialogue, plot, character are its stuff – more pliant, less palpable, undeniably more engaging. Yet they complement one another, Ezra-Nehemiah and Esther, in all kinds of obvious and subtle ways: Esther's 'secularity' to Ezra-Nehemiah's piety, Esther's evocation of mood to Ezra-Nehemiah's cumulation of detail, Esther's diaspora perspective from the Persian heartland to Ezra-Nehemiah's 'loyalist' focus on the Jewish homeland – and so on.

My thanks for the opportunity to write on these much neglected but rewarding books is gladly paid to Professor R. E. Clements, who honoured me with the invitation to contribute this volume to the New Century Bible series. He could not have known, at the time I undertook the assignment, how ignorant I was of one at least of the books here commented upon; but unwittingly he directed my attention to a book I have found more and more congenial and on which I discovered I had more to say than could be put into this commentary. Hence another study, *The Esther Scroll: The Story of the Story* (Sheffield, 1984).

This book is dedicated to my daughter Miriam, in happy memory of a long summer *en famille* in the Swiss Jura when, in between haymaking and hunting wild strawberries, the first pages were written.

Sheffield                                                    D.J.A.C.

# ABBREVIATIONS

## BIBLICAL

### OLD TESTAMENT (*OT*)

| | | | | | | |
|---|---|---|---|---|---|---|
| Gen. | Jg. | 1 Chr. | Ps. | Lam. | Ob. | Hag. |
| Exod. | Ru. | 2 Chr. | Prov. | Ezek. | Jon. | Zech. |
| Lev. | 1 Sam. | Ezr. | Ec. | Dan. | Mic. | Mal. |
| Num. | 2 Sam. | Neh. | Ca. | Hos. | Nah. | |
| Dt. | 1 Kg. | Est. | Isa. | Jl | Hab. | |
| Jos. | 2 Kg. | Job | Jer. | Am. | Zeph. | |

### APOCRYPHA (*Apoc.*)

| | | | | |
|---|---|---|---|---|
| 1 Esd. | Jdt. | Sir. | S 3 Ch. | Man. |
| 2 Esd. | Ad. Est. | Bar. | Sus. | 1 Mac. |
| Tob. | Wis. | Ep. Jer. | Bel | 2 Mac. |

### NEW TESTAMENT (*NT*)

| | | | | | | |
|---|---|---|---|---|---|---|
| Mt. | Ac. | Gal. | 1 Th. | Tit. | 1 Pet. | 3 Jn |
| Mk | Rom. | Eph. | 2 Th. | Phm. | 2 Pet. | Jude |
| Lk. | 1 C. | Phil. | 1 Tim. | Heb. | 1 Jn | Rev. |
| Jn | 2 C. | Col. | 2 Tim. | Jas | 2 Jn | |

### GENERAL

| | |
|---|---|
| *AASOR* | *Annual of the American Schools of Oriental Research* |
| *ABR* | *Australian Biblical Review* |
| *AD* | G. R. Driver, *Aramaic Documents of the Fifth Century B.C.*, Oxford, 1954 |
| *AfO* | *Archiv für Orientforschung* |
| *AJBA* | *Australian Journal of Biblical Archaeology* |
| *AJSL* | *American Journal of Semitic Languages and Literatures* |
| Akk. | Akkadian |
| *ANEP* | J. B. Pritchard, *The Ancient Near East in Pictures Relating to the Old Testament*, Princeton, 1954 |

| | |
|---|---|
| *ANET* | J. B. Pritchard, *Ancient Near Eastern Texts Relating to the Old Testament*, 2nd edn, Princeton, 1955 |
| *Ant.* | Josephus, *Antiquities of the Jews* |
| *AOTS* | D. W. Thomas, *Archaeology and Old Testament Study*, Oxford, 1967 |
| *AP* | A. E. Cowley, *Aramaic Papyri of the Fifth Century B.C.*, Oxford, 1923 |
| *ARAB* | D. D. Luckenbill, *Ancient Records of Assyria and Babylonia*, Chicago, 1927 |
| Aram. | Aramaic |
| Ass. | Assyrian |
| *ASTI* | *Annual of the Swedish Theological Institute* |
| *AUSS* | *Andrews University Seminary Studies* |
| *AV* | *Authorised* (King James) *Version* |
| b. | (Heb.) *ben*, 'son of' |
| *BA* | *Biblical Archaeologist* |
| *BANE* | R. de Vaux, *The Bible and the Ancient Near East*, London, 1972 |
| *BASOR* | *Bulletin of the American Schools of Oriental Research* |
| *BBB* | *Bonner Biblische Beiträge* |
| *BDB* | F. Brown, S. R. Driver and C. A. Briggs, *Hebrew-English Lexicon of the Old Testament*, Oxford, 1907 |
| *BHS* | K. Elliger and W. Rudolph, *Biblia Hebraica Stuttgartensia*, Stuttgart, 1977 |
| *Bib.* | *Biblica* |
| *BibRes* | *Biblical Research* |
| *BM* | *Beth Mikra* |
| *BMAP* | E. G. Kraeling, *The Brooklyn Museum Aramaic Papyri*, New Haven, 1953 |
| *BO* | *Bibliotheca Orientalis* |
| *BSOAS* | *Bulletin of the School of Oriental and African Studies* |
| *BTB* | *Biblical Theology Bulletin* |
| *BZ* | *Biblische Zeitschrift* |
| *BZAW* | *Beihefte zur Zeitschrift für die alttestamentliche Wissenschaft* |
| *CAD* | *The Assyrian Dictionary of the Oriental Institute of the University of Chicago*, 1956– |
| *CBQ* | *Catholic Biblical Quarterly* |
| *CTM* | *Concordia Theological Monthly* |
| *DOTT* | D. Winton Thomas (ed.), *Documents from Old Testa-* |

|         | *ment Times*, Edinburgh and London, 1958 |
|---------|-------------------------------------------|
| *EB*    | T. K. Cheyne and J. S. Black (eds), *Encyclopaedia Biblica*, 4 vols, London, 1899–1903 |
| ET      | English translation |
| *EVV*   | English Versions (used where *AV*, *RV* and *RSV* agree) |
| *ExpT*  | *Expository Times* |
| GKC     | W. Gesenius, E. Kautzsch and A. E. Cowley, *Hebrew Grammar*, Oxford, 2nd edn, 1910 |
| *HTR*   | *Harvard Theological Review* |
| *HUCA*  | *Hebrew Union College Annual* |
| *IB*    | *Interpreter's Bible* |
| *ICC*   | *International Critical Commentary* |
| *IDB*   | G. A. Buttrick (ed.), *The Interpreter's Dictionary of the Bible*, 4 vols, New York and Nashville, 1962 |
| *IDBS*  | K. Crim (ed.), *The Interpreter's Dictionary of the Bible. Supplementary Volume*, Nashville, 1976 |
| *IEJ*   | *Israel Exploration Journal* |
| *JAOS*  | *Journal of the American Oriental Society* |
| *JB*    | *Jerusalem Bible* |
| *JBC*   | R. E. Brown (ed.), *The Jerome Biblical Commentary*, London, 1968 |
| *JBL*   | *Journal of Biblical Literature* |
| *JESHO* | *Journal of the Economic and Social History of the Orient* |
| *JNES*  | *Journal of Near Eastern Studies* |
| *JPOS*  | *Journal of the Palestine Oriental Society* |
| *JPSV*  | *Jewish Publication Society Version* |
| *JQR*   | *Jewish Quarterly Review* |
| *JR*    | *Journal of Religion* |
| *JRAS*  | *Journal of the Royal Asiatic Society* |
| *JSOT*  | *Journal for the Study of the Old Testament* |
| *JSS*   | *Journal of Semitic Studies* |
| *JTS*   | *Journal of Theological Studies* |
| *KAT*   | *Kommentar zum Alten Testament* |
| *LTQ*   | *Lexington Theological Quarterly* |
| LXX     | Septuagint (pre-Christian Greek version of *OT*) |
| mg      | margin |
| *MGWJ*  | *Monatsschrift für Geschichte und Wissenschaft des Judentums* |
| MS MSS  | manuscript, manuscripts |

| | |
|---|---|
| MT | Massoretic text |
| *MVAG* | *Mitteilungen der Vorderasiatisch-Ägyptischen Gesellschaft* |
| *NAB* | *New American Bible* |
| *NEB* | *New English Bible* |
| *NIDNTT* | C. Brown (ed.), *New International Dictionary of New Testament Theology*, 3 vols, Exeter, 1975–8 |
| *NIV* | *New International Version* |
| *OLZ* | *Orientalische Literaturzeitung* |
| *OTS* | *Oudtestamentische Studiën* |
| *PEFQ* | *Palestine Exploration Fund Quarterly* |
| *PEQ* | *Palestine Exploration Quarterly* |
| Pers. | Persian |
| *PJB* | *Palästina-Jahrbuch* |
| *RA* | *Revue d'Assyriologie* |
| *RB* | *Revue Biblique* |
| *REJ* | *Revue des Études Juives* |
| *RES* | *Revue des Études Semitiques* |
| *RevBibl* | *Revista Biblica* |
| *RHA* | *Revue Hittite et Asiatique* |
| *RSV* | *Revised Standard Version* |
| *RTP* | *Revue de Théologie et de Philosophie* |
| *RV* | *Revised Version* |
| SB | H. L. Strack and P. Billerbeck, *Kommentar zum Neuen Testament aus Talmud und Midrasch*, 6 vols, Munich, 1922–61 |
| *SDB* | L. Pirot (ed.), *Supplément au Dictionnaire de la Bible*, Paris, 1928– |
| *SEA* | *Svensk Exegetisk Årsbok* |
| *SJT* | *Scottish Journal of Theology* |
| *ST* | *Studia Theologica* |
| Syr. | Syriac |
| TB | Babylonian Talmud |
| *TDNT* | G. Kittel and G. Friedrich (eds), *Theological Dictionary of the New Testament*; ET by G. W. Bromiley, 10 vols, Grand Rapids, 1964–76 |
| *TDOT* | G. J. Botterweck and H. Ringgren (eds), *Theological Dictionary of the Old Testament*; ET by J. T. Willis, Grand Rapids, 1974– |
| *TGUOS* | *Transactions of the Glasgow University Oriental Society* |

| | |
|---|---|
| *THB* | *Tyndale House Bulletin* |
| *ThSt* | *Theologische Studien* |
| *TynB* | *Tyndale Bulletin* |
| Ug. | Ugaritic |
| *UT* | C. H. Gordon, *Ugaritic Textbook*, Rome, 1965 |
| *VD* | *Verbum Domini* |
| *VT* | *Vetus Testamentum* |
| *VTS* | *Supplements to Vetus Testamentum* |
| Vulg. | Vulgate (Latin version) |
| *WA* | *Weimar Ausgabe (Luthers Werke*, 1957–) |
| *WO* | *Welt des Orients* |
| *WTJ* | *Westminster Theological Journal* |
| *WZKM* | *Wiener Zeitschrift für die Kunde des Morgenlandes* |
| *ZAW* | *Zeitschrift für die alttestamentliche Wissenschaft* |
| *ZDMG* | *Zeitschrift der deutschen morgenländischen Gesellschaft* |
| *ZDPV* | *Zeitschrift des deutschen Palästina-Vereins* |
| *ZNW* | *Zeitschrift für die neutestamentliche Wissenschaft* |

# SELECT BIBLIOGRAPHY

*In the text, commentaries and some monographs are cited by Author's name alone, or with abbreviated title added. Works not included below are cited in full in the text.*

COMMENTARIES

Ackroyd, P. R., *1 & 2 Chronicles, Ezra, Nehemiah (Torch Commentary)*, London, 1973

Anderson, B. W., 'The Book of Esther', *IB*, III, pp. 821–74

Bardtke, H., *Das Buch Esther*, KAT xvii/4–5, Gütersloh, 1963

Batten, L. W., *A Critical and Exegetical Commentary on the Books of Ezra and Nehemiah*, (*ICC*), Edinburgh, 1913

Bertholet, A., *Die Bücher Esra und Nehemia*, Tübingen, 1902

Bowman, R. A., 'The Book of Ezra and the Book of Nehemiah', *IB*, III, pp. 549–819

Brockington, L. H., *Ezra, Nehemiah and Esther (New Century Bible)*, London, 1969

Coggins, R. J., *Ezra and Nehemiah (Cambridge Bible Commentary on the NEB)*, Cambridge, 1976

Dommershausen, W., *Die Estherrolle: Stil und Ziel einer alttestamentlichen Schrift*, Stuttgart, 1968

Galling, K., *Die Bücher der Chronik, Esra, Nehemia (Das Alte Testament Deutsch)*, Göttingen, 1954

Gelin, A., *Le Livre de Esdras et Néhémie (La Sainte Bible)*, Paris, 1953

Gerleman, G., *Esther (Biblischer Kommentar, Altes Testament xxi)*, Neukirchen-Vluyn, 1973

Gordis, R., *Megillat Esther*, New York, 1972

Haller, M., *Die fünf Megilloth*, Tübingen, 1940

Moore, C. A., *Esther (Anchor Bible)*, Garden City, New York, 1971

Myers, J. M., *Ezra-Nehemiah (Anchor Bible)*, Garden City, New York, 1965

North, R., 'Ezra and Nehemiah', *JBC*, pp. 426–38

Paton, L. B., *A Critical and Exegetical Commentary on the Book of Esther*, (*ICC*), Edinburgh, 1908

Ringgren, H., 'Esther', in H. Ringgren and A. Weiser, *Das Hohe Lied, Klagelieder, Das Buch Esther (Das Alte Testament Deutsch xvi)*, Göttingen, 1958

Rudolph, W., *Esra und Nehemia samt 3. Esra*, Tübingen, 1949

Schildenberger, J. B., *Das Buch Esther (Die Heilige Schrift des Alten Testaments* iv. 3), Bonn, 1941

Schneider, H., *Die Bücher Esra und Nehemia*, Bonn, 1959

Wildeboer, G., *Das Buch Esther (Kurzer Hand-Commentar zum Alten Testament* xvii), Tübingen, 1898

Witton Davies, T., *Ezra Nehemiah and Esther (Century Bible)*, Edinburgh, 1909

Wright, J. S., 'Ezra and Nehemiah', *NBC*, pp. 365–79


OTHER STUDIES

Abel, F.-M., *Géographie de la Palestine*, 2 vols, Paris, 3rd edn, 1967

Ackroyd, P. R., *Exile and Restoration*, London, 1968

Aharoni, Y., *The Land of the Bible*, London and Philadelphia, 1966

Aharoni Y., and Avi-Yonah, M., *The Macmillan Bible Atlas*, London and New York, 1968

Albright, W. F., *The Biblical Period from Abraham to Ezra*, New York, 1963 (abbreviated *BP*)

Alt, A., *Kleine Schriften zur Geschichte des Volkes Israel*, Munich, 1953 (abbreviated *KS*)

Anderson, B. W., 'The Place of the Book of Esther in the Christian Bible', *JR* 30 (1950), pp. 32–43 (= Moore, *Studies*, pp. 130–41)

Avi-Yonah, M., *The Holy Land from the Persian Conquests*, Grand Rapids, 1966

Bardtke, H., 'Neuere Arbeiten zum Estherbuch. Eine kritische Würdigung', *Ex Oriente Lux* 19 (1965–6), pp. 519–49 (= Moore, *Studies*, pp. 91–121)

Bardtke, H., *Luther und das Buch Esther (Sammlung gemeinverständlicher Vorträge und Schriften aus dem Gebiet der Theologie und Religionsgeschichte*, 240–1), Tübingen, 1964

Berg, S. B., *The Book of Esther: Motifs, Themes and Structure (SBL Dissertation Series* 44), Missoula, Montana, 1979

Berg, S. B., 'After the Exile: God and History in the Books of the Chronicles and Esther', in *The Divine Helmsman*, ed. J. L. Crenshaw and S. Sandmel, New York, 1980, pp. 107–27

Bickerman, E. J., 'The Edict of Cyrus in Ezra 1', *JBL* 65 (1946), pp. 249–75

Bickerman, E. J., *Four Strange Books of the Bible: Jonah, Daniel, Koheleth, Esther*, New York, 1967

Bright, J., *A History of Israel*, 3rd edn, London 1971

Cazelles, H., 'Note sur la composition du rouleau d'Esther', in *Lex tua veritas: Festschrift für Hubert Junker*, eds H. Gross and F. Mussner, Trier, 1961, pp. 17–29 (= Moore, *Studies*, pp. 424–36)

Christian, V., 'Zur Herkunft des Purim-Festes', in *Alttestamentlichen Studien für F. Nötscher* (*BBB* 1), eds H. Junker and J. Botterweck, Bonn, 1950, pp. 33–7

Cohen, A. D., ' "Hu Ha-Goral": The Religious Significance of Esther', *Judaism* 23 (1974), pp. 87–94 (= Moore, *Studies*, pp. 122–9

Cook, H. J., 'The A-Text of the Greek Versions of the Book of Esther', *ZAW* 81 (1969), pp. 369–76

Cosquin, E., 'Le prologue-cadre des Mille et une Nuits. Les légendes perses et le livre d'Esther', *RB* 18 (1909), pp. 7–49, 161–97

Cowley, A., *Aramaic Papyri of the Fifth Century B.C.*, Oxford, 1923

Danby, H., *The Mishnah*, Oxford, 1933

Daube, D., 'The Last Chapter of Esther', *JQR* 37 (1946–7), pp. 139–47

de Vaux, R., *Ancient Israel. Its Life and Institutions*, London, 1961

Douglas, J. D. (ed.), *The New Bible Dictionary*, London, 1962

Driver, G. R., *Aramaic Documents of the Fifth Century B.C.*, Oxford, 1954

Ehrlich, A. B., *Randglossen zur Hebräischen Bibel*, 7 vols, Leipzig, 1908–14, rp 1968

Eissfeldt, O., *The Old Testament. An Introduction*, Oxford, 1965

Ellenbogen, M., *Foreign Words in the Old Testament*, London, 1962

Finkel, J., 'The Author of the Genesis Apocryphon Knew the Book of Esther' [Hebrew], in *Essays on the Dead Sea Scrolls in Memory of E. L. Sukenik*, ed. Y. Yadin, Jerusalem, 1961, pp. 163–82

Fohrer, G., *Introduction to the Old Testament*, London, 1968

Frye, R. N., *The Heritage of Persia*, London, 1966

Galling, K., *Studien zur Geschichte Israels im persischen Zeitalter*, Tübingen, 1964

Gan, M., 'The Book of Esther in the Light of the Story of Joseph in Egypt' [Hebrew], *Tarbiz* 31 (1961–2), pp. 144–9

Gaster, T. H., *Purim and Hanukkah in Custom and Tradition*, New York, 1950

Gehman, H. S., 'Notes on the Persian Words in the Book of Esther', *JBL* 43 (1924), pp. 321–8 (= Moore, *Studies*, pp. 235–42)

Gerleman, G., *Studien zu Esther: Stoff–Struktur–Stil–Sinn* (*Biblische Studien* 48), Neukirchen-Vluyn, 1966, pp. 1–48 (= Moore, *Studies*, pp. 308–49)

Gordis, R., 'Studies in the Esther Narrative', *JBL* 95 (1976), pp. 43–58 (= Moore *Studies*, pp. 408–23)

Gordis, R., 'Religion, Wisdom and History in the Book of Esther—A New Solution to an Ancient Crux', *JBL* 100 (1981), pp. 359–88

Gunkel, H., *Esther*, Tübingen, 1916

Harrison, R. K., *Introduction to the Old Testament*, London, 1970

Haupt, P., 'Critical Notes on Esther', *AJSL* 24 (1907f.), pp. 97–186
(= Moore, *Studies*, pp. 1–90)

Horn, S. H., 'Mordecai, A Historical Problem', *Biblical Research* 9
(1964), pp. 14–25

Hoschander, J., *The Book of Esther in the Light of History*, Philadelphia, 1923

Humphreys, W. L., 'A Life-Style for Diaspora: A Study of the
Tales of Esther and Daniel', *JBL* 92 (1973), pp. 211–23

Jeremias, J., *Jerusalem in the Time of Jesus*, London, 1969

Jones, B. W., 'Two Misconceptions about the Book of Esther',
*CBQ* 39 (1977), pp. 171–81 (= Moore, *Studies*, pp. 437–47)

Josephus, *Antiquities of the Jews*

Josephus, *The Jewish War*

Kellermann, U., *Nehemia Quellen Überlieferung und Geschichte*, 1967

Kent, R. G., *Old Persian. Grammar, Texts, Lexicon*, New Haven,
2nd edn, 1953

Kenyon, K., *Jerusalem*, London, 1967

Knox, R. A., *The Holy Bible. A Translation from the Latin Vulgate
in the Light of the Hebrew and Greek Originals*, New York, 1955

Kraeling, E. G., *The Brooklyn Museum Aramaic Papyri*, New Haven,
1953

Lebram, J. C. H., 'Purimfest und Estherbuch', *VT* 22 (1922), pp.
208–22 (= Moore, *Studies*, pp. 205–19)

Lewy, J., 'The Feast of the 14th Day of Adar', *HUCA* 14 (1939),
pp. 127–51 (= Moore, *Studies*, pp. 160–84)

Loader, J. A., 'Esther as a Novel with Different Levels of Meaning',
*ZAW* 90 (1978), pp. 417–21

Martin, R. A., 'Syntax Criticism of the LXX Additions to the Book
of Esther', *JBL* 94 (1975), pp. 65–72 (= Moore, *Studies*, pp.
595–602)

del Medico, H. E., 'Le cadre historique des fêtes de Hanukkah et
de Purim', *VT* 15 (1965), pp. 238–70

Meinhold, A., 'Die Gattung der Josephsgeschichte und des Estherbuches: Diasporanovelle II', *ZAW* 88 (1976), pp. 79–93 (=
Moore, *Studies*, pp. 284–305)

Meinhold, A., 'Theologische Erwägungen zum Buch Esther', *TZ*
34 (1978), pp. 321–33

Meyer, E., *Die Entstehung des Judentums*, Halle, 1896

Millard, A. R., 'The Persian Names in Esther and the Reliability
of the Hebrew Text', *JBL* 96 (1977), pp. 481–8

Miller, C. H., 'Esther's Levels of Meaning', *ZAW* 92 (1980), pp.
145–8

Moore, C. A., 'A Greek Witness to a Different Hebrew Text of
    Esther', *ZAW* 79 (1967), pp. 351–8 (= Moore, *Studies*, pp.
    521–8)
Moore, C. A., 'On the Origin of the LXX Additions to the Book
    of Esther', *JBL* 92 (1973), pp. 382–93 (= Moore, *Studies*, pp.
    369–86)
Moore, C. A., 'Archaeology and the Book of Esther', *BA* 38 (1975),
    pp. 62–79 (= Moore, *Studies*, pp. 369–86)
Moore, C. A., *Daniel, Esther, and Jeremiah: The Additions* (*Anchor
    Bible*), Garden City, New York, 1977
Moore, C. A., *Studies in the Book of Esther*, New York, 1982
Morris, A. E., 'The Purpose of the Book of Esther', *ExpT* 42
    (1930–1), pp. 124–8 (= Moore, *Studies*, pp. 142–6)
Mowinckel, S., *Studien zu dem Buche Esra-Nehemia*, 3 vols, Oslo
    1964–1965
Myers, J. M., *The World of the Restoration*, Englewood Cliffs, NJ,
    1968
Noth, M., *The History of Israel*, London, 2nd edn, 1960
Noth, M., *Die israelitischen Personnamen*, Stuttgart, 1928
Noth, M., *Überlieferungsgeschichtliche Studien I*, Halle, 1943
Oesterley, W. O. E., *A History of Israel*, London, 1932
Oesterley, W. O. E., and Robinson, T. H., *An Introduction to the
    Books of the Old Testament*, London, 1934
Olmstead, A. T., *History of the Persian Empire*, Chicago, 1948
Pfeiffer, R. H., *Introduction to the Old Testament*, New York, 1952
Porten, B., *Archives from Elephantine. The Life of an Ancient Jewish
    Military Colony*, Berkeley, Ca., 1968
Riessler, P., 'Zu Rosenthals Aufsatz, Bd. xv, S. 278ff.', *ZAW* 16
    (1896), p. 182
Ringgren, H., 'Esther and Purim', *SEA* 20 (1956), pp. 5–24 (=
    Moore, *Studies*, pp. 185–204)
Rosenthal, L. A., 'Die Josephsgeschichte mit den Büchern Ester
    und Daniel verglichen', *ZAW* 15 (1895), pp. 278–84 (= Moore,
    *Studies*, pp. 277–83)
Rosenthal, L. A., 'Nochmals der Vergleich Ester, Joseph, Daniel',
    *ZAW* 17 (1897), pp. 125–8
Rowley, H. H., 'The Chronological Order of Ezra and Nehemiah',
    in *The Servant of the Lord*, London, 2nd edn, 1965, pp. 135–68
Rowley, H. H., 'Nehemiah's Mission and its Background', in *Men
    of God*, London, 1963, pp. 211–45
Schaeder, H. H., *Iranische Beiträge*, I, Halle, 1930
    *Esra der Schreiber*, Tübingen, 1930
Simons, J., *The Geographical and Topographical Texts of the Old
    Testament*, Leiden, 1959

Simons, J., *Jerusalem in the Old Testament*, Leiden, 1952

Stiehl, R., 'Esther, Judith, und Daniel', in F. Altheim and R. Stiehl, *Die aramäische Sprache unter den Achaimeniden*, I, Frankfurt-am-Main, 1963, pp. 195–213

Striedl, H., 'Untersuchung zur Syntax und Stilistik des hebräischen Buches Esther', *ZAW* 55 (1937), pp. 73–108

Talmon, S., 'Wisdom in the Book of Esther', *VT* 13 (1963), pp. 419–55

Torrey, C. C., *The Chronicler's History of Israel*, New Haven, 1954

Torrey, C. C., *The Composition and Historical Value of Ezra-Nehemiah*, Giessen, 1896

Torrey, C. C., *Ezra Studies*, Chicago, 1910

Torrey, C. C., 'The Older Book of Esther', *HTR* 37 (1944), pp. 1–40 (= Moore, *Studies*, pp. 448–87)

Weiser, A., *Introduction to the Old Testament*, London, 1961

Wellhausen, J., *Prolegomena to the History of Ancient Israel*, Edinburgh, rp 1951

Wellhausen, J., 'Die Rückkehr der Juden aus dem babylonischen Exil', in *Nachrichten von der königliche Gesellschaft der Wissenschaften zu Göttingen. Phil.-hist. Klasse*, Göttingen 1895, pp. 166–86

Wright, J. S., *The Building of the Second Temple*, London, 1958

Wright, J. S., *The Date of Ezra's Coming to Jerusalem*, London, 1947

Wright, J. S., 'The Historicity of the Book of Esther', in J. B. Payne (ed.), *New Perspectives on the Old Testament*, Waco, Texas, 1970, pp. 37–47

Young, E. J., *An Introduction to the Old Testament*, London, 2nd edn, 1960

# INTRODUCTION
## to
## Ezra-Nehemiah

# INTRODUCTION TO EZRA-NEHEMIAH

## I. THE CANONICAL BOOKS OF EZRA-NEHEMIAH, AND THEIR RELATION TO EXTRA-CANONICAL LITERATURE

The books of Ezra and Nehemiah were, as the earliest Jewish and Christian lists of canonical books show, originally a single work called Ezra (see TB *Baba Bathra* 15a; Melito of Sardis (*c.* AD 170) in Eusebius, *Ecclesiastical History* 4.26.14). The division into two is first attested by Origen (AD 185–254; in Eusebius, *Ecclesiastical History* 6.25.2), and confirmed by Jerome (AD 342–420; *Prologus Galeatus*), whose Vulgate contained a 'book of Ezra' and a 'book of Nehemiah'. Only as late as AD 1448, and under the influence of the Vulgate division, did Hebrew Bibles begin to appear with Ezra and Nehemiah distinguished (see H. B. Swete, *An Introduction to the Old Testament in Greek* [1900], pp. 197–230).

Ezra-Nehemiah is obviously closely connected with Chronicles, not only because it shares its language, style, and interests, but also because it begins (Ezr. 1:1ff.) with a repetition of the concluding verses of 2 Chronicles (36:22f.). These facts make it likely that Ezra-Nehemiah originally formed part of the same work as 1–2 Chronicles, or at least that its narrative of post-exilic times was designed by the Chronicler as a sequel to his pre-exilic history. (For views that the Chronicler was not the author of the books of Ezra and Nehemiah, see below on Composition, Section III.)

Ezra-Nehemiah has always appeared in Jewish and Western Christian canonical lists, though in the Syrian church both it and Chronicles find no place. The position in the order of biblical books assigned to Ezra-Nehemiah has, however, varied greatly in different traditions. The order in our English Bibles, according to which Ezra-Nehemiah logically follows Chronicles, which is in turn preceded by the older history of Samuel and Kings, derives ultimately from the Alexandrian tradition (both in some important manuscripts of the Septuagint version and in Origen's canonical list), where the historical books preceded the poetic and prophetic books. The usual Jewish order, however, followed the division of the Old Testament into Law, Prophets, and Writings; this division allotted Joshua–2 Kings to the Prophets and left both Chronicles and Ezra-Nehemiah to the Writings (*Hagiographa*). The reason may be, as is commonly said, that the prophetic canon was closed by the time the Chronicler wrote his history. Even within the Writings, Ezra-

Nehemiah found no fixed place: in the Palestinian tradition, followed by Spanish Hebrew manuscripts, the Writings open with Chronicles and close with Ezra-Nehemiah, while in the Babylonian Talmudic tradition, followed by German and French manuscripts and by printed Hebrew Bibles, the Writings concluded with Ezra-Nehemiah and Chronicles—in that order.

Besides the canonical book of Ezra-Nehemiah, there are other works bearing the name of Ezra (or Esdras, as it is in Greek). 1 Esdras (which is to be found in the Protestant Apocrypha, but not among the Catholic deuterocanonical books) is a Greek work which contains material paralleled in Chronicles and Ezra-Nehemiah; its narrative begins with Josiah's Passover (2 Chr. 35) and ends with Ezra's reading of the law (Neh. 8), no reference being made to Nehemiah. The text keeps fairly close to the canonical books, and occasionally preserves readings superior to those of our manuscripts of Ezra-Nehemiah. Its major surplus to the canonical books is its insertion of a story concerning three pages of Darius (3:1–5:6), the third of whom is identified with Zerubbabel. It is currently a matter of debate whether 1 Esdras may be an earlier form of the canonical books (see K.-F. Pohlmann, *Studien zum dritten Esra* [1970]; H. G. M. Williamson, *Israel in the Books of Chronicles* [1977], pp. 12–36; F. M. Cross, *JBL* 94 [1975], pp. 11–14).

2 Esdras, which like 1 Esdras finds a place in the Apocrypha of the Protestant English versions, has nothing to do with the historical person Ezra. It is, with the exception of its first two and last two chapters, which are probably Christian in origin, a Jewish apocalypse recounting seven visions attributed to Ezra in the manner of anonymous authors of apocalypses (cf. 1 Enoch, 2 Baruch). The bulk of the book seems to have been composed in the late first century AD; it does not survive in its Hebrew original nor in its first translation into Greek, but only in secondary versions in Latin, Syriac, Ethiopic, etc.

The following table indicates the relationship among books bearing the name of Ezra:

| Hebrew | Greek (LXX) | Latin (Vulgate) | English |
|---|---|---|---|
| Ezra | = 2 Esdras | = 1 Esdras | = Ezra |
| (Ezra- | (later: 2,3 | 2 Esdras | = Nehemiah |
| Nehemiah) | Esd.) | = 3 Esdras | = 1 Esdras |
| 1 Esdras |  | (New | (Apocrypha) |
|  |  | Testament |  |
|  |  | appendix) |  |

| *Hebrew* | *Greek* | *Latin* | *English* |
|---|---|---|---|
| | | 4,5,6 Esdras | = 2 Esdras |
| | | (New | (Apocrypha) |
| | | Testament | |
| | | appendix) | |

2 Esdras is included in the *AV* and *RSV* Apocrypha; omitted by Luther in his 1534 Bible, it is called pseudepigraphical by many continental scholars. 4 Esdras is in the *AV* and *RSV* found in 2 Esdras 3–14, 5 Esdras is 2 Esdras 1–2, and 6, Esdras is 2 Esdras 15–16. 3–6 Esdras were added by the Council of Trent (AD 1546) to the New Testament as an appendix. But they are not deutero-canonical books (like Maccabees, Tobit) and so are omitted by many modern Catholic Bibles.

## II. SOURCES OF EZRA-NEHEMIAH

An attempt to discover the sources of the narrator and to distinguish those sources from his own editorial additions is—especially in the case of these books—not a matter of speculation and antiquarian interest, but can have a marked effect on the interpretation of particular passages. We may note, for example, the contrast between the Chronicler's assessment of the era of Nehemiah (Neh. 12:44–13:3) and Nehemiah's own record of events (13:4–31), where by recognising the tension between the editor and his source we gain a better perspective on the period than we would have if we had had only Nehemiah's or the Chronicler's account.

These appear to be the major sources of the books of Ezra and Nehemiah:

1. *The Nehemiah memoirs* (Neh. 1:1–7:73*a;* 11:1f.; 12:31–43; 13:4–31; on their exact scope, see below). This first-person narrative is unique in the Old Testament as an indisputably authentic record made by a leading statesman about affairs he was personally involved in. It has been subject to practically no editorial revision, and its vivid and direct style marks it off quite clearly from the work of the Chronicler.

The term 'memoirs' is misleading, for Nehemiah is not simply recording his reminiscences; the several appeals to God to 'remember' him (5:19; 13:14, 22, 31; cf. 6:9, 14) make it plain that the document is in some sense addressed to God. S. Mowinckel compared the form and style of the Nehemiah source with ancient Near Eastern royal inscriptions on which are narrated the king's deeds in first-person form, followed by a wish for good fortune and remembrance ('Die vorderasiatischen Königs- und Fürstenin-schriften', in *Eucharisterion* (Gunkel *Festschrift*), ed. H. Schmidt (1923), pp. 278–322; *Studien*, II, pp. 50–104). E. Sellin and others have been reminded, especially by the 'remember'-formula, of votive inscriptions (e.g. the inscription of Yehawmilk of Byblos, *ANET*, p. 502; see Sellin, *Geschichte des israelitisch-jüdischen Volkes*, II [1932], p. 159; Rudolph, p. 212; Fohrer, p. 243; Eissfeldt, p. 547), while G. von Rad has seen an analogy to biographical tomb-inscriptions from Egypt ('Die Nehemia-Denkschrift', *ZAW* 76 [1964], pp. 176–87; cf. on Neh. 2:12). Others have attributed a more legal character to the document, W. Erbt, for example, describing it as a document submitted for the defence in a lawsuit at the royal court ('Esra und Nehemia', *OLZ* 12 [1909], cols. 154–61, esp. col. 155), and M. Haller as a report made by Nehemiah to Artaxerxes to safeguard himself from possible recriminations by his opponents (*Das Judentum* [²1925], p. 149).

Objections may be raised to each of these analogies, as U. Keller-mann points out (pp. 76–84). His own view is that in form and content it is closest to the psalm type of the 'prayer of the accused' (e.g. Ps. 5), a legal appeal to God against his enemies (Kellermann's emphasis on the significance of the enemies is linked with his inter-pretation of Nehemiah as the victim in a conflict within the post-exilic community between messianic Zionism and an apolitical piety; see below, section IV). That one or more of the literary forms mentioned above may have been Nehemiah's prototype is quite probable, but it has not yet been clearly shown what the formal purpose of Nehemiah's memoirs was. The Chronicler's use of them suggests strongly that they were intended by Nehemiah from the first for publication.

The exact scope of the Nehemiah memoirs is disputed (see the commentary on the relevant passages). To this list given above, Rudolph, p. 211, adds 11:20, 25*a*, part of 12:27, 30, but subtracts 12:32–36, 38f., 41f. Kellermann, pp. 8–56, esp. pp. 55f., omits (if we take no account of glosses) 7:5*b*–73*a;* 11:1f., but is otherwise close to Rudolph's view. More radical omissions from the main bulk of the Nehemiah 'memoirs', such as 1:5–11 and 2:7–9a by Batten (pp. 188f., 15), and ch. 13 by Torrey (*Composition*, pp. 44–9), have not gained acceptance. Probably we do not have the complete 'memoirs'; e.g. a more ample account of the expansion of Jerusalem may be expected than that found in 11:1f.

Written sources for some material in the Nehemiah memoirs themselves may be discerned:

(a) *The wall-builders list* (Neh. 3). It is debated whether this list formed part of the memoirs or not (see commentary), but it is almost universally agreed that it preserves genuine historical material (Kellermann, pp. 14f. Torrey thought it an independent creation of the Chronicler [*Composition*, pp. 37f.]; and H. Lusseau, in *Introduction to the OT*, ed. A. Robert [1968], p. 487, speaks of its possibly 'fictional dress').

(b) *The homecomers list* (Neh. 7:6–73a). It is again open to question whether Nehemiah included this list in his memoirs, but the majority opinion is that he did. See the commentary on Ezr. 2, where the list is also found, for details.

2. *The Ezra memoirs* (used in Ezr. 7–10; Neh. 8–9). Some of the narratives concerning Ezra are written in the first person (Ezr. 7:27–9:15), which creates a presumption that there was also a collection of Ezra memoirs which has been used by the editor (the Chronicler). The most natural assumption is that where the first-person form is used the Chronicler has reproduced more or less exactly the wording of Ezra's account, and that where Ezra is spoken of in the third person (7:1–26; 10; Neh. 8–9) he has created his own account partly on the basis of that by Ezra; so, e.g., Oesterley and Robinson, *Introduction*, p. 125; cf. Rudolph, p. 165. Some have supposed a third-person narrative source written about Ezra by a contemporary and used by the Chronicler (so, F. Ahlemann, 'Zur Esra-Quelle', *ZAW* 59 [1942f.], pp. 77–98). For details of scholarly opinion on the distinction between Ezran memoirs and the Chronicler's additions, see Pfeiffer, pp. 830f., and especially W. T. In der Smitten, *Esra. Quellen, Überlieferung und Geschichte* (1973).

There is little scholarly agreement on these issues. It has been argued by A. S. Kapelrud that stylistically no differences between the first-person and the third-person blocks of the Ezra material can be discerned, a view which casts doubt on the authenticity of the first-person narrative (*The Question of Authorship in the Ezra Narrative* [1942], pp. 95f.; similarly already, Torrey, *Studies*, pp. 240ff.; Noth, *Studien*, p. 146). If the traditional identification of the Chronicler with Ezra himself (e.g. TB, *Baba Bathra* 15a) could be maintained, as W. F. Albright attempted to do ('The Date and Personality of the Chronicler', *JBL* 40 [1921], pp. 104–24), there would be no problem; but there is little modern support for this view. However, it has been adequately shown by W. Rudolph's investigation of the language of the 'Ezra memoirs' and of the Chronicler that, with one exception, all the linguistic items shared by Ezra and the Chronicler are shared as well with other post-exilic Hebrew writing (pp. 163ff.). This does not of course of itself prove that Ezra is the author of the first-person passages, but it makes it possible. Use of the first person in a narrative is also no clear proof that the passage is authentic; it can be a literary device to create

greater vividness (cf. Ecclesiastes). But there are no compelling
reasons, as in the case of Ecclesiastes, for supposing such a device
to be employed here.

Some have taken a much more negative view of the Ezra narratives. C. C. Torrey regarded them as the Chronicler's fiction, and
Ezra himself as a figment of the Chronicler's imagination, the
personification of his own interests (*Composition*, pp. 57–63; *Studies*,
pp. 238–48). No scholar today doubts that Ezra was a historical
personage, but the value of the Ezran material is still sometimes
minimised. Thus R. H. Pfeiffer thought that Ezra 'may well have
been a devout Jew . . . in the days of Nehemiah . . . The Chronicler
. . . apparently selected Ezra for the role of founder of the guild of
the scribes and concocted his fictitious biography' (p. 833). And
according to the author of the most recent monograph on Nehemiah,
U. Kellermann, the Ezra story is a 'free midrash' of the Chronicler's
based on the one authentic element, the firman of Artaxerxes (Ezr.
7:12–23, 26) (pp. 56–69, esp. pp. 68f.; he thinks the inventory in
8:26f. may also be authentic). These views rest heavily upon the
establishment of linguistic and literary parallels between the Chronicler and the Ezran material; but while dissimilarities of style are
*prima facie* evidence for difference of authorship, similarity of style
(especially in the light of Rudolph's study, cited above) can prove
nothing, and is merely negative evidence. Even if the Ezra narratives
were written in language distinctively characteristic of the Chronicler, one could not be sure that we were dealing with anything
more than an extensive linguistic revision of an authentically Ezran
document. Only historical implausibilities or impossibilities could
tell strongly against the supposition of an Ezran substratum to the
narrative, and it, in my opinion, tells a coherent and plausible story.

What was the purpose of Ezra's memoirs? W. Rudolph believes
that they were a report to the Persian government and to Babylonian
Jewry on the results of his mission (pp. 166f.; cf. on Ezr. 9:6–15),
while F. Ahlemann has regarded them as intended for the edification
of the Judean community (*ZAW* 69 [1942f.], p. 98); but there seems
to be no clear evidence either way. W. Erbt thought they formed
part of the official record of the high priest filed in the temple
archive (*OLZ* 12 [1909], col. 160).

Within the Ezra memoirs three written sources may be noted:

(a) *the firman of Artaxerxes* (Ezr. 7:12–26), written, like other
Persian correspondence quoted in these books, in Aramaic, and
widely acknowledged to be authentic (so, e.g., Eissfeldt, pp. 555f.;
Kellermann, pp. 56–9).

(b) *the list of those who returned with Ezra* (Ezr. 8:1–14), generally
assigned to the Ezra memoirs (e.g. Eissfeldt, p. 549; Rudolph, p.

79. Fohrer, pp. 243f., thinks it an artificial list on the basis of Ezr.
2.).

(c) *the list of those who had made mixed marriages* (Ezr. 10:18–43),
not certainly a part of the Ezra memoirs, but usually thought to
reproduce some contemporary list (Eissfeldt, pp. 544, 549, attributes it to a third-person source which told of the divorces; Schneider, pp. 48f., attributes it to Ezra; Fohrer, p. 244, thinks it an
artificial list).

3. *The 'Aramaic chronicle'* (Ezr. 4:7–6:18). This section of Ezra
is written in Aramaic, and contains a number of documents purport-
ing to be the official correspondence relating to Jerusalem, strung
together with linking narrative. The natural assumption is that the
editor of Ezra (the Chronicler) has here drawn upon an Aramaic
source, which presumably told more than the story of Ezr. 4:7–6:18,
and which may well have been a chronicle concerning the early
years of post-exilic Jerusalem. It is possible that the story of Ezr.
3:1–4:6 was also contained in the Aramaic chronicle, and that the
biblical Chronicler translated it with his own elaborations or correc-
tions in Ezr. 3:1–4:6, and reproduced it word for word in 4:7–6:18.
It is clear in any case that he is responsible for its place in Ezra,
since not only is it indispensable to the story, but it is preceded and
followed by the Chronicler's own writing (4:1–6; 6:19–22).

The Aramaic chronicle contains (following references in the
Hebrew text to an accusatory document addressed to Ahasuerus
(4:7), and a possibly exculpatory document addressed to Artaxerxes
(4:8), both of which have been reproduced in the Aramaic chronicle), four documents: 1. a letter of Rehum to Artaxerxes (4:8–16);
2. Artaxerxes' reply (4:17–22;) 3. a report from the satrap Tattenai
to Darius (5:7–17); 4. a reply from Darius (6:2–12), in which is
included a copy of an earlier rescript of Cyrus (6:2–5). The authenticity of these letters, written in the official Aramaic language in
bureaucratic terminology, is today generally accepted (e.g. Eissfeldt,
p. 555; Noth, *History*, p. 306 n.2; Bowman, p. 558), though older
scholars tended to regard them as free creations of the Chronicler
(Wellhausen, 'Rückkehr', pp. 175f.; Torrey, *Composition*, pp. 5–12,
55ff.; L. E. Browne, *Early Judaism* [1920], pp. 37ff.). With our
increasing knowledge of Persian administration and of Aramaic
correspondence it has become clear that they fit perfectly into the
period of the fifth century BC (thus, for example, discovery of the
so-called 'Passover Papyrus' (*AP* 30; *ANET*, p. 491; *DOTT*, p.
259), in which the Jews at Elephantine are commanded *by the
Persian government* to keep the festival of unleavened bread, has
quite removed any suspicion that the detailed knowledge of Jewish

ritual and custom in the Aramaic documents shows them to be spurious.

4. *Lists*. There are a number of lists which did not belong to any of the Chronicler's main sources and were probably obtained by him or a later editor of Ezra-Nehemiah from temple archives:

(a) *List of family heads resident in Jerusalem* (Neh. 11:3–19), a document from about the time of Nehemiah, and possibly incorporated already by him in his memoirs.

(b) *List of country towns with Jewish populations* (Neh. 11:25–36), possibly a pre-exilic town list of uncertain relevance to the story of Nehemiah, and perhaps inserted by an editor later than the Chronicler.

(c) *List of priests and Levites from the time of Zerubbabel* (Neh. 12:1–9).

(d) *List of high priests from Jeshua to Jaddua* (Neh. 12:10f.).

(e) *List of priests and Levites from the time of Joiakim* (Neh. 12:12–21, 24ff.). The insertion of these three lists is probably due to a post-Chronicler editor. All of them have a considerable claim to being genuine, even if not entirely relevant to the period of Nehemiah.

5. *The Nehemian pledge* (Neh. 10). Though associated with the activity of Nehemiah, it probably formed no part of his memoirs, but was derived by the Chronicler from an archival document. Many scholars have separated the list of names (10:1–27) from the pledge itself (10:28–39), but it seems more probable that the document containing the pledge also contained some such list of signatories to it (cf. commentary on 10:1–27).

## III. COMPOSITION OF EZRA-NEHEMIAH

### *1. Method of Composition*

The general view taken in this commentary is that the author of 1 and 2 Chronicles was responsible for the composition of the books of Ezra and Nehemiah in more or less their present form. This appears still to be the majority view of scholars, but some important disagreements with this position ought to be noted here. On the one hand is the view that the book of Nehemiah did not originally belong to the Chronicler's work, but was incorporated into it at a relatively late date. Thus, for example, F. M. Cross argues that while in the first edition of the Chronicler's history composed *c.* 520 BC (containing 1 Chr. 10–2 Chr. 34 plus the *Vorlage* of 1 Esdr. 1–5:65) neither Ezra nor Nehemiah found a place, a second edition (soon after 458 BC) included the Ezra material as narrated in the *Vorlage* of 1 Esdras. Only in the third edition of the work (*c.* 400) was the narrative of Nehemiah attached. W. T. In der Smitten also views the addition of the Nehemiah memoirs to the Chronicler's work as a secondary development ('Die Gründe für die Aufnahme der Nehemiaschrift in das chronistische Geschichtswerk', *BZ* 16 [1972], pp. 207–21). (Among older scholars who had developed the view that the Chronicler's book did not contain the story of Nehemiah at all are S. Granild, *Ezrabogens litereare genesis* [1949], followed by Bentzen, II, p. 210; similarly W. F. Albright, *JBL* 40 [1921], p. 123; V. Pavlovský, *Bib.* 38 [1957], pp. 280f.) On the other hand is the view that the Chronicler's work never contained either Ezra or Nehemiah; thus, for example, S. Japhet whose case is built upon supposed linguistic differences between Chronicles and Ezra-Nehemiah, though with insufficient discrimination between the writing of the editor and of his sources ('The Supposed Common Authorship of Chronicles and Ezra-Nehemiah Investigated Anew', *VT* 18 [1968], pp. 330–71), and H. G. M. Williamson, whose *Israel in the Books of Chronicles* (1977) considers besides linguistic matters the textual evidence, the relationship of the Greek versions, and the ideology of the Chronicler (see my review in *Themelios* 5 [1979], pp. 29f.).

It is difficult to keep all these options open during the course of a commentary, and the attempt made in this work is to offer a coherent account of the books on the basis of the working hypothesis that the author of Chronicles is also the author of Ezra and Nehemiah. It is of course an even more hazardous undertaking than the discovery of sources to attempt to reconstruct the method by which the sources which we have identified above were welded into our present book of Ezra-Nehemiah. But there is an intriguing aspect of the form of the book that compels us to offer some kind of an hypothesis and that in fact gives us some clues. It is that the narrative of Ezra (Ezr. 7–10; Neh. 8–9) is interrupted by most of the narrative of Nehemiah (Neh. 1–7). Several explanations of this interruption have been offered:

(i) The simplest explanation is that the events of Neh. 8–9 in which Ezra was involved actually took place after Nehemiah's wall-building and are therefore recounted in proper chronological sequence (so Wright, *Date*, p. 26; Harrison, p. 1149). This view, however, entails the acceptance of some historical implausibilities: e.g. that Ezra's reading of the law, for which he had been sent in 458 BC, was not carried out until Nehemiah's arrival in 445; and that the activities of Ezra and Nehemiah overlapped, for which there is only meagre and uncertain evidence (see further, Introduction,

IV). This explanation is accordingly not followed in this commentary, but it remains worthy of serious consideration.

(ii) Another possibility is that although the material about Ezra was originally a unit, part of it has accidentally been interposed in the Nehemiah material. So, for example, W. Rudolph (pp. xxiif.) argues that the Chronicler's book originally had the following neat schema. For each of the three great leaders of the post-exilic community, Zerubbabel, Ezra, and Nehemiah, there was an account of his successful accomplishment, despite opposition, of the task he had been commissioned to perform. Zerubbabel rebuilt the temple, Ezra reinstituted the law, Nehemiah rebuilt the city. In each case the completion of the work was marked by a festival. Thus the original order of the Chronicler's book was: Ezr. 1–8; Neh. 8 (with 7:73*b*); Ezr. 9–10; Neh. 9–10; 1–7 (minus 7:73*b*); 11–13 (thus also Gelin, p. 14; Myers, p. xlv; Bowman, p. 560. A closely similar view had been propounded by Torrey, *Composition*, pp. 29–34; *Studies*, pp. 30ff., 255–8; *History*, pp. xxviiif.).

This is an attractive view, but it is difficult to imagine how this accidental transposition occurred. Rudolph has to suppose, without any concrete evidence, that Ezr. 8 originally ended with a sentence like Neh. 7:73*a*, which led to the confusion (pp. xxii, 15, 143f.). His reconstruction is further open to the objection that Neh. 9 does not naturally follow Ezr. 10 (see commentary on Neh. 9:1–37). Another explanation on the basis of scribal error was offered by P.-P. Saydon, 'Literary Criticism of the Old Testament: Old Problems and New Ways of Solution', *Sacra Pagina* I (1959), pp. 316–24, esp. p. 321: Ezra-Nehemiah was written on five scrolls, the fourth before the third (Neh. 8–10). But on this view some of the scrolls would be improbably short (the third would contain only Neh. 8–9, since Neh. 10 is probably not related; cf. commentary) and would vary in length (e.g. the first, Ezr. 1–6, would be at least twice as long as the third).

(iii) It seems preferable to regard the order of the Ezra material, not as the result of scribal error, but as deliberately intended. But by whom? According to N. H. Snaith, by an editor later than the Chronicler who dislocated the Chronicler's order of Nehemiah narratives followed by Ezra narratives (which was the historical order, according to Snaith), in order to set Nehemiah in the last and climactic position ('The Date of Ezra's Arrival in Jerusalem', *ZAW* 63 [1951], pp. 53–66, esp. pp. 64f.). Unfortunately this leaves unexplained the interposition of Ezran material in the Nehemiah story.

(iv) There remains one further possibility, that the chronological rearrangement of the Ezran material is the Chronicler's doing (so e.g. Weiser, p. 322). It is usually agreed that the Chronicler believed that Ezra preceded Nehemiah and that both were active in the reign of the same king, Artaxerxes I. In this he was not mistaken, as will be argued below in section IV. But it would not have been unnatural or improper for him to write as if these two leaders were exact contemporaries, since their work was in fact complementary. It may be suggested, therefore, that the Chronicler transferred the law-reading and penitence ceremonies (Neh. 8–9) from their original place in the Ezra memoirs to a setting in the Nehemiah memoirs for a thematic reason: to emphasise that it was an obedient and penitent community that Nehemiah brought together to inhabit the 'holy city' (Neh. 11:1). These narratives are thus intentionally interposed between Nehemiah's finding of the register of those who were by birth entitled to live in Jerusalem (7:5) and the actual removal to the capital by those who were chosen (11:1). (One minor advantage of this reconstruction is that it may spare the necessity of finding two post-Chronicler editors. For if the removal of Neh. 8–9 to its present place was the work of a post-Chronicler editor, the copying of Neh. 7, with 7:73b and part of 8:1a, into Ezr. 2 with 3:1 must have been done by a later editor still; Rudolph's attempt, p. 145, to avoid this inference is unconvincing.) If such an explanation is correct, this would be the Chronicler's second major rearrangement of his material on thematic grounds (cf. on Ezr. 4:6–24).

For a fresh approach to the subject of the Chronicler's intentions in the arrangement of his total work, see P. R. Ackroyd, *The Age of the Chronicler* (1970); 'History and Theology in the Writings of the Chronicler', *CTM* 38 (1967), pp. 501–15; 'The Chronicler as Exegete', *JSOT* 2 (1977), pp. 2–32.

## 2. Date of Composition

Whatever the solution to the problem of the order of Ezra-Nehemiah may be, it is clear that most scholars assume the existence of two authors, or rather an author (the Chronicler, author also of 1–2 Chronicles), and an editor (the 'post-Chronicler editor'). Can any dates be assigned to these two?

If, with W. F. Albright (*JBL* 40 [1921], pp. 119f.; *BP*, p. 93), we hold that the Chronicler was none other than Ezra, there is no difficulty, except to establish the exact date of Ezra's activity. Given that Ezra in fact preceded Nehemiah and that the disorder in the Ezran material is due to an editor, there is no serious objection to this view. In language, style and outlook, the Chronicler is hardly distinguishable from Ezra; 'if he was not . . . Ezra himself, he was

Ezra's spiritual son' (F. F. Bruce, *Israel and the Nations* [1963], p. 111). Only in the Chronicler's absorbing interest in the non-priestly Levites may we find a mark of distinction from the priestly Ezra.

There is little internal evidence to help determine the date of the Chronicler's work. In 1 Chr. 3:10–24 a genealogy of the line of David and Solomon apparently extends six generations beyond Zerubbabel (*c*. 520 BC); reckoning 30 years to a generation this could bring us down to *c*. 340. But in fact we should count only four generations, and even allowing the liberal figure of 30 years for a generation (Albright, *BP*, p. 113 n. 198, allows 27½ years) we would come down only to *c*. 400, while *c*. 420 would be more realistic. Zerubbabel's son Hananiah was probably born in Babylon, i.e. before 520 BC at least, and possibly before 538, so no time need be allowed for that generation; and v. 22 contains only one generation once 'the sons of Shemaiah' are deleted (note the total of 6!). See W. Rudolph, *Chronikbücher* (1955), p. 28. A similar result emerges by reckoning seven generations from Jehoiachin, born in 616 BC (Bright, *History*, p. 397). The not improbable identification of Anani (1 Ch. 3:24) with the Anani of *AP* 30.19, dated 407 BC, would confirm the date. In any case some have argued that the genealogy is a later addition to 1 Chronicles (e.g. Noth, *Studien*, I, pp. 117, 120), and thus no indication of its date. The list of high priests in Neh. 12:10f. (cf. 22f.) certainly extends beyond *c*. 400 BC for it mentions three high priests later than Nehemiah's contemporary Eliashib. It is arguable whether the last in the list, Jaddua, was indeed contemporary with Alexander the Great (*c*. 332 BC); cf. on Neh. 12:10f. But even if he were, it could always be maintained that the list had been updated well after the completion of the Chronicler's book (so, e.g., Rudolph, p. xxiv).

Arguments from the development of language are notoriously shaky. H. H. Rowley was confident that the Aramaic of these books is 'demonstrably later than that of the Aramaic papyri from Elephantine of the fifth century B.C.' ('Nehemiah', p. 217). This is highly debatable (cf. K. A. Kitchen, 'The Aramaic of Daniel', in D. J. Wiseman *et al.*, *Notes on some Problems in the Book of Daniel* [1965], pp. 31–79), and in any case an orthographical revision (perhaps even unconscious) by a later copier would adequately explain the situation, and no argument about the date of composition can be drawn.

We may safely leave aside the argument that the Chronicler's attitude to the Samaritans presupposes an established rival Samaritan community, later than 350 BC (e.g. Fohrer, p. 239), since hostility between Jews and Samaritans may be traced much further back than the fifth century, and Ezra-Nehemiah refer simply to some of the events which hastened the process towards the eventual schism (cf. J. D. Purvis, *The Samaritan Pentateuch and the Origin of the Samaritan Sect* [1968], pp. 5f., 98f.).

If Ezra arrived in Jerusalem in 398 BC, obviously the Chronicler, even if he were Ezra himself, must have written his book somewhat later than that date; if the Chronicler himself confused the order of Ezra and Nehemiah, he must have lived at least two or three generations later than Ezra. If Ezra came in 458, 437, or 427 BC, there would be little reason to doubt that his book was completed about 400 BC. On all grounds it seems most reasonable to date the Chronicler's work within a few decades of Ezra and Nehemiah.

There is even less value in attempting to date the post-Chronicler editor, because we know so little of him. U. Kellermann (pp. 110f.) believes he was a Levite of the end of the second century BC; but that rests upon rather more confident identifications of his literary activity and theological opinions than can be allowed.

## IV. HISTORICAL BACKGROUND AND PROBLEMS

The books Ezra-Nehemiah cover a period of more than a century, perhaps 140 years. Ezr. 1–6, narrating the return from exile and the rebuilding of the temple, concerns the last third of the sixth century BC, while Ezr. 7 onwards, containing the narratives of Ezra and Nehemiah, belongs to the last half of the fifth century BC. From these books we learn virtually all we know about the history of the post-exilic community. The post-exilic prophets, Haggai, Zechariah, and Malachi, together with other Old Testament literature that may be dated after the exile, afford us quite deep understanding of the thought and life of the post-exilic age, but only from Ezra-Nehemiah do we discover the outline of historical events that holds the period together. Here is a sketch of the historical reconstruction adopted in this commentary.

1. 539–515 BC. On his accession to the throne of Babylon, Cyrus (550–530 BC), in accordance with his imperial policies, gave permission for Jewish exiles to return to Judea to rebuild the Jerusalem temple (Ezr. 6:2–5; 1:2–4). In charge of the restoration of objects plundered from the temple was Sheshbazzar (on his identity, see on 1:8; 5:14). Sacrifice was reinstituted at the first opportunity and a start was made on the repair of the temple (ch. 3), but for various reasons, not least the hostility of Judea's neighbours, the work lapsed, and was resumed only in 520 BC (4:24; 5:1f.), by which time Zerubbabel had become governor of Judea. In spite of renewed

opposition (5:3–17) the temple was completed in 515 BC (6:15), the sixth year of Darius I (522–486 BC).

2. 515–458 BC. Only one verse (4:6), mentioning an accusation against the Jews, possibly to the effect that they supported the Egyptian revolt against Persia in 486 BC, relates to this period.

3. 458–457 BC. Ezra, a Jewish priest and probably also a Persian official of high standing, was commissioned by Artaxerxes I (465–424 BC) to establish and enforce the Pentateuchal law as state law in the province of Judea and to regulate the temple cult (ch. 7). After a three-month period of preparation (cf. on Neh. 7:73*b*–9:37), Ezra read the law to the populace gathered for the autumnal Festival of Booths (September, 458 BC; Neh. 8), and presumably appointed judges to act in accordance with it (cf. Ezr. 7:25). Apart from the day of national confession apparently organised by Ezra later in the same month (Neh. 9), the only other activity of Ezra's that we know of was his action over marriages contracted by Jews with non-Jews (Ezr. 9–10); he learned of these in the December of 458 BC (cf. 10:9), and the commission of enquiry that was set up completed its work by the spring of 457 (10:17). On this reconstruction, his total recorded activity occupies only a year, from the first day of the year beginning Nisan, 458, to the first day of Nisan, 457. Possibly his legal work, which involved the interpretation of the law rather than its day to day administration, occupied him for some years more in Jerusalem, but it is equally possible that he returned before very long to Babylonia. It is open to doubt whether he is mentioned again (but cf. on Neh. 12:36). It may be observed that this analysis of Ezra's activity implicitly calls into question the pre-eminent position accorded him in later tradition as 'the father of Judaism'; his establishment of formal procedures for legal decision-making and biblical interpretation cannot have been entirely novel, and the development of these procedures must have owed more to his successors than to himself.

4. *c.* 445–*c.* 430 BC. The prelude to this period, the governorship of Nehemiah, was the abortive attempt made by the Jews to rebuild Jerusalem and repair its walls which had remained broken down since the destruction of the city in 587 BC. The Samarian government was able to play upon imperial fears of sedition in the west and easily obtained authorisation for the work to be stopped and, apparently (cf. on Neh. 1:3), for what had been built to be demolished (the relevant documents are reproduced in Ezr. 4:11–22). On hearing of this, Nehemiah, who was cupbearer (obviously no lowly office) to Artaxerxes I, asked permission to go to Judea to rebuild his ancestral city. The king fulfilled his request by appointing him governor of Judea and signified his approval of Nehemiah's plans

by making a grant of timber from the royal forest for the repairing of the walls.

Nehemiah was governor of Judea for twelve years, from the spring of 445 BC, Artaxerxes' 20th year, to 434 or 433 (Neh. 5:14). His first achievement was the rebuilding of the walls, accomplished in the remarkably brief space of 52 days (6:15), in spite of threats of armed intervention by the Samarians (chs. 3–4, 6), and celebrated with a dedication ceremony (12:27–43). No less important was his project for the resettlement of Jerusalem (ch. 11), which may have included some provision of housing. Only one other episode from this governorship is recorded: his economic measures to alleviate debt (5:1–13). At some unspecifiable date after his return to the Persian court in 434 or 433 BC, he came again as governor to Judea and carried out some reforms of the religious life of the community (ch. 13). The reform pledge of Neh. 10, which belongs to this 'second governorship', was probably much indebted to him for its ideals.

Some of the historical problems which this account raises will be noted in the commentary, but the most important problem, the date of Ezra's coming to Jerusalem, requires extended treatment, since it is fundamental to our understanding of these books.

## The Date of Ezra's coming to Jerusalem

In the present form of our books the plain story is that Ezra came to Jerusalem in the seventh year of Artaxerxes (458 BC), and carried out his mixed marriages reform; Nehemiah arrived in the 20th year of Artaxerxes (445 BC), built the city wall, and together with Ezra celebrated the Festival of Booths (Neh. 8:9) and dedicated the walls (12:36). The difficulties with this picture are these:

1. Except for passing mentions in Nehemiah 8:9 and 12:36 Ezra and Nehemiah ignore one another completely, which would be strange if they were contemporaries.

2. 'The powers granted Ezra and Nehemiah were so similar that it is improbable that they could have exercised them simultaneously' (Bowman, p. 562).

3. Why should Ezra, who came with imperial authority to impose the law, not have read the law to the people until 13 years after his arrival (Neh. 8)?

These difficulties appear insoluble; the dating of Ezra's mission to 458, and so the priority of Ezra, can be maintained only if his work and that of Nehemiah can be shown to have been entirely separate chronologically. Indeed, the references to their contemporaneity are very likely to be editorial or scribal additions (cf. on Neh. 8:9; 12:36; also 12:26); it follows that the recorded activity of Ezra may be compressed into the twelve months following his arrival. This is the position taken in this commentary, though it cannot be claimed to be certain.

Among recent advocates of the priority of Ezra we may mention Wright, *Date;* J. de Fraine, *Esdras en Nehemias* (1961), p. 15; A. Jepsen, *ZAW* 66 (1954), p. 84; M. Rehm, *BZ* 1 (1957), p. 65; H. H. Grosheide, *Ezra-Nehemia*, 1 (1963), pp. 49ff.; A. van Selms, *BO* 8 (1951), pp. 185ff.; A. F. Rainey, *AJBA* 1 (1969), p. 62; Porten, *Elephantine*, pp. 130, 280; M. Noth, *The Laws in the Pentateuch* (1966), pp. 74f. (but contrast Noth, *History*, p. 320); U. Kellermann, 'Erwägungen zum Problem der Esradatierung', *ZAW* 80 (1968), pp. 55–87; F. M. Cross, 'A Reconstruction of the Judean Restoration', *JBL* 94 (1975), pp. 4–18; S. Talmon, 'Ezra and Nehemiah', *IDBS*, pp. 317–28. Even such a list by no means represents a majority opinion.

However, from the standpoint of the present commentary it is possible to give an answer to all the arguments raised against the priority of Ezra. Some of them indeed favour the priority of Nehemiah, but none unequivocally demands it. We shall examine in turn (a) arguments against the priority of Ezra, (b) arguments for the priority of Ezra, and (c) arguments about the date of Ezra if Ezra was not prior to Nehemiah. In most cases it may be profitable also to consult the commentary on the verses referred to.

*(a) Arguments against the priority of Ezra*

1. Ezra found Jerusalem a populous city (Ezr. 10:1), while Nehemiah found it only thinly inhabited (Neh. 7:4), and took measures to repeople it (11:1). However, 'if some recent disaster [the destruction of the rebuilding of the walls] had befallen Jerusalem when Nehemiah came, its population might well have fallen considerably below what it had been in 457 B.C.' (Rowley, 'Order', p. 152). Also. Nehemiah is comparing its population before and after his resettlement; 7:3 shows that it was already inhabited to some extent.

2. In preparing for his census Nehemiah uses a population list nearly 100 years old (Neh. 7), but ignores the list of the homecomers with Ezra (Ezr. 8:1–14). But as pointed out on Neh. 7:5, Nehemiah did not use the Zerubbabel homecomer list for a census, but to establish genealogy; the Ezr. 8 list makes no additions to the family names (except in 8:2), so it would have been of no use to him.

3. The high priest contemporary with Nehemiah was clearly Eliashib (Neh. 3:1, 20), whereas Ezra was in Jerusalem during the high-priesthood of Johanan (Jehohanan, Ezr. 10:6), who appears to have been the grandson of Eliashib (Neh. 12:10f. (*q.v.*), 22), and to have

been high priest by 407 BC (*AP* 30.29). This was regarded by H. H. Rowley as the strongest argument for the priority of Nehemiah ('Order', pp. 153–9; in 'Nehemiah', p. 233, he rests his case entirely on the present argument). The current response to this argument is that while the Johanan contemporary with Ezra was Johanan I (son of Eliashib I), the Eliashib contemporary with Nehemiah was Eliashib II, and the Johanan who was high priest *c.* 407 was Johanan II (so Cross, *JBL* 94 [1975], pp. 10, 17; Talmon, *IDBS*, p. 327).

This reconstruction is not so certain, however, as its proponents allege, and we may suggest another line of argument. Thus, it may be doubted whether the Jehohanan of Ezra 10:6 was at that time the high priest. For one thing, it is strange that he is not called the high priest; omission of the title from his name at Neh. 12:23 is no parallel (*pace* Rowley, 'Order', p. 155), for there it is in the context of a list of high priests, not in a narrative; and for another, it is most unusual for a grandson to be called simply 'son' except in genealogical lists; see J. R. Porter, 'Son or Grandson (Ezra x.6)?', *JTS* 17 (1966), pp. 55–67, against the common assumption that 'son' often means 'grandson'. For a possible example, see Porten, *Elephantine*, p. 225 (and for a discussion of the possibility that Johanan was in fact the son of Eliashib, cf. on Neh. 12:10f.). It is further said that Ezra would not have lodged with some subordinate official but with the high priest. But if Jehohanan were, for example, the temple manager (like the Eliashib of Neh. 13:4, 7) he was no 'subordinate official'. Is it also possible that Ezra had a positive reason for not entering the high priest's house?: that is, by identifying himself with the guilt of those who had married foreigners, may he not have put himself in the category of the unclean? A quite different approach is taken by some who argue that the room was known as Johanan's in the Chronicler's day, and that there may have been no Johanan there in Ezra's time (Meyer, *Entstehung*, p. 91; F. Ahlemann, *ZAW* 59 [1942f.], pp. 97f.).

4. Nehemiah had to appoint a body of temple treasurers (Neh. 11:16; 13:13); Ezra found such a body in existence on his arrival (Ezr. 8:33). But there is no evidence that Nehemiah instituted that body (see on Neh. 13:13); he may simply have been making new appointments to a board which is inherently likely to have been in existence long before his time.

5. Meremoth b. Uriah belonged to the priestly family of Koz which had been unable to prove its ancestry in Zerubbabel's time (Ezr. 2:61f.). In Nehemiah's time Meremoth is not called a priest (Neh. 3:4, 21), but in Ezra's time he is (Ezr. 8:33). However, we may ask, what could have happened between the time of Nehemiah and that of Ezra to legitimise a family that had been excluded from

the priesthood for a century? The reference in Neh. 3 is inconclusive evidence, since that wall-builders list does not always specify the class of the builder; cf. Neh. 3:23. And are we to suppose as well that the Immer of 3:29 is a layman, though elsewhere the name is attested as priestly, not lay; and that neither Meshullam in 3:30 is a priest, and that *niskâ* does not have a religious meaning (A. van Selms, *BO* 8 [1951], p. 186)? Kellermann, *ZAW* 80 (1968), p. 69, evades the problem by supposing two men called Meremoth b. Uriah.

6. 'In Ezra 8:29; 10:5 the priests, Levites, and heads of families were dwelling in Jerusalem, while according to Neh. 11.1ff., Nehemiah had sent them to the capital' (Bowman, p. 562; cf. Rudolph, p. 69). But Neh. 11:1 speaks of family heads already living in Jerusalem, while the list of priests and Levites forms part of a census list of Jerusalem which does not specify whether those mentioned had lived in Jerusalem before Nehemiah's resettlement or not. Also, it is not clear that the family heads in Ezr. 8:29 were inhabitants of Jerusalem and had not rather assembled to Jerusalem to receive the gifts (A. van Selms, *BO* 8 [1951], p. 186).

7. 'Nehemiah would scarcely have designated the inhabitants of Jerusalem as those who had escaped exile (Neh. 1:2–3), if shortly before a great caravan had arrived there from Babylonia with Ezra' (Bowman, p. 562; cf. Rudolph, p. 69). But if 'escaped exile' means 'had not gone into exile', Nehemiah would be leaving entirely out of consideration not only Ezra's company of returning exiles, but Zerubbabel's as well, which is most unlikely. For a more satisfactory interpretation, see on Neh. 1:2f. (cf. also A. van Selms, *BO* 8 [1951], p. 187).

8. Ezra thanks God for the provision of a wall for Jerusalem (Ezr. 9:9), which presupposes Nehemiah's wall-building. However, the 'wall' in Ezr. 9:9 (*q.v.*) must be a figurative wall, since it is built 'in Judea and Jerusalem' (so also, U. Kellermann, *ZAW* 80 [1968], p. 67). Rudolph, while admitting that the wall is to be understood metaphorically, still thinks that the metaphor is more intelligible if the wall had actually been rebuilt. On the contrary, if Ezra has a literal wall in mind, he is hardly likely to speak of a wall 'in Judea'.

9. The rigorous reforms of Nehemiah would scarcely have been necessary if Ezra had already secured popular acceptance of the law—unless perhaps Ezra's work was a failure, of which there is no evidence. But, we may ask, is a reformer's work a failure, if 25 years or more later some individuals are found to be disregarding it? Ezra's activity was surely not confined to the mixed marriages issue, even though that is all the Chronicler tells us of. Ezra succeeded in establishing the law, and, apparently, methods of

interpretation and application of the law; he did not succeed in ensuring universal obedience to it in the following decades, and so the reforms of Nehemiah were necessary. The reforms of Nehemiah were obviously not fundamental but directed to small-scale abuses of a generally acknowledged and accepted way of life in conformity with the law. Had Ezra been a total failure, it is unbelievable that he would have become in Jewish tradition a second Moses (Bright, *History*, p. 393).

10. Nehemiah's name precedes Ezra's in Nehemiah 12:26 (W. F. Albright, *JBL* 40 [1921], p. 121, thought this the most conclusive argument; but cf. Rowley, 'Order', p. 153). Quite apart from the probability that the verse has been subject to editorial or scribal manipulation, by what means, may we suppose, has the correct order of Nehemiah-Ezra been preserved here when it has been systematically confused (on this view) by the Chronicler everywhere else?

11. 'The matter of tithes and the consequent flight of the Levites (Neh. 13:10–11) would be surprising so soon after the popular acceptance of the law . . . Nehemiah . . . was correcting a situation of long neglect and abuse' (Bowman, p. 563). But is it conceivable that for the twelve years of his first governorship Nehemiah tolerated the absence of Levites from the temple (which must have brought worship almost to a standstill), but at the beginning of his second term of office suddenly decided to rectify this long-standing abuse?

12. In the unsettled early years of the reign of Artaxerxes I, during which the empire was engaged in a struggle with Egypt, a journey by returning exiles in 458 BC and an official grant for the Jerusalem cult are said to be most improbable (e.g. V. Pavlovský, *Bib.* 38 [1957], pp. 283–9), whereas in 398 the recent defection of Egypt from the empire would provide an intelligible motive for imperial encouragement of Ezra (H. Cazelles, 'La mission d'Esdras', *VT* 4 [1954], pp. 113–40). But it is equally reasonable to regard the mission of Ezra in 458 as part of the imperial policy to strengthen the loyalty of the western provinces to itself (U. Kellermann, *ZAW* 80 [1968], p. 71. The return in 538 has also been viewed in the same light by R. Dunand, *VTS* 19 [1969], p. 69).

13. None of those who returned with Ezra is mentioned among Nehemiah's wall-builders (Rudolph, p. 69; Bowman, p. 562). But plainly those members, e.g. of the Parosh phratry (see commentary on Ezr. 2:3), who returned with Ezra would soon have merged with their kinsmen already in the land and have lost their identity as members of Ezra's company (A. van Selms, *BO* 8 [1951], p. 186; cf. also U. Kellermann, *ZAW* 80 [1968], p. 67).

*(b) Arguments for the priority of Ezra*

The arguments against the priority of Ezra are thus seen to have little weight; it remains to consider some positive arguments for placing Ezra before Nehemiah.

1. The order of the Chronicler's book. Especially if the Chronicler may be dated soon after 400 BC, it is inconceivable that he should have confused the chronological order of his heroes. Even if he lived a century or so later he is unlikely to have imagined that Ezra, nearly 50 years later than Nehemiah (if he came in 398), actually preceded him, though he may well have regarded the two men as contemporaries (cf. Wright, *Date*, pp. 9f.).

2. The returning exiles referred to in Rehum's letter (Ezr. 4:12) may naturally be taken as Ezra's company; they are unidentifiable if Ezra is later than Nehemiah.

3. If we have rightly understood Ezra's mission as the imposition of Pentateuchal law as state law in Judea by authorisation of the Persian government, Nehemiah's excursions into cultic and religious matters (especially Neh. 13) are not mere interference but part of his responsibility as a Persian official.

4. The community's pledge in Neh. 10, which forms part of the outcome of Nehemiah's work, presupposes a close and detailed knowledge of the law; if it preceded Ezra, Ezra's visit in order to teach and expound the law would have been unnecessary (these two objections do not apply to dating Ezra before 432 BC).

5. Ezra's commission by Artaxerxes I in 458 BC is intelligible as a public relations exercise towards one of his western lands (see no. 12 above), especially at a time when Egypt was attempting, with Athenian help, to break free of Persian control (cf. A. F. Rainey, *AJBA* 1 [1969], p. 62).

*(c) Arguments about the date of Ezra if Ezra was not prior to Nehemiah*

Those who are persuaded of the priority of Nehemiah still need to determine the precise date of Ezra's arrival. Three possibilities exist:

(i) *398 BC*. The most common view, and in my judgment the most credible alternative to 458 BC, is 398 BC, the 7th year of Artaxerxes II; so, e.g., Batten, pp. 28ff.; N. H. Snaith, *ZAW* 22 (1951), pp. 53–66; H. Cazelles, *VT* 4 (1954), pp. 113–40; Bowman, pp. 554, 561ff.; Galling, pp. 12ff.; Eissfeldt, pp. 553ff.; Rowley, 'Order'. See especially, for a critical review of the arguments, J. A. Emerton, 'Did Ezra go to Jerusalem in 428 B.C.?', *JTS* 17 (1966), pp. 1–19. No arbitrary emendation of the given dates is involved, though passages making Nehemiah and Ezra contemporaries must be regarded as secondary. Some objections have been raised to this particular date; only the last of them however is serious.

1. The 'Passover Papyrus' from Elephantine (419 BC) contains the Persian government's regulation for the observance of Jewish law there, the same kind of regulation as Ezra was empowered to enforce. 'Is it likely that Jewish practice was being regulated in a far corner of Egypt . . . before this had been done in Jerusalem itself?', it is asked (Bright, *History*, p. 384). But it is not clear how far the prescription of the 'Passover Papyrus', which is concerned with only one festival, is strictly comparable with the wide-ranging powers given to Ezra (cf. J. A. Emerton, *JTS* 17 [1966], pp. 8f.; Porten, *Elephantine*, pp. 128–33). It is however reasonable to claim that Hanani's instruction in this papyrus was simply an extension of the authority granted already to Ezra (so Porten, *op. cit.*, p. 130), and that the papyrus makes better sense on the supposition that Ezra had come to Jerusalem prior to 419 BC.

2. The Jehohanan b. Eliashib with whom Ezra stayed (Ezr. 10:6) is, if the date is on other grounds fixed at 398, likely to have been the high priest. But this is the Johanan who, Josephus says, murdered his brother in the temple (cf. on Neh. 12:10f.). Would Ezra have consorted with a murderer? (This is one of the chief objections of Bright, *History*, p. 399, to the 398 date.) Assuming, as most do, that the story in Josephus is historical, and that the event occurred before 398 BC (denied by Mowinckel, *Studien*, I, p. 161), it is possible that the killing would have been regarded as 'an act of self-defence against an attack by a godless would-be usurper' (J. A. Emerton, *JTS* 17 [1966], p. 12). Even if it were a sacrilegious act, as seems more probable, there are still two unprovable assumptions, and the argument, though apparently a weighty one, cannot be pressed.

3. The Davidide Hattush (Ezr. 8:2) would have been, by Bright's calculations (*History*, p. 385), well over 80 by 398 BC, and too old to travel with Ezra; but Emerton thinks it impossible to be so precise (*op. cit.*, p. 14).

4. It is hard to explain how Nehemiah ever came to be regarded as subsequent to Ezra if he preceded him by nearly half a century.

(ii) *428 BC*. Other scholars have thought that emendation of 'seventh' to 'thirty-seventh' in Ezra 7:7f. would provide a suitable date for Ezra's arrival, 428 BC, in the reign of Artaxerxes I, and thus during Nehemiah's second governorship (so Albright, *BP*, pp. 93, 112f.; Bright, *History*, pp. 369ff., 385f.; A. Lefèvre, *SDB*, VI [1960], cols. 416–21). This view enables references to Ezra and Nehemiah's contemporaneity to be retained, but it does not adequately explain why 'the two men are never brought into an organic relationship with each other' (Emerton, *op. cit.*, p. 16). Bright's explanations, that the Chronicler's interests were primarily ecclesiastical, to which Nehemiah's work was peripheral, and that perhaps Ezra and Nehemiah had clashed with one another, are unconvincing. Nehemiah, especially in the period when on this theory Ezra was present, was preoccupied by religious matters, and head-on collision with Ezra seems to have been a sure method for inclusion in his memoirs. And in any case, the proposal rests upon an arbitrary emendation which is more complicated than Bright implies, since it involves both accidental corruption and deliberate change (Emerton, *op. cit.*, pp. 18f.); it is easier to omit the two or three references to Ezra and Nehemiah as contemporaries (cf. on Neh. 8:9; 12:26, 36).

(iii) *Other dates.* Still others have suggested reading in Ezr. 7:7 'twenty-seventh' year, i.e. 438 BC (Wellhausen, 'Rückkehr', p. 186; T. K. Cheyne, *EB*, III, col. 3385; H. Lusseau, in *Introduction to the Old Testament*, ed. A. Robert [1968], p. 490; F. F. Bruce, *Israel and the Nations* [1963], p. 110). This is again a conjectural emendation; but the problem of the contemporaneity of the two men remains. It is eased somewhat if we locate Ezra in the interval between Nehemiah's first and second governorships, viz. in 432 BC (Rudolph, p. 71), but this suffers from the serious difficulty that Ezra's marriage reform would have been a thorough fiasco, a strange foundation for the high esteem in which Ezra came to be held in later tradition. A complex theory which evades this difficulty is that of V. Pavlovský ('Die Chronologie der Tätigkeit Esdras: Versuch einer neuen Lösung', *Bib.* 38 [1957], pp. 275–305, 428–56; followed hesitantly by Myers, pp. xlviff.). He thinks Ezra accompanied Nehemiah on his second governorship in 430 BC, and read the law in that year; then he returned to Susa, and again in 428 came to Jerusalem, this time with a caravan of exiles (Ezr. 7), and dealt with the mixed marriages. But this involves too many improbable hypotheses. A bold solution is that the dates of the two leaders have become confused, Nehemiah having come in 458, and Ezra in 445 (S. Jellicoe, 'Nehemiah-Ezra: A Reconstruction', *ExpT* 59 [1947–8], p. 54). Apart from the difficulty of imagining how this complex scribal error could have been made, this theory is in danger of overlapping Nehemiah and Ezra, Nehemiah's second governorship having begun, on these dates, *c.* 445!

None of these views is quite impossible, and so certainty is unattainable; in spite of the lengthy list of objections that have been made to 458 BC (most of them very weak), this seems to me to be still the most probable date for Ezra's coming to Jerusalem.

In recent years several radical reappraisals of the historical situation in the time of Ezra and Nehemiah have been proposed. One such depends wholly on a redating of Nehemiah's work. Although it has almost invariably been thought that it was Artaxerxes I under whom Nehemiah served, R. J. Saley has proposed that Nehemiah's governorship began in 384 BC, in the twentieth year of Artaxerxes II; Ezra's mission would have been in the seventh year of the same Artaxerxes (398) ('The Date of Nehemiah Reconsidered', in *Biblical and Near Eastern Studies* (LaSor *Festschrift*), ed. G. A. Tuttle [1978], pp. 151–65). This suggestion is made possible by the data from the Wadi Dâliyeh papyri which indicate a second Sanballat, governor of Samaria, in the reign of Artaxerxes II (F. M. Cross, 'The Discovery of the Samaria Papyri', *BA* 26 [1963], pp. 110–21; 'Aspects of Samaritan and Jewish History in Late Persian and Hellenistic Times', *HTR* 59 [1966], pp. 201–11; 'Papyri of the fourth Century B.C. from Dâliyeh: A Preliminary Report on Their Discovery and Significance', in *New Directions in Biblical Archaeology*, ed. D. N. Freedman and J. C. Greenfield [1969], pp. 41–62). This remains, at best, an alternative possibility, and perhaps too much is made to hang on the supposed practice of papponymy, which is not sufficiently attested as a custom that was strictly followed in the period in question.

Kellermann views all the data of Ezra-Nehemiah from the perspective of the theory of a major party conflict in post-exilic Judea between a priestly theocratic tendency and an eschatological messianic tendency (cf. O. Plöger, *Theocracy and Eschatology* [1968], and W. E. Rast, 'Developments in Post-Exilic Judaism', *JR* 50 (1970), pp. 101–11). Both Ezra and Nehemiah supported the latter party, Ezra being distinctly less successful than Nehemiah, though overshadowing Nehemiah in the Chronicler's account, which greatly elaborated the only piece of genuine information available to the Chronicler, the firman of Artaxerxes (Ezr. 7:12–23, 25f.). Nehemiah in rebuilding the walls of Jerusalem assisted the eschatological party, but was embarrassed by the messianic expectations some of that party entertained for him. His supposed pretensions to kingship brought about his recall to the Persian court; and his Memoir is an exculpatory document addressed to God, or, in a modified form, to the Persian authorities. The Chronicler, being of the theocratic party, approved only of the anti-Samarian activities of Nehemiah (Neh. 13). There are perhaps too many weaknesses and unverifiable hypotheses in this reconstruction: despite divergences in post-exilic thought, the theory of a party division is hard to substantiate; Kellermann's extreme scepticism about the Ezra material lacks sufficient foundation; and his account of the Chronicler's handling of the Nehemiah material contains considerable improbabilities (see also J. A. Emerton, *JTS* 23 [1972], pp. 171–65).

# V. PURPOSE AND THEOLOGY OF THE CHRONICLER

In addition to works cited below in this section, note also: D. N.
Freedman, 'The Chronicler's Purpose', *CBQ* 23 (1961), pp. 436–43;
D. F. Payne, 'The Purpose and Methods of the Chronicler', *Faith and
Thought* 93 (1963), pp. 64–73; R. North, 'Theology of the Chronicler',
*JBL* 82 (1963), pp. 369–81; P. R. Ackroyd, 'History and Theology in
the Writings of the Chronicler', *CTM* 38 (1967), pp. 501–15; 'The
Theology of the Chronicler', *LTQ* 8 (1973), pp. 101–116; J. Goldingay,
'The Theology of the Chronicler', *BTB* 5 (1975), pp. 99–126.

1. The purpose of the Chronicler's work (1–2 Chronicles; Ezra-
Nehemiah) is to assert the *legitimacy of his own community*, the
Judean state of the fourth century BC, as the sole heir of the true
theocratic Israel (we do not need to postulate a sociological dimension to this assertion, as though, for example, it must reflect conflict
with the Samaritans; cf. W. Rudolph, *Chronikbücher* [1955], p. ix).
Already in the genealogies of 1 Chr. 1–9 it is plain that for him the
whole movement of the history of salvation has been towards the
election of the Davidic state: Judah takes first place among the sons
of Jacob (1 Chr. 2:3; cf. 5:1f.) and little attention is paid to Ephraim
and Manasseh (7:14–27). The story proper starts, not with Patriarchs, Exodus, Sinai, or Conquest, but with the establishment of
the Davidic dynasty at Jerusalem and the organisation of the whole
structure of Israelite society and worship by David.

It was to the Davidic dynasty, the rightful rulers of Israel, that
God's promises were made (17:1–14; cf. 26f.), so the tribes that
remained faithful to the Davidic house are necessarily the legitimate
representatives of Israel. We are rather more dispassionate than the
Chronicler when we speak of the 'division' of the kingdom; for him,
it was a rebellion that had continued to his own day (2 Chr. 10:19).
Northern Israel had put itself outside the theocratic community and
only those individuals from the northern tribes who threw in their
lot with Judah (2 Chr. 11:13f.; 30:10) could share the blessings of
true Israel.

In the books of Ezra and Nehemiah the Chronicler is at pains to
stress the continuity between the pre-exilic Judean state and the
community of returned exiles. Their altar of sacrifice stands on the
traditional spot (Ezr. 3:3); their temple is not a new temple but
simply the Solomonic temple rebuilt on its site (5:2, 11, 15; 6:7);
their clergy are organised according to the ancient Davidic prescriptions (Neh. 12:24, 45); their sacrifices and festivals conform to the
Mosaic laws (Ezr. 3:3; Neh. 8:14). What is more, proof of descent
from Judahite, Benjamite, or Levite families can be offered by most
members of the community (Neh. 7:11; but cf. 7:61f.), and those

who are of plainly non-Israelite ancestry are excluded from the community (Ezr. 10; Neh. 13:1–3). Of those who had not been exiled but had remained in the land, only those who had 'separated themselves from the pollutions of the peoples of the land' had been admitted to full membership of the religious community (Ezr. 6:21). Here in Judah was to be found all that was truly Israel (Ezr. 2:70; 3:1; 4:3; 6:16, 21; 7:10; 9:1; 10:1, 2, 5, 10; Neh. 2:10; 9:1f.; 12:47; 13:3), dedicated to obedience to God's law (Neh. 10:29).

Is the Chronicler then a mere nationalist who writes to boost Jewish morale and to 'glorify the Jews in Jerusalem and Judea in a period of utter political and economic insignificance' (R. H. Pfeiffer, *IDB*, 1, p. 576)? Not so; for one thing, he has not written off entirely the rebellious tribes: there are still twelve tribes of Israel (Ezr. 6:17; 8:35; see further R. L. Braun, 'A Reconstruction of the Chronicler's Attitude Toward the North', *JBL* 96 [1977], pp. 59–62). For another, he does not imagine that to stand in line of succession to the pre-exilic theocracy exempts the community of his day from the necessity for sustained faithfulness to the law of God; for his community has inherited the guilt of Israel as well as its promises (Ezr. 9:6f., 13; Neh. 9:16ff., 26–30, 33) and stands where it does only by the grace of God (Ezr. 1:1; 3:11; 5:5; 6:22; 7:6, 9, 27f.; 8:18, 22, 31; 9:8f., 13; Neh. 2:8, 20; 4:9, 15, 20; 6:16; 7:5; 9; 12:43). Rather, the Chronicler's book should be seen as an attempt at self-understanding on the part of Ezra's community which has experienced a fulfilment of the divine promises of restoration, but is still 'in great distress' (Neh. 9:37) because of Persian overlordship.

2. Such a large role is given by the Chronicler to David and his dynasty that some have thought that the *Davidic house* must be the central theme of this book (so A.-M. Brunet, 'La théologie du Chroniste: Théocratie et messianisme', *Sacra Pagina*, 1 [1959], pp. 384–97; and cf. R. North, *JBL* 82 [1963], p. 376: 'The person and dynasty of David forms the heartbeat of all the Chronicler's theology'). To David and his son Solomon are devoted 1 Chr. 11–2 Chr. 9, one third of the whole work; the history is (unlike Kings) exclusively of the Davidic line; the oracle of Nathan, promising a perpetual succession of Davidic kings (1 Chr. 17), appears utterly unconditional. The figure of David is idealised, his misdemeanours and the scandals of his court go unmentioned, and his devotion to the cult becomes the standard by which his successors are judged (e.g. 2 Chr. 28:1; 29:2). The election of the Davidic house has almost completely eliminated reference to the election of Israel, and to David rather than Moses are attributed the institutions of temple worship (1 Chr. 16:4ff.; ch. 23–26; Ezr. 3:10; Neh. 12:45f.).

Yet the remarkable thing is that in the community of Ezra and Nehemiah, the Davidic line does not figure, and towards its one post-exilic representative, Zerubbabel, the Chronicler is distinctly cool: for him, Zerubbabel is merely 'son of Shealtiel' (Ezr. 3:2), not scion of David; he is never to be found acting as a Davidic ruler, but only in conjunction with others (Ezr. 5:2); and he is not even credited with the completion of the temple (Ezr. 6:14; cf. Zech. 4:9). Ezra the priest and scribe, and Nehemiah the imperial official, seem to have taken the place of the Davidic kings. What has happened to the divine promise of 1 Chr. 17?

There are several possible replies, quite apart from the view that the ideology of the Chronicler and of Ezra-Nehemiah are distinct (cf., e.g., J. D. Newsome, 'Toward a New Understanding of the Chronicler and His Purposes', *JBL* 94 [1975], pp. 201–17; H. G. M. Williamson, *Israel in the Books of Chronicles* [1977]). At the one extreme, it has been argued (by A. Noordtzij, 'Les intentions du Chroniste', *RB* 21 [1940], pp. 161–8) that the Chronicler's intention was to show that it was impossible for the theocratic ideal to be realised in Israel; the Davidic dynasty, in spite of its divine institution, proved a failure, and the efforts of Ezra and Nehemiah to restore a community in which God's will was followed have been equally unsuccessful. The Chronicler can have made such judgment upon the past and present only if he believed that the ideal could be fulfilled in the future; hence his ultimate intention was to point his readers towards a future scion of David (see especially R. Mosis, *Untersuchungen zur Theologie des chronistischen Geschichtswerkes* [1973]). However, few will agree that the Chronicler takes such a negative view of the history of his people; the idyllic picture of the restored community with which he concludes his work (Neh. 12:44–13:3; the remainder of ch. 13 is not the Chronicler's own writing) can leave us in little doubt that he believed his community was faithfully conforming itself to the Law.

But even if we reject the view that the Chronicler was portraying the failure of his community to be a true theocracy, may we agree that the role given to David is intelligible only if the author was firmly convinced that a son of David would one day re-establish the dynasty? (Thus A.-M. Brunet, *op. cit.*, p. 394; and cf. G. von Rad, *Old Testament Theology*, 1 [1962], p. 351: 'In his miserable age when there were no kings, the Chronicler is the guardian of the messianic tradition . . . We may certainly read off the picture of the one whom he awaited from his great original David'. See also W. F. Stinespring, 'Eschatology in Chronicles', *JBL* 80 [1961], pp. 209–19.) We may indeed note certain dissatisfactions with the present state of affairs expressed in Ezr. 9:8f. and in Neh. 9:36f., where the Levite prayer ends plaintively with 'We are all slaves this day . . . and we are in great distress' (though these passages are probably not the composition of the Chronicler himself). But we miss any genuine hopes for the restoration of the monarchy, and it is hard to imagine that all such expectations have been suppressed for prudential reasons. Freedom from imperial taxation and independence from foreign control are fervently desired, but for a true shepherd (Ezek. 34:23), a ruler in Israel (Mic. 5:1), a righteous branch (Jer. 23:5), there appears no longing.

Then may we go to the other extreme and claim that the Chronicler has no eschatological expectation because his community is so perfect an expression of the theocratic ideal? (So W. Rudolph, *Chronikbücher* [1955], p. xxxiii. Cf. A. Caquot, 'Peut-on parler de messianisme dans l'oeuvre du Chroniste?', *RTP* 99 [1960], pp. 110–20; and O. Plöger, *Theocracy and Eschatology* [1968], esp. pp. 37–43.) We can only say that if the Chronicler did entertain hopes for the future, he was remarkably reticent about them. David and the monarchy belong to the past, and it is the collective obedience of the people, rather than the personal devotion of the king, that is the measure according to which divine favour is experienced. But is it enough to say that for the Chronicler the Davidic dynasty is dispensable, so long as the second pillar of the theocracy, the temple, remains standing (Rudolph, *loc. cit.*)? What has become of the divine promises?

First, we should observe that the promises to the Davidic line, though sometimes expressed unconditionally (1 Chr. 17:11–14; 22:10; 2 Chr. 13:5; 21:7 ), at other times have conditions attached (1 Chr. 28:7; 2 Chr. 6:16; cf. 1 Chr. 22:12f.). It is plain by the end of 2 Chr. that the kings of Judah have failed to meet those conditions, and so have forfeited their right to rule. But, secondly, it is noteworthy that the Chronicler does not explicitly acknowledge that the promises have been frustrated; the Davidic dynasty ends not with a bang but a whimper, nothing is said of the fate of the last king Zedekiah, and by the time the Chronicler comes to recount the taking into captivity, his interest has shifted from the king to the people as a whole (2 Chr. 36:14–21).

The reason may well be that the Chronicler sees in his own time both a failure and a fulfilment of the divine promises: there is no king on the throne of David, and that is how it should be, since the house of David was not faithful to Yahweh; yet the purposes for which the monarchy was established—the building of the temple, the maintenance of worship, the preservation of the state—are all accomplished, and the divine promises have not entirely lacked fulfilment. The Chronicler's community has become the heir of the promises to David. A more satisfying future realisation of those promises is not excluded, though the Chronicler himself gives little thought to the future. It may be noted, though, that this preoccupation with the present, which 'directly identifies the kingdom of God with the empiric post-exilic Israel . . . comes dangerously close to Israel's conceptions of the period before the great prophets in which Yahweh's kingship assured Israel of its own unassailable position and its dominion over the nations' (T. C. Vriezen, *An Outline of Old Testament Theology* [1958], p. 350).

3. One of the prime functions of the monarchy, in the view of the Chronicler, was to establish and maintain the *temple worship*. This is clear from the space devoted to the cultic activities of David and Solomon (1 Chr. 23–26; 2 Chr. 2–7). Similarly, in the post-exilic community the Chronicler stresses the enthusiastic adherence of the people to the cultic regulations (Ezr. 3:2–6, 10f.; 6:16–22; 8:35; Neh. 12:27–30, 44–47), and obviously finds congenial material in the narratives of the rebuilding of the temple (Ezr. 5–6) and of the public services of worship (Ezr. 9; Neh. 8–9), and in the community's pledge to observe the details of the cultic law (Neh. 10). For him obedience to the will of God is first and foremost the correct performance of ritual, liturgy, and offerings. Doubtless this is largely because he himself belonged to a clerical order—most scholars see in the attention he pays to Levite activities an indication of his own class (there are more references to Levites in the Chronicler's work than in the rest of the Old Testament put together)—but he is not thinking only of the responsibilities of the clergy. For him, a theocratic community is one where 'divine service' is regularly performed according to ancient traditions. Must this not be called sub-prophetic? Has he never read any prophetic denunciation of cult for cult's sake (e.g. Am. 5:21–24; Isa. 1:12–17)? Indeed, his is a dangerous theology, since the transition from formal religion to *mere* formal religion is all too easy; yet it must also be said that the prophetic tradition is equally one-sided whenever it imagines that true religion can ever be merely a matter of inward disposition or of social action. 'Outward form is not a matter of indifference to the interior concerns of religion, but effectively mediates the presence of the divine' (W. Eichrodt, *Theology of the Old Testament*, i [1961], p. 404). Temple furnishings, sacrificial animals, Levite choirs, need not be mere externalities, but instances of faith searching for a 'body' by which to express itself. There is one sure sign that the Chronicler has not succumbed to a mere formalism in religion: his emphasis on joy in the performance of the divine will (Ezr. 3:11, 13; 6:16, 22; Neh. 12:27; cf. Neh. 8:10, 17; 12:43). That is what marks off obedience to God's law from legalism.

4. But are the existence of the community and the maintenance of the temple cult ends in themselves? They loom large in the Chronicler's mind, but not large enough to obscure the fundamental fact that the institutions to which he is devoted exist for the sake of *God* quite as much as they exist on account of God's gracious activity (see p. 29 above). The temple is after all the 'house of the *Lord*' (Ezr. 1:3, 5, 7; 3:8; etc.), the place of sacrifice is the 'altar of the God of Israel' (Ezr. 3:2), the festival seasons are the 'feasts of the Lord' (Ezr. 3:5) and the offerings of sacrifice and song are 'to the Lord' (Ezr. 3:3f., 11; Neh. 12:45f.). Likewise the orders of clergy exist 'for the service of God' (Ezr. 6:18; cf. Neh. 12:45), and the whole community, clergy and laity alike, is committed to the worship of God (Ezr. 3:11; 4:3; 6:16, 21; 8:35; Neh. 12:47; cf. 10:32–39). 'We will not neglect the house of our God' (Neh. 10:39) is the pledge of the whole people.

Yet for the Chronicler, God is not bound to his temple at Jerusalem; it is the Persian king who speaks of the 'God of Jerusalem' (Ezr. 7:19) and of 'the God who is in Jerusalem' (1:3). To the Chronicler, Yahweh is characteristically 'the God of Israel' (Ezr. 3:2; 4:1, 3; 5:1; 6:14, 21, 22; 7:6; 8:35), that is, the God of the community that is heir to the Davidic kingdom. (Elsewhere in Ezra-Nehemiah the term 'God of Israel' occurs only twice in Persian decrees (Ezr. 1:3; 7:15) and twice in the Ezra memoirs (Ezr. 9:4, 15). Ezra's characteristic phrase is 'our God' (Ezr. 8:17, 18, 21, 22, 23, 25, 30, 31, 33; 9:8, 9, 10, 13; 10:2, 3, 4), and Nehemiah's phrase is 'my God' (Ne. 2:8, 12, 18; 5:19; 6:14; 7:5; 13:14, 22, 29, 31).) The post-exilic Jews used the old term 'God of heaven and earth' (Ezr. 5:11), and Nehemiah speaks of 'the God of heaven' (Neh. 1:4f.; 2:4, 20; cf. Ezr. 5:12), a term employed in the Persian decrees within these books (Ezr. 1:2; 6:9f.; 7:12, 21, 23), but the Chronicler is less concerned with the universality of God's rule than with his particular relationship with Israel. Yahweh may 'stir up the spirit' of the Persian king (Ezr. 1:1), but the Chronicler speaks of that only because the resultant imperial decree impinges on the Jews.

The Chronicler's view of God plainly has not the width or depth of that of Isaiah 40–55, for example, yet his concentration upon God's relation to Israel is necessarily a concentration upon the divine-human encounter in the history of salvation, which prevents the development of a view of God as remote and purely transcendental. One of the Chronicler's characteristic emphases is upon the co-operation of God and man, which avoids both the negative standpoint of 'Man proposes, God disposes', and the anthropocentric attitude of 'God helps those who help themselves'. In that co-operation, God is the leading, prompting, encouraging partner, but his initiative does not stifle the free human decision to work with him. Perhaps the most striking example of this perspective of the Chronicler is his statement at the completion of the temple (Ezr. 6:14): 'They finished their building by command of the God of Israel and by decree of Cyrus and Darius king of Persia', where the divine and human are artlessly conjoined (cf. also Ezr. 1:5; 5:1f.; 6:22; 7:6, 27; and in the Nehemiah memoirs: Neh. 2:1–8, 18, 20; 4:9, 20; 6:16). Ezra and Nehemiah strike us, perhaps simply because of the intimacy of their 'memoirs', as men of deeper personal piety than the Chronicler, but their theological stance is the same: preoccupation with God's purposes for their own community shortens their perspective on the future, but relieves them of any charge of otherworldliness; their concern for outward forms, bricks and mortar, ritual observance, could easily have been an empty formalism, but in fact was a meaningful expression of the outwardness of genuine religion; and their emphasis on the obedience of the whole community and of its individual members to the divine law, which is always in danger of degenerating into an individualistic legalism, was a necessary and fruitful response to the divine mercy which had restored them to their homeland.


# VI. ANALYSIS OF EZRA-NEHEMIAH

## EZRA

### I. THE RETURN FROM EXILE AND REBUILDING OF THE TEMPLE
(ch. 1–6)

The return from exile under Sheshbazzar (ch. 1)
List of returned exiles (ch. 2)
The rebuilding of the temple planned and thwarted (ch. 3–4)
Restoration of the temple (ch. 5–6)

### II. EZRA'S MISSION AND ITS RESULTS (ch. 7–10)

Ezra's return (ch. 7–8)
Ezra's action over mixed marriages (ch. 9–10)

# NEHEMIAH

## I. NEHEMIAH'S MISSION (1:1–7:73a)

Nehemiah hears news from Jerusalem (1:1–4)
Nehemiah's prayer (1:5–11)
Nehemiah receives permission to visit Jerusalem (2:1–8)
Nehemiah arrives in Jerusalem, inspects its walls, and gains assent
    to his proposals (2:9–20)
The rebuilding of the walls (ch. 3)
Opposition from the Samarians (ch. 4)
Economic difficulties and Nehemiah's solution (5:1–13)
Nehemiah's unselfishness as governor (5:14–19)
In spite of traps for Nehemiah, the wall is finished (ch. 6)
Preparations for the peopling of Jerusalem (7:1–73a)

## II. EZRA'S ACTIVITY (CONTINUED) (7:73b–9:37)

Ezra's reading of the law (7:73b-8:12)
Celebration of the Festival of Booths (8:13–18)
A day of repentance and its penitential psalm (9:1–37)

## III. NEHEMIAH'S COMMUNITY (9:38–13:31)

The pledge of reform (9:38–10:39)
The population of Jerusalem and Judah (ch. 11)
The clergy of the post-exilic community (12:1–26)
The dedication of the wall (12:27–43)
An ideal community (12:44–13:3)
Reforms during Nehemiah's second governorship (13:4–31)

# EZRA

# I. THE RETURN FROM EXILE AND REBUILDING OF THE TEMPLE ch. 1–6

## ch. 1

The return from exile in Babylonia and the restoration of the Jewish community to its land were due to the enlightened repatriation policy of Cyrus II, newly installed as heir by conquest of the Babylonian empire. According to his own testimony, he 'gathered together all the [exiled] inhabitants' of various regions and 'returned them to their homes' (Cyrus cylinder, line 32; *ANET*, p. 316; *DOTT*, p. 93). Among the repatriates were the Jewish exiles. The royal decree authorising their return, and more particularly the rebuilding of the Jerusalem temple (for restoration of holy places was especially important to Cyrus; cf. the last two paragraphs of the Cyrus cylinder, lines 28–36), is here reproduced by the Chronicler (see Introduction, III) with perhaps some additions of his own.

### CYRUS' DECISION

#### 1:1

Cyrus II (the Great) had in the space of twenty years extended his rule from the kingdom of Anshan (Elam) to include Persia, Media, Lydia, Assyria, and finally Babylonia, whose capital fell to him in October 539 BC. **the first year of Cyrus**: For the Chronicler this was not Cyrus' first year as a king (559–558 BC) but his first regnal year as king of Babylon (538–537 BC), that is, when he first assumed power over the Jews and over Palestine. **king of Persia**: This title was more naturally used before his capture of Babylon; thereafter 'king of Babylon' (cf. 5:13; Neh. 13:6) seems to have been the more common form, though in the west 'king of Persia' was still frequently employed (Bickerman, *JBL* 65 (1946), pp. 255f.; R. D. Wilson, 'Titles of the Persian Kings', *Festschrift E. Sachau* [1915], pp. 179–207). **the word of the LORD by the mouth of Jeremiah**: The ending of the captivity is not due to some sudden relenting on God's part, but is in conformity with his word given by Jeremiah that there would be seventy years' exile in Babylonia (Jer. 25:11, referred to in what was the previous verse in the Chronicler's work, 2 Chr. 36:21), to be followed by a return to the land (Jer. 29:10). The 'accomplishment' of the prophetic word often occurs in two stages (cf. 1 Sam. 2:27–36 with 4:11, 18, and 1 Kg. 2:27); here the

negative aspect (captivity) of the 'seventy years' oracle has long ago
been realised, as the Chronicler has noted (2 Chr. 36:20f.), while
the positive side (release), which is now in view, will bring the
prophecy to its full accomplishment. Seventy years from 538 BC
takes us back to 608, but the first captivity we read of in 2 Kings
dates from 597 (24:12–16). Perhaps the years of captivity were
reckoned from the minor deportation referred to in Dan. 1:1, which
may have occurred in 605 BC (but see D. J. A. Clines, *AJBA* 2
[1972], pp. 20–8). The figure 70 would thus be a round number for
67 or 68 years.

On the period of captivity, cf. Josephus, *Ant.* 10.6.3; and see D.
J. Wiseman, *Notes on Some Problems in the Book of Daniel* (1965),
pp. 16ff. C. F. Whitley, 'The Term Seventy Years Captivity', *VT*
4 (1954), pp. 60–72 (additionally, *VT* 7 [1957], pp. 416ff.) finds an
exact period of seventy years, from the destruction of the temple to
the completion of its rebuilding (586–516 BC), and this period is
apparently in mind at Zech. 1:12; 7:5. But strictly speaking, the
Jeremiah prophecies refer not to the cessation of worship but to the
years of Babylonian rule (so, A. Orr, *VT* 6 [1956], pp. 304ff.). G.
Larsson's argument ('When did the Babylonian Captivity Begin?',
*JTS* 18 [1967], pp. 417–23) that that period is in fact exactly 70
lunar years is questionable.

**the LORD stirred up** (lit. 'awakened) **the spirit**: a phrase which is
several times used for God's prompting of foreigners to do his will,
of which they would otherwise be ignorant (1 Chr. 5:26; 2 Chr.
21:16; of Cyrus himself, Isa. 41:2, 25; 45:13). A decision of such
moment is necessarily regarded as motivated by God; the Chronicler
is not affirming that all the events of world-history are instigated by
God, but rather that where pagan history impinges upon Israel's
life God has exercised his sovereignty on Israel's behalf. **a proclamation . . . in writing**: Cyrus' permission for the exiles to return was
given both orally and in writing (cf. *NEB*): **he made a proclamation
throughout all his kingdom** (lit. 'made a voice pass through all
his kingdom') by dispatching a herald who would after the public
announcement of the royal edict have a copy of it posted on an
official notice board (for oral and written forms of a message, cf. 2
Kg. 19:9–14; the Greek inscription reproducing proclamations from
Seleucid kings *c.* 200 BC are probably of a similar type: Y. H.
Landau, *IEJ* 16 [1966], pp. 54–70). **throughout all his kingdom**:
Jewish exiles had settled mainly in Babylonia but the edict would
apply equally to Jews everywhere in the Persian empire (cf. Jer.
44:1; Est. 3:8).

THE EDICT

1:2-4

Another edict of Cyrus concerning the rebuilding of the temple in Jerusalem is reproduced in 6:3–5, in Aramaic; the relation of the two edicts constitutes a problem. See Bickerman, pp. 249–75; de Vaux, *BANE*, pp. 63–96; Galling, 'Die Proklamation des Cyros in Esra 1', in *Studien*, pp. 61–77; L. Rost, 'Erwägungen zum Kyroserlasses', in *Verbannung und Heimkehr* (W. Rudolph *Festschrift*, 1961), pp. 301–7. The fact that the Aramaic edict, which most scholars accept as authentic, provides only for the rebuilding of the temple, and does not specify the repatriation of the Jews, leads some to think that the present Hebrew decree, which does allow a return, is a Jewish expansion of the original edict (so, e.g., Noth, *History*, p. 308). There is undoubtedly a very marked Jewish colouring in the wording of this document: note especially **the LORD, the God of Israel** (v. 3), **each survivor, sojourns, freewill offerings** (v. 4). This fact may be explained by the suggestion that the edict was drafted by a Jewish secretary at the Persian court; but it remains possible that vv. 3*b*–4 may be an editorial addition to the original decree (so de Vaux, *BANE*, p. 95); the shorter form of the edict as it appears in 2 Chr. 36:23 is free of these more distinctively Jewish phrases. The Aramaic and Hebrew edicts in fact serve different functions: the Hebrew is the text of a herald's proclamation which is subsequently posted on a notice-board, while the Aramaic is an official memorandum (cf. on 6:2) filed in the royal archives. Naturally the proclamation encouraged Jews to return (though even in the Hebrew edict the building of the temple is the prime concern); the purpose of the memorandum was more limited, relating solely to the expense incurred by the royal treasury for the temple works. When the distinction between the two documents is recognised, as Bickerman points out, the essential authenticity of the one cannot be challenged by the provisions of the other.

**2. Thus says Cyrus king of Persia**: The decree begins with the conventional introductory phrase of the imperial style, **Thus says Cyrus (the) king**. (For examples, see *AP*, pp. 251–9 (i.7, 12; ii. 16); Kent, *Old Persian*, pp. 16, 19; Bickerman, p. 271). **of Persia**: This addition to the official phrase is perhaps the Chronicler's, though 'king of Persia' is attested occasionally in contemporary documents (Wilson, *op. cit.*, pp. 183, 188). **The LORD . . . has given me**: There is nothing improbable in Cyrus' professing before the Jews that **the LORD** (Yahweh) was responsible for his rise to power. Cyrus himself was probably a Zoroastrian (W. Hinz, *Zarathustra* [1961], pp. 146–9), a worshipper of Ahura-Mazda; but it was

part of his imperial policy to acknowledge with gratitude his blessings from the high gods of his realm. Thus at Babylon it is Marduk,
the god of Babylon, who chooses him and declares him to be ruler
of all the world; in a text from Ur, it is Sin, the moon-god worshipped there, who gives him victory (see, respectively, *ANET*, p.
315 [= *DOTT*, p. 92] and *DOTT*, p. 94). Cyrus may even have
been prepared to identify Ahura-Mazda, the 'lord of heaven', with
Yahweh, whom his worshippers called **God of heaven** (cf. also
5:11; 6:9; 7:11). This name for God had been avoided in Israel in
pre-exilic times, probably because it was a title of the Semitic god
Baal-Hadad; but it is frequent in the fifth-century Jewish papyri
from Elephantine, and in the post-exilic books is used especially by
Jews in conversation with foreigners (cf. Jon. 1:9; Dan. 2:37-44;
Nehemiah's use [1:4f.; 2:4, 20; cf. on 1:5] may be conditioned by
his expectation of a non-Jewish reading public for his memoirs).
See further, D. K. Andrews, 'Yahweh the God of the Heavens', in
*The Seed of Wisdom* (T. J. Meek volume), ed. W. S. McCullough
(1964), pp. 45-57; Porten, *Elephantine*, pp. 108f.; *AP* 30.2, 27f.;
**38.2f. all the kingdoms of the earth**: This claim, not at all unrealistic when one considers the vast sweep of Cyrus' empire from the
Mediterranean to the Indus, is paralleled by the text of an inscribed
brick of Cyrus at Ur: 'The great gods have delivered all the lands
into my hands' (C. J. Gadd and L. Legrain, *Ur Excavations Texts:
Royal Inscriptions* [1928], p. 58, no. 194). Cf. also Cyrus cylinder,
line 20: 'I am Cyrus, King of the world, great King, legitimate
King, King of Babylon, King of Sumer and Akkad, King of the
four rims (of the earth)' (*ANET*, p. 316; *DOTT*, p. 93).
**to build him a house at Jerusalem**: This divine charge was, from
Cyrus' point of view, merely one of the many responsibilities he
took upon himself for the restoration of local and national cults in
his empire. Referring to the lands of the west, he says: 'I returned
to (these) sacred cities on the other side of the Tigris, the sanctuaries
of which have been in ruins for a long time, the images which (used)
to live therein and established for them permanent sanctuaries'
(Cyrus cylinder, lines 31f. [*ANET*, p. 316; *DOTT*, p. 93]). Josephus' speculation (*Ant.* 11.1.1f.) that Cyrus was prompted to rebuild
the temple by reading the Isaianic prophecies which mentioned him
by name (Isa. 44:26ff.; 45:1-7) is by no means impossible, since
some of his highest officials were Jews; but a special concern on his
part for the Jewish cult is nowhere attested. On the interest of
Persian kings in oracles, cf. Bickerman, p. 269. **Jerusalem, which
is in Judah**: The specifying clause would not be natural to a Jewish
writer; it is official terminology, and may be a pointer to the authenticity of the decree (cf. the letter from the Jews of Elephantine to

the Persian governor of Judea: 'the temple of Ya'u the God which is in the fortress of Yeb'; *AP* 30.6).

**3.** The instruction for all Jews to return to their land reads as much like a royal command as the requirement to build the temple, which is indeed referred to as a 'decree' in 5:3. But since we know that many exiles remained in Babylonia (cf. 7:6f.), this part of the edict must have been construed as permission simply; the command is the only mode of speech suitable for an autocrat. The edict was directed to **all** the **people** of Yahweh to be found in the Empire, that is, exiles of the Assyrian captivity as well as of the Babylonian. Such a restoration of all Israel had been envisaged by Ezekiel (e.g. Ezek. 47). But it is not very surprising that the idea of returning to Judea and of restoring the Jerusalem temple did not appeal to the descendants of the ten northern tribes; in the event only members of Judah and Benjamin, together with some Levites, returned (1:5; 2:1). **may his God be with him**: To deportees other than the Jews, the phrase would have implied the restoration of the image of the national god to its shrine; here of course the phrase has a less concrete significance. **go up to Jerusalem**: not to Jerusalem as an elevated place, which is usually the meaning (e.g. Ps. 122:4); here the verb means 'to go up country', i.e. north (G. R. Driver, *ZAW* 69 [1957], pp. 74–7), following the Euphrates route northward before striking out to the west.

**4.** The natural sense is that Cyrus required his non-Jewish subjects to help provide for the returning exiles money, food, and transport, together with offerings for the Jewish temple (cf. *NEB*, 'every remaining Jew . . . may claim aid from his neighbours'). **each survivor** (*hanniššār*): as in 2 Chr. 36:20, those who had escaped the sword but had been brought into exile (cf. also Neh. 1:2); **the men of his place**: Gentile neighbours. Such an imposition seems incredible at first sight, but given Cyrus' determination to restore regional cults, and the necessity of a community of worshippers to maintain them, such a stipulation may have been a practical measure designed to ensure the success of his policy; needless to say, we would have to assume similar arrangements for the repatriation of other peoples and gods, and there is no extra-biblical evidence of such measures. It may be preferable to regard this verse as an addition by the Chronicler, intended to remind the reader of the exodus from Egypt; like Second Isaiah, he regards the return as a second exodus (Isa. 43:16–21; 48:21f.), in which the acceptance of Gentile aid corresponds to the exodus motif of 'the spoiling of the Egyptians' (Ex. 3:21f., etc.; and cf. G. W. Coats, 'Despoiling the Egyptians', *VT* 18 [1968], pp. 450–7). Alternative interpretations of the verse are rather unconvincing: the view that 'whosoever remaineth' (*AV*; **each survivor**, *RSV*) means those who cannot return for financial reasons, and that they are to be assisted by their richer Jewish neighbours (Bickerman, p. 260) breaks down on the fact that v. 3 does not envisage anyone being left behind. H. L. Ginsberg, *JBL* 79 (1960), pp. 169ff., is forced to postulate an emendation, a mistranslation from Aramaic, and an Aramaic original. M. D. Goldman, *ABR* 1 (1951), p. 58, interprets: 'And whoever remains in any of the places where he lives, the men of his locality shall impose a levy on him (*nāśā'*, lit. 'lift up', hence 'raise a tax') in silver, etc.'; but this usage of *nāśā'* is unattested.

## PREPARATION FOR THE RETURN
### 1:5–11

This was by no means the only occasion on which exiles returned to Judea (cf. on 2:1–70), but as the first return it has a special significance for the Chronicler who describes it, proleptically, as the return of all the exiles. Obviously not all the family **heads, priests** and **Levites** returned with Sheshbazzar, but the Chronicler is concentrating on the success of the return, and does not hint at the rather meagre response to Cyrus' decree. He is careful to insist, by describing the returning exiles as **every one whose spirit God had stirred** (v. 5), that the decision to return was no mere human decision, but due to the prompting of the divine will which was in course of reconstituting the theocratic community. It is the fulfilment of the divine promise that interests him, not the precise historical details of dates or route. We may take it, though, that the decree was issued by the spring of 538, and the return took place in the summer (cf. on 3:1).

**5.** That only members of the tribes of **Judah and Benjamin**, along with **Levites**, returned in significant numbers must be a matter of historical fact. It is not that the Chronicler has written off the other tribes as unworthy to participate in the return because of their faithlessness to the Davidic monarchy and the Jerusalem temple in pre-exilic times, as some have suggested. The Chronicler has been at pains to refer, whenever possible, to the involvement of northerners in worship at Jerusalem (e.g. 2 Chr. 15:9f.; 30:11, 18, 25; cf. J. M. Myers, *I Chronicles* [1965], pp. lxxiii ff.; H. G. M. Williamson, *Israel in the Books of Chronicles* [1977]). **fathers' houses**: what anthropologists call an 'extended family', that is, a group 'composed of all living persons, except married females, descended from a person still living, and including the family slaves' (F. I. Andersen, 'Israelite Kinship Terminology and Social Structure', *Bible Translator* 20 [1969], pp. 29–39, esp. p. 37, adding some precisions to the standard statement in de Vaux, *Ancient Israel*, pp. 7f.; and J. P. Weinberg, 'Das *bêit 'ābōt* im 6.-4. Jh. v.u.Z.', *VT* 23 [1973], pp. 400–14). **priests**: members of the tribe of Levi and descendants of the Aaron family according to the priestly law (Num. 3:10); **Levites**: The non-Aaronite members of the tribe of Levi were responsible for the more menial duties in the cult (Num. 3:5–9). **God** is the Chronicler's preferred term; earlier (v. 1) he has spoken of 'Yahweh', perhaps under the influence of the Jeremianic prophecy.

6. **all who were about them** probably includes Gentiles (cf. 'the men of his place', v. 4). **aided them**: One wonders how the Chronicler interpreted Isa. 52:11, which seems to forbid returning exiles to accept gifts from Gentiles. **vessels of silver**: Why these are specified is unclear; 1 Esd. 2:9 suggests that the Heb. *bkly ksp*, 'with vessels of silver', originally read *bkl bksp*, 'in everything, *or* in every respect, with silver . . .' (so *NEB*). Before **besides** the word *lᵉ̱baḏ*, 'only', unintelligible in the context, has been omitted by most versions; it is very probably a scribal error for the orthographically similar *lārōḇ*, 'in abundance' (cf. 1 Esd. 2:9; *NEB*). **all that was freely offered**: gifts for the temple, as distinct from assistance afforded to the exiles themselves. *NEB* has 'in addition to any voluntary service', taking *'al*, 'besides', as a noun meaning 'work, service' (following G. R. Driver, *VTS* 16 [1967], pp. 61f.); but this translates *'al* twice.

7. The contribution of **Cyrus** to the re-establishment of the Jerusalem temple was the sacred temple vessels that had been dedicated as a war trophy by **Nebuchadnezzar** in the **house**, the temple called Esagila, of his god (*NEB*; rather than **gods**, *RSV*) Marduk in Babylon, after his capture of Jerusalem in 587 BC and plundering of the temple (2 Kg. 24:13; 25:13–16; 2 Chr. 36:10, 18; Jer. 52:17ff.). According to Dan. 1:2, Nebuchadrezzar had already in 605 BC removed some of the vessels of the temple to Babylon. This is not recorded in the Babylonian Chronicle for that year; but see D. J. Wiseman, *Notes on Some Problems in the Book of Daniel* (1965), pp. 16ff. The return of the temple vessels formed part of Cyrus' original decree, according to the Aramaic memorandum (6:5).

8. **Mithredath**, a common Persian name meaning 'gift of Mithras', will have been temple **treasurer** (Heb. *gizbār*, a loanword from Pers. *ganzabara*, and the origin, through the LXX's misunderstanding of it as a proper name, of Caspar, the traditional name of one of the Magi).

**Sheshbazzar**: His identity is much disputed. The name is a Hebrew corruption of a Babylonian name, probably Shamash-aba-uṣur, 'May Shamash (the sun god) protect the father'. The superficially most attractive view is that it is another name for Zerubbabel. (So apparently already, I Esd. 6:18f., especially if the variant omitting 'and' after Zerubbabel is original; and Josephus, *Ant.* 11.1.5. So too in modern times, H. Ewald, *The History of Israel*, v [²1880], p. 87; H. E. Ryle, *Ezra and Nehemiah* [1893], pp. 12f.; J. Gabriel, *Zorobabel* [1927], pp. 48–79; and, most recently, M. B. Pelaia, *Esdra e Neemia* [1960], pp. 39f.) Both Zerubbabel and **Sheshbazzar** are said to have begun the rebuilding of the temple (3:10; 5:16), and the narrative of ch. 3 in which Zerubbabel plays the leading part appears to resume directly from ch. 1 without any hint that a new leader has come on the scene. This identification, however, is now largely given up. The major difficulty with it is that in ch. 5, set in the time of Zerubbabel, Sheshbazzar seems to be referred to as a governor of a former time (5:14, 16, *q.v.*). A further objection is that one person is not likely to have had two Babylonian names (Daniel, for example, had a Hebrew and a Babylonian name), but it is not so certain as many think that Zerubbabel is a Babylonian name: it could be Hebrew, a variant on *zᵉrû'bāḇēl*, 'born in (lit. sown of) Babylon'; and even if it is originally Babylonian (*zērbabīli*, 'seed of Babylon'; for attestation, see K. L. Tallqvist, *Assyrian Personal Names* [rp 1966], p. 321), the name sounds Hebrew, which Sheshbazzar certainly does not.

If however **Sheshbazzar** is not Zerubbabel, who is he? The title **prince of Judah** would suit Shenazzar, a son of Jehoiachin the exiled king of Judah (1 Chr. 3:18); interestingly, he is the only one of Jehoiachin's sons with a Babylonian name, and the name is close enough to Sheshbazzar to be identified, especially if one Septuagintal form of Sheshbazzar, Sanabassar, is regarded as more authentic. Shenazzar was the fourth of Jehoiachin's sons (1 Chr. 3:17f.), and must have been born before 592 BC, since a Babylonian ration list of that year provides for five sons of the king (E. F. Weidner, 'Jojachin, König von Juda, in babylonischen Keilschrifttexten', in *Mélanges Syriens* [R. Dussaud volume], II [1939], pp. 923–35; *ANET*, p. 309b). This assumes that the king in question was Jehoiachin, but it could possibly have been Jehoiakim (so Rudolph, p. 19 n. 2). Thus at the time of the return in 538 BC, Shenazzar/Sheshbazzar would have been at least 55, so it is not improbable that his death occurred soon after the return and his nephew Zerubbabel (cf. on 3:2) took his place as the 'prince' (*nāśî'*) or 'governor' (*peḥâ*, 5:14) of Judah. Certainty is impossible, however, and it can be argued that Sheshbazzar was simply a member of the Judean nobility, or even a Babylonian (see further, on 5:14).

**9.** The **number** of the temple **vessels** (or rather, 'utensils') is uncertain. The sum of the categories in the MT, 2,499 (so LXX, *AV*,

*NEB*), is very different from the total of 5,400 given in v. 11. *RSV* has attempted to amend the list by adopting from 1 Esd. 2:13f. several figures which add up to its total of 5,469. There is no guarantee, however, that 1 Esdras does not contain a secondary and artificial harmonisation of the list rather than the original text.

Many have regarded the numbers as the Chronicler's exaggerations in order to glorify the temple. But there is every reason to suppose that the inventory of Solomon's temple, including not only utensils specially made for cultic use (e.g. Exod. 25:29; 37:16; 1 Chr. 28:17; 2 Chr. 4:20ff.) and objects dedicated by worshippers (e.g. Num. 7:13f.) but also sacred objects brought back as booty from foreign wars (e.g. 2 Sam. 8:10ff.), ran into several thousands of items. For comparison, note the inventory of temple treasures plundered by Sargon from the temple of Haldia, god of Urartu, including $x + 4$ talents, 3 minas of gold, and 162 talents, 20 minas of silver, and hundreds of gold and silver objects (*ARAB*, II, pp. 96ff.). See also J. Bottéro, 'Les inventaires de Qatna', *RA* 43 (1949), pp. 1–40, 137–215, for a vast list of temple treasure; and Galling, 'Das Protokoll über die Rückgabe der Tempelgeräte', in *Studien*, pp. 78–88, arguing for the essential authenticity of the list as an inventory of Nebuchadrezzar's booty.

The types of temple utensils are well known from other passages (e.g. 2 Kg. 25:14ff., recording objects plundered from the temple), but nowhere else is there any indication of their number. These figures, therefore, though far from certain in detail, are valuable evidence for the vast wealth of the Jerusalem sanctuary. The list doubtless derives originally from an official receipt, probably in Aramaic, of which Mithredath the treasurer would have received one copy and Sheshbazzar the other.

The gold and silver **basins** (*AV* 'chargers') are probably libation vessels (as LXX *spondeia* in 1 Esd. 2:9); the Heb. *'aḡarṭēl* occurs only here, probably as a loanword from Persian (see Ellenbogen, *Foreign Words*, pp. 9ff.; C. Rabin, *Orientalia* 32 [1963], pp. 126ff., derives it from Hittite *kurtal*, 'container made of wood or basketwork', inappropriate in this context). The number of vessels, given in MT as 30, is emended by *RSV* to **a thousand**, following 1 Esd. 2:13; but this could be an inner-Greek corruption of ,A (1000) for Λ' (30) (J. A. Bewer, *Der Text des Buches Ezra* [1922], p. 16). **censers:** another obscure word, occurring only here. *AV*, 'knives', following Vulg., is still a more likely rendering (cf. N. Tromp, *VD* 41 [1963], pp. 299–304; and Ug. *ḥlp*, probably 'knife' [*UT* 19.402]). W. Rudolph suggests that the word, *maḥᵃlāp̄îm*, should be revocalised to *moḥᵒlāp̄îm*, 'to be altered', a marginal note (on **a thousand**) which

has mistakenly crept into the text. *NEB* also connects the word
with *ḥālap̄* 'to alter, change', and translates 'of various kinds'.

   **10. two thousand**: I Esd. 2:13 may well have correctly preserved
this numeral before **four hundred and ten bowls of silver**; MT 'of
a second sort' (so *AV*) makes little sense. Yet it is hard to see how
an original *'lpym*, 'two thousand', could have been corrupted to
*mšnym*, 'of a second sort'. *NEB*'s 'of various types' again traces the
word to a verb 'to change' (*šānâ*), and Rudolph finds here also an
intrusive marginal note, vocalising it as *mᵉšunnîm*, 'to be changed';
but it is a weakness in both suggestions that two different words
are used in successive verses for exactly the same thing.

   **11.** The MT total (5,400) is emended by *RSV*, following I Esd.
2:14, to 5,469, thus at least creating a self-consistent list, which is
perhaps the best that can be done with these recalcitrant figures.
Only **vessels of gold and of silver** are said to have been returned
(so, too, 5:14; 6:5); bronze vessels and objects taken by Nebuchadrezzar (2 Kg. 25:14f.) had either been melted down, as had presumably the bronze pillars and brazen sea (2 Kg. 25:13), or were not
valuable enough to be included in this list. The primary significance
of the list, for the Chronicler, lay in 'the completeness of restoration
without which the true continuity of worship might be in doubt'
(Ackroyd, *Exile*, p. 216).

   Not a word is said here of the circumstances of the journey,
though I Esd. 5:1–6 prefaces the homecomer list (= Ezr. 2) with a
romanticised description of the caravan, 'a thousand horsemen to
accompany them . . . , with a band of drums and flutes, and all
their brothers dancing' (*NEB*). The Chronicler's picture itself is
vivid enough: its term of exile having run its full course, vindicating
the prophetic word, Israel en masse returns to its homeland bearing
with it the blessing (how strange for Israel!) of a foreign yet God-
inspired emperor, and laden with goodwill gifts from Gentile neighbours and with all the treasures of the house of God. The Isaianic
vision that this would be an exodus to eclipse the exodus from
Egypt (Isa. 43:16–21) has become transformed, in the Chronicler's
narrative, into a historical reality.

### LIST OF RETURNED EXILES
#### ch. 2

This list of returned exiles is called in Neh. 7, where it is reproduced
with many minor variations, 'the book of the genealogy of those
who came up at the first' (Neh. 7:5). Is it then a list of those who
returned with Sheshbazzar? Its setting in Ezr. 2, immediately after
'all these did Sheshbazzar bring up' (1:11), would lead one to think

so, but this can hardly have been the case. For (i) Sheshbazzar is not mentioned among the leaders in 2:2; (ii) the total of 42,360 returning exiles (2:64) seems surprisingly large when compared with the numbers said to have been taken captive (2 Kg. 24:14; Jer. 52:28ff.); (iii) the frequent use in the list of the formula 'men of X-town' suggests that some parts of the list at least were compiled from a census of localities after the exiles had settled in their towns and villages; (iv) a list merely of those who had returned with Sheshbazzar would have been of little help to Nehemiah in establishing genealogies nearly 100 years later (cf. on Neh. 7:5).

The most probable explanation is that we are dealing here with a list of all those who returned between 538 and 520 or 515 BC (so, e.g., Rudolph, p. 17). By Nehemiah, nearly a century later, those returning groups could naturally be thought of as 'those who came up at the first' (Neh. 7:5). To these early years belong also the reference to freewill offerings towards the construction of the temple (Ezr. 2:68f.) and the allusion to the absence of a priest entitled to consult the holy oracle (2:63).

Various explanations of the purpose of the list have been offered. K. Galling thinks it was intended to prove to the Samarian adversaries of the returned exiles (cf. 5:3, 10) that they, the true Israel, capable of proving their legitimate descent, had sufficient material and human resources to rebuild the temple, and so had no need of help from the Samarians ('The Gōlā-List According to Ezra 2//Nehemiah 7', *JBL* 70 [1951], pp. 149–58). G. Hölscher supposed it was a Persian tax list (in *Die Heilige Schrift des ATs*, ed. E. Kautzsch, II [1923], pp. 503f.), and A. Alt thought it a list of Zerubbabel's to determine the rights of returning exiles to land (Alt, *KS*, II, pp. 334f.). W. F. Albright (*BP*, pp. 87, 110f.), followed by J. Bright (*History*, p. 376), took it to be a census of the population of Judah from about the time of Nehemiah; but we have already noted evidence suggesting the list originated long before his time. All the above proposals are quite speculative, and it seems improbable that it was originally a unified list with a single purpose; the different criteria by which the population is grouped suggests rather that it was compiled from independent registers of different kinds. What is agreed by most scholars today is that the list is no mere fiction of the Chronicler, as Torrey supposed (*Composition*, pp. 39ff.; *Studies*, p. 250), but is a collection, however incomplete and heterogeneous, of genuine contemporary lists.

Which, then, is its original place: Ezr. 2 or Neh. 7? In Neh. 7, the concluding verse (73*b*) is followed naturally by 8:1; but the same verse, with slight variations in Ezra (3:1), is not well suited to the context: in the book of Nehemiah as it stands 'the seventh month'

belongs to a stated year (445/4 BC), but in Ezra there is no indication
of the year. It would therefore appear that in Ezr. 2 the editor has
copied the list, together with the linking final verse, from its place
in the Nehemiah memoirs. It stands here in Ezra apparently, but
not in fact, as a list of the returnees under Sheshbazzar, because it
was the best list of exiles available to the editor.

For a similar account of how the list comes to be in Ezr. 2, cf.
e.g. Rudolph, pp. 11–15. Some support is still given to the view
that Ezr. 2 is its original place (e.g. Noth, *Studien*, pp. 124, 127ff.;
Mowinckel, *Studien I*, pp. 29–45), most recently by Kellermann (p.
25), who can prove only that the list is well integrated here, and
not that it was copied from here into Neh. 7. The other logical
alternative, that the list was copied from its archive original into
both positions, is held by Eissfeldt (pp. 550f.), who believes that
the Chronicler found the list both in his source for Ezr. 1:1–4:5 and
in the Nehemiah memoirs. The list proper, however, is followed in
both places by two narrative sentences (Ezr. 2:70–3:1; Neh.
7:72–8:1*a*) which are virtually identical; this makes one of the
'influence' theories much more likely.

There is considerable variation between the figures given here
and those in the parallel Neh. 7. Leaving aside the variations
between 2:68f. and Neh. 7:69ff., which are the result of editorial
manipulation, not scribal error, we may note that of the 49 figures
in 2:3–67, only 26 agree with those in the Nehemiah list (three are
missing altogether, and one is included in another figure; cf. vv.
30, 66, 21f.). The most common variants display a difference of ±1
in the units, tens, hundreds, or thousands (e.g. Adonikam, 666//667;
Bigvai, 2056//2067; Azgad, 1222//2322). Such differences will have
been due, as H. L. Allrik has shown (*BASOR* 136 [Dec. 1954],
pp. 21–7), to the employmnet in the original list of a numeral
notation rather like that attested in the Elephantine papyri (e.g. *AP*
28.1) in which units were marked by upright or oblique strokes
which could easily be miscounted, 'specially on ancient papyrus,
which tended to be fragile and quickly flaked, fractured, or wrin-
kled'. It is easier to assume, Allrik further argues, that signs have
been overlooked rather than added, so the significant number of
minuses in Ezr. 2 compared with Neh. 7 may be confirmatory
evidence of the priority of Neh. 7.

THE HEADING

2:1–2a

The list does not purport to be a census of a returning caravan of
exiles, but of **people of the province**, i.e. Jews already returned

and settled, at the time of compilation of the list, in their towns in Judah, a province of the fifth satrapy 'Beyond the River' (Aram. *'Aḇar-naharā'*) of the Persian Empire. The phrase **each to his own town** ought not to be pressed too literally, since some of the towns of returning exiles had never lain within the boundaries of Judah (especially Lod, Hadid, and Ono, v. 33), and doubtless a number of pre-exilic town-sites were never reoccupied, a fact still remembered in Talmudic times (TB, *Ḥullin* 7a). Nevertheless, there can be little doubt that exiles returned to their ancestral homes wherever possible.

Why are some homecomers numbered by family (or rather, phratry; see below on vv. 3–20) and others by town? Rudolph (p. 20) sees in the former the descendants of former landowners, the pre-exilic 'people of the land' (*'am hā'āreṣ*), and in the latter the landless 'poor of the land' (*dallat hā'āreṣ*). But the most natural solution is that the members of the seventeen (or eighteen) phratries are inhabitants of Jerusalem (so Batten, p. 78), whose lay citizens do not otherwise find a place in this list.

The ancestral towns of the returning exiles lie, with the exception of the three outposts mentioned in v. 33, within the borders of the late pre-exilic kingdom of Judah, and no more than 10 miles distant from Jerusalem. The fact that no towns south of Bethlehem and Netophah are named corresponds to Jeremiah's remark after Nebuchadrezzar's destruction of the Negeb in 598 BC that the 'cities of the Negeb are shut up' (Jer. 13:19) (see Noth, *History*, p. 283).

**2a.** To this list of eleven leaders of the exiles should be added, from Neh. 7:7 and 1 Esd. 5:8 (Eneneus), the name of Nahamani, which has dropped out here through scribal error. This is one of a score of points in this chapter at which 1 Esd. preserves a text older and more correct than our MT, and identical with MT of Neh. 7 (R. W. Klein, 'Old Readings in 1 Esdras: The List of Returnees From Babylon (Ezra 2//Nehemiah 7)', *HTR* 62 [1969], pp. 99–107). It can hardly be accidental that the leaders number twelve; such a number indicates that the Chronicler, and, before him, the original compilers of this list, regarded the homecoming exiles as representative of all Israel. It is possible that these names are those of the leaders of successive caravans of exiles (cf. Schneider, pp. 92f.); if so, it may be possible to recognise in **Nehemiah** the governor Nehemiah, and it is tempting for advocates of the priority of Nehemiah to Ezra to see in **Seraiah** (more obviously in the form the name is given in Neh. 7:7, viz. Azariah) the Biblical Ezra. But that is speculation; we do not even know that Nehemiah brought returning exiles with him, and it is safer to admit our ignorance of all but the first two names.

The exile has left its mark even on the names of the leaders of the returning exiles: **Bilshan** and **Mordecai** are Babylonian names, the latter containing the name of Marduk, god of Babylon; **Zerubbabel** is possibly Babylonian (cf. on 1:8), and **Bigvai** is Persian (cf. on v. 14). Myers notes throughout his commentary attestations of names in recently discovered documents, usefully supplementing the standard work on Israelite proper names, M. Noth, *Die israelitischen Personennamen* (1928).

**Reelaiah** is given as Raamiah in Neh. 1:7, **Rehum** as Nehum. In the latter case the Ezr. form, supported by 1 Esd. 5:8, is probably correct, since Rehum also occurs in Neh. 10:25 (different Rehums in Ezr. 4:8f. and Neh. 3:17).

LAYMEN

2:2b–35

The **men of the people of Israel** (v. 2b) are the laymen among the returned exiles, distinguished on the one hand from the returning priests and temple personnel (vv. 36–58) and on the other from the post-exilic 'people of the land' (4:4), i.e. Jews who had not been exiled, and non-Jews. The term **people of Israel** for the lay members of the community is an old priestly usage (cf. Num. 2:32f., 'The Levites were not numbered among the people of Israel'; similarly, 'Israel' in Ezr. 10:25). It is contrary to the Chronicler's custom to present lay members of the community before priests (cf. 1 Chr. 23–27), so we may assume that the list of this chapter was not compiled by him but found by him in its present form.

That this list is called the **number** of the people does not necessarily imply that its chief purpose is to count the number of returnees (*NEB* 'roll' is suitably vague). A census can have many purposes, e.g. it can be the basis for a taxation assessment. In Neh. 7:5 the same list is called a 'book of genealogy', but it is plainly not that either in the strict sense, for it contains no lines of descent. It could have functioned, however, at times as a genealogical list in the sense that if a Jew could trace his ancestry back to a family head mentioned in the list, he had proof of his membership of the true Israel in the most exclusive post-exilic sense.

In vv. 3–20 the exiles are classified by family ('the sons of . . .'), while in vv. 21–35 they are classified by town. In the latter case 'the sons of . . .' and 'the men of . . .' are used indiscriminately to signify the inhabitants of a town, but it is possible that in its original form the list used only the form 'men of . . .' before a town name. Certainly in Neh. 7 there is more consistency, in that all the town names from Bethlehem (v. 26//Ezr. 2:21) to Nebo (v. 33//Ezr. 2:29)

are preceded by 'men of . . .'; but thereafter, strangely, the indubit-
able place-names Jericho, Lod, Hadid, and Ono are preceded by
'sons of . . .' (so also here). It is very unusual to speak of the men
of a town as the 'sons' of that town, but perhaps the idiom was
used by analogy with the phrase that heads the list (v. 1), 'these
were the people (lit. 'sons') of the province' (*beñê hammedînâ*) and
with the similar phrase, 'sons of the exile' (*benê haggôlâ*) for 'exiles'
(Ezr. 4:1; 6:19–20; 8:35; 10:7, 16). It is therefore conceivable that
originally 'sons of . . .' was used throughout this list and that we
owe the intrusive 'men of . . .' to an overzealous scribe who knew
that that was the normal phrase for the inhabitants of a town.

## LAYMEN LISTED BY FAMILY (PHRATRY)

### 2:3–30

The term 'phratry' is used in this commentary as the translation of
Heb. *mišpāḥâ*, commonly translated as 'family' or 'clan'. The
*mišpāḥâ*, composed of several 'father's houses' or 'extended families'
(*bêt-'āḇ*; cf. on 1:5), was the primary division of the tribe (*šēḇeṭ*);
numbering as it must have in normal times 10,000 members or
more, it is too large to be called a 'family', or even a 'clan' (de
Vaux, *Ancient Israel*, p. 8). On the phratry, 'the most important
single group in Israelite society', see F. I. Andersen, *Bible Translator*
20 (1969), p. 35. Recognition of the nature of the phratry will
prevent astonishment at the size of the 'families' in this list (see B.
Mazar, *IEJ* 7 [1957], pp. 232f.). In most cases the names of these
phratries are to be found also in the parallel passages Neh. 7:8–25
and 1 Esd. 5:9–16 as well as in the lists in Ezr. 10:25–38 and Neh.
10:15–28.

   **3. Parosh** ('flea') is a common phratry name in post-exilic records
(8:13; 10:25; Neh. 3:25; 10:14) but unattested in pre-exilic times.

   **4. Shephatiah** ('Yahweh has judged') is found frequently in pre-
exilic and post-exilic texts. Other members of this phratry later
returned with Ezra (8:8).

   **5. Arah** ('ox' or 'traveller') appears in 1 Chr. 7:39f. as the head
of a 'father's house', but there in an Asherite list. A member of the
phratry is probably to be found in Neh. 6:18. The unusual form in
which the figure 775 is written suggests that the correct reading is
757, which differs from the 652 of Neh. 7 through the misreading
of only two signs, for 1 and for 5 (Allrik, *op. cit.*, p. 22).

   **6. Pahath-moab** is not a personal name, but means 'governor of
Moab'. Under David and Solomon Moab had been ruled from Judah
(2 Sam. 8:2), so perhaps this very large phratry of 2,812 (2,818 in
Neh. 7:11) traced its ancestry back to a governor of that period.

418 members returned with Ezra (Ezr. 8:4, 9), and some of its
members had married foreign wives (Ezr. 10:30). **Jeshua** (variant
form of Joshua) and **Joab** would be divisions of the phratry.

**7. Elam** has nothing to do with the country of Elam from which
Cyrus originated; it is the name in 1 Chr. 8:24 of a Benjamite family
head living in Jerusalem (cf. v. 28) at some indeterminate pre-
exilic time. One of the members of this phratry, Shecaniah, plays a
significant part in encouraging Ezra to annul the mixed marriages
(Ezr. 10:2).

**9. Zaccai** either means 'pure' or is a short form of Zechariah,
'Yahweh has remembered'; the Greek form is Zacchaeus (Lk. 19:2).
The wall-builder Baruch b. Zabbai (Neh. 3:20) may have been a
member of the phratry.

**10. Bani**, probably a short form of Benaiah, 'Yahweh has built',
is easily confused with the names Bunni and Binnui and with the
word *benê*, 'sons of' (cf. on v. 40). At first sight it appears that the
parallel Neh. 7:15 has Binnui instead of Bani; but if we take our
lead from Ezr. 10:34, 38, where both Bani and Binnui figure as
phratry names, it seems rather that scribes have mistakenly omitted
Binnui from Ezr. 2 and Bani from Neh. 7. The two names appear
again side by side as phratry names in Neh. 10:14, where, however,
Binnui has been corrupted to Bunni. To complicate the matter
further there are Levites called Bani (Neh. 3:17; 8:7; 9:4; 11:22),
Bunni (Neh. 9:4) and possibly Binnui (Neh 10:9).

**12. Azgad** is thought by some to mean 'the god Gad (*Fortune*) is
strong' (cf. Gaddiel, 'Gad is God', Num. 13:10, and the divine name
Gad in Isa. 65:11). With such a large phratry of 1,222 (or more
probably 2,322, Neh. 7:17), the eponymous ancestor is plainly pre-
exilic, so the name is no evidence for the worship of the god Gad
in exilic times. For the post-exilic cult of Gad (Isa. 65:11), cf. J.
Gray, *IDB*, II, p. 335.

**13. Adonikam**, 'The lord has arisen', an old Hebrew name type,
appears in Neh. 10:16 as Adonijah.

**14.** It is remarkable that one of the largest phratries (2,056
members; 2,067 according to Neh. 7) should bear a Persian name,
**Bigvai**, so early in the Persian period. In the form Bagoas the name
is known as that of the governor of Jerusalem *c.* 410 BC (*AP* 30.1;
32.1). Bagoas is usually said to be a Persian, but his name is not
sufficient evidence, and he may well have been a Jew. The name is
formed from the Persian *baga-*, 'god', and is probably a surrogate
for some older Hebrew theophoric name.

**16.** As with Bigvai, in this case also a foreign name, **Ater**, the
neo-Babylonian and Persian Etir, has replaced a Hebrew one. After
v. 16 two names, Azzur and Hodijah, attested in Neh. 10:17f. and

1 Esd. 5:15 (if Annias, i.e. Hananiah, represents Hodijah), are missing from Ezr. 2 and Neh. 7, possibly because these families were not among the earliest returning exiles.

17. **Bezai**, a short form of Bezalel 'in the shadow of God' (cf. Ps. 91:1), occurs in Neh. 7 after Hashum (v. 19).

18. In Neh. 7:24 the name that follows Bezai is Hariph, not **Jorah** as here. Since the number is the same in both cases (112), the names are probably applied to the same phratry. Hariph probably means 'autumnal' (cf. *ḥōreþ* 'autumn') and Jorah is very like *yôreh*, 'autumn rain', so they may well be alternative names.

20. The personal name **Gibbar**, unattested elsewhere (though cf. Aram. *gibbārā'*, 'hero'; Ass. Gabbaru), appears in Neh. 7:25 as the place-name Gibeon. It is difficult to decide between the two ('sons of', as distinct from 'men of', does not help much, as pointed out above), but since the list of places from Bethlehem on works northward, it is not likely that the northerly town of Gibeon should head the list. Since, however, three Gibeonite towns were settled (v. 25), Gibeon itself may also have belonged to the list originally.

LAYMEN LISTED BY TOWN

2:21–35

The place-names here, identified according to Aharoni, *Land*, unless otherwise indicated, may be found also in the parallel passages Neh. 7:36–38 and 1 Esd. 5:17–23. The four names in vv. 29–32 are perhaps additional phratry names rather than place-names.

Remarkably, only two towns in former Judahite territory, Bethlehem and Netophah (vv. 21f.) are mentioned, while the other nineteen, from Anathoth (v. 23) to Jericho (v. 34) or Senaah (v. 35), if that is a place-name, lie in Benjamite territory. Possibly the Benjamite towns surrendered more quickly to the invading Babylonians in 589 BC, and so were spared destruction (so A. Malamat, *JNES* 9 [1950], p. 227); alternatively, many Judahite towns may have been taken over by Edomites during the exile (so Brockington, p. 59); but the problem remains unsolved.

21–22. In Neh. 7:26 the totals of the inhabitants of **Bethlehem** (5 m. south of Jerusalem) and **Netophah** (3½ m. south-east of Bethlehem) are combined: 188, as against 123 + 56 = 179 in Ezra. Bethlehem, though never more than a village (cf. Mic. 5:2), had the distinction of being the birthplace of David. It was fortified by Rehoboam (2 Chr. 11:6). We do not know whether Micah's prophecy (5:2) of the rise of the messianic ruler from Bethlehem made any impression on returning exiles, but messianic expectations were certainly in the air (e.g. Zech. 6:11ff.), and it would have been strange if some had not looked for a fulfilment of the eighth-century prophecy. Netophah was resettled after the exile by Levites (1 Chr. 9:16) and, with its outlying hamlets, 'the villages of the Neto-phathites', by temple singers (Neh. 12:28f.).

**23. Anathoth**, a priestly city and the birthplace of Jeremiah (Jer. 1:1), lies 3 m. north-east of Jerusalem. For another list of Benjamite towns, see Neh. 11:31–35.

**24. Azmaveth**, or more fully Beth-azmaveth (Neh. 7:28; *NEB*, Beth-azmoth), is not mentioned in pre-exilic times, though the name is very old, but may be identified with modern Hizmeh, 5 m. north-north-east of Jerusalem. Temple singers settled there (Neh. 12:29).

**25.** These three towns were related to Gibeon (Jos. 9:17). **Kiriatharim** is clearly a scribal error for 'Kiriath-jearim' (*NEB*), as in Neh. 7:29. It lies 6 m. north-west of Gibeon on the boundary of Judah and Benjamin; it is Benjamite according to the town-list of Jos. 18:21–28, but included in Judah in Jos. 18:14; Jg. 18:12; 1 Chr. 2:50; 13:6. **Chephirah**, modern Kh. el Kefireh, was 5 m. west of Gibeon, and **Beeroth** is probably to be identified with the village of Nebi Samwil, a mile south of Gibeon and 5 m. north of Jerusalem.

**26. Ramah** and **Geba** were Benjamite frontier towns (cf. 1 Kg. 15:17, 22), both about 5 m. north of Jerusalem.

**27. Michmas**, about a mile north-east of Geba.

**28. Bethel** and **Ai** belonged originally to Ephraim, Bethel having been a famous sanctuary of the northern kingdom, but they were absorbed into the kingdom of Judah by Josiah in the closing years of the pre-exilic period (Noth, *History*, p. 273). **Bethel** lies about 12 m. north of Jerusalem. The location of **Ai**, usually identified with et Tell, 2 m. east of Bethel, is currently under discussion, J. A. Callaway denying there are any other suitable locations in the vicinity (*JBL* 87 [1968], p. 315), and J. M. Grintz (*Bib.* 42 [1961], pp. 201–16) and D. Livingston (*WTJ* 33 [1970], pp. 20–44) proposing alternative locations. See further, J. J. Bimson, *Redating the Exodus and Conquest* (1978), pp. 216–25.

**29. Nebo**, if a place-name, is very likely identical with Nob, a Benjamite settlement in Neh. 11:32, probably located on a hill overlooking Jerusalem from the north (cf. Isa. 10:32), possibly Mt Scopus (el Isawiyeh; mod. Heb. Har haZophim) or else modern Nuba, 15 m. south-west of Jerusalem (E. D. Grohman, *IDB*, III, p. 528; Simons, *Texts*, p. 380). It may be the place called in Neh. 7:33 'the other Nebo'; 'other' could be a scribal slip (since no other Nebo is mentioned), or perhaps a qualifier to distinguish it from the well-known Nebo in Moab (e.g. Isa. 15:2). In 10:43, and in Neh. 10:19 (in the form Nebai) it appears among personal names, so it could equally well be a phratry name (so e.g. Rudolph, p. 9, and presumably Aharoni, who does not offer an identification).

**30.** The entry for **Magbish** is missing in Neh. 7; as a place-name (meaning 'heaped up', i.e. hill) it is unidentified. A variant of the same name, Magpiash, occurs in Neh. 10:20, among a list of personal names of leading laymen; but since Anathoth and possibly Nebai in the preceding verse are place-names, one cannot be sure that Magbish is a personal name. It is not significant that it is here preceded by 'sons of'.

**31.** The **other Elam** may also be a phratry name, as is the first Elam (v. 7). A difficulty here is that exactly the same number (1254) is recorded of this Elam as of that in v. 7, a remarkable coincidence. While we ought not to delete v. 31 on this account, we must query the figure.

**32. Harim** ('dedicated') is a common personal and family name (Ezr. 2:39; 10:21, 31; Neh. 3:11; 7:35, 42; 10:6, 28; 12:15), both for priests and laymen; but no town of this name is known. It is possible to equate Nebo, Magbish, Elam and Harim with four modern place-names, 10–15 m. south-west of Jerusalem (Nuba, Kh. Maḥbiyeh or Kh. Qanan Mugheimis (Simons, *Texts*, p. 380), Beit 'Alam, Kh. Hôrân), but in the absence of evidence of Israelite towns of this name, the identification is precarious. If correct, it would add more Judahite towns to the list (cf. on vv. 21–35).

**33. Lod** (*NT* Lydda), **Hadid**, and **Ono** are towns within a few miles of one another, about 25 m. north-west of Jerusalem, thus much further from Jerusalem than any other towns settled by the returning exiles. A tradition preserved in 1 Chr. 8:12 assigns the foundation of Ono and Lod and its villages to a Benjamite, though they lay far outside Benjamite territory. Their Benjamite occupation in pre-exilic times is the most probable reason for their resettlement after the exile, though A. Alt also suggested that they were annexed by Josiah and so formed part of pre-exilic Judah (*KS*, II, p. 283). In post-exilic times they appear to have formed a neutral area between the provinces of Ashdod and Samaria (cf. Neh. 6:2; Alt, *KS*, II, p. 343 n.2). It is not surprising, in view of their remoteness from the capital, that townsmen from this area do not figure in any of the activities at Jerusalem (not even in the divorce of foreign wives, Ezr. 10). Jericho precedes these towns in Neh. 7:36f.

**34. Jericho**, 15 m. north-east of Jerusalem, theoretically part of the tribe of Benjamin (Jos. 18:21), belonged during most of the pre-exilic period to the northern kingdom (cf. 1 Kg. 16:34; 2 Kg. 2:4ff.), but shortly before the exile was probably included within Josiah's kingdom of Judah (cf. v. 28). Men of Jericho were involved in Nehemiah's wall-building (Neh. 3:2).

35. If **Senaah** is a place, it is probably to be identified with Magdalsenna, 8 m. north-east of Jericho; yet Neh. 3:3 speaks of the 'sons of Hassenaah' (i.e. 'the Senaah') among the wall-builders as if Senaah were a person (in that list 'men of' a town are clearly differentiated from 'sons of' a man). A Benjamite family of Hassenuah, mentioned in 1 Chr. 9:7; Neh. 11:9 may be identical with Senaah. It is most remarkable that the largest group of returning exiles (3,630 here, 3,930 in Neh. 7:38) should belong to a village otherwise unknown in Old Testament times, or to a Benjamite phratry rarely mentioned. Some have therefore thought that Senaah must be a term for a group not already listed, perhaps the lower classes or proletariat of Jerusalem; the form Hassenuah could mean 'the hated one' (feminine singular for collective), i.e. the rejected, despised ones. But it seems most unlikely that this could have been the official term for such a group (though Jerusalem as a whole is described poetically as *śᵉnûâ*, 'hated', in Isa. 60:15), and in any case there is no evidence that persons of all classes were not included in the phratry and town totals. The only group not represented in the whole list is of those individuals and small families resident in Jerusalem who did not belong to one of the phratries, i.e. people belonging to other Judahite and Benjamite phratries, possibly also to phratries from other tribes. We should perhaps find in Senaah/Hassenuah a reference to them. Those with an uncertain claim to membership of one of the phratries were a different category again (vv. 59f.).

### PRIESTS AND TEMPLE PERSONNEL
### 2:36–58

Those who served in the temple are now classified in groups (priests, Levites, singers, porters, temple servants, 'Solomon's servants'). The parallel lists are Neh. 7:39–60 and 1 Esd. 5:24–35.

**36–39. The priests**: To the four priestly phratries mentioned here are reckoned the returning priests. This genealogical division is to be distinguished from the functional division of the priests into 24 courses, as in Neh. 10:2–8; 12:1–7 (where only 21 and 22 names are preserved), following the traditional arrangements for temple service noted in 1 Chr. 24 (see further on Neh. 10:2–8). Some of the phratry names are to be found also in the course list, but obviously the Immer course (1 Chr. 24:14), for example, does not contain all the priests of the Immer phratry.

The large number (4,289) of returning priests, about ten per cent of the homecomers (if the list is complete), should occasion no surprise, since the prime object of the return was the re-establishment of the temple and its worship. On the priesthood, see further, A. Cody, *A History of Old Testament Priesthood* (1969).

**36.** The phratry of **Jedaiah** provided the second course of priests in the Solomonic temple according to 1 Chr. 24:7; **Jeshua** is Jeshua b. Jozadak (cf. Ezr. 10:18), the high priest contemporary with Zerubbabel (Ezr. 3:28). Naturally no one in his lifetime could have 973 adult male descendants, so **of the house of Jeshua**, which is syntactically awkward, must simply be intended to note that the high priest belonged to the Jedaiah phratry. In Ezr. 10:18 the phratry is referred to, not by its proper name, but, out of deference to the high priest, as the 'sons of Jeshua b. Jozadak and his brethren'.

**37-39.** The **Immer** phratry supplied the sixteenth course, according to 1 Chr. 24:14; **Pashhur** is not one of the 24 priestly courses, but probably represents the Malchijah course. Neh. 10:3 has both Pashhur and Malchijah, which could be a revival of the old course name; for a name ending b. Pashhur b. Malchijah, cf. Neh. 11:12; and for a pre-exilic Pashhur b. Malchijah, see Jer. 21:1; 38:1. On the name Pashhur, see S. Ahituv, *IEJ* 20 (1970), pp. 95f. **Harim** provided the third course (1 Chr. 24:8).

**40.** The number of **Levites** is remarkably small, **seventy-four**, compared with over 4,000 priests (contrast the 38,000 male Levites over 30 years of age numbered by David, according to 1 Chr. 23:3). Even if we accept with many scholars that the distinction between priests and Levites became operative only after the exile (the references to the establishment of this distinction by Moses being a retrojection of post-exilic practice), it would still be surprising that so many more descendants of priestly families (whatever criterion may have been used) returned than of the far more numerous non-priestly Levites. The Ezra memoirs (Ezr. 8:15) provide independent confirmation that the Levites showed no interest in returning to the land; only 38 Levites could be persuaded to join a caravan of about 1,500 (though 220 non-Levitical temple servants helped to swell the numbers).

Why did so few Levites return? If the degradation in their status had occurred during the exile, that would be a sufficient reason. Myers suggests it was because they were a neglected group in the exile and had turned their talents to other quarters (p. 18). Very probably it was not just a question of lack of interest, but rather that there were very few Levites any longer to be found. Ezr. 8 does not actually speak of unwillingness on the part of the Levites, but of difficulty in finding any. Since the Levites' temple duties would have ceased at the exile, they would have had to look for other work, and had presumably been absorbed into secular occupations.

There is also the reasonable possibility that since the Levites formed rather a lowly social class not many of them had been deported (cf. 2 Kg. 24:14; 25:12).

The lists of Levite names in Ezra-Nehemiah have been greatly corrupted in transmission, and certainty is unattainable. Perhaps we have here four Levite families **Jeshua**, **Kadmiel**, Bani or possibly Binnui (reading *bny* for *lbny;* Binnui is a well-attested Levite family name: e.g. 8:33; Neh. 3:17), and Hodaviah. This would correspond to four of the six Levite names in Neh. 12:8 (Hodaviah being a variant form of Judah). Another method of restoring order is to take a lead from Ezr. 3:9, and find here three families, Bani (revocalising *bny*, the first 'the sons of'), Jeshua, and Kadmiel. Ezr. 3:9 has three families: Jeshua, Kadmiel of the sons of Judah (= Hodaviah), and the sons of Henadad. The original pattern is clearly 'X of the sons of Y', three times repeated; we can supply the missing members f..m Neh. 10:9, where Jeshua's ancestor is given as Azaniah, and the Henadad family is called 'Binnui (= Bani) of the sons of Henadad'. So the fully-written list here would have been: 'Bani (family) of Henadad (phratry), Jeshua of Azaniah, Kadmiel of Hodaviah'. The three families Bani, Henadad, and Jeshua are to be found also in Neh. 3:17ff. But in Ezr. 3:9 'the sons of Henadad' is apparently a gloss, not being integrated into the syntax of the verse, and perhaps the simplest solution is to suppose that in the time of Zerubbabel there were only the Jeshua and Kadmiel families of Levites, the Henadad family forming a third group in Nehemiah's time. A scribe familiar with the threefold Levite division, missing the name of Henadad in Ezr. 3:9, will have simply inserted it.

**41–42.** The **singers** and **gatekeepers** were also Levites; so the Levites of v. 40 correspond to the groups of Levites of 1 Chr. 9:14–16 and 23:4a without specified tasks. In later lists (Neh. 12:8f., 24, 27; 1 Chr. 15:4f.; cf. Ezr. 3:10) singers and gatekeepers are included with Levites, which leads some (e.g. W. Rudolph, *Chronikbücher* [1955], p. 121) to suggest that it was only later than Zerubbabel's time that they were upgraded to Levite status. But the priestly legislation, probably earlier than Zerubbabel, does not distinguish them from Levites, while Ezr. 10:24 and Neh. 11:15–20 and 12:24f. from Nehemiah's time, include singers with Levites, but list gatekeepers separately. 1 Chr. 9:14–32, later than Nehemiah in its present form, does likewise, but insists that gatekeepers also are Levites. These are merely terminological differences, and no historical changes can be inferred (cf. J. M. Myers, *1 Chronicles* [1965], pp.120f.) Only one of the three family groups of singers mentioned in 1 Chr. 25:1 (cf. 6:31–47; 15:16–22), appears here, **the sons of Asaph.** A number of psalms (Pss. 50, 73–83) are ascribed to this guild (see M. J. Buss, 'The Psalms of Asaph and Korah', *JBL* 82 [1963], pp. 382–91), whose eponymous ancestor was not improbably a contemporary of David. The gatekeepers are also said by 1 Chr. 23:5 to have been appointed by David; their tasks, which included more than their name indicates (cf. 1 Chr. 9:17–32), were among the most humble of levitical chores (cf. Ps. 84:10, a psalm of the Korah guild of temple singers: 'I would rather be a doorkeeper in the house of my God than dwell in the tents of wickedness'). **Shallum, Talmon**, and **Akkub** are mentioned in 1 Chr. 9:17 among the gatekeepers. Shallum the Korahite, established as gatekeeper of the tabernacle in the time of David according to 1 Chr. 9:22, was the eponymous ancestor of the gatekeepers; in the late 7th century a Maaseiah b. Shallum is 'keeper of the threshhold' (Jer. 35:4). **Talmon** is Telem in 10:24.

**43–54.** The term for the hereditary caste of **temple servants** or slaves (*nᵉṯînîm; AV*, 'Nethinims') occurs first in post-exilic texts, but the institution is much older (by David, according to 8:20). The cognate term *ytmn* heads a Ugaritic list of temple slaves (*UT* 301, 1.1) in which, curiously, the name Hagab/Hagabah (vv. 45f.), not attested elsewhere in the *OT*, appears (*UT* 301, II.5). The name **Keros** (v. 44), previously unattested, has recently appeared on a Hebrew ostracon from Arad, which may afford a slight evidence of pre-exilic Nethinim (B. A. Levine, *IEJ* 19 [1969], pp. 49ff.) The Gibeonites were made slaves by Joshua in order to cut wood and draw water for the congregation and the shrine (Jos. 9:27), and it was normal practice in ancient warfare for sanctuaries to share in the booty, including prisoners (cf. Num. 31:25–47; Ezr. 8:20). On the Nethinim, see de Vaux, *Ancient Israel*, pp. 89f.; M. Haran, 'The Gibeonites, the Nethinim and the sons of Solomon's servants', *VT* 11 (1961), pp. 159–69; E. A. Speiser, *IEJ* 13 (1963), pp. 71f; J. Blenkinsopp, *Gibeon and Israel* (1972), pp. 106ff. The neo-Baby-lonian temple-servants called *širku* 'dedicated', like Heb. *nᵉṯînîm*, 'given', form a closely parallel group. Contrary to the general opinion, B. A. Levine, 'The Netînîm', *JBL* 82 (1963), pp. 207–12, argues that they were not slaves but 'a cultic guild whose members were devoted yet free'. The use of foreigners for the humblest jobs is strikingly confirmed by the names, which are either non-Israelite or nicknames such as servants might be given. Yet in spite of their mean status the Nethinim were members of the congregation of Israel who had 'separated themselves from the peoples of the lands to the law of God' (Neh. 10:28), and shared the priests' and Levites' immunity from taxation. The Nethinim lived on Ophel, from where access to the spring Gihon was easy via the Water Gate (Neh. 3:26).

Among the foreign names are the **Meunim** (v. 50), Arabs from

Ma'an (or perhaps inhabitants of the Negeb town Maon, Jos. 15:55; cf. 1 Sam. 23:24; see J. R. Bartlett, *JTS* 20 [1969], p. 6 n. 5), several times conquered by kings of Judah (2 Chr. 20:1–23; 26:7; possibly 1 Chr. 4:39–41); the **Nephisim** (v. 50), an Ishmaelite tribe also conquered by Israel (1 Chr. 5:18–22); **Ziha** (v. 43) and **Asnah** (v. 50) Egyptian; **Barkos** (v. 53) probably Edomite (the name means 'sons of Kos', the Edomite, or perhaps Arabian, god; cf. T. C. Vriezen, 'The Edomitic Deity Qaus', *OTS* 14 [1965], pp. 330–53; M. Rose, *JSOT* 4 [1977], pp. 28–34; J. R. Bartlett, *JSOT* 5 [1977], pp. 29–38); **Rezin** (v. 48) Aramaic (cf. the Aramaean king of that name, Isa. 7:1); **Sisera** (v. 53) (cf. Jg. 4, 5) perhaps Illyrian, certainly not Semitic; **Besai** (v. 49) possibly Babylonian. Among the nicknames are **Hasupha** (v. 43), 'Quick'; **Neziah** (v. 54), perhaps 'Faithful'; others are physical descriptions, as often in Israelite names (Noth, *IP*, pp. 224–8; L. Koehler, *Hebrew Man* [1956], pp. 64–7): **Lebanah** (v. 45), 'White'; **Nekoda** (v. 48), 'Spotted'; **Paseah** (v. 49), 'Lame'; **Hakupha** (v. 51), 'Stooped'. **Hatipha** (v. 54), 'Snatched', and **Mehida** (v. 52) (perhaps for Mehira, 'Bought') indicate the circumstances of acquisition. **Shamlai** (v. 46) appears as Shalmai in Neh. 7:48. **Akkub** (v. 45), **Hagab** (v. 46, possibly a mistaken repetition of Hagabah, v. 45), and **Asnah** (v. 50) are missing from Neh. 7.

**55–57.** The class known as **Solomon's servants** were originally Canaanites formed into a task-force (*corvée*) by Solomon (1 Kg. 9:20f.; 2 Chr. 8:7f.); they were state slaves who had become, perhaps during the exile, temple servants (and are so called in Ezr. 7:24). They bear slave names like those of the Nethinim: **Peruda** (v. 55) (probably Perida, as in Neh. 7:57), 'solitary'; **Darkon** (v. 56), 'rough'; perhaps 'stern'; **Hattil** (v. 57), 'talkative'. The feminine form names **Hassophereth** (v. 55), 'The Teacher', and **Pochereth-hazzebaim** (v. 57), 'Gazelle-hunter', may indicate an office or hereditary occupation (cf. Qoheleth, 'the preacher'?).

**58.** Only a small number of these lowest temple servants returned, an average of eight from each of the 45 families mentioned. Even of the doorkeepers each family averaged about 23 homecomers.

THOSE WITHOUT PROOF OF ANCESTRY

2:59–63

One of the chief functions of this list was to define who was and who was not a true member of Israel. It was apparently the responsibility of the heads of father's houses to keep genealogical records (cf. 1 Chr. 4:33; 5:7), and unless a line of descent reaching back to one of the certified phratry-founders could be produced by a *pater familias*, full enjoyment of the rights and privileges of members of the community could not be had. But besides establishing the legitimacy of individuals and families, such a list as the present one may be seen as an attempt to express the continuity between the old pre-exilic Israel and the new Israel of the restoration. See further, M. D. Johnson, *The Purpose of the Biblical Genealogies* (1969), esp. pp. 42ff.; A. Malamat, *JAOS* 88 (1968), p. 163.

With the priests it was far different, for uncertainty about a man's priestly descent involved a risk of contaminating the worship and the sacred objects (on the care with which priestly ancestry was investigated in later times, see Mishnah, *Qid.* 4.4f.; SB, 1, pp. 2ff.; Jeremias, *Jerusalem*, pp. 154ff.). These families were therefore desacralised by authority of the governor Zerubbabel until such time as a competent religious authority should decide their case by means of sacred divination. Neither they nor the laymen (vv. 59f.) were excluded from the community. Even under the regime of Ezra only those whose ancestry could be proved to be non-Jewish were expelled (10:16f.).

**59.** These five Babylonian towns cannot be identified; the element *tel* ('mound') suggests that at least two of their villages were Jewish settlements on the site of ruined Babylonian towns (cf. Tel-abib, Ezek. 3:15).

**60.** We have no evidence that these families who had lost trace of their ancestry were ever able to prove their descent. **Delaiah** is attested elsewhere only as a personal name from Nehemiah's time (Neh. 6:10; and 1 Chr. 3:24, a seventh-generation descendant of Zerubbabel; and one of Sanballat's sons; *AP* 30.29). The Tobijah of Zech. 6:10, 14 could possibly belong to the **Tobiah** family. **Nekoda** is known only as the name of a Nethinim family (v. 48). Those who failed to prove their ancestry came to constitute the ninth degree of genealogical purity according to one rabbinic formulation (Mishnah, *Qiddushin*, 4.1; Danby, *Mishnah*, p. 327).

**61. the sons of** seems to be a scribal addition and should be omitted with Neh. 7:63. The family of **Hakkoz** ('the thorn') was later reinstated, for we find that in the time of Ezra a certain Meremoth b. Uriah of the Hakkoz family (cf. Neh. 3:4) is acting as a priest (Ezr. 8:33). The **Barzillai** family traced their ancestry to Barzillai the Gileadite (2 Sam. 17:27ff.; 19:31–39), a nobleman contemporary with David, and their claim that one of the sons of Barzillai was actually a priestly Levite by birth could not be checked. The taking of the name of one's wife's family is not paralleled.

**62. unclean** (*AV* 'polluted') of course refers only to ritual purity, and even so only to the absence of proof of descent.

**63. the governor** translates the Persian honorific *tiršāṯā'*, 'His Excellency, His Reverence', the title of a provincial governor (cf. Neh. 8:9). Exclusion from partaking of the most holy food, the portion designated for the male Aaronic priests (Lev. 2:3; 7:1, 6) would still allow them to eat the ordinary holy food reserved for priestly families and Levites (cf. e.g. Neh. 12:44, 47). In any case this exclusion was only temporary until the establishment of a high priest with **Urim and Thummim**, the sacred lot, according to the fall of which decisions beyond the reach of human wisdom could be made. The use of this method of discovering the will of God is attributed only to times no later than the time of Saul (1 Sam. 28:6); Josephus' claim (*Ant.* 3.8.9) that it ceased only *c.* 100 BC is dismissed by most scholars. Perhaps the existence of the law, or of prophecy, had rendered use of the lot unnecessary (cf. the Rabbinic tradition that it ceased from the time of the 'first prophets': Mishnah, *Soṭah* 9.12, though according to TB, *Soṭah* 48b the 'first prophets' include all but Haggai, Zechariah, and Malachi). If the Urim and Thummim were not preserved into post-exilic times (and biblical evidence is completely lacking), we can only assume that it was expected that with the restoration of the temple would come the restoration of the priesthood's hereditary privileges. A Talmudic interpretation that **until there should be a priest to consult Urim and Thummim** means 'until the dead rise and the Messiah, the son of David, comes' (TB, *Soṭah* 48b), indicates the virtual disappearance eventually of the hope of restoration of the Urim and Thummim. If the legitimacy of these families was in fact solved, as Ezr. 8:33 suggests, and not left in permanent abeyance, some other method of determining the issue must have been used. In that case it is not the Chronicler, but his source, who holds the hope of the restoration of Urim and Thummim; thereby a potential indicator of the Chronicler's eschatological expectations evaporates (cf. Coggins, p. 20). **Urim and Thummim** appear to be two small objects kept in a pouch of the high priest's ephod (Exod 28:30; Lev. 8:8). By casting these objects like dice an oracle indicated 'Yes' (e.g. 1 Sam. 23:9–12; 30:7–8) or 'No' (no example) or 'No answer' (e.g. 1 Sam. 14:36f.). It is plausibly suggested that each object was marked identically, one side negatively (**Urim** probably means 'curses'), the other positively (**Thummim** meant 'perfection[s]'); if both displayed the same face, the answer was plainly Yes or No, but one Urim and Thummim meant 'no reply' (cf. J. A. Motyer, *NBD*, p. 1306). Less plausible suggestions have been made by E. Robertson, *VT* 14 (1964), pp. 67–74; J. Maier, *Kairos* 11 (1969), pp. 22–8.

## THE TOTALS
### 2:64–67

The figure of 42,360 is not the sum of the individual totals of
the list, viz. 29,818 (or 31,089 according to Neh. 7). Attempts at
harmonisation are unconvincing. By emending three figures (in
2:12, 16, 31) J. Bewer arrived at a total of 32,360 for which 42,360
would be a simple scribal error involving only one digit (*Der Text
des Buches Ezra* [1922], p. 33). W. Rudolph's suggestion (p. 25)
that the difference is due to the inclusion of women in the grand
total suffers from the improbability that three times as many men
as women would have returned from exile. The large number of
male and female **servants** (7,337) implies a higher standard of living
among the homecomers than has often been realised (cf. Hag. 1:4,
'panelled houses'). Of similar significance is the number of **singers**,
200 (245 in Neh. 7:67) secular musicians belonging to families, not
temple singers (2:41) (women singers were not to be found in the
temple). Obviously the social status of such minstrels, mentioned
only at the foot of the list, cannot have been very high. Ezr. 1:6
speaks of cattle accompanying the returning exiles, since the description there is to some extent patterned on the exodus from Egypt
(cf. 'very many cattle, both flocks and herds', Exod. 12:38). Here
only animals for riding and bearing loads are mentioned, as would
be appropriate in a caravan inventory, which this part of the list
perhaps was originally. **horses** and **mules** (for riding, cf. 2 Sam.
13:29; 18:9) are lacking in Neh. 7:68; but that may be a scribal
omission. **asses** are beasts of burden (cf. 2 Sam. 16:1). Reference
to beasts of burden would suit Galling's theory of the original
significance of the list (see ch. 2, p. 44 above), but the mention of
animals for riding would be out of place.

## GIFTS FOR THE TEMPLE
### 2:68–69

This paragraph is an editorial abbreviation of its equivalent in Neh.
7:70ff. Here we have 61,000 gold darics, 5,000 silver minas, 100
priests' garments. Neh. 7, analysing the contributions of the
governor, the heads of fathers' houses, and the rest of the people,
gives totals of 41,000 gold darics, 4,200 silver minas, 50 basins, 597
priests' garments. Most commentators bring the lists into harmony
thus: the last words of Neh. 7:70 are literally: 'priests' garments,
thirty and five hundred'. If we suppose that 'silver minas' (*ksp
mnym*) has dropped out before 'five hundred', Neh. 7 has 30 priests'
garments given by the governor and 67 by the family heads, making

a total of 97 (roughly equivalent to the 100 of Ezr. 2:69), and 4,700 minas of silver (roughly equivalent to the 5,000 of Ezr. 2). The difference between the 61,000 gold darics of Ezra and the 41,000 of Nehemiah may be due to scribal error, or to the editor's valuation of the 50 (gold?) basins of Neh. 7:70 at 4,000 darics apiece (Rudolph, p. 26). But there is a better explanation: **some of the heads of families . . . made freewill offerings** implies that some did not, which is unbelievable; the fuller Neh. 7:70f. shows that there were in fact two categories of family heads. Some 'gave to the work', while some gave 20,000 gold darics and 2,200 minas of silver 'to the treasury of the work'. There is apparently a distinction between gifts to two different funds. K. Galling, *JBL* 70 (1951), p. 151, suggested a building and a furnishing fund (priests' garments are natural gifts to the latter); cf. *NEB*, 'the work, the fabric fund' (Neh. 7:70f.). So it may reasonably be suggested that the total of gifts to the first fund has dropped out of our present text, and that their total was also 20,000 gold darics (+ perhaps 300 minas of silver). These figures were however included by the editor of Ezr. 2 when he compiled his totals.

The **daric** was a gold coin of 8.424 grams. The name is usually derived from Darius I (521–486 BC) who is represented on the daric half-length or kneeling with a bow and arrow (illustration: *IDB*, III, p. 431, fig. 2; a similar representation on the silver siglos in *NBD*, p. 838, fig. 145 no. 4). The anachronistic reference here to darics at a period earlier than Darius may be accounted for by supposing that the editor simply employs the term for a gold coin that was common in his time. The total weight of gold would be 1,133 lbs. The **mina** is not a coin like the daric, but a weight of *c.* 570 gm (20 oz.), fifty times the common shekel of *c.* 11.4 gm; 5,000 minas of silver would weigh 6,250 lbs. The giving of freewill offerings for the temple is reminiscent of the accounts of the tabernacle preparations in Exod. 25:2–7; 35:21–29, and of the temple building in 1 Chr. 29:2–9; the similarity is natural, since such undertakings were likely to have prompted, or demanded, such gifts.

**69.** The **priests' garments**, or rather tunics (*keṯōneṯ*, usually translated 'coat' in *RSV*) were made of intricately embroidered linen (Exod. 28:4; cf. 28:39; 39:27).

SETTLEMENT IN THE LAND

2:70

Once he has given an account of funds for the temple, the rebuilding of which was one of the main purposes of the return, the compiler of the list can conclude by mentioning where the homecomers actually

settled, for of course there was no room for them all in ruined
Jerusalem. Verse 70 says in MT: 'The priests, the Levites, some of
the people, the singers, the gatekeepers, and the temple servants
lived in their towns, and all Israel in their towns'. Neh. 7:73 is
almost the same, except that 'and all Israel' follows 'the temple
servants' and 'in their towns' appears only once. The problem is:
what can 'some of the people' mean as distinct from 'all Israel'? It
is likely that the author was in this last verse referring back to v.
1, 'they returned to Jerusalem and Judah, each to his own town',
and that while priests and Levites and some of the people returned
to Jerusalem, the rest of the people returned to their own villages
in the province of Judah. *RSV* therefore adopts the longer reading
of 1 Esd. 5:46: 'the priests, the Levites, and some of the people
lived in Jerusalem and its vicinity . . .' (cf. *NEB*). Religious and
civil leaders would naturally congregate at the capital, where sacrifices were reinstituted soon after the return and administrative tasks
must have needed attention immediately. For the **towns** of the
**singers**, cf. on Neh. 12:28f.

Nothing is said by the Chronicler, in incorporating the list of
Ezr. 2 into his narrative, of the vast difficulties that must have
attended this process of resettlement. Of course, it is not his purpose
to describe the home-coming in detail. Nevertheless, in viewing this
period of the re-establishment of the Jewish state on Palestinian soil
as an ideal period in Israel's history (cf. also Neh. 12:44–13:3), he
omits, of necessity, any hint of the grave economic and social
difficulties (especially of adjustment with those who had remained
in the land) the returning exiles must have faced. (Cf. the idealism
of 'all Israel in their towns', 2:1.)

Already in this list of homecoming exiles, one of the great virtues
of the post-exilic community as viewed by its historian may be
discerned: it is a community where what matters is the response of
everyone, from princes (v. 2) to temple servants (vv. 55–58), to the
new act of creation and redemption which God has performed. No
longer can the only evaluation of the worth of a community be a
verdict on the religious activities of a king, as is so often the case
in the Books of Kings: now those who are registered as the 'Pilgrim
Fathers' of the community and who will determine the moral and
religious condition of their nation are family groups of villagers and
temple servitors, not just nobles and priests (see further, Introduction, V; and on Neh. 10:32f.).

But at the same time, this list shows us a community that is much
concerned to draw lines of demarcation both between itself and
outsiders and between groups within Israel. It is nothing strange
that the hereditary priesthood should survive into the post-exilic

period, but it was all too easy for a caste of professional religious men to arrogate to itself the privileges and responsibilities of all the people of God and to look with disdain upon laymen—such was to happen in Judaism in the development of the class of the scribes, and Christianity also has suffered from similar tendencies. Furthermore, in the concern, very evident here, for testimony of pure Israelite descent, the spectre of racialism is visible, however large a measure of praiseworthy insistence upon purity of worship is mixed with it (cf. also on 4:1–5; ch. 9–10). This is a community that is building into its understanding of God's will elements that threaten to mask the purposes for which God has chosen it.

## THE REBUILDING OF THE TEMPLE PLANNED AND THWARTED ch. 3–4

### RE-ESTABLISHMENT OF WORSHIP

### 3:1–6

The restoration of the temple and its worship was the *raison d'être* of the return; the Chronicler therefore stresses that at the first opportunity after arrival in Jerusalem, even before the temple-building could be set under way, the returning exiles signified their preoccupation with spiritual matters by reinstituting the daily and festival cult. It is possible that the altar of the Solomonic temple had not been destroyed and sacrifices had in fact been offered in the temple ruins from time to time during the exile (cf. Jer. 41:5; so Bright, *History*, p. 344; Noth, *History*, p. 291; E. Janssen, *Juda in der Exilszeit* [1956], pp. 94–104. But note the contrary argument of D. R. Jones, 'The Cessation of Sacrifice after the Destruction of the Temple in 586 B.C.', *JTS* 14 [1963], pp. 12–31; cf. also on 4:2). But even so, the men of the return, and the Chronicler after them, would doubtless have regarded such sacrifices and the altar on which they were offered as illegitimate and polluted; so the first necessity was the building of an altar. A good biblical precedent for the offering of sacrifices before the building of a temple existed in the case of David (2 Sam. 24:18–25), and would have provided confirmation to the returned exiles that they were involved in nothing less than a restitution of the most splendid period of Israel's history.

1. The **seventh month** is, in the context, the seventh month (Tishri; September/October, 538 BC) of Cyrus' first regnal year (cf. 1:1), or of the first year of the return, if that is different (cf. 3:8). Rudolph (p. 29) thinks six months does not give enough time for

the return, and suggests the events of Ezr. 3 occurred in the second or third year of Cyrus. But curiously, the register in Neh. 7 is also succeeded by a reference to the seventh month, there apparently related to the sixth month (Elul) (Neh. 6:15) of 445 BC. Some therefore suggest that with the copying of the list from Nehemiah, this date also has been transferred, erroneously, to Ezra; even if that is the case, the seventh month, being the most important month in the liturgical year (cf. Num. 29; Lev. 23:23–43), is a quite likely time for the resumption of sacrifice. And it is perhaps not improbable that the exiles timed their return so as to coincide with the beginning of the seventh month.

**2. Jeshua** (a variant of Joshua, as he is called in Hag. 1:1, 12, 14, etc., 'Yahweh is salvation') and **Zerubbabel** ('Seed, i.e. offspring, of Babylon'), usually appear in the reverse order (2:2; 3:8; 4:3; 5:2; Neh. 7:7; 12:1; Hag. 1:1, 12, 14; 2:2, 4), but here where cultic affairs are directly concerned Jeshua takes the precedence. Jeshua's father **Jozadak** (= Jehozadak) was high priest at the time of the exile in 587 BC (1 Chr. 6:15), and Jeshua is called high priest elsewhere (Neh. 12:10; Hag. 1:1, 14; 2:2). **Zerubbabel** was the grandson of the exiled king of Judah, Jehoiachin (Jeconiah) (1 Chr. 3:17ff.), and thus in Jewish eyes the legitimate secular ruler. He is usually called son of Shealtiel (Ezr. 3:2, 8; 5:2; Neh. 12:1; Hag. 1:1, 12, 14; 2:2, 23) but once (1 Chr. 3:19) son of Pedaiah; perhaps we should admit that we do not know the truth about his parentage, but the suggestion is worth mentioning that though he was the physical son of Pedaiah, he was legally Shealtiel's son, Shealtiel's widow having married her brother-in-law Pedaiah (a levirate marriage, Dt. 25:5–10).

The Chronicler takes a much less excited view of Zerubbabel than did the prophets of the time, Haggai and Zechariah. For the Chronicler, Zerubbabel is simply the Persian governor; even his descent from the Davidic line is not mentioned. Kellermann has supposed therefore a large-scale conflict between messianic and anti-messianic interpretations of Zerubbabel (and Nehemiah) in their time (pp. 96f.). But this is to go too far; the Chronicler takes such a dispassionate view of Zerubbabel simply because events have proved that he was not a messianic figure. For the prophets and Zerubbabel's contemporaries, however, the office given to Zerubbabel is an integral part of the fulfilment of the divine promises of restoration—no perfect fulfilment, for Judah is still a Persian province, but a partial fulfilment that contains both satisfaction and expectation (cf. Ackroyd, *Exile and Restoration*, p. 190).

Jeshua and Zerubbabel are usually mentioned in connection with the period *c.* 520 BC, the beginning of the reign of Darius I, so many scholars regard this reference to them in 538 as anachronistic, perhaps due to a faulty identification by the Chronicler of Zerubbabel with Sheshbazzar. A. Alt (*KS*, II, p. 335), for example, linked the coming of Zerubbabel with the activity of Cambyses in Palestine and Egypt *c.* 524 BC, and K. Galling would bring the arrival of Zerubbabel down into the age of Darius I (*Studien*, pp. 58ff. See further, P. R. Ackroyd, *JNES* 17 [1958], p. 21).

The link between this account of Zerubbabel and the beginning of Cyrus' reign is indeed weak (cf. on v. 1; v. 8 may not be independent evidence), and the absence of Sheshbazzar from the scene of restoration of the temple foundations is surprising in view of his clear connection with that activity in 5:14–16, in a document older than the Chronicler's work. Nevertheless, we may certainly accept the Chronicler's claim that sacrifice was reinstituted and temple-building begun very soon after the arrival of the homecomers in the land, even though we have no supporting evidence that Zerubbabel himself was involved in these activities.

Had the altar been demolished at the sack of Jerusalem, and did it have to be rebuilt by Jeshua and Zerubbabel? We have no direct evidence, but the deliberate demolition of the altars of one's enemies was an attested practice (2 Kg. 23:15; cf. Hos. 10:2; Ezek. 6:6), and even had the altar survived destruction, it would probably have been pulled down by the returning exiles because of the likelihood of its having been defiled by heathen worship in the absence of legitimate Israelite priests (cf. the procedure after the defilement of the altar by Antiochus Epiphanes IV, 1 Mac. 4:42–47). The altar would have been rebuilt of unhewn stones, according to the **law of Moses** (Exod. 20:25; cf. Dt. 27:6; 1 Mac. 4:47). **man of God**: The term signifies that he possessed some superhuman qualities or functions (cf. the 'man of God' in Jg. 13:6 who is 'the angel of God', 13:9). Usually it is prophets who are thus termed (e.g. Samuel, Elijah, Elisha; 1 Sam. 9:6; 1 Kg. 17:18; 2 Kg. 4:7; etc.); so too Moses in his prophetic capacity (Dt. 33:1; Ps. 90 title; Jos. 14:6); perhaps this is also the background of the use of it in reference to Timothy (1 Tim. 6:11; 2 Tim. 3:17). But without particular prophetic significance it is applied by the Chronicler to Moses (also 1 Chr. 23:14; 2 Chr. 30:16) and to David (2 Chr. 8:14; Neh. 12:24, 36), in all cases in connection with their commandments, thus stressing the divine authority of the laws established by them, rather than simply their 'special nearness to the Godhead' (R. Hallevy, 'Man of God', *JNES* 17 [1958], pp. 237–44).

**3.** Implicitly, the new altar was built on the foundations of the old still remaining, which means **in its** former **place**, not only for convenience, but as a mark of the continuity of the worship there

offered. In restoring the worship of Yahweh in Jerusalem the
returned exiles were acting under imperial authority; but not unnaturally **fear was upon them because of the peoples of the lands**,
the neighbouring nations of Edom, Ammon, etc., the traditional
enemies of Israel, not to be confused, as apparently by *NEB*, 'the
foreign population', with 'the people of the land' (cf. on 4:4). The
remarkable reading of 1 Esd. 5:50, 'they were joined by men from
the other peoples of the land', is no independent evidence for a co-
operation with other Palestinians such as is rejected in 4:3, for it
seems to be due to a scribal variant (see R. H. Charles, *The
Apocrypha and Pseudepigrapha of the Old Testament*, 1 [1913], p. 39).
A more ready and ultimately more effective defence against any
hostility was the protection of God, ensured by faithful obedience
to the ritual law (cf. the protective function of the temple, 9:8). It
is a mark of the homecomers' intention of strict adherence to the
law that they built the altar 'as it is written' (v. 2), in the traditional
place (v. 3), and that they offered the daily and festival sacrifices
'according to the ordinance, or custom' (vv. 4f.). The **burnt offerings morning and evening**, the 'perpetual offering' (*tāmîd*), were of
a lamb accompanied by flour, oil and wine (Exod. 29:38–42; Num.
28:3–8); they were reinstituted on the first day of Tishri, the seventh
month (v. 6).

**4.** The **feast of booths** (Tabernacles) took place from the 15th
day to the 22nd of the seventh month (Lev. 23:33–36, 39–43), the
**daily burnt offerings . . . as each day required** being detailed in
Num. 29:12–38 and totalling in the week 71 bulls, 15 rams, 105
lambs, and 7 goats, no vast quantity compared to the 22,000 oxen
and 120,000 sheep said to have been offered by Solomon at the
dedication of the temple (1 Kg. 8:63). By comparison, the sacrifices
at the cleansing of the temple under Hezekiah, 670 bulls, 100 rams,
200 lambs, 3,000 sheep as recorded by the Chronicler (2 Chr.
29:32f.) were meagre! Many think that the numbers are too huge
for the tiny resources of the community and are a reading back of
the Chronicler's own situation (e.g. Bowman, pp. 590f.), but we
have no real evidence that the homecomers were too few or too
poor to offer this quantity of sacrificial animals. The first festival
celebrated by Solomon after the building of the temple was this
festival of Tabernacles (1 Kg. 8:2), the most important festival in
Israel's liturgical year (known often as 'the feast') and so called
because it was originally a Semitic harvest festival (cf. Jg. 9:27)
celebrated when booths were set up in the fields for the temporary
lodging of the harvesters. In Israel, while it remained an agricultural
festival (Dt. 16:13ff.), it was associated in thought with the 'booths'

in which Israel lived during their march through the wilderness (Lev. 23:42f.). A later celebration is described in Neh. 8:13–18.

5. We have here a generalising account of the types of sacrifice offered throughout the year: the public **continual burnt offerings** daily (cf. v. 3), the **new moon** monthly, the **appointed feasts** seasonally, and the private **freewill offerings** irregularly. **new moon**: observed in pre-exilic times as a regular festival (cf. Hos. 2:11; Am. 8:5; Isa. 1:14); the sacrifices prescribed for the day are found in Num. 28:11–15. **appointed feasts**, or festivals; enumerated in Lev. 23 as Passover (with Unleavened Bread), Weeks (Pentecost), Tabernacles (Booths) (preceded by Day of Atonement and a special celebration of new moon). It would be surprising if the Day of Atonement was celebrated by the exiles a mere ten days after the resumption of worship, without high priest or temple (cf. Lev. 16; 23:26–32); its absence from v. 4 would suggest that it was not. We miss from the list of special offerings the sabbath offerings (Num. 28:9f.), though 1 Esd. 5:52, followed by *NEB*, inserts them before 'new moon offerings', thus conforming the phrase to the Chronicler's usual formula (2 Chr. 2:4; 8:13; Neh. 10:33); possibly it has been accidentally omitted from Ezra, or else it is included among the 'appointed festivals' (as in Lev. 23:3). **freewill offerings**: As neither prescribed nor vowed, but a spontaneous (though sometimes customary, cf. Dt. 16:10) expression of gratitude, they did not have to meet all the usual exacting standards for sacrifices (cf. Lev. 22:23).

6. According to the Chronicler's statement here, sacrifice was resumed on 17 September 538 BC. The Heb. does not speak precisely of a **foundation of the temple not yet** being **laid**, but only of the temple not yet being repaired (see further on 5:16). *yāsad*, 'to found', used of Zerubbabel's work in Zech. 4:9 also, may refer not only to the commencement of work, but also to the repairs as a whole and their completion; see F. I. Andersen, 'Who Built the Second Temple?', *ABR* 6 (1958), pp. 1–35; A. Gelston, 'The Foundations of the Second Temple', *VT* 16 (1966), pp. 232–5.

### THE BEGINNING OF TEMPLE BUILDING

### 3:7–13

This narrative of the initiation of the work of rebuilding is obviously very dependent upon that of the building of Solomon's temple (1 Chr. 22; 2 Chr. 2), but it is not necessarily on that account simply a free creation of the Chronicler's on the basis of the old tradition. Indeed, many (e.g. Wellhausen, 'Rückkehr', p. 175) have doubted that temple repairs were begun so soon as 537, arguing that 3:8 may refer to the arrival of Zerubbabel shortly before 520, and even that the Chronicler was misled by the reference to temple building in his Aramaic source at 5:16, which was designed to mislead the Persians (N. H. Baynes, *JTS* 25 [1924], pp. 154–60). But not only is it probable that much the same problems would have been faced and the same solutions found by the post-exilic temple builders as by Solomon, but also we doubtless have here an instance of history being determined by scriptural tradition: if timber for the first temple was transported from Tyre and Sidon, so too must the timber for the second temple. Nothing is said here of the use of local timber (Hag. 1:8).

7. **money**: probably an anachronistic translation; the Heb. is simply 'silver', which would have been weighed out as wages. Coinage seems to have come into existence by this time (cf. 2:69), but it was in common use only somewhat later. **masons**: Stone-cutters are included (as in 1 Chr. 22:2). **carpenters** (*ḥārāš*): workers in wood, metal and stone (cf. 1 Chr. 22:15). Solomon too paid the Sidonian and Tyrian workmen in kind (wheat and oil, 1 Kg. 5:11). The tall and robust **cedar trees from Lebanon** were ideal for roof beams (they were used also in the Jewish temple at Elephantine; *AP* 30.11), and had for long been highly prized throughout the ancient Near East (in Egypt, see the tale of Wen-Amon [*ANET*, pp. 25–9]; in Assyria, see *ANET*, p. 307 [= *DOTT*, p. 87]; by Darius, see Kent, *Old Persian*, pp. 142ff. A comprehensive collection of texts is given by J. P. Brown, *The Lebanon and Phoenicia*, 1 [1969], pp. 175–212). **to the sea, to Joppa** (*'el-yām yāpô'*): probably correctly translated by *NEB* 'to the roadstead at Joppa', i.e. Port Joppa (cf. modern Heb. Ashdod-Yam). Logs bound together as rafts had been towed in Solomon's time also (2 Chr. 2:16) to Joppa, Tell Qasile, just north of modern Tel Aviv. **the grant . . . from Cyrus**: probably not the money grant (6:4) but his 'permission' (as the otherwise unknown Heb. *rišyōn* probably means) for timber to be taken free from Lebanon. In Solomon's time Hiram had to be paid for the timber; now, since Lebanon forms part of the Persian domains, Cyrus only needs to give permission. The prophetic word, 'The glory of Lebanon shall come to you . . . to beautify the place of my sanctuary' (Isa. 60:13), thus begins to take effect.

8. The building of the temple under Zerubbabel and Joshua plainly took place not in 538 BC but from 520 onward, as Haggai's reference to the temple lying waste in his days makes certain (Hag. 1:4, 9). The present chapter, if chronologically accurate, must describe an attempt made in 538 which proved abortive when opposition was encountered (4:1–5). The building of a temple, which has been described as a 'task for gods and kings' (A. S. Kapelrud,

*Orientalia* 32 [1963], pp. 56–62), is consonant with Zerubbabel's near-royal status. Cf. also K. Galling, 'Königliche und nichtkönigliche Stifter beim Tempel von Jerusalem', *ZPDV* 68 (1950), pp. 134–42; D. L. Petersen, 'Zerubbabel and Jerusalem Temple Reconstruction', *CBQ* 36 (1974), pp. 366–72. **the second month**: In the same month Solomon began work upon his temple (1 Kg. 6:1; 2 Chr. 3:2); again the ancient pattern is followed, though not just blindly, for this season (April-May) was a most suitable one for building, after the spring rains and the early harvest of flax and barley (cf. Gezer calendar, *DOTT*, pp. 201ff.). **made a beginning**: Heb. has simply *hēḥēllû*, 'they began', probably to be closely connected with **they appointed**, viz. 'they first of all appointed'. **twenty years old**: Elsewhere also the Chronicler takes 20 as the minimum age for levitical duties (1 Chr. 23:24, 27; 2 Chr. 31:17), but in his account of David's organisation of the Levites he speaks of 30 (1 Chr. 23:3), in accord with the priestly legislation (Num. 4:3, 23, 30), though there too there is some variation (25 years in Num. 8:24). The lowering of the age limit may plausibly be accounted for by the extreme paucity of Levites (2:40ff.).

**9.** In accordance with his custom, the Chronicler lingers over the functions and names of the Levites. For **Jeshua** (not the priest Jeshua b. Jozadak) and **Kadmiel**, see on 2:40. **Judah** is the same name as the Levite family name Hodaviah (2:40). The **sons of Henadad** are not mentioned in 2:40, though they appear later in Neh. 3:18, 24; 10:9, and may have been inserted here by a scribe to conform with those references to Levites; the syntactical unevenness of the verse suggests that they were not originally mentioned here (*NEB* omits the phrase).

**10.** The prototype for this ceremony marking the beginning of repair work, and of course also for the Chronicler's description of it, is the dedication of Solomon's temple (1 Kg. 8; 2 Chr. 5–7). A similar ceremony celebrated the cleansing of the temple under Hezekiah, according to the Chronicler (2 Chr. 29:25–30). **the builders laid the foundation**: The Hebrew, however, does not speak specifically of a foundation, and says simply that the builders 'restored, repaired' (cf. on 3:6; 4:12), which can only mean in the context that they began to repair (cf. 4:1–3 where the temple is still in course of repair). The foundations of Solomon's temple would hardly have been uprooted by the Babylonians (cf. 2 Kg. 25:9 which speaks only of the burning of the temple), and the large dressed foundation stones (1 Kg. 5:17), perhaps up to 12 or 15 feet in length (cf. 1 Kg. 7:10), would not have suffered damage even from the collapse of the upper parts of the temple. Almost certainly the builders used the same ground-plan as Solomon's temple (cf. on

5:15; 6:4). **in their vestments**: disguises the fact that MT has simply 'clothed', surely too unremarkable an occurrence to be worth recording! The similar verse 2 Chr. 5:12 suggests that *bûṣ* 'linen' has accidentally dropped out of the text here. **came forward** (*wayya'ᵃmîḏû*): should probably be slightly revocalised to *wayya'amᵉḏû*, 'and they stood' (cf. *NEB*). **trumpets**: Silver trumpets (*ḥᵃṣōṣᵉrôṯ*) are prescribed in Num. 10:1–10 for use as signals for summoning the congregation and breaking camp; here and in 2 Chr. 5:12f. they figure as musical instruments used as accompaniment for vocal music. **sons of Asaph**: the levitical musicians (cf. on 2:41), with their characteristic instruments, the cymbals (1 Chr. 15:19), which they sounded in traditional fashion, according to the directions of David who had specified, according to the Chronicler, the use of trumpets by the priests and cymbals by the Levites (1 Chr. 16:5f.; 25:1, 6). In Israelite music the instrumental sound did not 'accompany' the vocal music as in western music; at best it can be described as a creation of sound synchronous with the vocal praise. 1 Esd. 5:58f. gives the impression that the Levites provided 'music while you work' throughout the whole building programme (as Ashurbanipal claimed was done during the repair of his royal harem; *ARAB*, II, p. 322 §836).

11. **and they sang responsively**: lit. 'and they answered'; this could mean simply that the singers responded vocally to the instrumental music. **for he is good, for his steadfast loves endures for ever**: doubtless only the refrain of such a psalm as Ps. 136, obviously intended for responsive singing (cf. also Ps. 106:1; Jer. 33:11). *NEB* adopts an improbable translation (cf. Brockington, p. 70), to make it appear that Ps. 106 is being precisely quoted.

As so often, the praise is anticipatory; Israel is not simply thanking God for blessings already received, but at a time of crisis (cf. 3:3) praising him for his expected favour in the future. Praise in such a situation is an affirmation of faith in a trustworthy God whose covenant love endures for ever (cf. S. B. Frost, 'Asseveration by Thanksgiving', *VT* 8 [1958], pp. 380–90). The thought of the covenant and Yahweh's pledged loyalty to it is strong here, both in the term **good**, which seems to have often the specific meaning of 'faithful to a covenant', and in the term *ḥeseḏ*, **steadfast love**, or 'pledged love', not simply 'mercy' (*AV*). On 'good' in a covenant context, cf. W. L. Moran, *JNES* 22 (1963), pp. 173–6; A. Malamat, *BA* 28 (1965), p. 64; A. R. Millard, *TynB* 17 (1966), pp. 115ff. On 'steadfast love', see N. H. Snaith, *The Distinctive Ideas of the Old Testament* (1944), pp. 94–130; N. Glueck, *Ḥesed in the Bible* (1967); A. R. Johnson, 'Ḥesed and ḥāsîd', *Interpretationes ad VT pertinentes S. Mowinckel . . . missae* (1955), pp. 100–12. For the conjunction of the two, cf. Ps. 23:6, where goodness and *hesed* are possibly represented as the faithful bodyguards of the psalmist (M. Dahood, *Psalms I* [1966], p. 148). **shout:** Heb. *terû'â* is often a shout of victory in war, and is associated with the presence of the ark of the covenant, the throne of the divine King (e.g. 1 Sam. 4:5f.). It is the cry of acclamation of Yahweh's kingship when the ark is brought to Zion by David (Ps. 47:5; cf. 132:16; 1 Chr. 15:28), and probably signifies here also that through the restoration of the temple Yahweh the king will resume his seat upon Zion (cf. Isa. 52:7f. where the 'return of the Lord to Zion' means 'Your God reigns'). **because the foundation . . . was laid:** rather, 'because of the rebuilding' (cf. on verse 10).

12. Why did the old men weep, who had seen the Solomonic temple fifty years previously? Because they knew they would not live to see the rebuilding completed (Solomon's temple had taken seven years, 1 Kg. 6:38), or simply because of the memory of its former splendour (cf. Hag. 2:3)? Or was it weeping for joy? Certainly the Chronicler regards the weeping as being drowned by the triumphal shouting (v. 13). If this picturesque detail of the weeping of the old men has any historical value, it suggests that the date is 537 rather than 520 BC, by which time it could hardly have been true that many who remembered the Solomonic temple were still alive (Myers, p. 26). **when they saw the foundation of this house being laid:** The Heb. is difficult, lit. 'at its repair (cf. on v. 10) this the house in their eyes'. This could mean 'as it (viz. this house, temple) was being repaired before them', the phrase 'this house' being a gloss. But preferably we should revocalise *bysdw*, 'at its repair', to *bîsōdô*, 'on its foundation', translating 'old men who had seen the first house on its foundation (i.e. still standing)—that was the temple in their sight (i.e. as far as they were concerned)—wept'.

13. With some literary art, the Chronicler concludes the episode with a remark, **the sound was heard afar**, which prepares for the 'hearing' by the adversaries of the Jews (4:1), and thus takes on a more ambiguous aspect than is at first apparent. (In 1 Esd. 5:66 the connection is much more explicit: 'The enemies of Judah and Benjamin heard the noise of the trumpets and came to see what it meant', *NEB*.)

With all the emphasis in this chapter upon the restoration of ancient religious practices, has not the Chronicler depicted a group of reactionaries? The altar is rebuilt in its traditional place, and offerings are set upon it according to the law of Moses (vv. 2f.); they keep the festival of booths 'as it is written' and offer 'according to the ordinance' (v. 4); the same arrangements for the rebuilding of the temple are made as were made for its first building by

Solomon (v. 7), even to the month in which work is begun (v. 8); the ceremony to mark the commencement of repairs follows a pattern from Solomon's time and even the praises that are sung follow the directions of David (v. 10). What has happened to the 'new song' of Isa. 42:10?

Yet for the Chronicler all these are signs, not of a backward-looking conservatism, but of the continuity of his community's worship with what had been divinely authorised in ancient times—and so of the legitimacy of his community (see Introduction, V). According to him, the real reactionaries are the old men for whom Solomon's temple was still *the* temple (v.12); but drowning their nostalgia is the shout of the vast majority of the people, who are looking toward the future, not mainly in fear of the 'peoples of the lands' (v. 3), but in that kind of confident joy which can thank God even at the beginning of a work (v. 11) when there is as yet nothing much, to all appearances, to thank him for.

### CONFLICT WITH THE SAMARIANS AND OTHERS

### 4:1-5

After the splendid start to the restoration of the temple, with which the first three chapters have been concerned, the Chronicler must now explain how it was that nearly twenty years later (520 BC) the temple was still in a desolate state (Hag. 1:4) and was not fully repaired until the sixth year of Darius I (515 BC). The explanation lies for him in the opposition of the enemies of the returned exiles, namely, the inhabitants of the province of Samaria who 'discouraged' the Jews from their task. We may be sure that there were other reasons too; Haggai blames the spiritual indifference and self-centredness of the people (Hag. 1:3f., 9), and there were probably economic factors as well. In a period of inflation (cf. Hag. 1:6) brought about by the necessarily low productivity in a country long desolate and lately afflicted by some bad harvests (cf. Hag 1:6, 9, 10f.), money must have been scarce and the temple funds themselves decreasingly adequate. But the Chronicler, dominated as he is by the importance of the purity of cult and community, sees the failings of the community as due to external opposition, and there is doubtless some truth in that. Many however think it improbable that opposition was expressed so early as the reign of Cyrus; nevertheless if the narrative of the offer of assistance in 4:1ff. has any germ of historical truth in it, we must place it at the very beginning of the temple rebuilding, since everyone would have expected the temple repairs to be completed in a comparatively short period.

Remarkably enough, opposition came from people who had begun by offering to co-operate (v. 2). The categorical rejection of 'the people of the land' (v. 4) who claimed to be Yahweh-worshippers seems offensively exclusivist and even racialist (see e.g. C. W. Gilkey, 'Ezra and Nehemiah. Exposition', *IB*, III, pp. 596f.). But in order to form a reasoned judgment on the issues involved, we need to ask: who were 'the adversaries of Judah and Benjamin', and what is implied by 'building with you'?

Obviously the term 'adversaries' is the Chronicler's categorisation; though some scholars have attempted to distinguish them from 'the people of the land' (v. 4), it seems more probable that the Chronicler intended us to identify the two groups. By their own admission, as reported by the Chronicler, the 'people of the land' were colonists of the former northern kingdom of Israel, imported from some other part of his empire by the Assyrian king Esarhaddon (681–669 BC) to settle the land left vacant by the deportation to Assyria at the fall of Samaria (721 BC), and only partly repeopled by Sargon (2 Kg. 17:24) at the time of his conquest. We do not have independent evidence of settlement in Israel (now part of the Assyrian empire) in the time of Esarhaddon, but it is quite probable; we do know that he settled people from the east at Sidon after a Syro-Palestinian campaign (*ANET*, p. 290), and a settlement of colonists in Israel could be connected with his Egyptian campaigns in 673 and 671 BC (*ANET*, pp. 291ff.). The arrival of such colonists may also be connected with the final dismemberment of northern Israel referred to parenthetically in Isa. 7:8 as occurring 65 years after *c.* 735 BC, viz. *c.* 670 BC. In any case the 'people of the land' cannot be clearly identified with the Persian officials in Samaria whose later antagonism to the Jews is dealt with in vv. 7–23, and certainly not (as is often done) with the Samaritans of much later times (see R. J. Coggins, *Samaritans and Jews* 1975, esp. pp. 37–57).

As for the religious practices of such Assyrian settlers, they are likely to have been similar to those of colonists of Sargon who 'feared the Lord, and also served their graven images' (1 Kg. 17:41; cf. 17:24–40). For a non-Israelite the worship of the gods of one's homeland together with the god of one's adopted country was entirely natural. And it was by no means unknown for communities calling themselves Jewish to revere other deities beside Yahweh, as the documents of the fifth-century settlement of Elephantine in Egypt make abundantly clear (see Porten, *Elephantine*, pp. 173–9). We might think it a nice question whether worship of Yahweh in such a context has the right to be called worship of Yahweh, but for the returned exiles the answer was clear, that since Yahweh demanded exclusive worship, and moreover had driven his people into exile because of their disobedience on this very score, the

restored community was obliged to separate itself from those who
did not share its understanding of Yahweh's exclusive claims.

Further, co-operation in the actual work of rebuilding would
naturally involve co-operative arrangements about the cultus of the
restored temple; the returned exiles took their stand on the view
that official permission and directives had been given to them alone
to restore the worship. Rudolph (p. 33) and others argue that the
offer of assistance must also have had political significance, though
the Chronicler says nothing of this; the arrival of a fairly large band
of settlers directly answerable to the Persian king himself must have
been an embarrassment and potential source of humiliation to the
government of the province of Samaria, of which Judah had been,
and perhaps still remained, a part; the help, if inspired by the
Samarian officials, may have been therefore a subtle attempt at
manipulation of the affairs of the Jewish community, just as foreign
aid to developing countries is still often advanced largely in the
interests of the donors.

While we may thus offer some positive evaluation of the behaviour
of the returned exiles, as faithful to the commission with which they
had been charged by the Persian king and to their understanding
of God's nature that had been won from the suffering of exile, we
may admit that an exclusive community of this type runs a grave
risk of losing sight of the positive ideals for which it has been created
in its efforts to keep out those not in full sympathy with its ideals.

**1. the adversaries:** probably the same as 'the people of the land'
(v. 4 *q.v.*). **the returned exiles:** Nothing is said of the Judeans who
had not been exiled. This does not imply hostility towards or a
deliberate ignoring of such people on the part of the Chronicler.
Whatever may have been the actual tension between the returning
exiles and the non-exiled Judeans, the Chronicler says nothing of
that, but assigns the creative impulses to the homecomers (cf. also
3:8)—which may well correspond to the truth. Certainly the
returned exiles represent all Israel (cf. v. 3, 'heads of fathers' houses
in Israel').

**2. Zerubbabel:** add 'and Jeshua' (cf. v. 3 and I Esd. 5:68).
Zerubbabel, as civil head, precedes the other leaders. **Let us build**
can be read as a very deferential request; the Hebrew has rather
'We will build', which is in the context still a request, but considerably more self-confident. **worship** (Heb. *dāraš*, lit. 'seek, enquire'):
a characteristic expression of the Chronicler for to 'revere' in any
way; in earlier times it meant to 'consult, inquire of' for oracles on
a specific occasion (e.g. Gen. 25:22; I Sam. 9:9). **we have been
sacrificing to him:** MT actually reads 'not (*lō'*) sacrificing', though
'to him' (*lô*; pronounced identically) is without doubt the original

reading. The present text is probably a tendentious alteration from a time when the episode was interpreted of the Samaritans. **Esarhaddon**, Akkadian Aššur-aḥ-iddina, '(The god) Asshur has given a brother,' king of Babylonia, 681–669 BC.

**3. You have nothing to do with us:** lit. '(it is) not for you and for us', i.e. 'we have nothing in common' (cf. Jos. 22:2–4; 2 Kg. 3:13; Jn 2:4). **we alone** follows 1 Esd. 5:71; the Heb. rather says 'we as a community' (S. Talmon, *VT* 3 [1953], pp. 133–40; but cf. J. C. de Moor, *VT* 7 [1957], pp. 350–61). Strictly, of course, it was the returning exiles whom Cyrus had directed to rebuild the temple, but his decree would hardly have been compromised if the northern Yahweh-worshippers had helped. The exiles take their stand on the technicality of the letter of the Persian law. But instinctively also, it might be argued, they feel that the blandishments of northerners are to be resisted as they should have been in the days of the divided kingdom.

**4. the people of the land:** most probably the non-Jewish inhabitants of Palestine. Even if 'the people of the land' was a technical term in pre-exilic times for the political entity of free landed citizens (so E. Würthwein, *Der 'Am Ha'arez im Alten Testament*, BWANT 17, 1936; and more recently, S. Talmon, 'The Judean 'am ha'areṣ in historical perspective', *Fourth World Congress of Jewish Studies. Papers*, 1 [1967], pp. 71–6), which seems in any case unlikely (see R. de Vaux, 'Le sens de l'expression "peuple du pays" dans l'Ancien Testament et le rôle politique du peuple en Israël', *RA* 58 [1964], pp. 167–72; E. W. Nicholson, 'The Meaning of the Expression *'am hā'āreṣ* in the Old Testament', *JSS* 10 [1965], pp. 59–66; cf. Ackroyd, *Exile and Restoration*, p. 150 n. 50), there is no good reason to give it that sense here (but see R. J. Coggins, *JTS* 16 [1965], pp. 124–7). **discouraged:** lit. 'relaxed the hands of', i.e., 'weakened the morale of' (Neh. 6:9; 2 Sam. 4:1; Jer. 6:24; 38:4; and a fine example in one of the 'Lachish letters' [ostracon vi: *ANET*, p. 322; *DOTT*, pp. 212–17]).

**5.** The adversaries' method of opposition is expressed very vaguely, and the Chronicler gives no concrete example from the time of Cyrus of 'hiring of counsellors' against the Judeans nor of any action by the provincial administration to hinder their work. Since the Chronicler is able to furnish us with accounts of effective opposition from later periods (4:6–23) we may assume that he knew none from the relevant period. He is doubtless generalising, on the principle that the enemies of God's people use the same tactics over and over again. Since in the reigns of Darius (ch. 5), Ahasuerus (4:6), and Artaxerxes (4:7–24*a*), ill reports of the Judeans' activity were forwarded to the central government, one may assume (so the

Chronicler apparently thinks) that in the time of Cyrus the same procedure was adopted. As a matter of plain historical fact, however, it may well be that the greatest obstacle in the time of Cyrus lay in the minds of the returned exiles. **counsellors** who are bribed (**hired**) are probably envisaged as officials at the royal court (cf. *NEB* and 7:14, where the equivalent Aramaic term for 'counsellor' is used); for examples from Egypt, cf. Porten, *Elephantine*, pp. 282f.

## SIMILAR CONFLICTS IN LATER TIMES
### 4:6–24

The notice (v. 6) and the narrative (vv. 7–24*a*) of opposition to the Jews are not chronologically relevant here. They concern the period of Ahasuerus, i.e. Xerxes I (486–465 BC), and of Artaxerxes I (465–424 BC), by which time the temple had long been built (completed in 515 BC; Ezr. 6:15), and the opposition was no longer to the temple, but to the rebuilding of the walls of Jerusalem (4:12). This digression, however, functions in the present narrative as an illustration of the methods of the provincial government in resisting the plans of God, and on the literary plane it serves the purpose of filling the gap between 537 and 520 occasioned by the lack of evidence for that period available to the Chronicler.

The passage 4:8–6:8 is in Aramaic (see note on 4:7). The most reasonable explanation for the change from Hebrew is that the Chronicler now began to draw upon another source (the 'Aramaic Chronicle'; see Introduction, II). Unless perhaps his source was itself ill-arranged chronologically, whether by design or accident, it would seem that the Chronicler has transferred the passage 4:8–24*a* from the end of the Aramaic document (or such portion of it as he wished to use) to the beginning (so Rudolph, p. 40; Fohrer, p. 243).

**6. Ahasuerus** ('*ăḥašwērôš*): the Persian name *khšayārša*, which came into Greek as Xerxes. It is difficult to know what the content of the **accusation** was; Xerxes had become king in December 486, and at **the beginning of his reign** (i.e. in his 'accession year' which ran to 6 April 485), a natural time for raising complaints, the temple had been completed thirty years, and there is no evidence that the idea of repairing the walls had occurred to anyone before the time of Artaxerxes (cf. on vv. 8–16). There was indeed a revolt by Egypt in the year of Darius' death (486), which was not put down until the end of 483; the accusation may well have been that the Jews were favourable to the Egyptian cause, though it is going too far to claim, as J. Morgenstern does (e.g. *HUCA* 31 [1960], pp. 1–29), that the Jews actually joined the rebellion.

**7. Artaxerxes**: the Greek form of the Old Persian *artakhšaśśa*, 'having just rule'; it has nothing to do with the name Xerxes (Persian *khšaya-* and *aršan-*, 'hero among rulers'). Justice was the principal element in the public image of the Persian kings (cf. G. G. Cameron, 'Ancient Persia', in *The Idea of History in the Ancient Near East*, ed. R. C. Dentan [1955], pp. 77–97). **Bishlam**, unattested as a name, may be the Aramaic *bišlām* 'in peace', i.e. 'Mithredath and Tabeel wrote in peace'; *NEB*'s translation 'with the agreement of' (cf. Brockington, p. 74) cannot be paralleled. This letter, which appears to have nothing to do with the letter of Rehum and Shimshai (vv. 8–16), may then possibly be a letter favourable to the Jewish community (cf. F. Rosenthal, *Die aramaistische Forschung* [rp 1964], p. 64). An alternative suggestion is that *bšlm* represents Belshunu, whom we know to have been governor of Abar-nahara in Artaxerxes' third year (A. F. Rainey, *AJBA* 1 [1969], p. 58). **Mithredath**: not the same person as in 1:8. **Tabeel**, 'God is good': an Aramaean name. **Aramaic**: the official *lingua franca* of the Persian empire in which correspondence, especially from the West, was written. The final words **in Aramaic** (cf. *RSV* mg) are simply a scribal note that the following passage is in Aramaic (cf. the similar note at Dan. 2:4). Probably the letter was translated at the royal court into Persian. Though the verse is in Hebrew, it contains a number of Aramaisms (*keṉôṯā[y]w*, 'associates'; *'al*, 'to'; *ništewān*, 'letter'; and possibly *bišlām*, 'in peace'), which suggests that it originally formed part of the Aramaic document (4:8–6:18).

**8–16.** This letter, quite different from that of v. 7, is an accusation by officials and settlers of the Samaria province (not of the satrapy as a whole) that the Jews intend by rebuilding the walls of Jerusalem to revolt from Persian authority. The accusation may well have been made *c.* 448 when Megabyzus, satrap of Abar-nahara, was in rebellion, and it therefore was bound to be acted upon by a nervous Persian administration. The charge was almost certainly spurious and the Samarians' assessment of the threat to the stability of the satrapy was ludicrously exaggerated (v. 16), so it is difficult to know what reliance to put on the 'facts' of the letter. For example, it is very doubtful that the rebuilding of the walls was the activity especially of those who had migrated to Judea in the time of Artaxerxes (v. 12); is this phraseology only a way of placing responsibility for the new situation in Jerusalem foursquare on the central government (cf. **from you to us**)? The only return of exiles in the time of Artaxerxes I known to us was with Ezra (8:1–20)—that is, if Ezra's activity is to be dated to 458–457 BC (see Introduction, IV)—but it is unlikely that Ezra himself had initiated the rebuilding of the walls, since that lay quite outside the authority given him by the king. Possibly the reference is to the returned exiles generally (see further, on v. 12). The abortive attempt at wall-building described in the present letter may well be that attested also in Neh. 1:2f. (*q.v.*). V. Pavlovský, *Bib.* 38 (1957), p. 446, thinks that those responsible for the wall-building were Jews who had returned with Hanani, Nehemiah's brother (cf. Neh. 1:2).

We are to imagine the exchange of official letters spoken of in this Aramaic document as taking place with great rapidity and efficiency. Herodotus (*Hist.* 5.52) describes the excellent road system of the Persian empire: at posting stations every 14 miles or so waited messengers with fresh horses to speed the royal post on its way. A letter from Samaria or Damascus would reach the Persian king at whichever capital he was residing well within a week.

**8.** The letter is prefaced, rather awkwardly, by two introductions. Probably the substance of vv. 9f. originally headed the letter and therefore belongs after v. 11*a*, while v. 8 looks as if it may have been drawn from the kind of information that appears on the outside of Aramaic papyri letters: writer's name, addressee, brief statement of contents, introduced by '*al*, 'concerning' (*RSV* 'against'). For an example of such data, cf. *AD* 5.1 'From 'Aršam the prince to 'Artahant who is in Egypt. Concerning the Cilicians who were on my domain, who did [not] succeed in entering Mispeh'. On the form of Aramaic letters, see Porten, *Elephantine*, pp. 158ff. **Rehum** (short form of Babylonian Rahim-ili, 'my god is merciful', or Rahim-šarri, 'my lord is merciful') bears the title *be'ēl ṭe'ēm*, lit. 'master of an order', i.e. probably 'holder of a firman, or royal decree'. **commander:** a misleading translation, for he is a civil official highly placed in the satrap's office, and responsible for the routine correspondence of the satrapy; 'chancellor' (*AV*) or 'high commissioner' (*NEB*) are more appropriate terms. He would draft letters on behalf of the satrap, adding his name at the foot (e.g. *AP* 26.23; cf. Porten, *Elephantine*, pp. 55ff.). **Shimshai:** Akk. Shamshai; the name is connected with the name of the sun-god Shamash. **scribe:** He would in some cases have to translate documents into or from Aramaic, and in others merely write out a fair copy.

**9.** As is usual, the Persian officials appear in a group (cf. the seven advisors of the king, 7:14; also 4:17; 5:3, 6; 6:6, 13) (cf. Porten, *Elephantine*, pp. 46f.), clearly reflecting a system of checks and balances designed to prevent subversion. **judges** (vocalising *dayyānayyā'* rather than *AV* 'Dinaites', following MT's gentilic *dînāyē'*): a well-attested class of Persian officials known as *dātabara* (e.g. *AP* 6.6; 27.9; cf. Dan. 3:3, *de̱tāḇe̱rayyā'*; cf. Kraeling, *BMAP*, pp. 36f.). **governors:** not a people, Apharsathchites (as *AV*), but rather, 'commissioners', the Persian term *fraištaka* or *fraistaka*, 'envoy' (W. Eilers, *Iranische Beamtennamen*, I [1940], p. 40). **officials** (lit. Tarpelites): an unidentified class of officials (less probably a gentilic, 'men of [Syrian] Tripolis'; K. Galling, *VT* 4 [1954], pp. 418–22). **Persians:** probably 'the imperial officials', generalising the previous signatories (unless the word, not the usual word for 'Persians', masks another official title; cf. Bowman, p. 601; *NEB* 'chief officers'). **the men of Erech, the Babylonians . . . :** The men of these cities mean communities from those places exiled in Assyrian times, but still, interestingly, preserving their national identity (for similar cases, see E. J. Bickerman, *JBL* 65 [1946], pp. 261f.). **Erech:** ancient Uruk in southern Babylon. **Susa:** Shushan, capital of Elam (see on Neh. 1:1).

10. **Osnappar deported:** Though there is no external evidence of this transference of peoples by Osnappar, i.e. Asshurbanipal (669-*c.* 633 BC), the last of the great Assyrian kings, it is not unlikely, since he could easily have imposed upon his 22 kingly vassals in Syro-Palestine (*ARAB*, II, pp. 340f., §87b) deportees from Babylon, where he quashed a rebellion in 648, or from the Elamites and Persians defeated in 641–639 (see A. Malamat, *IEJ* 3 [1953], pp. 28f.). **great and noble:** probably reflects a Persian phrase, e.g. 'Cyrus, great King, Achaemenian' (cf., e.g., E. Herzfeld, *Altpersische Inschriften* [1938], p. 2, no. 2). **cities:** *RSV* rightly emends MT *kiryāh* 'city', to *kiryetâ* (cf. LXX and 2 Kg. 17:24); but *NEB* retains the singular. **the province Beyond the River** (Euphrates): the official name (Abar-nahara) of the satrapy of which Samaria and also Judea were sub-satrapies or provinces. In the time of Cyrus, and still for some time in Darius' reign, Abar-nahara was combined with Babylon for administrative purposes, and the governor of Abar-nahara (cf. on 5:3) was a subordinate of the governor or satrap of the whole area (see A. F. Rainey, 'The Satrapy "Beyond the River" ', *AJBA* I [1969], pp. 51–78).

11. Cf. a typical salutation to a superior in an Aramaic letter: 'To our lord Bigvai, governor in Judea, your servants Yedoniah and his colleagues . . . The health of your lordship may the God of Heaven seek after exceedingly at all times' (*AP* 30.1). **and now** (*AV*, wrongly, 'at such a time', at end of vv. 10, 11, as also MT) usually introduces the body of a letter after the introduction (as in vv. 12, 18; 5:17). Here it is probably a scribal error.

12. **be it known to the king:** perhaps a fixed formula for introducing reports (cf. v. 13; 5:8; and the concluding formula in 4:16; and the Assyrian concluding formula 'May the king my lord know'). **Jews** (*yehûḏîm*) originally meant 'men of Judah,' but after the exile referred to the community as a whole; only rarely is it used in *OT* for the inhabitants of the southern kingdom before the exile, though

Assyrian texts do so. **from you to us** does not imply necessarily a migration in the time of Artaxarxes; the Jews responsible for the wall-building could have been those of any previous return; **from you** could mean 'from Babylonia generally'. Certainly the Jews were not **finishing the walls**, for we can hardly suppose that a work the magnitude of Nehemiah's was nearly completed. Is this then an exaggeration by the Jews' enemies, or does the word (*šaklēl*) mean simply 'repair'? Or should we perhaps suppose that 'they have begun' (*šryw*) has accidentally dropped out after the very similar word 'walls' (*šwry'*), and translate 'they have begun to finish' (Rudolph, p. 38)? Probably mention of **repairing the foundations** after restoring (?) the walls indicates that the work was not very far advanced. G. R. Driver, *JTS* 32 (1931), p. 364, saw in the *hapax ḥiṭ* (*RSV*, 'repair') the Akk. *ḥâṭu*, 'to examine', sometimes used of inspecting foundations, and thought that 'the natural order of the operation is inverted in order to assign the first place to the completion of the task . . . , the culmination of the builders' offence'. *NEB*, 'surveyed the foundations', follows Driver, emending *yaḥiṭû*, 'are surveying', to *ḥāṭû*, 'have surveyed', and reversing the order of the clauses without saying so. Note that in the Gilgamesh epic (I.i.16–19; *ANET*, p. 73) walls are examined (Akk. *ḥâṭu*) after they are completed. **foundations:** *'uššayyā'*, a loanword from Akk. *uššu*, possibly signifying a subfoundation double the thickness of the upper wall (S. Smith, 'Foundations. Ezra iv, 12; v, 16; vi, 3', *Essays in Honour of. . . J. H. Hertz*, ed. I. Epstein *et al.* [1944], pp. 385–96). If so, this was Mesopotamian building practice not pertinent in Jerusalem, but possibly assumed by the Persian authors of the letter (cf. Darius' account of his palace building: Kent, *Old Persian*, pp. 142ff.). But more probably the term refers to the rubble fill against the wall which served as a substructure for dwellings (cf. on 5:16).

**13. tribute, custom, or toll:** These three terms for income (also at 4:20; 7:24) are probably used rather loosely, but may bear specific meanings: **tribute** is a semi-voluntary gift, **custom**, fixed tax, and **toll** is rather 'duty', the corvée service or its money equivalent owed by vassals (cf. Neh. 9:37). **revenue:** a guess at an uncertain word (*'app<sup>e</sup>tōm*) which is more probably a Persian loanword (*apatom;* H. S. Nyberg, *Hilfsbuch des Pehlevi. II* [1931], p. 1), meaning 'finally' (so *NEB*); the rest of the clause may then be translated 'it [the city] will harm kings' (*NEB*, 'the monarchy').

**14. we eat the salt of the palace** is misleading (suggesting *AV*, 'we have maintenance'), and may be improved by a slight revocalisation, *milḥanā'*, 'our salt', for *m<sup>e</sup>laḥnā*, 'we have salted'; *RSV*, 'we eat') to mean 'we are under obligation to the king' (Myers); i.e. the

king and they are partners (metaphorically) in a covenant of salt (cf.
Lev. 2:13; Num. 18:19; 2 Chr. 13:5; *TDOT* II, p. 263) pledging
perpetual mutual support; for not all the signatories of the letter are
financially maintained by the Persian government, as *RSV* might
suggest. **fitting** (Aram. *'ᵃrîḵ*) may be the Persian *ariyaka*, 'worthy of
an Aryan'. **dishonour:** lit. 'nakedness'. The letter insists that the
Jewish affair is the concern of a wider circle than the provincial
administration.

**15. the book of the records,** i.e. the memoranda, **of your
fathers,** i.e. your 'predecessors' (*NEB*), the Babylonian kings whose
legitimate heirs the Persian kings believed themselves to be, would
have been available in tablet or scroll form in the royal archives (cf.
6:1f.; Est. 6:1; G. G. Cameron, *Persepolis Treasury Tablets* [1945],
pp. 9ff., 20–3). **why this city was laid waste:** a secular interpretation
of Jerusalem's history, but not far different from the Chronicler's
religious interpretation (2 Chr. 36:15–20).

**17. greeting,** lit. 'Peace' (*AV*), a brief salutation attested in the
Aramaic papyri (e.g., *AP* 39.1; cf. also on v. 7; 5:7). The curt
greeting is typical of a superior's address to an inferior (cf. *AP* 26.1;
*AD* 3.1).

**18.** The letter was sent to **us**, the king and his government, and
read before **me**, the king personally; **us** is probably not a royal
plural, despite *NEB* 'sent to me' (cf. D. J. A. Clines, *TynB* 19
[1968], p. 65). **plainly read** is inexact for the technical term for
'translated' (*mᵉp̄āraš*), here from Aramaic to Persian, probably in a
sentence by sentence extempore translation (cf. Neh. 8:8).

**19. made a decree:** cf. on 5:3.

**20.** Had Artaxerxes' officials records going back as far as David?
It is not impossible, but even in David's time the kingdom of Israel
was considerably smaller than the satrapy of Abar-nahara. Some
think we have a Jewish exaggerating interpolation here; but even
Batten believes that the inscriptions of Sennacherib would be
enough 'to arouse the apprehensions of a king who was always
fearing rebellion in the subject provinces' (p. 179). Alternatively,
Artaxerxes' response could be seen simply as 'part of a universal
tendency to exaggerate the power of one's enemies' (Coggins, p. 32;
and cf. v. 16).

**21.** Would a mere **decree** by the provincial government stop the
work? Perhaps not; a slight emendation (*śym ṭʿm* for *śymw ṭʿm*) would
give the preferable meaning 'a decree is made', viz. by this rescript.
1 Esd. lacks **until a decree is made by me**, which could suggest
that the MT phrase is a later addition to conform to the later granting
of permission to Nehemiah (Neh. 2:5f.); but if the 'law of the Medes
and Persians' was really as unalterable as represented in Dan. 6:8f.,

12, 15 and Est 1:19; 8:8, escape clauses like this must often have been written into decrees.

**22.** The irony of the king's strictly enjoining upon the Samarians their own dearest desire is reminiscent of the fine ironies of the tale of Esther. For conclusions of letters with warnings against disobedience, cf. 6:11; 7:26; Dan. 3:6; 6:7; *AD* 7.8f.

**23. Rehum:** Add, with some versional support and *NEB*, his title *b'l t'm*, 'the ambassador' (cf. v. 8). **force and power** means military strength; in the Aramaic papyri 'power' (*ḥayil*) means the 'army', such as that with which the Egyptian governor is known to have been provided (*AD* 4.1f.; 5.6), and 1 Esd. 2:30 adopts this sense also: 'with cavalry and a multitude in battle array'. It is a reasonable assumption that the military method of terminating a project was to destroy what had already been accomplished; but it is only an assumption, and on its strength depends the important correlation of these events with the news which prompted Nehemiah's mission (Neh. 1:3).

**24.** At this point we must observe that the narrative resumes from v. 5: we are taken back to the time of Cyrus and to the cessation of temple-building, not of wall-building. It is the Chronicler's addition (in Aramaic nevertheless) to prepare for ch. 5. The only problem is **then** (*bē'dayin*), which, if taken literally, gives an impossible chronology; it is incredible that the Chronicler believed that the temple was not built till the reign of Darius II (423–404 BC) with Darius (522–486 BC) succeeding Artaxerxes (465–424 BC). Not entirely convincing is Schaeder's suggestion that the verse comes from the Aramaic document, in which **then** referred to previously mentioned events from the time of Cyrus; the Chronicler would, he thinks, have omitted them as irrelevant but have failed to delete the linking word **then** (*Iranische Beiträge*, p. 23). Rudolph argues (pp. 35f.) that the Chronicler actually wrote 'thus' (*kāzō't*) in Hebrew, which was corrupted to 'then' in Aramaic translation. Certainly the meaning must be that just as the rebuilding of the walls was hindered by the Samarians, so the temple rebuilding came to a halt through their interference. **king of Persia** (cf. on 1:1) is a phrase the Chronicler has made his own (cf. 4:5, 7), and points to his authorship of this verse.

Opposition to the work of God, the Chronicler has shown in this chapter, can take many forms, from outright violence (v. 23) to overtures of co-operation (v. 2), and forms even more subtle. For every religious community has a right to exclude from its fellowship those who do not share its faith, but every act of exclusiveness damages those who are in as well as those who are kept out. So the work of God can be opposed also by those who are doing the work of God. For the work of God is not only the building of the temple and the maintenance of worship but also the spiritual development of the people of God, and if the purity of worship can be achieved only at the cost of religious pride, we are entitled to ask: in what sense has the work of God been advanced?

## RESTORATION OF THE TEMPLE
### ch. 5–6

The account of the rebuilding of the temple is resumed from 4:5, and the Chronicler, following his Aramaic source (see Introduction, II.3) gives us an account in Aramaic of the new prophetic stimulus for the work in the time of Darius (5:1f.), an investigation of the work by the provincial government (5:3ff.), and a report to the central government questioning the Jews' authority to proceed (5:6–17). Darius' rescript authorising the work (6:1–12) is followed by the account of the completion and dedication of the temple (6:13–18), to which the Chronicler adds in Hebrew a note about the subsequent celebration of the Passover (6:19–22).

## A NEW BEGINNING TO THE TEMPLE BUILDING
### 5:1–2

1. A new stimulus to restore the temple appeared in the second year of Darius (520 BC), when **Haggai** began to prophesy, blaming the lack of prosperity on neglect of the temple, and urging immediate resumption of repairs. His first prophecy is dated 29 August 520 BC (Hag. 1:1), and by September 21 building was in progress (1:15). The author of the Aramaic source of the Chronicler has obviously depended on the prophecies of Haggai and Zechariah for his dates and his knowledge of the prophets' role. Thus he speaks of the **second year** of Darius (4:24), of Haggai simply as 'the prophet' (as Hag. 1:1; *RSV* omits without comment; cf. *NEB*) without father's name, and of **Zechariah** as **the son of Iddo** (cf. Zech. 1:1 'Zechariah the son of Berachiah son of Iddo'); Iddo may be not the grandfather of Zechariah (as *NEB*), but the tenth-century prophet of that name (2 Chr. 13:22), and his **son** may here mean simply 'descendant' (for a Zechariah of the Iddo family, see Neh. 12:16). **who** (or, which) **was over them**: an ambiguous phrase (over the prophets? Or the Jews? And was it God or his name that was over them?); *NEB* simply omits it. Even though the prophets spoke as those sent by God, the changed political situation with a new king on the throne, and probably a new governor in Damascus (cf. on v. 3), may have played its part in convincing the prophets that

the time was ripe. More precisely, it may not be coincidence that Haggai's prophecy followed Darius' stabilisation of his rule at the beginning of 520 BC (A. F. Rainey, *AJBA* 1 [1969], p. 56). For a probable recent influx of exiles, cf. Zech. 6:10.

**2. Zerubbabel . . . Jeshua:** cf. on 3:2. **began to rebuild** (cf. on 3:10) means the repairing of the superstructure, and does not imply that no repairs had previously been made (cf. in the same Aram. document 5:16, where Sheshbazzar is credited with beginning the repairs, and in the Chronicler's own account 3:8, where Zerubbabel and Jeshua themselves are active 18 years previously). Hag. 1:4, 9 gives the impression that no building had previously been done, but that is probably prophetic hyperbole; 2:3 makes better sense if the temple is in serviceable condition, though far from complete (F. I. Andersen, *ABR* 6 [1958], pp. 22–7). **helping them:** presumably by impressing on the people that neglect of the temple was a token of neglect of God (cf. *NEB*, 'unbraided', v. 1, lit. 'prophesied against'), but also to assure them of God's protective presence (Hag. 1:13) as they rebuilt and of the future splendour of the temple in God's purposes (Hag. 2:9).

## INVESTIGATION BY PROVINCIAL OFFICIALS

### 5:3–5

We do not know if this visitation of Jerusalem was part of a regular tour of inspection or the result of a tip-off that something was amiss at Jerusalem. But in the unsettled early years of Darius (cf. the revolt of Babylon until late 521 BC; see Olmstead, *History*, pp. 112, 115; Kent, *Old Persian*, pp. 126ff.), a provincial governor would keep his ears and eyes open for signs of incipient rebellion, and the temple under construction would have looked suspiciously like a fortress. Judging by the governor's report (5:7–17), which largely allows the Jews to plead their own case, and which, apparently in expectation of a positive reply from the king, did not forbid the building (v. 5), there does not seem to have been much hostility about the visitation (cf. especially 5:17); these officials represent the administration of the whole satrapy based on Damascus, and are doubtless not so personally involved in the Jewish question as were the representatives of the Samaria government in ch. 4.

**3. At the same time:** The date cannot be fixed, but the outer walls of the temple were now being laid (v. 8). **Tattenai,** whose office as governor (*peḥâ*) of the province (satrapy) of Abar-nahara (**Beyond the River**; cf. on 4:10) is confirmed by a cuneiform document dated 502 BC (see A. T. Olmstead, *JNES* 3 [1944], p. 46), was at this time probably still subordinate to Ushtannu, satrap of

Babylonia with Abar-nahara. **Shethar-bozenai** (probably a Persian name, Xšathra-baujana, 'enjoyment of the kingdom') would have been the governor's 'scribe' (cf. Shimshai, 4:8) or 'First Secretary'. Their **associates** or 'colleagues' are the 'investigators' or 'trouble-shooters' (v. 6; cf. on 4:9). **gave you a decree**: It was really permission but autocratic Persian kings commanded rather than allowed (cf. on 1:3). **structure** (*'uššarnâ*): a term signifying woodwork (as in *AP* 26.9, 21; etc.) lining the interior walls as in Solomon's temple (1 Kg. 6:14–18), or beams laid in the stone walls (cf. on v. 8; cf. also *BMAP*, p. 101 n. 6), or perhaps the roofing (*BMAP* 12.12f.; Porten, *Elephantine*, p. 97).

**4. They . . . asked**: an emendation of MT *'ªmarnâ'*, 'we said' (so *AV*), corrupted by the wording of v. 9. **the names** of the builders were not given in the Jewish reply (vv. 11–16), and perhaps were supplied separately (cf. 1 Esd. 6:12, where a list in writing is demanded); K. Galling, *JBL* 70 (1951), pp. 149–58, thought that Ezr. 2 was in essence such a list (cf. on 2:1–70).

**5. the elders of the Jews**: The replacement at this point of Zerubbabel by **the elders** suggests to many that Zerubbabel had by now either died or fallen out of favour with the Persians, and it is indeed strange that he should not be mentioned when his restoration of the temple was completed (6:14–18), all the more so when Zechariah had affirmed (4:9): 'his hands shall complete it'. It may be that Zerubbabel's messiah-like traits are being deliberately played down by the Chronicler (cf. Kellermann, *Nehemia*, pp. 96f.). If Zerubbabel had in fact by this time disappeared from the scene, we may well have to lay some of the responsibility upon the royalist, not to say messianic, prophecies of Zechariah concerning Zerub-babel. **the eye of their God**: his watchful providence (cf. Dt. 11:12; Ps. 33:18f.).

OFFICIAL REPORT TO DARIUS

5:6–17

The Persian governor Tattenai hopes to impress Darius by the efficiency with which he has enquired into the Jerusalem affair, making a personal visit to the city, enquiring about the authorisation of the building, taking a statement from the Jewish leaders, and dispatching his report with a request for a central government decision, leaving the matter strictly alone until word arrives from Darius.

**6. the governors** (*AV*, 'Apharsachites') are not the same group as the 'governors' in 4:9 and the 'governors' (*peḥâ*) in 5:3; the term here is a loanword from Persian *frasaka*, 'investigator, inquisitor' (cf. *NEB*, 'inspectors'); they are the imperial troubleshooters, armed

with powers of punishment. For an example of their activity, see
*AP* 37.3ff. as translated e.g. by Porten, *Elephantine*, p. 54 n. 100.

7. **all peace**, a greeting otherwise unattested in Aramaic letters,
may be short (cf. 4:17) for the pagan formula 'The welfare (*šᵉlāmā*',
lit. 'peace') of X may (all) the gods seek abundantly (at all times)'
(e.g. *AP* 17.1f.; cf. J. A. Fitzmyer, *Bib*. 38 [1957], pp. 178ff.).

8. **Be it known**: see on 4:12. **we went**: cf. on Neh. 3:7. **Judah**
(*RSV*) or 'Judea' (*AV*) was a province (*mᵉdînā*') of the satrapy
'Beyond the River' (cf. on 4:10), the fifth satrapy according to
Herodotus (*Hist*. 3.91). We should add, from 1 Esd. 6:8, after
**Judah**, 'and we found in the city of Jerusalem the elders building'
(the great house of God) (cf. *NEB*); for the reference to 'those
elders' (v. 9) demands a previous introduction of them, and a report
to the king must specify that the temple is at Jerusalem (contrast
*NEB*). Though not at all impossible that a Persian official should
call Yahweh **the great God** (cf. on Neh. 8:6, and note that Cyrus
calls Marduk 'the great lord'; *ANET*, p. 315), it is more natural to
translate 'the great house of God'. **huge**: *'eḇen gᵉlāl* looks like
'stone(s) of rolling', i.e. too heavy for carrying (BDB), and they
certainly were huge, if Zerubbabel's wall has been correctly identified (cf. on v. 16); but we should probably connect the term with
Akk. *galālu*, 'stone treated in a specific way' (*CAD* v, p. 11), perhaps
smoothed or polished. **timber laid in the walls**: Apparently Tattenai
observed the same architectural feature as stipulated in the decree
of Cyrus: the walls were to be built 'with three courses of great
stones and one course of timber' (6:4), a feature specified also of
the porch of Solomon's temple as well as of the walls of the outer
and inner courts (1 Kg. 6:36; 7:12). This design, which may have
been repeated all the way up the wall, seems to originate in Anatolia,
possibly as a protection against earthquake damage (S. Smith,
'Timber and Brick or Masonry Construction', *PEQ* 73 [1941], pp.
5ff.; R. Naumann, *Architektur Kleinasiens* [1955], pp. 83ff.).
Another interpretation is that above the stone that formed the wall
base lay a row of timber, surmounted by mud-bricks (so H. C.
Thomson, 'A Row of Cedar Beams', *PEQ* 92 [1960], pp. 57–63,
with examples of the technique). **diligently** (Aram. *'āsparnâ*) belongs
to the number of technical and bureaucratic Persian words which
were borrowed by Aramaic; strictly it means 'in full measure',
'thoroughly' (*NEB*).

11–16. This long reply by the Jews, probably a written statement
by them incorporated into the Persian report, does not limit itself
to answering the first question of the Persian officials (vv. 3, 9). To
reply simply 'Cyrus commanded us to build this temple', would be
misleading, since in Jewish eyes it was Yahweh himself who author-

ised the temple, and Solomon an Israelite king who gave instructions about its building. The Jews begin conciliatorily by professing themselves worshippers of **the God of heaven and earth** (cf. on 1:2), no petty tribal deity but a universal God who is God of Persians also; such a God must have a large and beautiful temple. But since a deity who cannot preserve his own temple from the hands of desecrators might well be thought ineffectual, the Jews hasten to add that the destruction of the temple had been actively willed by their God (v. 12). In more direct answer to the question they refer to the decree of Cyrus (6:3ff.) who had, by restoring the temple treasures to the returning exiles (5:14f.), left no doubt about his support for the Jewish temple.

**12.** The understanding of past history as prosperous or tragic according to Israel's obedience to the covenant is one we usually identify with the Deuteronomistic historians of Deuteronomy to 2 Kings; the allusion to it here shows how it has permeated the thought of the post-exilic community (cf. also Neh. 1:5–10; 9:6–37) for two further independent witnesses). The underlying covenant theology also becomes visible in the reference to the wrath of God (see *TDOT*, I, pp. 348–60) as provoked by breach of covenant (cf. e.g. Dt. 1:34–37; 2 Chr. 34:24f.; 36:14ff.). That God should give Israel **into the hand of** another king implies that he controls at least at crucial moments the events of foreign history (cf. more explicitly 2 Chr. 36:17, 'He brought up against them the king of the Chaldaeans'). This is not a peculiarly Israelite conception (cf. the Moabite inscription, lines 4f.; *ANET*, p. 320; *DOTT*, p. 196; B. Albrektson, *History and the Gods* [1967]), but it plays an important role in the *OT* understanding of God (cf. also on 1:2). **Nebuchadnezzar** (more usually spelled Nebuchadrezzar) II reigned 604–562 BC, and captured Jerusalem in 597 BC, taking many inhabitants of Judah into exile (2 Kg. 24–25). **Chaldean** denotes Nebuchadrezzar's tribal affiliation; Chaldeans (Kaldai) lived in southern Babylonia, and founded the neo-Babylonian empire after the fall of the Assyrian empire (see *IDB*, I, pp. 549f.).

**13. king of Babylon:** cf. on 1:1. The **decree** refers specifically to 6:3ff.

**14. vessels:** cf. on 1:9. The **temple of Babylon** (cf. on 1:7), dedicated to Marduk the city god, was under the patronage of Nebuchadrezzar. **one whose name was Sheshbazzar,** lit. 'Sheshbazzar his name', is an unusual idiom, but one which, very curiously, is found regularly in contemporary papyri in reference to slaves (e.g. *AP* 28.4; *BMAP* 5.2, 4; 8.3; *AD* 5.2f.; 8.1; 9.1. Cf. *BMAP*, pp. 145, 208); so the possibility must be considered that he was a high-ranking Babylonian official of slave status (cf. also with 'that

Sheshbazzar' (v. 16) the use of 'that X' for further references to a slave [*AD* 5.7, 9; 8.4, 5; *BMAP* 8.7, 8; *AP* 28.11]). **Sheshbazzar** is referred to by the Chronicler in 1:8 (*q.v.*) as 'prince of Judah', but here he is called **governor** (*peḥâ*), a term with a wide range of applications; it may mean the satrap himself (5:3), the governor of a province (e.g. Nehemiah, Neh. 5:14), or a royal commissioner with a specific task. The last is the most probable sense here.

**15.** Of course the **temple** has to be **rebuilt** before the vessels can be deposited in it, but the thought of depositing the vessels most naturally takes first place at this point, following v. 14 which recounts the delivery of them to Sheshbazzar. It is much to the Jewish advantage to stress the continuity of the new temple with the old (**rebuilt on its site;** cf. on 3:3); but we may note also the 'great concern of the neo-Babylonian rulers . . . to find the most ancient foundations possible and to match them exactly in rebuilding' (R. S. Ellis, *Foundation Deposits in Ancient Mesopotomia* [1968], p. 161). The same Aramaic phrase is used in connection with the rebuilding of the Elephantine temple (*AP* 32.8). See K. Galling, *Studien*, pp. 69ff.

**16.** The term for **foundations** (*'uššayyā'*) occurs only here and in 4:13; 6:3 (*q.v.*). It has been suggested previously (on 3:10) that the foundations of the temple walls would not need to be laid again, and perhaps *'uššayyā'* should be identified with the podium or platform on which the temple was built; cf. C. G. Tuland, *JNES* 17 (1958), pp. 269–75. M. Dunand, 'Byblos, Sidon, Jerusalem. Monuments apparentés des temps achéménides', *VTS* 17 (1969), pp. 64–70, has identified (p. 70) the pre-Herodian remains of the wall of the temple terrace (the podium, as he calls it) as the 'foundations' referred to here; the style of the stone-working is very similar to that of temples built in Persian times at Byblos and Sidon (see also Sir. 50:1f.).

Direct biblical evidence for such a platform is lacking, but it is a feature of Ezekiel's temple (Ezek. 40:49; 41:8) which was very probably derived from Solomon's temple (cf., e.g., the Stevens-Wright reconstruction of the temple, *NBD*, p. 1244, fig. 206; *IDB*, IV, p. 545, fig. 30). The retaining wall for this platform is likely to have been broken down either in the destruction of Jerusalem or by the elements during the time of exile, and its fill greatly damaged. This interpretation of the term will fit well with 6:3 (*q.v.*), 'let its substructure or platform be raised, i.e. built up, to its former height', and with 4:13, where as the town wall is completed fill is dumped behind it as a substructure for building.

Who built the second temple? (See Wright, *Second Temple;* and references on 3:6.) According to the Chronicler in 3:8 and to Zech.

4:9, it was Zerubbabel; but in the Chronicler's Aramaic source it was Sheshbazzar. If Zerubbabel and Sheshbazzar are identical (cf. on 1:8), there is no problem; it would be natural for the Jews to use Zerubbabel's Persian name in dealing with Persian officials. Nevertheless, the identification is very uncertain and we must reckon with the likelihood that Sheshbazzar and Zerubbabel were different persons. If so, we would have to suppose that Sheshbazzar's responsibility was an official one as governor, Zerubbabel's a less official one as leader of the Jewish community, and that the Jewish elders in replying to Tattenai refer, not unnaturally, only to the Persian official. It should be noted also that while Sheshbazzar is said to have laid or set the foundations, or rather the temple-platform (*'uššayyā'*), Zerubbabel 'restored' (*yāsaḏ*, cf. on 3:6) the temple.

**from that time,** i.e. since 537 BC, **until now it has been in building:** this is rather misleading, for on the testimony of both Haggai (1:2, 4, 9) and the Chronicler (Ezr. 4:4, 24) work had long ceased. The Jews obviously do not want it reported to Darius that they had neglected to carry out the edict of his predecessor Cyrus, nor do they mention the Palestinian opposition (in so far as it was responsible for the cessation; cf. on 4:1–5) lest the issue that aroused that opposition (4:1ff.) should again be opened up, and be adjudged unfavourable to Jewish opinion by the king. In so far as work begun and not yet completed is work in progress, the Jews do not actually tell an untruth; but they sail as close to the wind as possible.

**17. Therefore,** lit. 'and now' (cf. on 4:11), marking the transition from the Jewish statement to the official letter. **if it seem good:** the typical deference of the Persian official (cf. *AP* 27.21f.; 31.22). **the royal archives:** literally 'the king's treasure house' (*AV*) (cf. on 6:1). The governor suggests that the archives at **Babylon** would be the best place to locate documents from the early years of Cyrus, but in fact the document had been filed at Ecbatana (6:2), the former capital of Media, and now the summer residence of the Persian kings (Xenophon, *Cyropaedia* 8.6.22). The reason may be that documents were filed where the king was residing when they were written, though this explanation presupposes a rather tight timetable for the return: viz., that Cyrus entered Babylon in the autumn of 539, and in the spring of 538 apparently left for Ecbatana where he issued his decree which was carried out, according to 3:1 (*q.v.*), by the seventh month (Sept.-Oct.) of 538. A more likely explanation is that in these early months of his reign Cyrus had only a skeleton administrative staff in Babylon, and documents were still filed in his Median headquarters (similarly, Kraeling, *BMAP*, p. 35 n. 46); two decades later Tattenai naturally assumes that documents relating to the Babylonia region (the province Abar-nahara probably still forming part of the Babylon satrapy; cf. on 4:10) will be located at Babylon.

### RESCRIPT OF DARIUS
### 6:1–12

The finding of a financial document (cf. on 1:2–4) giving Cyrus' authorisation for the rebuilding of the temple is first narrated (vv. 1–2), followed by a copy of the document (vv. 3–5). Darius' own reply (vv. 6–12) is introduced rather abruptly, suggesting that the text is here defective, but the purport of his letter is plain: he is unconvinced that the Jews are disaffected, so he endorses the decree of Cyrus, adding grim sanctions for disobedience, and stipulates that offerings on his behalf be made in Jerusalem at royal expense. For evidence of Darius' friendly attitude to the religions of his empire and his involvement in temple building, cf. R. de Vaux, 'The Decrees of Cyrus and Darius on the Rebuilding of the Temple', in *The Bible and the Ancient Near East* (1972), pp. 63–96. On the relation of the Aramaic memorandum of Cyrus (vv. 3–5) to the Hebrew edict (1:2–4), see on 1:2–4.

1. Even matters of routine administration demand a decree (cf. 4:19 and on 5:3). **the house of the archives where the documents were stored:** The order of MT 'the house of the rolls, where the treasures were laid up' (cf. *AV*) is transposed, with some MS support, presumably on the ground that the sentence should lead up to the location not of the treasures, but of the rolls, which is what we are interested in at this point. **archives** should be replaced by 'treasury', part of which building housed the documents (cf. on 5:17; and cf. the archival rooms in the Persepolis treasury; E. F. Schmidt, *Treasures of Persepolis* [1939], pp. 33ff.). The present document is of course germane to a ministry of finance, and we do not know that archives in general were kept in the treasuries. This document may therefore well be of the class of treasury documents recording payments made; cf. R. T. Hallock, *JNES* 19 (1960), p. 90.

2. **Ecbatana** (Aram. *'aḥmᵉtā'*, *AV* Achmetha), modern Hamadan (cf. on 5:17), is called strictly 'the fortress', or 'fortified city', though it was also a **capital** (*RSV*). The **scroll,** or rather 'roll', would have been a rolled piece of leather or papyrus written on in Aramaic, and kept in a clay sealing shaped like a napkin ring (R. A. Bowman, *JNES* 7 [1948], p. 77; G. G. Cameron, *JNES* 17 [1958], p. 163). **A record** (*dikrônâ*) is regarded by most as the first word of the document itself (cf. *RSV* punctuation) and often translated 'memorandum' (because of its connection with Heb. *zākar* 'to remember'),

though it is more of an official document than that term may suggest. A similar *dikrônâ* gives permission to the Jews at Elephantine in Egypt to build a temple there (*AP* 32).

3. **In the first year of Cyrus:** as in 1:1; 5:13, the first year of his reign over Babylon. **the house of God at Jerusalem** looks like a title for what follows (*RSV*, 'concerning', is not in MT) and the reasonable suggestion is made that vv. 3–5 constitute an extract from a longer document authorising the restoration of other temples in the empire (K. Galling, *Syrien in der Politik der Achaemeniden* [1937], p. 31; Bowman, pp. 614f.). **the place where sacrifices are offered** seems a somewhat pointless explanation of **the house of God,** though perhaps it is not entirely so: the Persians themselves did not sacrifice, and they knew of non-sacrificial Jewish worship in Babylonia, so this may have been a distinguishing feature; cf. the phrase 'the altar-house of the God of Heaven', used of the Elephantine temple (*AP* 32.3f.). Nevertheless, it is preferable to translate: 'rebuild the house . . . as (*or,* to be) a place where sacrifices are offered' (cf. *NEB*). We know that Cyrus returned images of the gods of Sumer and Akkad to their temples so that prayer might be offered in those temples on his behalf (Cyrus cylinder, lines 33–36; *ANET,* p. 316. Cf. Herodotus, *Hist.* 1.132). His motive here was doubtless similar (cf. also Darius, v. 10). **burnt offerings are brought:** *RSV* unnecessarily and without comment emends *'uššôhî,* 'its substructure', to *'ešôhî,* 'its burnt offerings' (so 1 Esd. 6:24). The MT furnishes a good sense: 'let the house be rebuilt . . . and its platform be built up [to its former height]' (see on 5:16). Only two dimensions of the temple appear here, though all three must have been specified. If the missing dimension is supplied from Solomon's temple, a length of 60 cubits (1 Kg. 6:17, 20), the temple is a cube, a 'symbol of perfect space' (T. C. Vriezen, *An Outline of Old Testament Theology* [1958], p. 151; cf. G. R. H. Wright, *ZAW* 80 [1968], pp. 9–16) as in Solomon's temple the 'holy of holies' was. But a building of these dimensions would be six times bigger than Solomon's temple, which is most improbable, and would have required quite new foundations for most of the walls. Most probably the temple was rebuilt to the same size as Solomon's temple, length (excluding the porch) 60 cubits, breadth 20, height 30 (1 Kg. 6:2), the figures here being scribal alterations (perhaps intentional). By way of comparison we may note that the more modest Elephantine temple seems to have been sited in a courtyard measuring the traditional 60 x 20 cubits (see Porten, *Elephantine,* p. 110). **A cubit** was *c.* 17.5 ins., or, if the 'royal' or 'great' cubit was used (Ezek. 41:8), *c.* 20.4 ins.; the temple would therefore have been about 90 (or 102) ft. long (105 or 119 including the porch), 30 (or 34) ft.

wide and 45 (or 51) ft. high. The porch may have been higher, though hardly the 120 cubits of 2 Chr. 3:4. Though we hear comparatively little of Zerubbabel's temple, it is worth noting that it stood for almost 500 years, nearly a century longer than Solomon's temple, and of course much longer than its successor, Herod's temple.

**4. three courses of . . . stones and one course of timber:** The technical term for course (*niḏbāḵ*) specifies the type of construction Tattenai observed (see on 5:8). **one course of timber:** *RSV, NEB* rightly emend MT *hᵃḏat*, 'new' (cf. *AV*), to *ḥaḏ*, 'one'; new (unseasoned) timber set in the walls would be disastrous! The detailed knowledge of the specifications of Solomon's temple here implied is probably to be explained not as due to a later Jewish elaboration of Cyrus' decree, but as the result of Cyrus' sounding out Jewish opinion before framing the decree. That the **cost** is to be **paid from the royal treasury** will explain the necessity for details of size and building materials in the edict. L. Rost, 'Erwägungen zum Kyroserlass', in *Verbannung und Heimkehr* (W. Rudolph *Festschrift*), ed. A. Kuschke (1961), p. 302, remarks that this is the first time in recorded history when a ruler not only approved the performance of a foreign religion in his empire but devoted state resources to its maintenance. Why then, we may ask, if the temple rebuilding was to be undertaken at imperial expense, did the Jews for so long after 538 fail to take advantage of this provision? The explanation may partly be that finance would have come not directly from Persia, but from the revenues of the satrapy Beyond the River. Since, in the early years especially, Judea does not appear to have been on an equal footing administratively with the other provinces of the satrapy, any opposition from Samaria, a well-established and influential province, would have effectively cut off funds from higher sources.

**5. vessels . . . which Nebuchadnezzar took:** cf. on 1:7f. **each to its place; you shall put them** (*l'trh wtht*): the sudden (indefinite) second-person injunction, though paralleled (E. J. Bickerman, *JBL* 65 [1946], p. 251), is awkward; a small emendation (*l'trh ynht*) is preferable: 'let them be put in their place' (so Torrey, *Studies*, p. 193).

**6.** This abrupt transition from the Cyrus decree to the rescript of Darius to the satrap **Tattenai** is awkward. The Aramaic document may well have introduced his rescript with some such words as are added by *NEB:* 'Then King Darius issued this order.' Perhaps the names of the addressees have slipped out of the missing superscription of the letter and have been inserted after **now,** where they do not naturally belong; note that MT has 'their [not **your,** as *RSV*] associates'. **keep away** is a technical formula in Aramaic, meaning 'renounce all claim' (F. Rundgren, *ZAW* 70 [1958], pp. 209–15; cf. *AP* 13.6f.; 25.4).

**7.** **the governor of the Jews** seems to be a gloss since it is not syntactically integrated with the sentence, and only the elders figure in v. 8; note on 5:5 how Zerubbabel, to whom the phrase would have to refer, has by this stage disappeared from the scene. If the phrase is original, however, it would refer in Darius' understanding of the situation to Sheshbazzar, said in 5:14 to be governor, and not explicitly said to have ceased to be such. Translate the verse: 'Let [the governor of the Jews and] the elders of the Jews alone for the work of that house of God; let them build that house of God on its site.'

**8.** Darius repeats Cyrus' undertaking to pay the cost of the temples, adding only (something probably implicit in Cyrus' decree; cf. on 6:4) that the cost was to be deducted from the **royal revenue**, lit. 'king's goods' (*AV*) of the satrapy, and was to be paid **in full** and 'without interruption' (preferable to *RSV*, 'without delay').

**9.** The details here could well have been supplied by a Jewish official, like the comparable specifications in the Persian documents from Elephantine (*AP* 21, the 'Passover papyrus', and *AP* 32, prescribing sacrifices). So it is unnecessary, though not of course impossible, to suppose that the Chronicler himself is here expanding the original decree. For the use of **wheat** offered as flour, alone or mixed with olive **oil**, and baked or unbaked, see Lev. 5:11; 2:1–7. **salt** was specified with cereal offerings (Lev. 2:13) and **wine** formed a libation with daily and festival burnt offerings (Exod. 29:38–41; Lev. 23: 13, 18, 37). **the God of heaven**: cf. on 1:2.

**10.** **pleasing sacrifices**, lit. 'sweet savours' (*AV*), the technical Jewish term for sacrifices in general. **pray for the life of the king and his sons**: cf. Cyrus Cylinder (*ANET*, p. 316): 'May all the gods whom I have settled in their sacred cities ask daily Bel and Nebo for a long life for me and may they recommend me (to him).' Such prayer in the Jerusalem temple would accompany the daily ritual, which may explain the absence of imperial provision for the festival cult which was more specifically Jewish. There is no reason to doubt that this condition of the grant was fulfilled; it sheds an interesting sidelight on so-called post-exilic 'exclusivism' that, while co-opera-tion with the Palestinians (4:1ff.) was refused, the offer of large-scale maintenance of the cult by royal Persian provision could be accepted; in this case no unwelcome conditions were imposed. For expression of a similar attitude by Jeremiah to the (neo-Babylonian) state, see Jer. 29:7; and for prayers by Elephantine Jews for a Persian governor, cf. *AP* 30.25f.

**11.** Savage punishments for any who would **alter** (i.e. essentially, disobey) royal decrees were a conventional threat at the end of such documents (cf., e.g., Old Aramaic inscriptions: *ANET*, pp. 500, 502, 504); here the offender's house must first be made a ruin (cf. Dan. 2:5; 3:29), and he himself is to be **fastened erect** to a beam from it and **impaled** upon a beam set upright in the ground. Darius says in his Behistun inscription that he impaled an enemy, having cut off nose, ears and tongue, and put out one eye (Kent, *Old Persian*, p. 124: DB 2.76); according to Herodotus (*Hist.* 3.159), he impaled 3,000 citizens of Babylon. Further, the offender's house is to become a **dunghill** or public lavatory (cf. 2 Kg. 10:27; the word is translated 'ruin' in Dan. 2:5; 3:29); *NEB*, 'his house shall be forfeit', following 1 Esd. 6:32, seems a lame conclusion to such a threat.

**12.** The most Jewish element in the whole decree is the description of Yahweh as **the God who has caused his name to dwell there,** especially common in Dt. (12:11; 14:23; 16:2; etc.), but not a phrase of the Chronicler's (though a similar idea occurs in 2 Chr. 6:5; 33:4; etc.); so again a Jewish secretary of Darius is likely to have been responsible for the wording of the decree; the phrase refers to Yahweh's ownership of the temple (R. de Vaux, *BZAW* 105 [1967], p. 221). **to alter this** (the decree): translate 'to act contrary thereto so as to destroy that house of God' (Myers, p. 48). **with all diligence:** better, 'thoroughly'; cf. on 6:8 'in full' and 5:8.

### COMPLETION AND DEDICATION OF THE TEMPLE

### 6:13–18

The ready response of the Persian officials to Darius' decree confirms the impression that no hostility prompted their referral of the Jerusalem question to the king (cf. on 5:3). The author of the present Aramaic source gladly aknowledges the vital contribution of the Persian government: the temple was completed both **by command of the God of Israel and by decree of Cyrus and Darius** (v. 14), a conjunction which, without theological elaboration, expresses simply a typical biblical view of how the divine will is accomplished in history: along with God's command goes the free human decision. Cf. G. Fohrer, 'Action of God and Decision of Man in the Old Testament', *Biblical Essays* (Die Ou-Testamentiese Werkgemeenskap in Suid-Afrika) (1966), pp. 31–9. A comparable combination of piety and practicality is seen in the Old Aramaic inscription of Barrakab: 'Because of the righteousness of my father and my own righteousness, I was seated by my Lord Rakabel and my Lord Tiglath-Pileser upon the throne of my father' (*ANET*, p. 501). If the Chronicler himself rather subordinates the acts of the

Persian government to the divine prompting (v. 22), that is a theological refinement which is valid on another level.

After the completion of the temple in 515 BC, its dedication followed the pattern of Solomon's service (1 Kg. 8; 2 Chr. 7:4–7), though on a much less lavish scale (cf., e.g., 1 Kg. 8:63). Noteworthy is the significance of the reinstitution of the temple worship as a mark of the restoration of the true Israelite community; note **people of Israel** (v. 16), and **twelve he-goats, according to the number of the tribes of Israel** (v. 17).

**13. with all diligence:** cf. on 6:12.

**14.** The absence of Zerubbabel as the chief temple-builder is remarkable (cf. Zech. 4:9); as in 5:5, 9 (*q.v.*) it is **the elders of the Jews** who are responsible. No prophecies of Haggai and Zechariah of a suitable date are known to us; Haggai's activity belongs to 520 BC, and the latest dated prophecy of Zechariah comes from December 518 BC (Zech. 8–9). It is not impossible that both continued their prophesying beyond these years, but the reference in the present verse may be simply a generalizing one, implying nothing more than the prophecies referred to in 5:1. In the context of the Aramaic document, the **command of the God of Israel** must refer to the prophetic words (5:1; but cf. also 1:2), and the **decree of Cyrus and Darius** to 6:3–5 and 6:6–12 respectively. **Artaxerxes king of Persia** (464–423 BC), ruling long after the completion of the temple (515 BC), is quite out of place here, and should be omitted (*NEB*); the reference was probably inserted in view of the provisions made by the Artaxerxes of Ezra's time for the temple worship (7:12–24, 27).

**15.** The temple was finished about four and a half years after the resumption of work noted in 5:2, on **the third day of the month of Adar** (the twelfth month), **in the sixth year . . . of Darius,** 12 March 515 BC. But since that day was apparently a sabbath (F. X. Kugler, *Von Moses bis Paulus* [1922], p. 215), many read with 1 Esd. 7:5 'the twenty-third day', viz. April 1, a Friday. Nevertheless, since God is said to have 'finished' his work of creation on the seventh day (Gen. 2:2), without implying that he worked on that day, the same idiom may be used here.

**16.** The service of dedication, like that accompanying the commencement of work (3:10–13), would naturally have been modelled on Solomon's dedication (1 Kg. 8; 2 Chr. 7:4–7). Such a ceremony must have taken place, and possibly a report of it was among the documents used by the author of this Aramaic section. The author of these verses regards the returned exiles, for practical purposes, as the totality, or at least the real successors of, true Israel; they are not here 'Jews', but **the people of Israel,** in their three categories (cf. 3:10f.) of priests, Levites, and laymen (**the rest of the returned exiles**). **with joy:** cf. 1 Kg. 8:66.

**17.** The number of sacrificial animals is minimal compared with that said to have been offered at the dedication of Solomon's temple (1 Kg. 8:63; and cf. on Ezr. 3:4). The **sin offering** of a **he-goat** (cf. Lev. 4:23; 9:3) would have been made in order to decontaminate the temple or altar from any impurity brought upon it during its building (cf. Ezek. 43:18–27). All **twelve tribes** are intended to be represented by the sacrifice of the post-exilic community (cf. 8:35), which historically included only Judah, Benjamin, and Levi, and then not all members of these tribes.

**18.** The Pentateuch itself speaks only of the two classes, **priests** (Exod. 29; Lev. 8) and **Levites** (Num. 3; 4; 8), and of the duties of the various levitical families in relation to the tabernacle. It was David who, according to the Chronicler, first arranged the divisions and courses of priests and Levites (1 Chr. 23–26). The Aramaic author may well have been aware of this tradition of David's role, but his mention only of **the book of Moses** contrasts with the Chronicler's frequent attribution of cultic practices to David (cf. Ezr. 3:10; 8:20; Neh. 12:24, 45), and confirms that the present paragraph (vv. 16ff.), though somewhat out of character with the rest of the Aramaic document, is at least not the work of the Chronicler.

THE FESTIVALS OF PASSOVER AND UNLEAVENED BREAD CELEBRATED

6:19–22

With v. 19 the Hebrew language is resumed, and the Chronicler himself recounts the celebration of the first festival that fell due after the completing of the temple, just as he had narrated the observance of Tabernacles as the first festival after the erection of the altar (3:1–4). By making this addition to his Aramaic source he underlines the purpose for which the temple had to be rebuilt: it was in order that the daily and festival cult, in which the communion of God and people was realised, might be fittingly renewed.

**19.** On the prescribed day (Exod. 12:6), viz. 21 April 515 BC, the **passover,** originally a shepherds' festival, but in Israelite usage a joyful memorial of the deliverance from Egypt (Exod. 12:25ff.), was celebrated for the first time, in the Chronicler's view, after the return from exile. The pre-exilic model for this special celebration of the festival was not in this case connected with Solomon's completion of the temple, since that was finished in the seventh month (1 Kg. 8:65; 2 Chr. 7:8ff.), but rather the rededications of the temple by Hezekiah (2 Chr. 30:13–22, here celebrated a month late, according to the provision of Num. 9:9ff.) and by Josiah (2 Chr. 35:1–19). The latter passage gives a vivid description of the celebration of Passover once it had become an ecclesiastical rather than a lay, family festival (cf. Exod. 12:1–27; Dt. 16:1–8).

20. While priests and Levites alike had to purify themselves before offering sacrifice (Lev. 22:1–9; cf. Num. 8:5–13), the slaying of the Passover lamb was specifically the Levites' task, while the priests busied themselves with the manipulation of the blood and with the burnt offerings (cf. 2 Chr. 30:16f.; 35:3–6, 10–14). Interest in the activities of Levites is often regarded as an indication of the authorship of the Chronicler. **together:** 'as one man', 'without exception'.

21. For the first time, now that the temple has been completed, the presence of a wider circle of Jews than those who returned from exile is explicitly acknowledged (cf. on 1:5). **every one who had joined them and separated himself** will include, of course, proselytes, whose presence is envisaged in Exod. 12:43–49 and Num. 9:14, but also Jews who had not gone into exile, who no less were under an obligation to participate in any passover (Num. 9:13). Heathen **pollutions** mean essentially the worship of foreign gods, which involves ritual uncleanness; perhaps circumcision, the chief criterion for participation in the passover (Exod. 12:44, 48) is specially in view as a sign of separation from pagan uncleanness. **worship,** lit. 'seek': cf. on 4:2.

22. The festival of **unleavened bread,** originally a harvest festival, was in Israel virtually an extension of the Passover, celebrated from the 15th to the 21st of the first month (Exod. 12:15–20; Lev. 23:6ff.; Num. 28:17; Dt. 16:1–8). Passover with its vivid memorial of the escape from Egypt, and unleavened bread with its memory of the 'bread of affliction' (Dt. 16:3), must have taken on new meanings to the exiles who had now experienced a second exodus and settlement in the land. They would share Second Isaiah's view of the exodus from Egypt and the new exodus: 'Remember not the former things, nor consider the things of old' (Isa. 43:18). **turned the heart:** i.e. 'directed the purpose' (cf. Prov. 21:1), the heart being for the Israelite the seat of reason and will. The **king of Assyria** must be, especially in view of the close relation of this verse to 1:1, Cyrus; but the Assyrian empire was long defunct when Cyrus ruled. Some ancient parallels to a loose usage of 'Assyria' may be adduced (cf. Zech. 10:10f.; Herodotus, *Hist.* 1.178; Xenophon, *Cyropaedia* 2.1.5), but more probably the Chronicler deliberately employs this term to show how Cyrus, eventual heir of the Assyrian empire, has finally undone the evil against Israel initiated by the Assyrian kings.

With this verse the Chronicler concludes the first major section of the book of Ezra. In speaking of the God-inspired assistance of King Darius toward work upon 'the house of God, the God of Israel', he is referring back, by the literary device of *inclusio* or 'cyclic composition' to the first verses of the book where another God-inspired king, Cyrus, has decreed the rebuilding of 'the house of the LORD, the God of Israel' (1:3). The implication is that all that has been narrated in between has been the activity of God, however much its causation and outworking may seem to have developed on the purely human plane. A story that could have been told simply in terms of imperial policy (ch. 1), national feeling (ch. 3), petty provincial feuding (ch. 4), bureaucratic oversights (ch. 5, and royal generosity (ch. 6), is only fully told as a story about the action of God. He is the one who has 'stirred up' Cyrus (1:1), 'stirred the spirit' of the returning exiles (1:5), continued his covenanted mercies (3:11), raised up prophets to encourage the people (5:1), set his eye upon the elders of the Jews (5:5), 'turned the heart' of Darius toward them (5:22), and brought about the completion of his temple (5:14). See further, Introduction, V.

## II. EZRA'S MISSION AND ITS RESULTS ch. 7–10

### EZRA'S RETURN

### ch. 7–8

#### EZRA THE MAN

#### 7:1–10

In moving now to the second major section of the book of Ezra, the Chronicler passes over in silence a long interval of time, from 515 BC (the completion of the temple) to the seventh year of Artaxerxes, i.e. 458 BC, if it is Artaxerxes I; 398 BC, if it is Artaxerxes II; or 438 or 428 BC, if **seventh year** should be emended to 'twenty-seventh' or 'thirty-seventh' (see Introduction, IV). He can do this because his interest is not so much in narrating the history of the post-exilic community, as in presenting the religious ideals which brought into existence the community of which he is a member. He is emphasising that the renewed Israel is founded upon obedience to the law as the revealed will of God. He has therefore begun by describing how as soon as the exiles returned they resumed the cultic means of communion with God, according to the law (ch. 1–6); and now that the temple, as the prerequisite for complete obedience in matters of sacrifice and ritual, has been completed, the

Chronicler can introduce Ezra as the one who above all others was responsible for the establishment of the Pentateuchal law as the norm for all religious and social life in the post-exilic community. There underlies the Chronicler's view of the law the tragedy of pre-exilic Israel which was removed from God's land and its cultic communion with Yahweh precisely because of its disobedience to the law; only through unfaltering observance of the law can the new Israel stand.

**1–5.** Ezra's lineage is traced back to Aaron by way of the high-priestly line, though he himself was not high priest but simply a member of the high-priestly family. This genealogy, listing sixteen names between Aaron and the second-last pre-exilic high priest Seraiah, parallels the fuller, though still incomplete, list of 1 Chr. 6:3–15, where twenty-three high priests from Aaron to the time of the exile are recorded. See further, H. J. Katzenstein, 'Some Remarks on the Lists of the Chief Priests of the Temple of Solomon', *JBL* 81 (1962), pp. 377–84. Between Seraiah and Ezra himself, a period of 150 or 200 years, no lineage is given, which may suggest that Ezra belonged to a collateral branch of the family from Seraiah (*c.* 600 BC) onward. Possibly Seraiah was also the name of Ezra's own father, and a scribe's eye has jumped from the later to the earlier Seraiah, omitting the intervening names, in the same way as the names between Amariah b. Azariah and Amariah b. Meraioth (1 Chr. 6:7–14) were omitted in v. 3. A genealogy of this kind does not record physical descent, but rank and status, as for example when Zadok the priest of Solomon's time is called in 1 Chr. 6:7f. 'Zadok the son of Ahitub' because he was given the high priesthood of Abiathar, the real son of Ahitub (1 Kg. 2:35). A reasonable supposition is that the Chronicler himself wrote only **Ezra the son of Seraiah went up from Babylon** (vv. 1, 6), and that the lineage, which disrupts the sentence, is a later addition on the basis of 1 Chr. 6:3–15.

**6.** Ezra's office in Babylonia was that of **scribe,** a term which can signify a high official of state (like Shimshai, 4:8). In Ezra's case it has often been suggested (following Schaeder, *Esra*, pp. 39–59) that it implies that he was a Secretary of State for Jewish affairs at the Persian court (cf. also on Neh. 11:24). If so, the expression translated 'a ready scribe' (*AV*) would not refer to his speed or skill as a writer (as e.g. in Ps. 45:1), but to his sagacity as a statesman. That remains uncertain; but for the Chronicler the term **scribe** has a precise meaning: viz. doctor of the law (*NEB* mg), Torah-expert (cf. also Sir. 39:1–11). For the Chronicler, Ezra is something more important than a Persian official: he is one who had **set his heart to study the law of the LORD** (v. 10) and to **teach**

it (cf. also Neh. 8:13–18). This latter sense predominates in the Chronicler's usage. The teaching function of the priest, attested at many periods in Israel (cf. Dt. 33:10; Mal. 2:7) acquired a new lease of life in the post-exilic period. **Ezra**: a short form of Azariah, 'Yahweh has helped', a name borne by at least three of his ancestors (1 Chr. 6:3–15), and one of the commonest *OT* names. **law of Moses:** Some would restrict the law here mentioned to Deuteronomy or the priestly legislation, but it seems most likely that what is meant is the Pentateuch as a whole (cf. on v. 14). **all that he asked:** What that was is not said directly, and can only be inferred from Artaxerxes' letter (vv. 12–26). Perhaps the memoirs of Ezra gave some account of his request (cf. Nehemiah's memoirs, Neh. 2:4–8). In any case, it is plain that the initiative in Ezra's mission came from Ezra himself, so the generous response of the king was a matter for acknowledging divine favour (**because the hand of the LORD his God was upon him:** also at 7:28; 8:22, 31 and cf. 7:9; 8:18; Neh. 2:8, 18). The 'hand' or the 'good hand' (v. 9) of a king is his royal bounty (1 Kg. 10:13; Est. 1:7).

**7.** The caravan of exiles whom Ezra assembled is a reminder that many pious Jews, who could still be called 'Israel' (v. 28), had for long freely chosen to stay in Babylonia without the benefits of temple worship and residence in the holy land. **there went up:** As the verse stands, this return of exiles seems to have nothing to do with Ezra; since that differs from the picture in 8:1, 15, 21 of Ezra as the undoubted leader, we should probably emend **there went up** (*wyʿlw*) slightly to read 'and he brought up' (*wyʿl*). **seventh year of Artaxerxes:** See Introduction, IV; in this commentary the view is taken that Artaxerxes I is meant and that therefore Ezra came to Jerusalem in 458 BC. **priests and Levites . . . temple servants:** The Chronicler has before him in the Ezra memoirs a list of those who returned with Ezra (8:1–14), so he contents himself here with noting the classes involved, using the same categories as in Ezr. 2. The **people of Israel,** as there, are the laymen; the **singers and gatekeepers** belong to the class of Levites (cf. on 2:41f.). The **Levites** in Ezra's caravan (8:18f.) are not specified as singers or gatekeepers, so one wonders how the Chronicler knew. Perhaps he reasoned that since Hashabiah and Jeshaiah bore the names of pre-exilic musicians (1 Chr. 6:45; 25:3), they were musicians; or perhaps he was only reproducing a stereotyped classification (cf. v. 24).

**8–9.** The dates of departure and arrival must have been excerpted by the Chronicler from the Ezra memoirs. **he began to go up:** RSV suggests this translation since the MT, 'that was the foundation of the going up' (*RSV* mg), lacks a main verb; but a simple revocalisation of the Heb. (*yissaḏ* for *yᵉsuḏ*) will yield a preferable translation:

'on the first day . . . he had fixed the going up' (so *NEB*; cf. *NAB*);
from 8:31 we learn that the returning exiles did not actually get
under way till the twelfth day, the intervening time being spent by
the canal Ahava (8:15–30). The fourteen-week journey led the exiles
across *c.* 900 miles of steppe and desert at the rate of about ten
miles a day. In spite of Persian administrative efficiency the journey
must have been hazardous and exhausting; hence the acknowledgement of **the good hand of his God** (cf. on v. 6); the phrase derives
from the laying on of hands in blessing (e.g. Gen. 48:14). If the
calculations of F. X. Kugler (*Von Moses bis Paulus* [1922], pp.
218f.) are correct in reckoning that the day of their arrival, **the first
day of the fifth month,** was a sabbath in 398 BC, this verse offers
one piece of evidence for the early date of Ezra, since it is improbable
that he would have travelled on the sabbath (cf. on Neh. 13:15).
(The reply by A. van Hoonacker, *RB* 33 [1924], pp. 39f., seems
rather forced and unconvincing.) On the assumption that Ezra's
journey occurred in 458 BC, the date of his departure from Babylonia
was April 8, and of his arrival in Jerusalem August 4.

   10. Ezra and his party complete their journey under divine
protection because Ezra has devoted himself to learning and obeying
the law of God. To **study** (lit. 'to seek'), i.e. to learn and interpret,
and to **do** are the twin ideals of post-exilic Judaism; cf. the opening
sentence of the Qumran *Manual of Discipline*: 'The Master is to
teach his brethren according to the rule-book of the community to
seek God [i.e. by studying the Scriptures] with all their heart and
soul, and to do what is good and upright in his sight as he
commanded by Moses and all his servants the Prophets' (1QS
1.1–3). For Ezra, as for the later rabbis, study without action was
worthless. Cf. Rabban Gamaliel: 'All study of the Torah without
work must in the end be futile and become the cause of sin' (*Ethics
of the Fathers, Pirqe Aboth* 2.2). **statutes and ordinances** was an
ancient description of the totality of the law, **statutes** originally
meaning divine decrees, and **ordinances** (lit. 'judgments, customary
decisions') meaning case law; but no distinction is intended here.


### EZRA'S COMMISSION FROM ARTAXERXES
### 7:11–26

After an introductory verse in Hebrew (v. 10), there follows a long
official document in Aramaic (vv. 11–26), the language in which all
such documents in Ezra (except 1:2–4) are found. This is Artaxerxes' firman or letter of authorisation under which Ezra travelled
to Judea and set about reforming aspects of religious and social life
there.

The authenticity of this document has often been questioned, partly on the ground of the enormous sums of money and produce promised to Ezra (v. 22), and partly because of the Jewish character of much of the wording of the decree. The first point is a serious one, which will be examined below on v. 22. The second point may be adequately explained by the supposition that the decree was drafted by a Jewish official at the Persian court, possibly even by Ezra himself. (So Meyer, *Entstehung*, p. 65; Schaeder, *Esra*, p. 55; Rudolph, pp. 73, 76.) Only in this way, short of suggesting large-scale revision of an original decree by a Jewish editor or outright fabrication, can one explain the references to priests and Levites (v. 13) and other temple officers (v. 24), and the detailed knowledge of the types of Jewish offerings (v. 17). It is noteworthy that U. Kellermann, who rejects the rest of the Ezra narrative as fictional, sees in this document the one authentic piece of evidence about Ezra (*Nehemia*, pp. 60ff.).

**12. king of kings:** a title frequently used by Persian kings of themselves (cf. Dan. 2:37; Kent, *Old Persian*, p. 119 [Darius]; p. 153 [Artaxerxes I]). Through use of the title for the emperor in eastern parts of the Roman empire, the term came into the *NT* (1 Tim. 6:15; Rev. 17:14; 19:16; cf. also Dt. 10:17). **scribe of the law of the God of heaven:** The terminology suggests strongly that this is an official title of Ezra. **the God of heaven:** the name by which Yahweh is referred to in Persian correspondence; see on 1:2. After **heaven** the Aramaic has a word (*gᵉmîr*) not translated by *RSV*. It means literally 'complete, perfect', and so could mean 'etc.', abbreviating the formulaic address (like Heb. *wᵉḡômar*, 'etc.'), but preferably is to be taken as an office mark meaning 'completed, dealt with', which has crept into the text from the margin. We may compare the Akk *dinu gamru*, a title to certain official documents (G. Rinaldi, *Bibbia e Oriente* 3 [1961], p. 85). *NEB*, 'this is my decision', is a less plausible interpretation. **And now:** a normal word in official documents for introducing a new paragraph; it properly belongs with v. 13. *AV* took the official terms *gᵉmîr ukᵉᶜᵉneṯ* together as a greeting: 'perfect peace, and at such a time', the word 'peace' being inserted (cf. 5:7).

**13.** Artaxerxes renews the permission to return granted by Cyrus (1:3) to Jews anywhere in the empire, though in practice the Jewish population was concentrated in Babylonia. The distinction between **priests** and **Levites,** and the use of **people of Israel** for laymen and of the typically Hebrew expression **freely offers** (cf. Jg. 5:2; Ps. 110:3; Ezr. 1:6; 2:68; 3:5; 8:28; but also in the Cyrus decree, 1:4) point to a Jewish drafting of this decree.

**14.** What kind of **enquiries** is Ezra to make? He is to discover to what extent Jewish law is being observed in Judea, and more importantly (see on vv. 25f.) to ensure that in all respects the Pentateuchal law becomes the sole religious and civil authority. That Ezra's law was the complete Pentateuch in more or less its final form is fairly widely agreed, by e.g. Wellhausen, *Prolegomena*, p. 405; Eissfeldt, pp. 256f.; Bright, *History*, p. 390; Mowinckel, *Studien*, III, pp. 124ff. For a survey of opinion, see U. Kellermann, 'Erwägungen zum Esragesetz', *ZAW* 80 (1968), pp. 373–85. He himself concludes that Ezra's law was some form of Deuteronomy, but only at the cost of regarding all the Ezran material except Ezr. 7:12–26 as unhistorical, an extreme hypothesis. **the law . . . which is in your hand** does not point to a scroll which Ezra will carry to Judea, but means the law, already known (cf. v. 25), and in large measure observed, by the Jews in Judea; **in your hand** means 'of which you have the mastery'. The Deuteronomic law in particular seems to have already been the guide of the community; Ezra's special task was to make the priestly law also the concern of 'all Israel' and not only of the priests and Levites. **his seven counselors,** Persian and Median nobles (Est. 1:14) representing the leading aristocratic families, lend by their assent extra weight to the king's firman. For the role of the **counselors,** see Herodotus, *Hist.* 3.71, 76, 83f.; Xenophon, *Anabasis* 1.6.4; Frye, *Heritage of Persia*, p. 124.

**15–16.** Ezra is to convey gifts for the temple from three sources, gifts from the king and his counsellors (v. 15), a collection from the people of Babylonia (v. 16*a*), and freewill offerings by Babylonian Jews (v. 16*b*). **find** means simply 'acquire'. For the offering of gifts for the temple by non-Jews, remarkable as it seems, cf. on 1:4. There is no question of any forcible extraction of money from unwilling donors, but simply of permission to export from Babylonia to Judea whatever gifts can be secured. The total sum received as gifts is given in 8:26f. Ezra has obviously represented to the king that a display of magnanimity towards Jewish worship would be advantageous to the well-being of the empire. Many scholars, however, find the notion of charitable donations by non-Jews to the returning exiles hard to accept, and suggest that we have here a further use of the theme of 'spoiling the Egyptians' that may be developed also in Ezr. 1:4, 6. Nevertheless, Artaxerxes' decree concerns *permission* only, and guarantees nothing.

**17–18.** The money is to be spent upon sacrificial animals (goats are missing, by comparison with 5:17) with **their** accompanying **cereal offerings** and libations (cf. Num. 15:1–10), and since it is not a question here of providing for the daily maintenance of the cult (cf. vv. 20–24), what is left over (the majority of the money, one would imagine) may be applied to sacred purposes (**according to the will of your God**) at the discretion of Ezra and his **brethren** the priests.

**with all diligence** is better translated 'faithfully' (cf. on 5:8), i.e. strictly for the purposes for which the money had been given (*NEB*, 'solely').

**19.** These **vessels,** or rather 'utensils' (cf. 1:9), are votive offerings of Artaxerxes for the temple; they are itemised in 8:26f. Yahweh is never referred to elsewhere in the Aramaic documents as **the God of Jerusalem,** so this is perhaps a scribal error for 'the God who is in Jerusalem', or 'the God of Israel who is in Jerusalem' (cf. v. 15).

**20.** A new paragraph, dealing with provision for the regular maintenance of the cult, should begin here. Funds for this purpose would come from the income of the satrapy (cf. 6:4).

**21–24.** Darius had already made such an edict (6:9f.); **Artaxerxes** confirms it, adding restrictions upon the total amounts to be granted. These verses are cast in the form of a memorandum to **treasurers** (cf. **you,** v. 24) of the satrapy **Beyond the River**; it would have been excerpted as a separate document (cf. on 6:3) as well as being incorporated in the firman given to Ezra. To be of any real use, such a grant would have to have been a recurrent one, and if it were not for the huge sum of **silver** we could easily assume it to be an annual grant. **a hundred cors** (Heb. *cor* is a measure of capacity) **of wheat** is about 380 bushels, 100 **baths** (Heb. *bath*, a liquid measure *c.* 21–23 litres) about 480 gallons of **wine** and **oil,** generous but not huge annual donations.

**one hundred talents** (*c.* 7,500 lbs) **of silver** is by comparison enormous, especially when we learn from Herodotus (*Hist.* 3.91) that the annual income of the whole satrapy was only 350 talents. This figure however probably refers in fact to the satrapy's contribution to the central treasury, but nonetheless 100 talents must have formed a significant part of the satrapy budget. (By way of comparison, we may note that the whole state of Judah had yielded only 100 talents of silver and one of gold as tribute to Pharaoh Neco in late pre-exilic times, 2 Kg. 23:33.) The suggestion is worth considering that **talents** is a transmissional error for 'minas', one-sixtieth the weight, which would seem more in keeping with the quantities of produce prescribed. **salt:** The Persian government perhaps had a monopoly on this commodity, as did the Ptolemies later (cf. A. Dupont-Sommer, *RES* [1942–5], pp. 73f.; Porten, *Elephantine*, p. 86 n. 121). No limit is set on the quantity, since comparatively little was needed, though a later donation by Antiochus III (223–187 BC) specified 375 bushels, according to Josephus (*Ant.* 12.3.3). The generosity of the Persian government towards the worship at Jerusalem is no figment of Jewish imagination; it may be paralleled from Egyptian documents also (cf. Olmstead, *History*, p. 91).

**23.** Artaxerxes puts negatively what Darius had put positively (6:10); the object of the gift is to win the favour of the God of the Jews and thus of the Jews themselves for the empire. Political considerations, especially the role of Judea on the fringe of the empire, undoubtedly played their part (cf. H. Cazelles, 'La mission d'Esdras', *VT* 4 [1954], pp. 113–40, though with reference to the 398 date), but we need not doubt some genuine religious feeling on the part of the Persian kings. **in full** (*RSV; AV, NEB*, 'diligently') ('*adrazdā*', a Persian loanword) means 'faithfully, zealously' (P. Nober, *BZ* 2 [1958], pp. 134–8).

**24.** Immunity of temple personnel from taxation may be paralleled from elsewhere in the Persian empire; cf. Darius' reproach of his official, Gadatas, for exacting tribute from the 'sacred gardeners of Apollo' at Magnesia (de Vaux, *BANE*, p. 77; Olmstead, *History*, p. 156; text and translation in W. Brandenstein and M. Mayrhofer, *Handbuch des Altpersichen* [1964], pp. 91–8). For the terms for taxes, cf. on 4:13. The temple personnel are listed as in 2:36–57, **other servants** corresponding to 'the sons of Solomon's servants' (2:55). Only a Jewish secretary would be familiar with these details.

**25.** The most important responsibility of Ezra is left until last in Artaxerxes' letter. He is to set up Jewish **magistrates and judges** (the terms are synonymous) who will ensure that the Mosaic law becomes the rule of life throughout the Jewish communities in Palestine. For a similar involvement by the Persian government with local law, we may compare Darius' instigation in 518 BC of the codification of Egyptian land (the 'Demotic Chronicle') (see Olmstead, *History*, ch. 9). **judge all the people in the province Beyond the River:** Though the decree is not entirely explicit, we must not suppose that Ezra's authority extended over all the inhabitants of Beyond the River but only over those in that province who **know,** i.e. acknowledge, the Mosaic law. **all such as know the laws of your God** are the Jews themselves; those who **do not know them** would appear to be non-Jews (and also semi-paganised Jews) who live in Jewish communities, though the reference may be simply to Jewish children who have yet to learn the Torah. It is not likely that Ezra was given permission to proselytise (**teach**) throughout the province, but rather that for the sake of harmony and justice within the Jewish communities all inhabitants, whether Jewish or not, should be under the same law. It is necessary to give Ezra powers for the province of Beyond the River in general, for some Jews had settled outside the province of Judea (cf. on 2:33), and

previously in the letter Ezra's authority had been restricted to that
province (v. 14). **the wisdom of your God** is usually thought to be
a synonym for the law which is also 'in your hand' (v. 14) (cf. the
law as a source of wisdom or as wisdom itself in post-exilic Judaism,
Ps. 119:98; cf. 2 Tim. 3:15), but the Mosaic law will not help Ezra
appoint judges, and it is preferable to take **wisdom** as the wisdom
Ezra has acquired (**in your hand**) through divine aid.

**26.** In thus recognising the Mosaic law, the Persian king makes
it part of his own law; sanctions against disobedience are therefore
to be no less rigorous than those applied by the Persian government
itself. The penalties are listed in decreasing order of severity,
**confiscation** of property appearing as a greater evil than **imprisonment. banishment** is not normally a Jewish punishment (but cf.,
e.g., 10:8; Neh. 13:3, 28), and perhaps the term means 'physical
punishment, correction' (1 Esd. 8:24 has *timōria*, 'punishment')
which is typically Persian and also Israelite (scourging, Dt. 25:1ff.).
On the term for 'punishment' (*šᵉrōšî*, from Pers. *srausya*), cf. *srwšyt*
in *AD* 3–6; and F. Rundgren, *VT* 7 (1957), pp. 400–4; P. Nober,
*VD* 36 (1958), pp. 103f.; Z. W. Falk, *VT* 9 (1959), pp. 88f.
**imprisonment** as a punishment is unknown in *OT* law, though
temporary holding in custody is attested (Lev. 24:12; Num. 15:34),
and Israelite kings sometimes imprisoned political enemies (e.g. 1
Kg. 22:27); mention of this particular punishment is thus a minor
confirmation that the decree is authentically Persian. Yet to what
extent Artaxerxes' decree was carried out is impossible to judge; the
only evidences we have of Ezra's work (Ezr. 8–10; Neh. 8–9) amount
to nothing like fulfilment of his commission. But absence of historical corroboration of Ezra's commission does not necessarily mean
that the firman itself is a Jewish fantasy; it only shows that we are
too ill-informed to pass a judgment.

EZRA'S PRAISE OF YAHWEH

7:27–28

**27.** With the transition here from the Aramaic document to a
Hebrew doxology in the mouth of Ezra, we encounter for the first
time the 'memoirs of Ezra' (see Introduction, II §2). They cannot
have begun like this, and it may reasonably be supposed that their
opening sentences have been drawn upon by the Chronicler for his
introduction to the story of Ezra (vv. 1–10). Probably too Ezra
would have included the king's firman (vv. 11–26) in his memoirs,
but certainly now in this first person account it is Ezra who is
speaking. **God of our fathers:** Ezra uses this particular title of
Yahweh because permission and encouragement to restore the

community of Israel in its land is a fulfilment of God's promises to the patriarchs (**our fathers**). **heart:** cf. on 6:22. **beautify:** The idea of beautifying the temple by supplying a rich sacrificial cult may be founded on Isa. 60:7.

The addition by the *NEB* at the beginning of the verse 'And Ezra said', following some MSS of 1 Esd. 8:25, is inappropriate, since there is here no narrative sequence, and the 'life-setting' of the doxology is Ezra's writing of his memoirs (cf., e.g., Neh. 6:14); moreover the phrase is only redactional in 1 Esd. itself (cf. A. Rahlfs, *Septuaginta*, 1 [1935], p. 894).

**28. king and his counselors:** cf. on vv. 15f. **hand of the LORD:** cf. on v. 6. **gathered:** Some Jewish interpreters took this to mean that Ezra himself chose his company: 'Ezra did not go up from Babylon until he made it like pure sifted flour' by sifting out those of pure lineage from those who had intermarried with pagans (TB, *Qiddushin* 69b). But the word need only mean that he assembled his caravan.

It must have been difficult for those whose spirit the Chronicler regarded as having been 'stirred' (1:5) by God in the days of Cyrus to return to Palestine from Babylonia not to imagine themselves more dedicated to the will of God than those who remained behind in Babylon. But from the descendants of those who remained in Babylon—through indifference or lack of courage or simply because God had not 'stirred' their spirit—came the two great leaders of the Judean community, Ezra and Nehemiah. Even within the Babylonian community that had failed to respond to God's act of deliverance from exile, and whose eyes were blind to the 'new thing' God had done (Isa. 42:18ff.; 43:19), it was possible for Ezra to 'set his heart to study the law of the LORD, and to do it' (Ezr. 7:10). For God's purposes included the Babylonian Jews also, and his directing and guarding 'hand' (7:28) is upon a Jew who, from the point of view of the Judeans, has attained high office in the Persian government at the cost of 'forgetting' Jerusalem (Ps. 137:5f.). Should Ezra not have left the Persian court long before the seventh year of Artaxerxes to throw in his lot with the returned exiles? Many Judeans may well have thought so. But it is before his own Master that he stands or falls (Rom. 14:4). God works out his purpose through men of mixed motives and characters not above suspicion—through ordinary human beings, that is to say.

LIST OF EXILES WHO RETURNED WITH EZRA

8:1–14

Ezra's company numbered about 1,500 men, so about 5,000 people in all, no large number compared with the 42,000 returning exiles of ch. 2, but there cannot have been much in Judea in Ezra's time to attract back families that had decided some decades previously that life in Babylonia was more advantageous for them.

Here, in contrast to Ezr. 2, the priests are mentioned first, doubtless because this list was compiled by the priest Ezra. The names of clans differ also in order from those in Ezr. 2, though Bani, Bebai, Azgad, Adonikam, and Bigvai stand in the same sequence in both places, perhaps as a Benjamite group.

**2. Gershom** and **Daniel:** These priests (also Neh. 10:6) are listed according to their descent from Aaron, and not by course name (as in Ezr. 2:36–39). Eleazar and **Ithamar** were Aaron's only two sons who had children (1 Chr. 24:1f.) and Eleazar's only son was **Phinehas** (Exod. 6:25), so Phinehas and Ithamar represent the two branches of the Aaron family. Ezra himself also belonged to the Phinehas branch (7:5). **Gershom** and **Daniel** must have been heads of families, since Ezra was able to choose twelve **leading priests** from the company (v. 24). **Hattush** precedes the other laymen since he is a prince of the Davidic line, a nephew of Zerubbabel's nephew Peletiah and son of Shecaniah (*NEB* is to be preferred to *RSV;* cf. 1 Chr. 3:19–22, as emended; see Rudolph, *Chronikbücher*, p. 28). But he plays no special role in the Chronicler's history, and certainly does not represent a revival of the Davidic monarchy.

**3–14.** There are twelve lay families mentioned here, though this can hardly be due to Ezra's penchant for the number twelve as representative of all Israel (cf. vv. 24, 35). All twelve names are found among the thirteen names of Ezr. 2:3–15, but strangely no families mentioned in 2:16–20 are included here. The formula 'of the sons of X, Y son of Z, and with him *x* men' indicates: first, X, the name of a phratry (of which some members had already returned with Zerubbabel); then, Y, the name of a 'head of a father's house' (cf. on 2:3–20), i.e. living patriarch; then, Z, his own father's name; then, *x*, the number of males in his extended family, which could include his father, sons and grandsons, his younger brothers and their sons and grandsons, and in some cases the husbands of his daughters and brothers' daughters. These extended families average 125 male members. Cf. J. R. Porter, *The Extended Family in the Old Testament* (1967).

**3.** Zechariah's father's name is missing.

**4. Pahath-moab** must stand here for the Jeshua branch (2:6), since the Joab branch is given separately (8:9). Such a complete separation between the two branches is not surprising in view of the very large numbers in this phratry (cf. on 2:6).

**5. Zattu:** This phratry name is restored on the basis of 2:8 and I Esd. 8:32.

**7. Jeshaiah:** alternatively spelled Isaiah.

**10. Bani:** This name, lacking from MT, may be supplied from 2:10 and I Esd. 8:36. **Shelomith:** a feminine name (I Chr. 3:19); it should probably be revocalised to Shelomoth (I Chr. 24:22) (Noth, *IP*, p. 165).

**13.** It is unknown why the formula is abandoned here, three names being given. **those who came later** makes no sense in a list of those who returned with Ezra (v. 1); the phrase is preferably translated 'the last' ones in the list (*NEB*). Perhaps, however, it means that no members of the Adonikam phratry (2:13) now remained in Babylonia.

**14. Zaccur:** *RSV* adopts here in preference to the Kethiv form Zabud (cf. *RV*, *NEB*); probably we should also read 'Uthai the son of Zaccur, and with him . . .'.

### ENLISTMENT OF LEVITES

#### 8:15–20

When Ezra reviewed and registered his company at their assembly point not far from Babylon, he discovered that Levites were totally unrepresented. For possible reasons for the paucity of Levites both now and in the time of Zerubbabel, cf. on 2:40. Their absence would have made little difference to the success of his mission, though a plentiful supply of temple officials was necessary to implement the decree of Artaxerxes (cf. 7:17). But Ezra obviously believed that any company of returning exiles should be genuinely representative of all classes of Jews. Even though he could persuade only 41 Levites to join him, their presence is clearly indispensable, ideologically speaking.

**15. the river:** It cannot be the Euphrates or Tigris, otherwise it would be so called, so it may be a canal; but the name **Ahava** is unknown. The place must have been some convenient open space where the caravan could assemble, possibly the classical Scenae (e.g. Strabo, *Geography*, 16.1.27), an important caravan junction not far from Babylon.

**16.** The names of Ezra's deputies seem to have become greatly corrupted in transmission. There are three called **Elnathan** as well as a **Nathan**, a **Jarib** and a **Joiarib**, which are really two forms of the same name; and nine men are said to be **leading men**, while

two others are called intelligent (**men of insight**), which rather
reflects upon the 'leading men'! Probably the list originally
mentioned only six men, all called 'intelligent leaders'; only two of
them (**Zechariah** and **Shemaiah**) are heads of father's houses in the
preceding list.

**17. sent them:** The consonantal MT (Kethiv) has 'I sent them'
but the Massoretes preferred the Qere reading 'I commanded them'.
Some translations have attempted to incorporate both verbs (cf. *AV*,
*NEB*, *NAB*). While the sense plainly includes both, a translator
will have to settle for one only (cf. *RSV*). **Casiphia** is unknown;
that it is called **the place** need not mean that it contained a Jewish
sanctuary, like Jerusalem, called a 'place' in 9:8 (cf. L. E. Browne,
*JTS* 17 [1916], pp. 400f.; but see de Vaux, *Ancient Israel*, p. 339).
The Chronicler would in any case hardly have regarded any temple
outside Jerusalem as legitimate. **to Iddo and his brethren the
temple servants** (*nᵉtînîm*): *RSV*, like *AV* and *NEB*, emends,
without indication, a meaningless Hebrew text, 'to Iddo his brother
the Nethinim'; but further correction is needed. Since the Nethinim
were among the most lowly temple servants (cf. on 2:43) they are
hardly likely to be the **brethren** of **Iddo,** a leading man; so read
probably 'to Iddo and his brethren [the priests] and to the Nethinim'
(cf. *NAB*). **ministers:** a term that could be used of priests (e.g.
Exod. 28:35), but here it plainly means priests' assistants, i.e.
Levites.

**18.** Ezra knew he was asking a lot in expecting families to uproot
themselves at a few days' notice, and it is remarkable that he got
the response he did. This is therefore an occasion for acknowledging
the special favour of God upon his plans (**the good hand of our
God upon us,** cf. on 7:6). **namely Sherebiah:** lit. 'and Sherebiah'
(so *AV*); but the 'and' is explicative. Sherebiah figures several times
in Ezra's story (v. 24; Neh. 8:7; 9:4f.; cf. Neh. 10:12; 12:8–24).
He belonged to the line of **Mahli,** the son of **Merari** and grandson
of **Levi** (Exod. 6:16–19; 1 Chr. 6:16, 19; 'son' can of course mean
any descendant). The descendants of Merari were traditionally
responsible for porterage of the tabernacle (Num. 4:29–33).

**19.** These Levites are also of the line of **Merari**, and it is impossible to say why they should be so named when the sons of Mahli
(v. 18) are equally sons of Merari. The syntax of the verse is
awkward; a slight revocalisation (*'āḥîw*, 'his brother', for *'eḥāyw*,
'his brothers') would yield 'Hashabiah together with his brother
Jeshaiah [Isaiah] of the sons of Merari, and their sons' (cf. *JB*). The
size of these 'extended families' of Levites is small compared with
the lay families (vv. 3–14), which suggests that Levite families were
far from responsive to Ezra's summons.

**20.** As in the list of returning exiles in Ezr. 2, **temple servants** outnumbered Levites; for **Nethinim,** cf. on 2:43. **whom David and his officials** (cf. 2 Chr. 30:12) **had set apart to attend the Levites** is probably the Chronicler's or an editor's addition to Ezra's narrative; the form of the relative pronoun (*še-* instead of *'ªšer*) suggests that the phrase is not the Chronicler's. **mentioned by name:** in a list known to Ezra but presumably too lengthy to be reproduced here.

PREPARATIONS FOR DEPARTURE

8:21–30

To lead a company of 5,000, including women and children, in a four-month trek through uninhabited regions was a hazardous business (cf. v. 31*b*), especially when the company was carrying vast quantities of money and precious objects. Ezra would have been entitled to a military escort, such as accompanied Nehemiah (Neh. 2:9), and in the circumstances it is surprising that the king did not insist on supplying one, to ensure that his gift to the Jerusalem temple arrived intact. It speaks very well of Ezra's courage as well as of his piety that he could set out in reliance solely on God's ability to protect his people and what was after all now his property (**the vessels are holy,** v. 28). But one man's expression of piety cannot be used as the yardstick to measure another man's faith; Nehemiah was not, by comparison, lacking in faith because as a practical administrator he took for granted human aid.

**21.** Whatever the origins of fasting as a religious custom, it seems to have been used in Israel as a means by which a man might put himself by starvation in a 'death-situation', either because he felt that life was no longer worth living (thus fasting as a mourning rite, e.g. 1 Sam. 31:13), or because he wished to represent himself to God as one who was in extreme danger and thus had a special claim upon divine protection or deliverance (e.g. Jg. 20:26; 2 Chr. 20:3). **humble:** literally, 'afflict' oneself (*NEB* 'mortify'), i.e. put oneself in the position of the poor or afflicted man (*'ānî* or *'ānāw*), i.e. the underprivileged, so often encountered in the Psalms, who is specially under the divine care (e.g. Ps. 14:5; 25:16). The real-life situation of the economically underprivileged in pre-exilic Israel had become an ideal for all classes of society, since it was the literally poor who could be most acutely conscious of their dependence on God. A **straight** (*AV*, 'right') **way** means a favourable journey (*NEB*, 'safe journey') (cf. Ps. 107:7). Cf. further the contrast in the Psalms between the slippery, rough paths of death (116:8; 56:13) and the path of life (16:11), a level path (143:10), paths of 'right-ness', i.e. straight or level paths (23:3).

**22.** Ezra does not expect an uneventful journey; even **a band of soldiers** would only be able to *help* (AV, NEB, not **protect**, RSV); so Ezra must have been prepared for occasional skirmishes with brigands. Strange that he should call potential enemies **all that forsake him,** which suggests that the enemies were once Yahweh-worshippers. If a traditional poetic couplet is being used (cf. 2 Chr. 13:10f., where the 'forsakers' are the northern tribes), no specific enemies may be in mind.

**23. God . . . listened to our entreaty:** This can be said only in retrospect after arrival in Jerusalem.

**24–30. Commissioning of those who carry the treasure.** Ezra takes only religious measures to protect the property. By placing **holy** property in the hands of **holy** men (v. 28) he hands over responsibility for its protection to the Holy One. This would also have certain practical effects: it would impress upon the bearers of the treasure the importance of taking good care of the holy objects, and it would warn off any light-fingered members of the company.

**24.** The translations of *RSV* and *AV* are impossible, since **Shere-biah** and **Hashabiah** are not priests, but Levites (vv. 18f.); by emending the meaningless 'to' ($l^e$) before Sherebiah (not in *RSV*) to 'and' ($w^e$), we make clear that the guard consisted of twelve priests plus twelve Levites (so *NEB*, *JB*; cf. v. 30). Perhaps the number **twelve** signifies that they were representative of all Israel (though in fact they were all of one tribe, Levi), or perhaps it was just a conventional number.

**25.** The **lords,** as distinct from the **king and his counselors,** seem to have made the donation mentioned in 7:16a. This gift parallels the gift made for the first temple by various classes of people (1 Chr. 26:26). The weighing shows that the **gold** and **silver** was not in minted form but in bars or wedges.

**26, 27. six hundred and fifty talents of silver,** reckoning the talent as 65 lb, is about 19 tons. **silver vessels worth a hundred talents** (*RSV*, cf. *AV*): This translation misrepresents the MT, which has 'silver vessels, one hundred, worth talents'; either the number is missing or else the word for **talents** (*kikkārîm*) should be revocal-ised as *kikkerayim*, 'two talents' (so *NEB*, *JB*). A **hundred talents of gold** is *c.* three tons. The final two vessels are of fine red (*NEB*; *RSV*'s **bright** is inexact) copper (*AV*, *NEB*; not **bronze**, *RSV*), an expensive metal perhaps incorporating copper and gold or else a highly prized type of copper (like 'orichalc', *NEB* mg) (see also B. Pelzl, *ZAW* 87 [1975], pp. 221–4). Modern monetary equivalents of these sums are totally misleading, but some contemporary comparisons are possible: a skilled workman earned between 12 and 84 silver shekels a year, so Ezra's treasure (equivalent—as the figures stand—to 2,083 silver talents, viz. *c.* 6,500,000 shekels) would represent the annual income of, say, between 100,000 and 500,000 men (see further, V. Pavlovský, *Bib.* 38 [1957], pp. 297–300). Such figures are astounding, and while extraordinarily large-scale payments of silver and gold are attested in the Assyrian, Babylonian, and Persian empires (see D. J. Wiseman, *BSAOS* 30 [1967], p. 499), it is more likely that some figures in this list have been corrupted in scribal transmission, or that 'talents' has been substituted for 'minas' (cf. on 7:22). Such reduced figures for gold and silver would harmonise better with the 100 silver vessels worth two talents (v. 26), if that is the right reading, and with the 20 gold bowls worth 1,000 darics, both reasonable sums. The varying details suggest that we are dealing with corrupted figures that were once genuine, rather than with deliberate hyperbole (as e.g. in 1 Chr. 22:14 or 1 Chr. 21:25 compared with 2 Sam. 24:24).

**28.** Holiness is not an attribute of God, but his essence. He is holy in that he is divine, so his holiness involves his majesty, his uniqueness, his awe-inspiring character. Anything that is dedicated to God is transferred into the sphere of the holy, and so becomes unusable by men except on pain of the divine wrath. Thus **vessels** given for the temple are **holy**, and likewise the priests and Levites who are dedicated to God. A good example of the dangers of secular use of 'holy' objects is that of Achan (Jos. 7, where the 'holy' things are spoils dedicated to Yahweh). Holiness is not necessarily a moral quality, as may be seen from the application of the term to material objects; but when it is applied to people it is often implied that since the Holy One himself is a righteous God, those who come within the sphere of his holiness in any way conform (or ought to conform) to his character. **the silver and the gold** cannot be called holy in the sense the vessels are, for the money may be spent and so pass into secular use. But this gift also has been offered **to the LORD,** and must therefore be carefully guarded.

**29. heads of fathers' houses** do not appear in the account of the delivery of the temple gifts (v. 33), and perhaps do not belong here. **the chambers** of Solomon's temple were the three-storeyed storerooms against the back and side walls of the temple (1 Kg. 6:5f., 8ff.); probably Zerubbabel's temple was similarly designed.

DEPARTURE FROM BABYLONIA AND ARRIVAL IN JERUSALEM
## 8:31–36

On the nature of the journey, see on 7:8f.

**31. departed:** lit. 'pulled up tent pegs'. **Ahava:** cf. on v. 15.
**deliver** is a stronger word than 'protect', and usually suggests that
the person is already in the grip of enemies or afflictions; thus when
a psalmist is delivered from death, he feels that he has been under
its power and has now escaped (e.g. Ps. 56:13; 18:4f., 16f.).

**32.** Ezra's memoirs must have noted at this point the date of his
arrival in **Jerusalem,** but the Chronicler has already given this
information in 7:8f. ('on the first day of the fifth month'), so need
not repeat it here. Nehemiah also seems to have rested **three days**
after his arrival before beginning his work (Neh. 2:11; cf. also Jos.
3:1f.); it may be a customary period after a long journey.

**33–34.** After the rest period and demobilisation of the caravan,
the gifts for the temple were delivered to temple representatives,
two priests and two Levites, and were carefully checked. (On the
significance of the existence of four temple treasurers for the question of the date of Ezra, see on Neh. 13:13.) Verse 34 especially
suggests to many that Ezra's memoir was not simply a personal
record, but a report for the king on the successful completion of
the mission. The contrary impression is however created by v. 22,
but at least it is noteworthy how important Ezra thought accuracy
in divine affairs was. **Meremoth . . . son of Uriah:** of the Hakkoz
family (Neh. 3:4–21) which in the time of the first returns had been
unable to prove its line of descent (Ezr. 2:59–63) but since then had
presumably been legitimised by a high priest. It is remarkable that
a family of dubious status a century previously could now produce
one of the leading priests. See also Introduction, IV. **Eleazar:** otherwise unknown, unless he is the priest Eliezer in 10:18 who had
married a foreign wife. **Jozabad,** elsewhere mentioned as one of the
overseers of the 'outside work' of the temple (Neh. 11:16), is from
a family mentioned in the list of early homecomers (Ezr. 2:40), and
possibly **Noadiah**'s family, **Binnui,** is also mentioned in that list
(though the name is corrupted in MT to 'sons of'); cf. also on Neh.
11:15.

**35–36.** These verses may well be from the Chronicler, not from
the Ezra memoirs; here it is the **exiles** rather than Ezra himself who
figure. The content of these verses, even if not from Ezra himself,
is no doubt correct in substance: the exiles are bound to have offered
sacrifices to celebrate their arrival, and Ezra to have informed the
satrap of Abar-nahara and his treasurer of the wishes of Artaxerxes
(cf. 7:21–24).

**35. At that time** belongs to this verse (as *RSV;* cf. *NAB*), not to
the end of v. 34 (as MT, *AV, NEB*). **offerings:** free-will thanksgiving
offerings or sacrifices in payment of vows made in expectation of a
safe journey (cf. Ps. 66:13). **twelve bulls . . . twelve he-goats:** the
number expresses the view, common to Ezra and the Chronicler,
of the new community as representative of all Israel (cf. on vv.
3–14, 24; 6:17); **ninety-six** is also a multiple of twelve, and **seventy-
seven** should probably be 'seventy-two' (*NEB, JB;* similarly some
MSS of 1 Esd. 8:65). **sin offering** (cf. Lev. 4): for the cleansing of
ritual defilement contracted through living in a foreign country.

**36. satraps:** There was of course only one satrap of the **province**
or satrapy Abar-nahara (**Beyond the River**), the governors of the
various sub-provinces being subordinate to him. The plural **satraps**
may be a scribal mistake or else is used loosely by the Chronicler
(cf. the wide range of meanings of *peḥâ*, 'governor, commissioner',
etc.; see on 5:14. **the king's commissions** (lit. 'laws, decrees') would
have been delivered to their addressees during the course of the
journey, not after arrival in Jerusalem. The main point of the verse
is to record how **they,** the Persian officials, **aided the people and
the house of God.**

At this point in the Ezra memoirs, according to the view taken
in this commentary, there probably followed originally the account
of the law-reading ceremony of Neh. 8 (cf. on Neh. 8:1–18) and
perhaps also that of the penitential service of Neh. 9 (cf. on Neh.
9:1–37); see further, Introduction, III.

As in the previous chapter grateful acknowledgement is made of
the assistance of the Persian government toward the upkeep of the
temple. Yet the gift has brought a responsibility with it: it is Ezra's
task to convey the money safely to Judea. The risks and hardships
involved in crossing the desert are fully realised by Ezra, but he
counts it better to run the risks unaided by Persian soldiers than to
allow any aspersions to be cast on the faithfulness of his God to
protect his property and his servants. But, we may ask, did Ezra
not have a responsibility also to the members of his caravan to make
their journey as safe as possible? He could surely have obtained an
escort if he had asked. A more practically-minded age such as our
own might find Ezra's decision too idealistic and lacking in common-
sense precautions; some might observe that 'God helps those who
help themselves'. But it would be a pity if we could not also admire
this calm confidence (v. 28) that does not 'rely on horses' but 'looks
to the Holy One of Israel' (Isa. 31:1).

## EZRA'S ACTION OVER MIXED MARRIAGES
### ch. 9–10

The book of Ezra concludes with the account of Ezra's response to the news that many of the Jewish community had married foreign women. Ezra's memoirs we may well suppose to have included other episodes beside this, but unless we are dealing with a scribal disarrangement of the material, we have to observe that the Chronicler has deliberately chosen this episode as a prime illustration of the work of Ezra. The Chronicler of course did not regard the dissolution of mixed marriages as a trivial matter, nor did it offend his moral sensibilities.

Many modern readers, who have perhaps accepted the understanding of the exclusivism of the post-exilic community outlined on 4:1ff., and who see that Ezra's strict obedience to the law is no mere 'legalism', may nevertheless be appalled by the personal misery brought into so many families by the compulsory divorce of foreign wives, and will be outraged at Ezra's insistence on racial purity, so uncongenial to modern liberal thought. We cannot lightly neglect such reactions, but we need to clarify the situation before we make judgments upon the actions taken.

First, what was the law (i.e. the Pentateuchal law)? Marriage with foreigners was not categorically forbidden; Joseph (Gen. 41:45), Moses (Num. 12:1ff.), and the sons of Elimelech (Ru. 1) had non-Israelite wives, and Abraham an Egyptian concubine (Gen. 16:3). But marriage with the non-Israelite inhabitants of Canaan was clearly disallowed (Exod. 34:11–16; Dt. 7:1–6); and not only law but patriarchal example stood opposed to such marriages (cf. Gen 24:2ff.; 27:46–28:9 specifically rejecting marriage with Canaanites). The fundamental distinction between marriage with Palestinians and with other foreigners is drawn also in Dt. 20:10–18 in reference to women captured in war.

The reason given for this prohibition was consistently a religious one: 'that they may not teach you to do according to all their abominable practices which they have done in the service of their gods' (Dt. 20:18; cf. 7:4; Exod. 34:16). The history of the Israelite monarchy amply illustrated how easily Israelite religion could be corrupted through royal marriages of alliance (1 Kg. 11:1–8; 16:31ff.; cf. Jg. 3:5ff.). In strict logic, the evil of foreign cults could not be measured by their geographical distance from Israel; nevertheless in practice the chief danger was that Israel would adopt the religions of its closest neighbours, so they were the cults to which the law was most sharply opposed. It is noteworthy too that the marriages with foreigners referred to above were contracted outside Israel in places where Hebrew wives were unavailable; while in the case of Abraham, nothing but trouble resulted from his concubinage with Hagar, so no Jew would have claimed that as a good precedent.

It could have been argued by those who had married non-Jewish wives that the law did not specifically proscribe those nations from which their wives had come. But that would have been seen by Ezra as a mere technicality; his interpretation and extension of the Pentateuchal law (cf. on 9:1) could well have been argued to be far more in keeping with the spirit of the Pentateuchal provisions. Certainly the laws must have been known in Palestine: even if Ezra's law-book was a new compilation, the relevant material must have already been familiar, since it is contained in parts of the Pentateuch that few scholars would date later than the ninth-eighth centuries (Exod. 34) and the seventh (Deuteronomy). A further point influencing the community of Ezra's time towards taking a rigorous decision may have been the fact that 'the leaders and magistrates have been the chief offenders' (v. 2, *NEB*). Higher standards of obedience to the law, especially in ritual matters—of which this was plainly one—may have been required of them, as it was of the priests (see further, Ackroyd, pp. 262f.)

Ezra was not some self-appointed reformer and custodian of other people's morals. He came to Jerusalem as a commissioner of the Persian king, with instructions, and not just permission, to insist that in the sub-province of Judea the Pentateuchal law was state law (7:25f.), 'the law of the Medes and Persians' (cf. Dan. 6:8). He was therefore legally entitled to compel obedience on this issue; a specific penalty is not laid down in the law, and it would have been left to his discretion.

In this context must be set the account of how Ezra proceeded. Far from using the force of his authority, he persuades the leaders of the people to take the responsibility upon themselves. They in turn demand only that the Jews should attend an assembly (10:7f.), and in the end it is those who themselves have broken the law who make their own decisions (10:14). Ezra's handling of the mixed-marriage question is often contrasted unfavourably with Nehemiah's; but it is not clear that Nehemiah took a more tolerant view, and certain moreover that he exerted his authority more forcibly than Ezra (cf. on Neh. 13:23–29).

Is there not still, however, a strong 'racialist' motive behind the divorce of foreign wives (cf. especially 9:2: 'the holy race has mixed itself with the peoples of the lands')? That can hardly be denied, but the defence of the 'holy race' is engaged in more strictly on religious grounds than has been the case with most so-called 'reli-

gious' persecutions and wars. It is noteworthy that Ezra's prayer in
response to the news (9:6–15) speaks not of Jewish racial superiority
but of the community's unfaithfulness to God, nor of any inferiority
of foreign nations, but simply of their religious 'abominations'
(9:14). We must also remember that racial purity, in a genetic sense,
was not at all claimed by the Israelite people (cf. Dt. 26:5; Exod.
12:38; Ezek. 16:3, 45).

But when all is said and done, there is no denying that the
breaking up of families was a horrible thing. Yet both Ezra and
those who had married foreign wives agreed that it was a lesser evil
than to break the law of God. One must be careful, though, not to
be too glib about such agonising matters. R. North says, 'The
dangerous and casual claim that "God's rights outweigh all human
considerations" can only be called fanaticism, (p. 433)—fanaticism
indeed if it is casual and is made a rule for the behaviour of others,
but it may well form part of the life-style of one who has taken
upon himself the yoke of the kingdom of God (cf. e.g. Lk. 14:26).
Modern readers are caught in a dilemma between imposing their
own moral standards upon an alien age and negating their legitimate
impulse to make moral judgments about human behaviour. Perhaps
rather than making judgments, it would be more rewarding to
attempt to sympathise both with Ezra and with those whose marriages were broken up. See further on Neh. 13:23–29.

## A REPORT MADE TO EZRA

### 9:1–2

This report, as is shown by 10:9, was made in the middle of the
ninth month, presumably of the year of Ezra's arrival in Jerusalem.
Two questions arise: (i) What had Ezra been doing in the interval
of four months? (ii) Why had it taken so long for news of these at
least 113 marriages (10:18–43) to reach his ears? The following
answers can be suggested:

(i) The appointment of judges (7:25) cannot have taken so long,
and it is reasonable to suppose that the reading of the law and the
observance of the festival of booths in the seventh month, as
narrated in Neh. 8, intervened (see further, Introduction, III, IV).

(ii) It may be inferred from 10:3 that Ezra not only knew about
the mixed marriages before the report of 9:1f. was made to him,
but also had made suggestions about what should be done. If this
inference is correct, the report in 9:1f. is an official report, to which
Ezra responds with a public manifestation of grief. We may think
that only spontaneous expressions of emotion are likely to be

genuine. But formalised weeping has always been a part of oriental life, and can hardly be dismissed as unreal.

The setting of the episode in 9:1–10:5 is the court in front of the temple (10:1), which suggests strongly that this is a formal report made to Ezra as a kind of test-case.

**1. After these things had been done** (lit. 'at the completion of these things') is a favourite expression of the Chronicler's (cf. 2 Chr. 7:1; 20:23; 24:10, 14; 29:29; 31:1), so this may be the Chronicler's editorial phrase to bridge the gap left by the omission of the law-reading narrative that is now to be found in Neh. 8. The **officials** (*śārîm*, 'chiefs, princes') are probably (as in Neh. 3:9, etc. 'ruler'; cf. 12:31) the chief administrators of the six districts, each divided into two, which comprised the province of Judea (cf. Avi-Yonah, *Holy Land*, pp. 19–23). **the peoples of the lands** (cf. 3:3): the non-Jewish or part-Jewish descendants of races like the Moabites and Edomites, whether living within the territory of Judea or not. The list of races given here bears little relationship to the races inhabiting Palestine in the time of Ezra. **Canaanites, Hittites, Perizzites, Jebusites, and Amorites** no longer existed as racial groups, but we need not regard the list on this account as a worthless scribal addition to the narrative. It is a stereotyped list of heathen nations (Gen. 15:19ff.; Exod. 3:8, 17; 33:2; 34:11; Neh. 9:8; etc.) drawn upon especially in Dt. 7:1 in connection with the prohibition of intermarriage (usually seven nations [cf. Ac. 13:19], including Girgashites and Hivites, are mentioned). Its use here is to refer formally to the relevant law, and to express the legal opinion that the contemporary non-Jewish population, though not mentioned expressly in the Mosaic law, comes within its provisions. Many think the term **Amorites** is here a scribal error for the similarly written word 'Edomites', who were still in existence (cf. on Neh. 2:19), but this is unlikely, since marriage with Edomites is not prohibited by the law (Dt. 23:7f.). **Ammonites** and **Moabites** do not belong to the stereotyped list, but are here grouped with the pagan nations on the basis of Deut. 23:3–6 which excludes them and their offspring from Israel (cf. on Neh. 13:1). Inclusion of **Egyptians** in such a list is unique and puzzling: marriage with Egyptians is not expressly forbidden (Dt. 23:7f.), but the episode of the half-Egyptian law-breaker in Lev. 24:10–23 displays strong disapproval (cf. the rejection of Egyptian customs in relation to marriage, Lev. 18:3). The list affords a fascinating glimpse into the way the law was being systematised and integrated by Ezra and his fellow 'scribes' of the law (cf. also on Neh 8:15); disparate sections of the Pentateuch, sometimes from widely differing historical origins, were being welded into a unitary system of legal prescription. **with their abomi-**

**nations** underlines the religious implications of mixed marriages (on *tô'ēḇâ*, 'abomination', see P. Humbert, *ZAW* 72 [1960], pp. 217–37).

**2.** Though the giving of daughters in marriage to pagans is forbidden (Dt. 7:3), the emphasis is usually on the dangers of taking pagan wives for one's sons (cf. Dt. 7:4; Exod. 34:16), since in the latter case pagan ways would be introduced into the Israelite family, whereas in the former the girl would be virtually lost to Israel. The principle of Israel's separation (v. 1) from the other nations of the world, a theme of the Chronicler's, has been undermined by this mixture (cf. Lev. 19:19) of the **holy race** with pagans; the term is literally 'holy seed' (*AV*), a phrase from Isa. 6:13, but with overtones of the blessings to Abraham (Gen. 12:7; 13:14ff.; 17:1–8; *RSV*, 'descendants', is lit. 'seed'). The measure of disobedience is the greater in that it is the leaders who have chiefly offended. At Elephantine also, lay leaders and temple officials are known to have married non-Jews (Porten, *Elephantine*, p. 250). **officials** (*śārîm*): possibly in the same sense as in v. 1; for of the eight district officials mentioned in Neh. 2, four can be identified as husbands of foreign wives (cf. on Ezr. 10:25, 41f.). But since it is not likely that a formal complaint should be brought by a group against some of its members, the term is perhaps used in a less specialised sense. **chief men** (*s*ᵉ*ḡānîm*), a term originally Babylonian, are minor officials, such as village elders (*NEB*, 'magistrates').

EZRA'S RESPONSE

9:3–5

Ezra responds to the officials' report with the formal behaviour customary at times of mourning or severe distress (cf. 2 Chr. 34:19). He does not assert himself against the offenders, but movingly identifies himself with the community in its sinfulness, and confesses the communal guilt. It is not simply that certain individuals have broken the law, but that the community has sinned in being the kind of community where such actions could occur and be tolerated. Ezra has a strong sense of the role of the group, the people of Israel, as the object of God's election; in contrast, Nehemiah seems more concerned with the role of the individual in determining the kind of society Judah will be (cf. on Neh 13:23–27; but see also Neh. 1:6).

**3.** Here the scribe Ezra enacts a typical piece of prophetic symbolism (e.g. Isa. 20:1–4; Ezek. 4–5). He rends not only his **mantle** (*mᵉ'îl*), the outer garment or cloak, which would usually be torn at times of distress (cf. Job 1:20; 2:12), but also his 'garment'

(*AV*, not *RSV* **garments**), i.e. his undergarment or tunic (*beḡeḏ*). See M. Jastrow, 'The Tearing of Garments as a Symbol of Mourning', *JAOS* 21 (1900), pp. 23–39; 'Baring of the Arm and Shoulder as a Sign of Mourning', *ZAW* 22 (1902), pp. 117–20. The tearing of garments is a stylised stripping oneself naked, which is a token of humiliation and death (e.g. Ezek. 16:39; Job 1:21). **pulled hair:** The common ancient practice of shaving the head in mourning (cf. Job 1:20; Isa. 15:2; Jer. 47:5; Mic. 1:16) was forbidden to Israel because of its pagan associations (Lev. 19:27; 21:5; Dt. 14:1), and was modified into pulling off some of the hair of head and beard. **appalled** (*NEB*, 'dumbfounded'): the conventional shocked silence at a time of lamentation (N. Lohfink, 'Enthielten die im Alten Testament bezeugten Klageriten eine Phase des Schweigens?', *VT* 12 [1962], pp. 260–77, esp. 265–9; for sitting appalled, cf. Ezek. 26:16; Job 2:12f.). See also on Est. 4:1.

**4.** Ezra's public demonstration of grief, though sincere enough, was also an effective means of rallying support, as Josephus observed (*Ant.* 11.5.3). There gathered about him a group of likeminded Jews who themselves had been concerned about the mixed marriages and had needed no Ezra to expound the law on the matter. **all who trembled at the words of the God of Israel:** the strict adherents of the law; it is almost a technical term (cf. 10:3; Isa. 66:2, 5). **because of the faithlessness** is to be connected closely with **gathered round me** (cf. *NEB*), not with **trembled. returned exiles:** Here they are of course those who had come back in earlier migrations: the 'exiles' in 8:35 are those returning with Ezra. **appalled until the evening sacrifice:** Ezra sat in silence, a symbol, like tearing the clothes and pulling out hair, of extreme grief, until the appropriate time to offer a prayer, the time of the **evening sacrifice,** the ninth hour, i.e. about 3 p.m. (cf. 1 Kg. 18:36; Mt. 27:46; Ac. 3:1).

**5. fasting,** rather than 'humiliation' (*NEB*), 'heaviness' (*AV*); 'wretchedness' (*NAB*): a natural accompaniment of grief; on its significance, see on 8:21. Ezra's fast continued throughout that night (10:6). **fell upon my knees and spread out my hands:** Various postures in prayer are attested in the *OT:* standing (e.g. 1 Sam. 1:26), sitting (1 Chr. 17:16), kneeling (1 Kg. 8:54). The hands were lifted (e.g. Neh. 8:6; Ps. 28:2) or spread out, palms upward (e.g. Isa. 1:15), perhaps as a sign of helplessness or need. Standing and kneeling postures for prayer are both found elsewhere in the ancient Near East: cf. Tukulti-ninurta (*ANEP*, p. 192, fig. 57*b*), standing and kneeling; and a man of Larsa (*ANEP*, p. 204, fig. 622) kneeling. For the lifting of hands, cf. Esarhaddon's Prism B (*ANET*, p. 289).

## EZRA'S PRAYER
### 9:6–15

Ezra is throughout this prayer quite conscious of his human audience, which is not improper, for it is a public prayer, designed in
part to enable his hearers to share his spiritual feeling. He begins
with a very personal expression of emotion, which assures us that
this is a prayer of genuine spirituality, but immediately proceeds to
identify himself with the community's sinfulness. Ezra shows his
instinctive psychological skill, which cannot be too sharply differentiated from his religious sensitivity, in making this prayer simply a
confession of sin and not a prayer for forgiveness; the gravity of
Israel's sin, which has called into question its whole existence as the
people of God (v. 14), must not be minimised by too ready an
appeal to the divine mercy (cf. on Neh. 9:32–37). That would be
to cheapen grace. It is no doubt a weakness of modern spirituality
that it regards a real fear of God's wrath which does not immediately
lead to assurance of God's forgiveness as somewhat fanatical.

Is the prayer, however, Ezra's own, or has it been composed by
the Chronicler as appropriate for the occasion? While it has been
argued that in it 'from the beginning to the end we have characteristic Chronicle terminology' (Kapelrud, *Authorship*, p. 70), and
it was certainly a normal practice for ancient historians to compose
suitable speeches for their characters (cf. the prayers of the Chronicler, 1 Chr. 29:10–19; 2 Chr. 20:6–12), there are good grounds for
supposing the prayer to be authentic in the sense of having formed
part of Ezra's memoirs (what relation this written prayer bore to
the prayer uttered on that occasion we cannot say). This prayer,
compared with others in *OT* historiography, is uniquely related to
its setting (cf. Plöger, 'Reden und Gebete'; In der Smitten, *Esra*,
p. 25). Furthermore, the reference to the generosity of the Persians
(v. 9) would be particularly significant if Ezra's memoirs were
intended as a report of his activities to the Persian government (see
Introduction, II.2). Some such climax to his demonstration is in
any case necessary both historically and psychologically.

**6. ashamed:** Shame is often in *OT* the objective act of humiliation, disgrace, or disappointment (e.g. Ps. 6:10; Isa. 45:16f.); but
here is the subjective feeling not so much of guilt (as e.g. Jer. 31:19)
as of embarrassment (as in Ezr. 8:22). See *TDOT*, II, pp. 50–60.
Though Ezra himself is innocent, he regards himself as involved in
the sin of his people.

**7.** Ezra, like most survivors of the exile, has made his own the
view of history which dominates the 'Deuteronomistic history'
(Jos.–2 Kg.); see Ackroyd, *Exile and Restoration*, pp. 73–8): the

disasters that have overtaken Israel are divine punishment for her faithlessness to God since **the days of our fathers** (cf. Jg. 2:11–23). While Ezra does not blame the evils of the present on the sin of former generations, he sees the men of his own generation as united in a sinful solidarity with their fathers. He cannot speak merely of the guilt of the individual offenders, for he is very conscious of the stranglehold of sin on the whole community. **kings of the lands:** foreign kings, Assyrian, Babylonian, and Persian (cf. Neh. 9:32). **as at this day** is in view of the next verse a strange addition (perhaps a later scribe's interjection), unless perhaps Ezra is thinking of the many Israelites (especially of the northern tribes) who still remain in exile.

**8.** He now turns to the change in Israel's fortunes brought about by the decree of Cyrus. A century or more has passed since that time, but it seems only **a brief moment** compared with the centuries of Assyrian and Babylonian oppression. **leave us a remnant** (*haš'îr pᵉlêṭâ*): Terms for remnant (*pᵉlêṭâ, šᵉ'ērît*), originally meaning the survivors of any disaster, become technical terms for the post-exilic community (e.g. Hag. 1:12, 14; 2:2; Zech. 8:6, 11f.; Neh. 1:2f.). Both returned exiles and descendants of the survivors of the fall of the southern kingdom can be included. **remnant** can have a positive or negative sense: negatively it emphasises the fewness of those who are delivered, positively it stresses that they are delivered; the latter sense is present here. See further, G. F. Hasel, *The Remnant* (1972). **secure hold** (lit. 'nail' or rather 'tent-peg', cf. *AV, RSV* mg): the rebuilt temple, the sign of God's presence in the midst of his people, guaranteeing their stability. We may compare the use of a nail or peg in the foundations of early Mesopotamian temples as 'the outward sign of a pact between the devout builder and his deity' (E. A. Speiser in *The Idea of History in the Ancient Near East*, ed. R. C. Dentan [1955], p. 47); see also R. S. Ellis, *Foundation Deposits in Ancient Mesopotamia* (1968), pp. 46–93. *NEB*, 'foothold', changes the metaphor and weakens the sense. **brighten our eyes:** i.e. increase the vitality, revive the spirits (cf. 2 Sam. 14:27; Ps. 23:3). **bondage:** In spite of these evidences of divine favour, the fact is (cf. Neh. 9:36) that the Jewish people is still in subjection (**bondage**) to foreign rulers. On the question whether this statement points to some future hope, see Introduction, V.

**9. forsaken:** God is pledged not to forsake his faithful servants (cf. Ps. 16:10; 37:25), but it is often said, 'If you forsake him, he will forsake you' (2 Chr. 15:2; cf. 12:5; 24:20; 1 Chr. 28:9). That Israel has not been forsaken, i.e. left to its own devices, in exile, is understood by Ezra to be a remarkable example of God's freedom to bypass the working of the law of retribution, and to bless those

who did not deserve it. **protection** (lit. 'a wall'): Some have regarded
this as a city-wall, arguing that the reference to it shows that Nehemiah's wall must already have been built when Ezra arrived. See H.
Kaupel, *BZ* 22 (1934), pp. 89–92; *Bib.* 16 (1935), pp. 213f.; A.
Fernández, *Bib.* 18 (1937), pp. 207f.; N. H. Snaith, *ZAW* 63
(1951), pp. 58f. But it is more likely that the term is being used
metaphorically (as in Ps. 80:12) for the protection afforded by the
Persian government; for a city-wall would hardly be called a wall
**in Judea and Jerusalem.** Another interpretation is based on the use
of the word (*gāḏēr*) in inscriptions from Gibeon for not only the
wall of a vineyard but the vineyard itself (like the French *clos*) (H.
Michaud, *VT* 10 [1960], p. 103); thus 'revived Israel is the vineyard
of Yahweh with its enclosure' (Myers, p. 75; cf. Isa. 5:1–7).

**10.** After these tokens of God's favour, what response will the
people make? Thanksgiving? Profession of obedience to the law?
No, they can only say that (not 'for', *AV, RSV, NEB*) **we have
forsaken thy commandments.**

**11–12.** Since the words of Scripture which Ezra here brings
together come chiefly from the Pentateuch, we must infer that he
regards Moses as a prophet, as does Deuteronomy (18:15; 34:10;
cf. Hos. 12:13). For a similar inclusion of the law within the category
of prophecy, cf. Dan. 6:10. Of the prophets in the strict sense, only
Malachi speaks against mixed marriages (2:11). Verses 11*b*-12 are a
mosaic of biblical phrases: **the land which you are entering, to take
possession of it** echoes Dt. 7:1; **a land unclean with the pollutions
of the peoples of the lands,** Lev. 18:24–30 (though **the peoples
of the lands** is typical of Ezra and the Chronicler; cf. 9:1; 3:3);
**abominations,** Dt. 18:9; Ezek. 16:47; etc.; **filled . . . from end to
end** (lit. 'mouth to mouth', 'edge to edge'), 2 Kg. 21:16; **give not
your daughters,** etc., Dt. 7:3 (though the marrying of Israelite
women to foreigners is not apposite here); **never seek their peace
or prosperity,** Dt. 23:6 (there specifically of Ammonites and Moabites); **that you may be strong,** Dt. 11:8; **eat the good of the land**
(i.e. its best produce), Isa. 1:19 (cf. Dt. 6:11; Gen. 45:18); **leave it
for an inheritance to your children,** Dt. 1:38f. (cf. Lev. 25:46;
Ezek. 37:25; and closest of all, 1 Chr. 28:8, David's prayer, perhaps
modelled on Ezra's by the Chronicler; cf. on 9:6–15).

**13–14.** The sense is: 'Now that we have experienced the misery
of punishment for our sins—and even so (*AV, RSV* **seeing that** is
better translated 'yet') we did not receive the full punishment (otherwise we would have been exterminated)—how can we be foolish
enough to bring similar (or rather, more devastating) punishment
upon ourselves?' (similarly, *NEB*). While Second Isaiah had said
that Israel had 'received from the Lord's hand double (i.e. a

sufficient punishment) for all her sins' (Isa. 40:2), Ezra knows that the suffering of exile was **less than our iniquities deserved**, that the 'double' is no exact requital (cf. Ps. 130:3) but the gracious reckoning of God ('the free gift is not like the trespass', Rom. 5:15). **Wouldst thou not be angry**: The negative question form is not hypothetical, but expresses a strong conviction. **angry**: cf. on 5:12.

**15. thou art just, for we are left a remnant**: This can hardly mean that God's justice is expressed by leaving a remnant; for God's righteousness (*sᵉḏāqâ*) does not here mean 'salvation' as it does e.g. in Isa. 46:13; 51:5. Rather, **for we are left** should be translated 'yet we are left', and the thought is parallel to v. 13. God is righteous, therefore only punishment for sin can be expected; he has been merciful, but his mercy cannot be presumed upon a second time (cf. on 10:2). Alternatively, the sense may be, 'Thou art just, in that we are virtually destroyed; only a remnant of the nation is left' (cf. *NEB*).

**our guilt**: The guilt is that of the whole community. But it need not be thought that with his stress on corporate responsibility, Ezra had little concern for the individual; after all, only those who had actually broken the law had to divorce their wives. It is of the essence of sin, though, that it can affect and harm those who are not responsible for it.

**stand**: a legal term meaning 'to be acquitted' (cf. Ps. 1:5; 130:3).

The prayer of Ezra is of interest for its psychological perception and its religious sensitivity. It also reflects a realistic appraisal, which may well have been shared by many of Ezra's contemporaries, of the political possibilities for Judea. In being at the Persian's government's mercy—which had in fact turned out to be clemency, so far—the Jews realise that there is no likelihood of a restoration of the splendours of the Davidic monarchy, and have decided to make the best of the 'day of small things' (Zech. 4:10). Above all, they realise that the favour of the Persians is the form in which they experience the favour of their God.

### PUBLIC REACTION TO EZRA'S CONFESSION
### 10:1–6

The narrative now returns to the third-person form, which suggests (as in ch. 7) that the Chronicler is adapting the Ezra memoirs rather than quoting verbally from them (Noth, *Studien*, pp. 146f.). It is not, however, impossible that Ezra's memoirs themselves used first and third person speech indiscriminately (cf. Dan. 4; for an ancient Near Eastern parallel, see the Cyrus cylinder; *ANET*, pp. 315f.; *DOTT*, pp. 92f.). Less probable are the views that the Chronicler was now using a source other than the Ezra memoirs (Eissfeldt, p. 544), or was freely composing (Fohrer, p. 243).

In any case, it is clear that Ezra's prayer had its desired repercussions among the bystanders, for by the end of the day he had gained a mandate from a sizable proportion of the people to deal firmly with the problem. We do not by any means have a full account of the events of these hours; how Shecaniah was able to speak for the people is obscure, and whether his response was spontaneous or to some extent arranged already with Ezra must be left an open question. The Ezra memoirs themselves may have told the story more fully.

1. **casting himself down** suggests prostration on the ground, but may simply refer to his kneeling posture (9:5; cf. Neh. 8:6). **the people wept bitterly**: presumably Ezra's like-minded friends of 9:4; the sound of their sustained high-pitched weeping attracted people **out of Israel**, i.e. of the Israelite nation, 'Israelites' (*NEB*).

2. One of the company, presumably acting as spokesman, accepts Ezra's statement of the nation's guilt and promises that the people will conform themselves to the law. It is extraordinary that the spokesman should be **Shecaniah** b. **Jehiel** of the family of **Elam** (2:7), since a Jehiel of the family of Elam was among those who had married foreign wives (10:26); Shecaniah himself in this case would have been advocating his own excommunication, so we can only suppose that his father was another Jehiel of that family (it is a fairly common Israelite name, meaning 'May God keep [X] alive'). Certainly he himself was not among the offenders, but like Ezra he identifies himself with the faithlessness of the community. **have broken faith** (*mā'al*): a technical term for the violation of an oath, often in the context of a covenant; see J. Milgrom, *JAOS* 96 [1976], pp. 236–47. **hope . . . in spite of this** (*RSV;* cf. *NEB*) gives the sense, though MT has 'but now there is hope . . . concerning this (matter)' (cf. *AV*) or perhaps 'in addition to this (sin)'. Shecaniah, in holding out some hope, goes further than Ezra; though God's forgiveness cannot be compelled, repentance (involving concrete action as well as a change of mind) is at least a prelude to forgiveness.

3. **make a covenant with our God**: Divine covenants in *OT*, whether with individuals, the nation, or the Davidic dynasty, are usually made by God as the superior partner; men's part is simply to keep the covenant. Very occasionally, though, kings are said to 'make a covenant' 'to' or before the Lord, pledging their obedience to the covenant that already exists (2 Kg. 23:3; 2 Chr. 29:10; cf. 15:12; 23:16; see *TDOT*, II, pp. 253–79). 'Let us pledge ourselves to our God' (*NEB*) is a preferable translation (cf. also on Neh. 9:38). **to put away all these wives**: Divorce is not prescribed in the

law, but is sanctioned as an existing practice (Dt. 24:1-4; cf. Mt. 19:8) in the event of a husband's finding some 'indecency' or 'uncleanness' in his wife. Perhaps Shecaniah is appealing to this passage in saying **let it be done according to the law**, for it is now the case that Jewish husbands have recognised their foreign wives to be (ritually) 'unclean'. Shecaniah is not speaking contemptuously of the foreign wives, as *NEB* suggests with 'dismiss all these women and their brood'. **those who tremble . . . :** see on 9:4.

**4. your task:** Now that marriage with foreign women has been recognised by the community to be an infringement of the law. **arise . . . be strong:** The exhortation does not imply any unwillingness on Ezra's part (cf. Jos. 1:9).

**5.** The **oath** given by 'the leaders of the priests, of the Levites, and of the lay Israelites' (*RSV* misleadingly restricts 'chief' or **leading** to the priests) affirms the covenant of v. 3. It is not that Ezra takes advantage of the emotional state of the people to extract from them an oath lest they should later think better of a hasty decision (contrast Neh. 5:12) but simply that he, as chief justice, administers the oath of the covenant proposed by Shecaniah. On *OT* oaths, see M. H. Pope, *IDB*, III, pp. 575ff.; M. R. Lehmann, 'Biblical Oaths', *ZAW* 81 (1969), pp. 74-92; and for an oath document, see *AP* 44 (Porten, *Elephantine*, pp. 317f.).

**6.** Ezra continues his fast (9:5) throughout the night since it remains to be seen whether the law will be universally obeyed. **spent the night** (*RSV*, cf. *NEB*, plausibly emending *wylk*, 'went', to *wyln*) in one of the rooms attached to the temple; as in Solomon's temple (1 Kg. 6:5f.), there was presumably a three-storeyed structure against the side and rear temple walls used for storage and for accommodating priests and Levites (cf. on Neh. 3:30). **Jehohanan b. Eliashib:** His identity is problematic. We know that an Eliashib was high priest in Nehemiah's time (Neh. 3:1), and that his grandson (or perhaps, son) was named Johanan, a short form of Jehohanan (Neh. 12:32; Jonathan in 12:11 is probably erroneous for Jehohanan), whose high priesthood *c.* 411-408 BC is attested by an Aramaic letter from Elephantine (*AP* 30.18). If Ezra came to Jerusalem in 398, J(eh)ohanan would be the contemporary high priest, and certainly it is likely that Ezra should retire to the quarters of the high priest rather than to those of an otherwise unknown person of that name. This identification of Jehohanan is presupposed by *NEB*'s 'grandson' (lit. 'son'). But the date of 458 is not ruled out: since Jehohanan is not called high priest here, it is arguable that he became high priest only at a later date; in 458 he may have been a young member of the high priestly family with some responsibilities in the administration of the temple (thus not a

nonentity). His sympathy with Ezra's cause, which we may naturally
assume, would fit well with the picture of the high-priest Johanan
in *AP* 30.18f. as a rather unco-operative rigorist. Nevertheless,
perhaps the best solution is that recently suggested by F. M. Cross
(*JBL* 94 [1975], pp. 10, 17), that the high-priestly genealogy of
Neh. 12:10f. omits two names: Eliashib, brother of Joiakim (born
*c.* 545), and Johanan his son, born *c.* 520. The J(eh)ohanan b.
Eliashib here mentioned would thus have been the high priest
contemporary with Ezra in 458. See further, Introduction, IV.

## THE PUBLIC ASSEMBLY AND THE COMMISSION

### 10:7–17

By summoning an assembly of the returned exiles who themselves
call for the dissolution of mixed marriages, Ezra withdraws from
the limelight, and refuses to impose his views by force of authority
(even the compulsion to attend is **by order of the officials and the
elders**, v. 8); all the same, he makes no secret of his opinion, and
exerts heavy moral pressure. As far as we can tell, he was under no
obligation to gain the assent of the people, but it is strongly emphasised that the policy of divorce and its implementation was the
responsibility of the whole community (cf. vv. 12, 14, 16f.; cf. also
on Neh. 8:1).

7. Striking while the iron was hot, so it seems, Ezra dispatches
heralds (cf. on 1:1) throughout the province to make an oral **proclamation** of a mass assembly in Jerusalem, analogous to the compulsory 'presentation' of Israelite men at the sanctuary (Exod. 23:17;
Dt. 16:16). Such assemblies, well-attested in Israel (cf. C. U. Wolf,
*JNES* 6 [1947], pp. 98–108; A. Malamat, *JNES* 22 [1963], pp.
247–53), are not expressions of democracy, but resemble rather the
'palaver', in which the opinions of all sections of the community
can be expressed before those in authority make the decision. Ezra
is through and through a priest, so he naturally stages what is
virtually a cultic assembly (it meets in the square fronting the
temple, v. 9), even though it is legal business that it has met to
transact.

**returned exiles**: by this phrase the whole community, whether
they or their ancestors had ever been in exile, is designated by Ezra
and the Chronicler; it is equivalent to 'the people of Israel' (9:1),
'Israel' (10:2), or 'all the men of Judah and Benjamin' (10:9). The
Chronicler does not pretend that Judea was inhabited only by
returned exiles, and it is unwise to make too much out of his
terminology.

8. **three days** seems to be the conventional period of notice for

an assembly of Israel (cf. 2 Sam. 20:4; 1 Kg. 12:5; also the Qumran *Manual of Discipline*, 1QS 1.25ff.); it would allow ample time to travel from the remotest districts of Judea. **his (movable) property . . . forfeited**: literally, 'devoted' to Yahweh, i.e. the sacred ban (*ḥērem*) would be applied to it, rendering it unusable for secular purposes. Objects devoted in this way to God were apparently sometimes entirely burnt or destroyed (Jos. 6:21; 7:25), but often accepted for temple use (Num. 18:14; Ezek. 44:29). See further, A. Malamat, 'The Ban in Mari and in the Bible', *Biblical Essays* (1966), pp. 40–9; M. H. Pope, *IDB*, 1, pp. 838–9. To be **banned** (lit. 'separated', *AV*) from the community (cf. on 7:26), the earliest attestation of excommunication (cf. Jn 9:22; 12:42), is probably a modification of the more ancient capital punishment, 'to be cut off from Israel' (e.g. Exod. 12:15; Gen. 17:14; see J. Skinner, *Genesis* [²1930], pp. 294–5).

**9.** The gravity of the situation outweighed the inconvenience of travel in bad winter weather (cf. Mt. 24:20). **the ninth month**: December, when the heavy winter rains, and sometimes snow, fall in Jerusalem, lying 2,000 ft. above sea level. **the open square** before the temple had been the scene of Ezra's prayer (v. 1), and perhaps also of his reading of the law (Neh. 8).

**because of this matter** and **because of the heavy rain**: the conjunction of these two reasons is a curious zeugma, but adds a vivid touch. P. Joüon, *Bib.* 12 (1931), p. 85, ingeniously emended *dābār*, 'matter', to *bārād*, 'hail', but that remains conjectural.

**10–11.** Ezra, assured of the support of the leaders, speaks more bluntly now. The weight laid upon the people's solidarity in sin is striking; only one hundred or so, as far as we know, had actually transgressed, yet Ezra accuses the whole assembly of some tens of thousands, **You have trespassed**. This is because marriage with foreigners is not a private matter, but determines the character of the community. **increased the guilt of Israel**: This sin is one further item in the already formidable catalogue of national sin. **make confession**: literally, 'give praise' to God as righteous judge and maintainer of justice, who has uncovered the evil deed (cf. Jos. 7:19). But mere confession is inadequate; if repentance is to be genuine it must be accompanied by a positive obedience to the divine **will**, which Ezra typically sees not as essentially a 'putting away' of the foreign wives (cf. Mal. 2:16) but rather as a separating of Israel from the heathen (contrast Neh. 13:3).

**12–14.** The assembly accepts Ezra's analysis of the situation (**we have greatly transgressed**), and since the vast majority of them have nothing to lose by insisting on strict adherence to the law, it is not surprising that they should accede to his suggestion with a

loud shout of 'Yes' (*NEB*; **it is so**, *RSV*). The wrongdoers now
have ranged against them not only Ezra and the law but also the
collective will of their community. It would be rash to assume
that every member of the assembly appreciated the serious human
consequences of his response. But on the other hand it would be
wrong to speak of the assembly as 'excited by a kind of mob
psychosis' (North, p. 433), since, far from a summary execution of
rough justice, the assembly called for a legal commission which
would have time to deliberate over each case (v. 13). Its mode of
operation is unclear: the **officials** delegated by the **whole assembly**
are apparently the family heads of v. 16 who will constitute the
commission which will sit in Jerusalem; they will take each village
in turn, summoning before them those believed to have married
foreign women. The local **elders** and **judges** (cf. 7:25) would be
able to offer evidence from their personal knowledge of family and
village history. **till the fierce wrath . . . be averted**: rather, 'so that
. . .'. The Hebrew does not imply that God's good favour will
automatically be restored when the marriages have been annulled.

**15.** The only opposition (if indeed it was opposition) came from
two otherwise unknown men, **Jonathan** b. **Asahel** and **Jahzeiah** b.
**Tikvah**; the fact that they were supported by **Meshullam**, presumably (since his patronym is omitted) the companion of Ezra in 8:16,
and by the Levite **Shabbethai**, who appears in Neh. 11:16 among
the leading Levites, could suggest that they were more zealous, not
more lax, than Ezra and demanded more summary treatment of
the offenders. Shabbethai's name suggests he came from a strictly
observant family, that 'called the sabbath a delight' (Isa. 58:13); cf.
Porten, *Elephantine*, p. 124. It is possible that the whole verse
reports not opposition but support (as 1 Esd. 9:14 has it).

**16–17. Ezra the priest**: He acts here not simply as a Persian
official or as a 'scribe' of the law, but in a priestly role in order to
decontaminate Israel from ritual impurity (cf. In der Smitten, pp.
31f.). **Ezra . . . selected**: According to MT, the popular assembly
chose the members of the commission (cf. *AV*, *JPSV*); but the
absence of 'and' before **heads of fathers' houses** prompts the
suggestion that we read *wayyabdēl*, 'and he (Ezra) selected' (cf. 1
Esd. 9:16), instead of *wayyibādᵉlû*, 'and they were selected'.

**heads of fathers' houses**, i.e. heads of 'extended families' (cf. on
1:5), whose names were recorded (**designated**) in a list known to
the author, perhaps in the Ezra memoirs.

Ezra's administrative efficiency ensured that the commission sat
for the first time no later than ten days after the public assembly;
but its business was not transacted in haste, the detection of one
hundred or so offenders occupying a full three months (or perhaps

four, if Ezra's work is dated to 398; cf. Bowman, p. 658). How
many cases were dismissed by the commissioners we cannot say,
but it cannot always have been easy to determine the racial status
of a woman who was partly of Jewish and partly of Gentile descent.

LIST OF THOSE MARRIED TO FOREIGN WIVES
10:18–44

Unlike the list of Ezr. 2, but like that of Ezr. 8, the names of priests
and Levites precede those of the laity. The numbers in the text as
it stands amount to 27 clergy and 86 laity, 113 in all; some textual
corruptions make the exact figure uncertain. Many find it incredible
that the misdemeanour of so few, out of a population of at least
30,000 (cf. on 2:64–67), could have constituted such a national crisis
as is depicted in these chapters. It is accordingly suggested that the
present list is incomplete, either being restricted to the names of
twelve representative lay families in addition to the priests, or omitting names from the lower classes of society. Indeed, none of the
lowest classes of cultic personnel, the Nethinim and 'sons of Solomon's servants' (2:43–58), is mentioned, but it is not surprising that
such a small group should have contained no members who had
contracted mixed marriages, and there is no good reason to doubt
that the list is complete.

**18–22.** All four priestly clans mentioned in 2:36–39 appear here.

**18. the sons of Jeshua the son of Jozadak and his brethren:** By
this circumlocution the priestly clan of Jedaiah is called, because its
most distinguished member was Jeshua b. Jozadak, the contemporary of Zerubbabel (see on 2:36).

**19. pledged themselves:** We may take it that all who were found
guilty, and not just the four priests of v. 18, **pledged themselves**
(lit. 'gave their hands', AV) and sacrificed. Very probably the list
derives from a formal document which would have recorded similar
details for each family (cf. Num. 7).

**a ram . . . for their guilt,** i.e. guilt-offering: This sacrifice is
prescribed 'if any one commits a breach of faith' unwittingly or 'if
any one sins, doing any of the things which the LORD has
commanded not to be done, though he does not know it' (Lev.
5:14–19; cf. Num. 5:8); the present offence is categorised as an
'unwitting' offence presumably because there was no explicit legal
prohibition of marriage with the particular nations in existence at
that time (cf. on 9:1).

**23–24. that is, Kelita:** a gloss to identify this Levite with the one
in Neh. 8:7; 10:10. **Judah:** the first example of the common post-
exilic use of patriarchal names (see Noth, *IP*, p. 60); cf. Manasseh

(v. 30), Shimeon (= Simeon) (v. 31), Benjamin (v. 32), Joseph (v. 42). **the gatekeepers** (cf. on 2:42) seem to bear family names; **Shallum** and **Telem** (= Talmon) are mentioned among Zerubbabel's caravan, and can hardly be the same individuals (cf. also on Neh. 11:19).

**25–43.** The names of the lay phratries (e.g. **the sons of Parosh**) are mostly to be found also in Ezr. 2; possibly we should by emendation bring the lists into closer relationship. **Bani** (v. 34) can hardly be correct, since it has already appeared (v. 29); perhaps the name of the large phratry Bigvai (2:14) belongs in one or other of these places. **Binnui** (v. 38) may be correct, if we restore that name to the list of the homecomers from Neh. 7:15, or Bunni from Neh. 10:15 (cf. on Ezr. 2:10); in any case it is fairly certain that we should read **of the sons of** (v. 38, *RSV, NEB*) rather than MT 'and Bani and'. The impossible name **Machnadebai** (v. 40), though still in *NEB*, is a simple corruption of 'of the sons of Dakkai (= Zakkai)' (cf. on 2:9). **Nebo** (v. 43) is probably the only phratry name which is not originally a personal, but a village, name (cf. on 2:29). In all, therefore, twelve phratries are mentioned, which some have taken as a sign that the original list has been shortened to create a representative list. Members of twelve phratries also returned with Ezra (cf. on 8:3–14), but neither there nor here is it necessary to regard the number as artificial. On the names of individuals we may note: **Malchijah** appears twice in v. 25 (cf. *AV*), and *RSV*, following 1 Esd. 9:26, correctly emends the latter to **Hashabiah**, elsewhere usually a priestly or Levite name. **Zabad** (v. 27) and **Zabbai** (v. 28) are two short forms of the name Zebadiah (cf. 8:8) ('Yahweh has given'); in Greek the name becomes Zebedee (e.g. Mt. 4:21). **Meshullam** (v. 29) is the name of one of the apparent opponents of Ezra's reform (v. 15), but it is so common a name that nothing much can be made of that. The unique **Sheal** (v. 29) is probably a corruption of Yishal; **Uel** (v. 34) should be Joel.

**44.** The second half of the verse reads literally 'and some of them were wives and they (masc.) set children'. Even if this could mean 'some of them had wives by whom they had children' (*AV*), that is an improbable note on which to conclude the story of Ezra's reform. *RSV*, following 1 Esd. 9:36, emends to **they put them away with their children** (similarly, *NEB*), reading *wyšlḥm nšym wbnym* for MT *wyš mhm nšym wyśymw bnym*. Perhaps a simpler solution is to reverse the order of two words that begin with the same three letters and read 'and they put their wives from them, even if there were children', Heb. *wyśymw mhm nšym wyš bnym* (Schneider, p. 160). It is not certain, however, that *śym* can mean 'to put away'. For the formula of divorce among contemporary Jews at Elephantine, see

*BMAP* 7.21–4; cf. *AP* 15.26–9; Porten, *Elephantine*, pp. 209f. The corruption of the text has suggested to some that Ezra's reform was a failure, but its success is already attested by v. 19, which is to be taken as applying to all those listed.

Enough has been said above (on 9:1–10:44) of the rights and wrongs of the mixed-marriages question. Here, at the end of the account, we may reflect on the difficulty that faced Ezra as one of the early interpreters of Scripture, the same difficulty that confronts all those who regard Scripture as in any way authoritative. There was no clear biblical text to meet the crisis of the day. Scripture had been framed to suit the conditions of an earlier time, and no law or narrative was directly applicable to the current situation. Scripture did not consist of general principles, but of concrete particulars which could not be transmuted into general principles that would necessarily command the assent of everyone. Scripture taught that marriage with certain foreigners was unlawful; did it mean thereby to prohibit marriage with all foreigners? Scripture showed that marriages with foreigners usually proved disastrous; did that mean that such marriages were not allowed? And even assuming that all marriages with foreigners were contrary to Scripture, what was to be done once such marriages had been contracted? Scripture was silent about that.

Who had the authority to decide how Scripture was to be interpreted? Ezra had been given that authority by the Persian king (7:25), but had a foreign king the right to bestow such authority? Ezra, as we have noted (on 9:1–10:44), did not act upon such authority in this matter. Instead, it is the community that regards Scripture as authoritative (9:10; 10:3) that decides how Scripture is to be applied to the situation (10:1–4); it is a matter of the consensus of opinion. It is not that there is a simple democratic referendum, in which each man's opinion is worth the same as his neighbour's; for opinion is formed by the leaders. In fact it is the 'officials' who effectively determine the applicability of the law (cf. on 9:1), and it is another leading layman who first mentions the matter of divorce (10:2f.). Thus Scripture is here of no 'private interpretation' (2 Pet. 1:20); as we might put it, the same Spirit who inspired the creation of Scripture works also in the community of believers for the interpretation of Scripture. That does not set a mark of infallible wisdom upon the decision reached by Ezra's community or upon the interpretation of any other believing community, but it does make the profound point that the biblical text is not only the object of the community's interpretation, but also an active subject in the life of the community. As contemporary hermeneutical theory argues, in matters of interpretation there is not only a movement from the interpreters to the text as object, but a movement from the text as subject to the interpreters as object, as if the text, or its author, were interpreting them.

Finally, we may observe a striking paradox: in the unrecorded conflict of interpretations that lies behind 9:1, a rigorous literalist interpretation of the law would have resulted in a laxer policy (the law forbade marriages only with races extinct in Ezra's time), while a more free interpretation, according to the 'spirit' of the law, resulted in more stringent policy (the law is to be extended to cover races not explicitly mentioned).

# NEHEMIAH

NEHEMIAH HEARS NEWS FROM JERUSALEM

1:1–4

Whether the heading **the words** (or perhaps 'the acts') **of Nehemiah the son of Hacaliah** is the Chronicler's or Nehemiah's own, we cannot tell. But we certainly encounter very soon the 'memoirs of Nehemiah', our most valuable and clearly authentic source for the history of the post-exilic age. Unlike Ezra, Nehemiah was not a priest, but like Ezra he belonged to that group of exiled Jews who had risen to high office in the Persian administration (cf. on v. 11). The date of Nehemiah's activity is noted as beginning in the 'twentieth year of King Artaxerxes' (2:1); the king is probably Artaxerxes I, though the possibility must now be entertained that Artaxerxes II is meant (see R. J. Saley, 'The Date of Nehemiah Reconsidered', in *Biblical and Near Eastern Studies. Essays in Honour of William Sanford LaSor*, ed. G. A. Tuttle [1978], pp. 151–65; see also on Neh. 12:10f. below). On the later view Nehemiah's narrative begins in 384 BC, but on the more usual view the 'twentieth year' is 445 BC. If it was the reign of Artaxerxes I in which Nehemiah was active, the background of Neh. 1 can be reconstructed. According to Ezr. 4:8–23, during the reign of Artaxerxes I a successful attempt was made by the authorities in Samaria to prevent the rebuilding of Jerusalem's walls. Though nothing is said there explicitly of a breaching and burning of the partly rebuilt walls, it is reasonable enough to suppose that this was involved in the 'force and power' which the Samarians exercised (Ezr. 4:23), and that it is this episode which is reported to Nehemiah in v. 3.

1. **Nehemiah** means 'Yahweh has comforted', a name expressing rather more assurance than that of his father **Hacaliah**, which possibly means 'Yahweh is dark, i.e. hidden, ambiguous' or perhaps 'wait for Yahweh' (on the name form, see Porten, *Elephantine*, pp. 144f.). What the circumstances were that suggested such names to the respective parents we cannot tell, for we know nothing further of his lineage. Nehemiah's patronym serves only to distinguish him from other Nehemiahs (Ezr. 2:2; Neh. 3:16; 7:7). For the view that Nehemiah came of the Judean royal line, see v. 6. **Chislev**: the ninth month (November/December) of the year, which at this period was regarded as beginning in Nisan, in the spring. It is therefore impossible that the Nisan of the **twentieth year** should have followed the Chislev (cf. 2:1 with 1:1)—unless, perhaps Nehemiah was using,

contrary to common Persian and Jewish custom, a reckoning of the
year from Tishri, in the autumn (so, e.g., E. R. Thiele, *The
Mysterious Numbers of the Hebrew Kings* [1965²], p. 30). But that is
unlikely, and since, surprisingly, no mention is made of the king
whose twentieth year it is (cf. 2:1), most scholars believe that **twentieth** here must be a scribal slip for 'nineteenth'. Less plausible is
the suggestion of G. da Deliceto, *Laurentianum* 4 (1963), pp. 431–68,
that it was the twentieth year since Hanani's departure and that the
abortive wall-building of Ezr. 4 had occurred soon after 465 BC in
the early years of Artaxerxes' reign. **Susa the capital**: the spring
residence of the Persian kings, and one of the three capitals of the
empire, the scene also of the story of Esther and of Daniel's vision;
cf. on Ezr. 6:2.

   **2.** Though 'brother' can have a wide range of meanings, **Hanani**
appears to be Nehemiah's blood brother, whom he later appointed
as his deputy (7:2). Was Hanani like Nehemiah a resident of Susa,
who had not been to Jerusalem himself, but had thought his brother
should hear at first-hand the news he had learned from returning
pilgrims (Batten, p. 183)? Or was this an official delegation led by
Hanani from Jerusalem (Myers, p. 94)? We cannot tell for certain,
but the fact that Nehemiah **asked** them for news may suggest that
the initiative was not theirs. **the Jews that survived, who had
escaped exile**: The enquiry concerned not only descendants of those
who had not been taken into exile but also returned exiles; 'escaped
exile' (*niš<sup>a</sup>rû min-haššebî*) can also mean 'have survived from the
exile'.

   **3. the province of Judea**: cf. on Ezr. 2:1. **shame**: the objective
humiliation of the people at the hands of their enemies (cf. on Ezr.
9:6).

   **4.** Nehemiah's reaction to the bad news about Jerusalem is that
of a pious Jew who has not allowed preferment at a foreign court
to dampen his ardour for Jerusalem and its honour (cf. Ezr. 9:3;
Dan. 6:10; Ps. 137:5f.). **sat down**: a customary posture in mourning
and fasting (cf. Job 2:8, 13; not here as an act of worship, as L. H.
Brockington, in *Essays in Honour of G. W. Thatcher*, ed. E. C. B.
MacLaurin [1967], pp. 119–25). **fasting**: cf. on Ezr. 8:21.

### NEHEMIAH'S PRAYER

#### 1:5–11

Some have suggested, on the basis of the frequent use of Deutero-
omic phrases in the prayer, that these verses are the Chronicler's
expansion of a briefer, more pointed prayer by Nehemiah. Verse
11 could be regarded as this original kernel, itself perhaps Nehem-

iah's silent prayer in the presence of the king (2:4*b*); **this man** and **today** (v. 11; contrast **day and night**, v. 6) would point to such a situation. But regardless of what Nehemiah may have said on that particular occasion, he is likely to have used traditional religious language when praying. Many of the features of the prayer may also be observed in Dan. 9, for which the Chronicler can bear no responsibility.

The use of stereotyped phrases in prayer does not necessarily imply poverty of feeling or of religious experience; in an age of priestly formalisation of religion, the layman Nehemiah nevertheless reveals an intimate consciousness of the presence and guidance of God (2:8, 12, 18, 20; 4:14, 15, 20; 5:13, 15; 6:16; 7:5), and has frequent recourse to personal prayer (2:4; 4:4f., 9; 5:19; 6:9, 14).

The essence of Nehemiah's prayer is the appeal in vv. 8f. to God's promise of restoration of his people, if they will 'return' and keep his commandments. That believing return of heart has now taken place, being symbolically represented by the return of exiles to Jerusalem. But the God who keeps covenant has not yet fulfilled his promise, since to 'gather' the exiles and bring them to Jerusalem must imply the rebuilding of the city, including its walls. Nehemiah therefore prays (v. 11) that God will prosper his plans for bringing about the rebuilding of Jerusalem. Nehemiah's confession of his own sin and that of his people expresses his consciousness that Israel, in spite of its 'return' to God, is still defective and sinful, and must therefore acknowledge that the restoration has been due to God's promise and not to any perfect obedience on its part.

Nehemiah's prayer may, however, be expressing a greater sense of crisis than that. He may be meaning: Yahweh keeps covenant with those who keep his commandments (v. 5), indeed, but Israel has not done so (vv. 6f.). God's promise of restoration to the land was conditional upon Israel's obedience (v. 9). Nehemiah is in desperation therefore and can appeal only to the mercy of God, as revealed in the event of Israel's redemption from Egypt (v. 10).

**5. great and terrible** (lit. 'feared, to be feared'): a Deuteronomic phrase (Dt. 7:21; 10:17; cf. Neh. 4:8; 9:32; Dan. 9:4); so also **keeps covenant and steadfast love** (cf. on Ezr. 3:11) . . . **commandments** (Dt. 7:9; cf. 1 Kg. 8:23; Dan. 9:4). Nehemiah does not elsewhere use the personal name of God, Yahweh (**LORD**) (though cf. 5:13), and its use here is plainly dependent on passages like Dt. 7:9. **God of heaven**: Though a customary title at this period (cf. on Ezr. 1:2), it may have in this context the added significance that God is also lord of the kings of the earth and may dispose their plans as he wills.

**6.** Prayer is not simply a verbal matter, but is also expressed by ritual actions and postures (cf. v. 4); thus Nehemiah prays not only **let thy ear be attentive**, but also **and thy eyes open, to hear** (cf. Isa. 37:17; 2 Chr. 6:40; 7:15), i.e. 'to hearken, respond', to his evident signs of grief. **we have sinned**: While it is usual in post-exilic times for pious Israelites to identify themselves with the sinful people of Israel (cf. Ezr. 9:6f., 10, 13; Est. 14:6, LXX), it is strange that Nehemiah should confess, **I and my father's house** in particular **have sinned**. Some infer from this that Nehemiah's 'father's house' must be some very important family in Israel, even the Davidic line (cf. on 2:3). But there is no evidence for this, and we may recall that Daniel also confesses his own sin when making confession of the national guilt (Dan. 9:20; cf. also Tob. 3:3).

**7. commandments, statutes, ordinances**: common Deuteronomic terms (e.g. Dt. 5:31; cf. also Ezr. 7:10f.).

**8–9.** Typically, now that the whole Pentateuch is coming to be regarded as law (and not, as originally, *tôrâ*, 'instruction'), a sentence which is really a promise is now spoken of as a *commandment* (**the word which thou didst command**).

We have here not a literal quotation, but a free summarising quotation from Dt. 30:1–5 (cf. also Lev. 26:14f., 33). In the *OT* the idea of repentance, which in modern thought is often rather individualistic (being sorry for what one has done, determining to change one's ways), is expressed by the relational term **return** (to God); in this sense *šûb*, 'return', appears especially in the context of the covenant (W. L. Holladay, *The Root Šubh in the Old Testament* [1958]). That is, sin is not seen primarily as a failure to meet standards, but as a breaking off of personal relations with God. **the place which I have chosen** is again typically Deuteronomic language for a legitimate sanctuary of Yahweh (e.g. Dt. 12:11, 14), though increasingly restricted in use to Jerusalem (cf. 1 Kg. 11:13), which is of course what it denotes here. On **to make my name dwell there**, also Deuteronomic, cf. on Ezr. 6:12.

**10–11.** Verse 10 echoes Dt. 9:29, to which Nehemiah adds two other Deuteronomic terms, **redeemed** and **strong hand** (cf. Dt. 7:8), and a favourite term of his own, **servants** (cf. 6, 11; 2:20). Ultimately Nehemiah's faith rests on what God has long ago done for his people. He therefore prays for himself in the context of his people, and associates with his prayer the prayers of his countrymen for the welfare of Jerusalem (cf. Ps. 122:6–9).

In referring to the king simply as **this man**, Nehemiah artlessly reveals his conception of God as the omniscient one who well knows already who is meant (cf. Ps. 139:4), even though the reader has not yet been plainly told; but also there is perhaps a hint of Nehemiah's inmost feeling, never publicly expressed (cf. 2:3, 5), that the king, after all, is a mere man who is of small account before God (note the frequent use of 'this one' (Heb. *zeh*) contemptuously, e.g. Exod. 10:7; 1 Sam 10:27; see BDB, p. 260*b*).

The office of **cupbearer** was a very important one in the Persian court, involving, according to Xenophon (*Cyropaedia* 1.3.8ff.), responsibility for tasting the king's wine and for guarding the royal apartment (Herodotus, *Hist.* 3.34; H. Zimmern, 'Über Bäcker und Mundschenk im Altsemitischen', *ZDMG* 53 [1899], pp. 115–19).

Since Nehemiah also served in the presence of the queen (2:6), many think that he was a eunuch (cf. also 6:11), like Xerxes' eunuch chamberlains (Est. 1:10) (see Myers, p. 96, and Kellermann, p. 154 n.17, for differing views. On the oriental eunuch, see E. Weidner, 'Hof- und Harems-Erlasse assyrischer Könige aus dem 2. Jahrtausend v. Chr.', *AfO* 17 (1954ff.), pp. 257–93, esp. 264f.). The cupbearer of Xerxes is for that reason portrayed in reliefs at Persepolis as beardless (*ANEP*, p. 159, fig. 463). In later Judaism Nehemiah seems to have been regarded by some as a eunuch, since one important LXX manuscript has *eunouchos*, 'eunuch', instead of *oinochoos*, 'cupbearer'. The law excluded eunuchs, along with various other physically handicapped persons, from the congregation (Dt. 23:1), but Isa. 56:3ff. represents a post-exilic relaxation of that rule.

It is surely worthy of remark that a courtier in such a position in a foreign court should feel himself so involved in the fate of his people as Nehemiah does! Perhaps his haughtiness and temperament, of which we shall catch glimpses in his narrative, are reflections of his experience of high office, but they are small eccentricities beside the considerable impression Nehemiah makes on us as an ardent believer both in his nation and in God's purposes for his people. How had Nehemiah retained his intense Jewishness, what contact with the Jewish community did he have, or, for that matter, how much private life did an oriental cupbearer have? For the most part we can only speculate, but there is one clue which may provide the best explanation for the fact that Nehemiah is fundamentally simply a God-fearing Jew: his practice of private prayer (cf. on vv. 5–11).

### NEHEMIAH RECEIVES PERMISSION TO VISIT JERUSALEM

### 2:1–8

Nehemiah waited four months for an answer to his prayer. As a court official he doubtless knew the value of silence about plans until the time is ripe, and his planned, deliberate methods are elsewhere obvious too (cf. 2:12–16; 6:1–14). When the opportunity to intervene personally in the affairs of Jerusalem arises, he has his rather daring plans already laid. His mourning and fasting have been genuine enough, yet he has not been despairing, but quietly 'trusting in God and keeping his powder dry'.

It has often been noticed with what skill he conducts himself before the king, 'the eunuch's subtlety', says Olmstead (*History*, p. 314). He never mentions Jerusalem by name, for that name is all too notorious at the court of Artaxerxes (cf. Ezr. 4:19f.); instead, in speaking of the city as the place of his fathers' graves (vv. 3, 5), he appeals to a common human interest of ancient peoples, and especially of kings, in the preservation of ancestral tombs. The rebuilding of the walls, which had provoked the damaging report of Rehum (Ezr. 4:9–16), is passed over in silence, and though Nehemiah's informants had spoken particularly of the breaching of the wall, and of the burning of its gates, Nehemiah mentions simply **the city** in general (v. 3), and asks to be sent to **Judah, to the city of my fathers' sepulchres** (v. 5). What is most remarkable is that the apparently simple request in v. 5 seems to be a polite way of asking for governorship of Judea. It is possible that Nehemiah left Susa as royal commissioner for reconstruction and only became governor after his arrival in Jerusalem; certainly by his own account, he became governor that same year (5:14). And surely Nehemiah himself already realised that without the full powers of a governor he would lack the necessary authority to superintend the rebuilding of a capital city?

**1–2.** Why did Nehemiah have to wait so long before he could make his request of the king? Perhaps he was simply waiting for an opportunity to present itself; an unconscious lapse from the courtier's officially cheerful appearance prompted the king to take the initiative. As if to emphasise that this was no manoeuvre on his part he says **I had not been sad** previously **in his presence**. *NEB*, 'I was feeling very unhappy', takes *lō*, 'not', as the affirmative particle *lā'* or *lu'* (cf. T. F. McDaniel, *Bib.* 49 [1968], pp. 206f.), but the existence of this particle in late prose Hebrew is doubtful. Nehemiah is afraid because he had not intended to show his depression to the king. 'An Oriental monarch did not expect his servants to carry their personal troubles to him or to reveal them in his presence' (Batten).

Other possible interpretations of the long delay are: Nehemiah probably served permanently in the palace at Susa, and perhaps the king did not reside there until the month of Nisan, in the spring; we know that Persian kings often spent the winter in Babylon. Alternatively, Nehemiah's request may have been made at the birthday or accession day banquet of the king on the first of Nisan;

on such occasions in Persia, according to Herodotus, 'every boon asked must of necessity be granted' (*Hist.* 9.110f.; cf. Mk 6:23ff.).

3. Now that the king has displayed his personal interest in Nehemiah by probing beneath the surface and correctly diagnosing Nehemiah's unaccustomed demeanour as due to depression of spirit, Nehemiah is emboldened to reveal the cause of his distress. It is the partial destruction of Jerusalem, lately ordered by the king himself, though Nehemiah does not so far forget himself as to mention that fact! The customary oriental wish, **Let the king live for ever!** (cf. 1 Kg. 1:31; Dan. 2:4), though doubtless rarely more than an empty formula, invokes not merely a long life, but a royal vitality which will bring blessing to his kingdom (cf. Ps. 72:5f., 15ff.); see P. A. H. de Boer, ' "Vive le roi!" ', *VT* 5 (1955), pp. 225–31.

Some see in the reference to Jerusalem as **the place of my fathers' sepulchres** a hint that Nehemiah belonged to the royal house (cf. 1:6; 3:16; 6:6).

4. The king realises that Nehemiah's response is no resigned sigh but itself demands a reply. His question **For what do you make request?** is therefore not abrupt, but the natural sequel to Nehemiah's response. Nehemiah's momentary turning to prayer (one of the few silent prayers in the Bible; cf. 1 Sam. 1:13) marks the critical stage in the interview and prefaces the bold request of v. 5. **God of heaven**: cf. on Ezr. 1:2.

5. To **rebuild** Jerusalem would not simply be a pious act in memory of his fathers, but would involve rulership of the rebuilt city. The founder or builder of a city in ancient times had great authority in the city, and was revered throughout its history (cf. W. Forster, *TDNT* III, p. 1026; N.D. Fustel de Coulanges, *The Ancient City* (rp 1955), pp. 142–6). Nehemiah thus stands to gain great personal prestige from his proposed visit to Jerusalem, and his motives therefore are not entirely unmixed (cf. also his repeated prayer, 'Remember for my good, O my God, all that I have done for this people'; 5:19; etc.). In the Judeo-Christian tradition, it is indeed more noble to do good without thought of reward (Lk. 6:35), but it is not ignoble or immoral to 'seek, by patience in well-doing, glory and honour and immortality' (Rom. 2:7; cf. Heb. 12:2).

6. Nehemiah can hardly have thought at this time that his absence from the Persian court would last twelve years (5:14); doubtless his leave was later extended. The presence of the **queen** Damaspia (her name is known from Ctesias, *Persika* 15.44; F. Jacoby, *Die Fragmente der griechischen Historiker*, III.c [1958], p. 468) seems to have been significant, at least in Nehemiah's eyes. Ancient historians depicted this ruler as especially pliable to feminine wishes (Ctesias,

*Persika* 14.39; Jacoby, III.c, p. 467); even if she said nothing the king probably wanted to make a display of his generosity before her. The fact that the king asks only **how long** Nehemiah expects to be absent plainly signifies a certain affection for his cupbearer.

**7–8.** Nehemiah loses no time in gaining the king's approval for his plans. Perhaps it is modesty on Nehemiah's part (or perhaps it is civil service etiquette!) that he does not explicitly ask for the official status of governor of Judah. His account here possibly compresses several conversations, and the whole arrangement may not have been made with such remarkable rapidity as depicted here.

His first request is for **letters**, addressed to the **governors of the province Beyond the River** (cf. on Ezr. 4:10), i.e. to the satrap and the governors of the various sub-satrapies (cf. on Ezr. 8:36), guaranteeing him safe passage through their territories and authorising provisioning for himself and his company. For one such 'passport', see *AD* 6, which instructs officials to give a king's envoy 'provisions from my estate in your provinces every day two measures of white meal, three measures of inferior (?) meal, two measures of wine or beer, and one sheep . . . in accordance with the stage of his journey until he reaches Egypt'.

The second request is for a requisition order for **timber** to the **keeper of the royal forest**, lit. 'park, pleasure-garden' (Persian *paridaida-*, whence English 'paradise'), probably the Lebanon forest (cf. on Ezr. 3:7). **Asaph**, the keeper of the forest, bears a Hebrew name, which could, however, be an assimilation to Hebrew of some Phoenician or Persian name. If he is indeed a Jew, it is perfectly natural that Nehemiah should know his name, not only through official channels, but also as a fellow Jew who like himself had attained high position in the Persian administration. **timber** is needed for the gates of the fortress of the temple (rather than *NEB*, 'the citadel, which adjoins the palace'); the **fortress** is here mentioned for the first time in *OT* (cf. also 7:2), and had presumably been built since the return from exile. It may have stood north of the temple, perhaps on the site where later John Hyrcanus built a fortress and Herod built the Antonia tower (Josephus, *Ant.* 18.4.3; 15.11.4); it is probably identical with the Tower of Hananel (3:1). **timber . . . for the wall of the city**: principally its gates (cf. 1:3). **the house which I shall build**: Probably his ancestral home is to be rebuilt; *NEB*, 'the palace', may mean a governor's residence, or leave open the possibility that Nehemiah was of royal blood (cf. on v. 3). Certainly the king is giving Nehemiah a free hand in the fortification of Jerusalem, perhaps to secure Persian authority on the borders of Egypt.

**the good hand of my God**: Using the same phrase as Ezra

(Ezr. 7:9; 8:18; and cf. on 7:6), Nehemiah acknowledges that only God's good hand has determined so successful an issue to his requests. If Persian decrees were indeed as unalterable as was traditionally believed (Dan. 6:9; Est. 1:19; 8:8; cf. also Diodorus Siculus, xviii.30), it was providential that Artaxerxes' original decree contained the escape clause, 'until a [another] decree is made by me' (Ezr. 4:21).

### NEHEMIAH ARRIVES IN JERUSALEM, INSPECTS ITS WALLS, AND GAINS ASSENT TO HIS PROPOSALS
#### 2:9–20

The journey passes without incident, except that at some point Nehemiah seems to make contact with the officials who are to be his chief opponents (v. 10). On arrival in Jerusalem he carries out a secret reconnaissance of the state of the walls of Jerusalem. When he announces his plans to rebuild, public morale is boosted and he is assured of support (vv. 17, 18)—but not by all, for there is a powerful opposition which makes its presence felt whenever Nehemiah achieves some success.

**9.** In each province through which his route lay Nehemiah displayed his royal 'passport' to the governor. Unlike Ezra (Ezr. 8:22), he saw no reason to refuse a military escort.

**10.** His mission could not be kept secret from the local authorities, since wherever he displayed his 'passport' his intentions would be known. Opposition came principally from **Sanballat** (a Babylonian name, 'Sin [the moon god] has given life'), the governor of the province Samaria (cf. 4:2). Nehemiah never accords him his official title, and most agree that **the Horonite** is a contemptuous term, whether it refers to the Moabite town Horonaim (prophesied for destruction in Jer. 48:3) or to the insignificant village of Upper or Lower Beth-Horon, c. 18m. north-west of Jerusalem. For other interpretations of **Horonite**, cf. J. Gray, *JNES* 8 (1949), pp. 27–34; Kraeling, *BMAP*, p. 107 n. 17. We know from the Elephantine papyri that Sanballat was still governor of Samaria, though probably only nominally, in 407 BC (*AP* 30.29; *ANET*, p. 492), and also that his sons' names were Delaiah and Shelemaiah, which show, being compounded with Yah (short form of Yahweh), that Sanballat was a worshipper of Yahweh. A further confirmation of this may be the marriage of his daughter into the family of the high priest (13:28). He may have been descended from an Israelite family that had not been exiled in 722 BC, or from the foreign settlers imported by Esarhaddon in the seventh century (cf. on Ezr. 4:1–5). The story of his opposition to Nehemiah is recounted in chs. 4 and 6.

**Tobiah** is usually thought to have been the Persian governor of the province of Ammon; **the servant** would then be some official title expressing his relationship to the Persian emperor (cf. Darius' Behistun inscription, line 38: *AP*, pp. 253, 259; and Z. Zevit, *JBL* 88 [1969], pp. 74–77). The name Tobiah was certainly a famous one in Moab, with the family of the Tobiads exercising authority there for several generations in Hellenistic times, and many have seen this Tobiah as an ancestor of that family (B. Mazar, *IEJ* 7 [1957], pp. 137–45, 229–38; C. C. McCown, *BA* 20 [1957], pp. 63–76). But Tobiah ('Yahweh is good') is a common name, and it is more likely that he is rather a Samarian official subordinate to Sanballat (cf. also on 4:7; 6:1). **the servant**, which could equally well mean 'the slave' (so *NEB*), and **the Ammonite** (cf. Dt. 23:3) may then be Nehemiah's derisory titles for a half-Jew (with a Jewish name and a non-Jewish parent) who had insinuated himself into the confidence of the upper classes in Jerusalem (6:17f.; 13:4f.).

Both Sanballat and Tobiah must have seen the advent of Nehemiah as a commissioner, if not already a governor, appointed directly by the king, as a threat to their status and economic power in the satrapy, and their hostility was doubtless largely against him personally. But he, not improperly, regards their opposition as directed against **the welfare of the children of Israel**, using the ancient religious name. On Nehemiah's opponents, see Kellerman, pp. 166–73; H. H. Rowley, *Men of God*, pp. 246–76; F. M. Cross, *BA* 26 (1963), pp. 110–21.

**11–12.** After a short rest (cf. on Ezr. 8:32), Nehemiah's first action was to inspect the city walls. We may be sure from the close connections of Sanballat and Tobiah with leading members of the Jerusalem community (cf. 6:10–14, 17–19; 13:4f., 28) that Nehemiah's arrival was not greeted with universal joy, so he needed to be wary. His moonlit night-ride, in the company of only a few men who followed on foot, is one of the most dramatic scenes in Nehemiah's brilliantly evocative memoirs. Though the provincial authorities will have known of Nehemiah's intentions, which like all good intentions are seen as originating with God (cf. 7:15; Ezr. 1:15; 6:22; 7:27; for Egyptian parallel see G. von Rad, *ZAW* 76 [1964], pp. 183f.), no one yet knew (cf. v. 16) that his plans for rebuilding the city included supplying it with fortifications to replace those recently demolished by royal authority (cf. on 1:1–10)!

**13–15.** The exact course of Nehemiah's tour is subject to several uncertainties; but since the excavations of Kathleen Kenyon in 1961–7, major advances have been made. She has shown that the walls of Nehemiah's city enclosed a relatively small area, principally the eastern ridge (viz. the temple area and the south-east spur, loosely called Ophel), together perhaps with a small extension to the north-west (cf. on 3:3). See her *Jerusalem. Excavating 3,000 Years of History* (1967). Discovery in 1969–70 of a very substantial wall on the western hill has indeed established that pre-exilic Jerusalem incorporated further areas to the west than has often been thought; see N. Avigad, *IEJ* 20 (1970), pp. 129–40; M. Avi-Yonah, *IEJ* 21 (1971), pp. 168f. But it still remains likely that Nehemiah's Jerusalem was considerably contracted, and Avi-Yonah's study, published even before Kenyon's work, remains the most useful for our period (*IEJ* 4 [1954], pp. 239–48).

**13.** Since it is plain that the last section of wall Nehemiah inspected was the eastern, beside the Kidron valley (v. 15), and he seems to have travelled anti-clockwise around Jerusalem (vv. 14f.), he must have begun his tour at the north or west of the city. His starting point, **the Valley Gate**, is said in fact in 3:13 to lie 1,000 cubits (*c.* 1,500 ft.) from the **Dung** (or, Rubbish) **Gate**, probably identical with the Potsherd Gate (Jer. 19:2) and suitably located near the southern tip of Ophel; so the Valley Gate would have been in the western wall, giving access to the central valley, the Tyropoean. **Jackal's Well**: *RSV* unnecessarily emends *tannîn*, 'dragon' (cf. *AV*, *NEB*), to *tannîm*, 'jackals'; the name does not occur elsewhere, but it is probably to be identified with En-rogel, 'the fuller's spring', modern Bir 'Ayub, 'Job's well', *c.* 250 yds. south of the southern tip of the city. This lies too far off Nehemiah's route; so, unless the identification is incorrect, we should translate: 'I went out by the Valley Gate in the direction of Dragon Well [i.e. south and east] as far as the Rubbish Gate.' The gates, partially constructed of timber, and thus easily damaged by fire, needed special observation.

**14.** As he rode by the southern tip of the city into the Kidron valley, Nehemiah had on his left hand **the Fountain Gate**, giving access to En-rogel (cf. on 3:15), and on his right **the King's Pool**, doubtless identical with the 'pool of Shelah of the king's garden' (3:15), fed by an aqueduct (the 'waters of Shiloah that flow gently', Isa. 8:6) from the spring Gihon further up the valley, and also presumably by the overflow from the Siloam pool to which water was led from Gihon via Hezekiah's tunnel.

As he proceeded up the Kidron valley, Nehemiah was compelled to dismount and continue his reconnaissance on foot. For already in this day, the eastern slope of the city was, as it is today, a vast tumble of stones, in places up to 15 ft. deep, where the ingeniously constructed system of terraces extending pre-exilic Jerusalem two-thirds of the way down the slope had collapsed after the destruction of the city wall by the Babylonians. 'A breach in the city wall at the base would bring down the structures supported against its rear, and it would need only a few winters' rains for the chain of collapse to spread up to the summit and far to either side' (Kenyon, *Jerusalem*, p. 108; pl. 9). The outcome of Nehemiah's inspection of the walls was a decision to abandon the part of the town that lay on the eastern slope and to make the boundary on the east the crest of the comparatively level summit.

**15.** Dismounting, Nehemiah continued on foot northwards up **the valley** of the Kidron **and inspected the** eastern **wall** of the city. Whether he **turned back** (*RSV*), retracing his steps to the Valley Gate, or whether he completed the circuit of the walls and 'came back through the Valley Gate' (as MT may mean and *NEB* suggests) is uncertain.

**16.** His repeated insistence (cf. v. 12) that no one knew of his plans is perhaps intended to stress that the rebuilding of Jerusalem's walls was entirely due to his initiative. We should probably make v. 16*a* the conclusion of v. 15: 'and so returned, without the officials knowing . . .'. These **officials** may be taken to be Persian officials with whom Nehemiah, as an imperial official himself, would have been lodging. They are distinct from **the Jews**, of whom he specifies four groups, **priests, nobles**, i.e. the heads of leading families (not hereditary aristocrats; cf. J. van der Ploeg, *RB* 57 [1950], pp. 40–61; *OTS* 9 [1951], pp. 49–64), local **officials** (cf. Ezr. 9:2), and **the rest that were to do the work**, i.e. probably, the rest of the people designated thus by way of anticipation! For a similar division, see 4:14, 19; 7:5.

**17–18.** Frustratingly, Nehemiah does not tell us how he publicised his plans for Jerusalem. Did he call an assembly like Ezra (Ezr. 10:7), or did he discreetly approach the leaders and officials? Certainly in promoting his plan he did not appeal to military or political considerations, but to national and religious honour (cf. 1:3). The state of their city was an unflattering reflection on the worth of their religion. But now, says Nehemiah, the Jews have nothing to fear from the Persian government if they rebuild the walls, and, more positively, the guiding hand of God can already be plainly seen in Nehemiah's personal experience down to this moment. We observe again the divine and human co-operation (**the hand of . . . God**, cf. v. 8; **the words which the king had spoken**) so frequent in these books (cf. on Ezr. 6:13–18). The response to Nehemiah's proposal is enthusiastic. **strengthened their hands**: took fresh courage (cf. on Ezr. 4:4).

**19.** As a counterpoint to his recording of his moments of triumph, Nehemiah is in the habit of recalling the attacks of his opponents. A new face appears among them, **Geshem**, or Gashmu (6:6), the

Arabian, who proves to be not a Persian official, but 'king of Qedar', the ruler, under nominal Persian control, of a vast territory occupied by Arabian tribes, incorporating N. Arabia, Edom, and the Negeb of Judah, and extending as far west as Egypt (see I. Rabinowitz, *JNES* 15 [1956], pp. 1–9; Kellerman, pp. 170–3). This status and provenance will explain both the considerable awe shown of Geshem at 6:6, and also how he comes to be proposing a conference at Ono (6:2), not so far from his own territory as it seems at first sight. Nehemiah's enemies' mocking questions make it plain that rebellion by Judah was never a dangerous threat to the Persian empire (cf. Ezr. 4:16), but at the same time there is an ominous implication of how Jewish actions could be construed. The question **What is this thing that you are doing?** is the conventional way of making an accusation; cf. e.g. 13:11; Jg. 8:1; see H. J. Boecker, *Redeformen des Rechtslebens im Alten Testament* (1964), pp. 25–34.

**20.** Nehemiah knows full well that their zeal for the Persian emperor is only a cloak for their personal ambitions, so he does not bother to defend himself against their accusation by reiterating his royal authorisation, which they must have already been aware of, but declares his faith that God will prosper the work which he has initiated (v. 12). The same **God of heaven** (cf. on Ezr. 1:2) who oversaw the rebuilding of the temple by and for the Jews alone will ensure that the rebuilding of the city will likewise be accomplished without foreign help or hindrance, and that foreigners will have in Jerusalem no **portion**, i.e. property or possessions, **right**, i.e. legal authority (cf. 2 Sam. 19:28), or **memorial** (*zikkārôn*), some long-standing traditional right (*NEB*) which may be remembered (*zākar*) in their favour, as Nehemiah hopes will be the case with him (e.g. 5:19).

These scenes from Nehemiah's life, his request of the king, his night-ride around Jerusalem, his stimulation of the rebuilding of the city walls, and his confrontation with Sanballat, Tobiah, and Geshem, have all displayed a man conscious of the active influence of God upon his life. Before the king he finds that he is granted what he asks because 'the good hand of my God was upon me' (v. 8). What he plans for the city as he inspects its desolated walls is 'what my God had put into my heart' (v. 12). And it is the fact that 'the hand of my God . . . had been upon me for good' (v. 18) that constitutes the success of his appeal to the citizens of Jerusalem, and that assures him that 'the God of heaven will make us prosper' (v. 20). The courtier Nehemiah knows well how much his fortunes have depended upon the good-will of his superiors, and is well practised in recognising that his masters' good-will has depended on the favour of God. He is the opposite of a self-made man.

## THE REBUILDING OF THE WALLS
### ch. 3

The dry and lengthy list of wall-builders and their allotted sections of wall seems intrusive into Nehemiah's dramatic narrative, so most think it formed no part of his memoirs. We may admit that the chapter is something of a literary misfit, in that while in its present context it is set between the decision to build (2:18) and the events which occurred during the building (4:1), it actually views the wall-building as completed, and records for example the consecration of part of the wall (v. 1) and speaks of the setting in place of the doors (vv. 3, 6, etc.), though at 6:1 the doors have not yet been hung.

So it is quite possible that it formed no part of his 'memoirs' and that this list is an editorial addition. Nevertheless, Nehemiah himself must have drawn up such a list as this when planning the operation, and on completion of the work may well have made a fair copy by way of record. It is reasonable therefore to regard Nehemiah as the original 'author' of the list, whether or not he is responsible for its present place in his memoirs. The view taken here is that Nehemiah himself may well have incorporated this list into his memoirs (so Rudolph; Kellermann, pp. 15f.), for in spite of the minor discrepancies with the surrounding narrative it well serves his purpose of creating a 'memory' for himself if he can show how he was able to inspire and co-ordinate the work of virtually the whole population. May not the childless Nehemiah (if he was; cf. 1:11) have regarded all these as his sons, in whom his name lived on?

Whatever the precise literary origin of the list, all recognise that it is our most valuable source for the topography of ancient Jerusalem. Although many of the gates and other features along the line of wall cannot be identified with certainty, and some remain totally enigmatic, a reasonably clear picture may be gained. Increasingly too the details of the text and archaeological evidence are becoming mutually illuminating. An interesting example is afforded by the contrast between the repairs of various sections of wall. In this chapter the rebuilding of the north and west walls is represented as largely a repair of walls and gates still recognisable (vv. 1–14), while on the eastern side the gangs worked not from gate to gate but from landmark to landmark or from house to house (e.g. vv. 19, 23). This distinction, long thought to be essentially literary and stylistic (e.g. M. Burrows, *AASOR* 14 [1933f.], pp. 116–21), corresponds to the new archaeological evidence that the western wall of post-exilic Jerusalem lay on the line of one of the walls of the pre-exilic city, whereas on the eastern side much of the pre-exilic wall with

its gates was abandoned in post-exilic times, and a new city wall
was built along the eastern crest.

Part of Nehemiah's eastern wall has been identified by Kathleen
Kenyon, who describes it as 'solidly built, *c.* 2.75 metres thick, but
its finish was rough, as might be expected in work executed so
rapidly' (*Jerusalem*, p. 111; pls. 54, 55).

This chapter also sheds some welcome light on the Persian administrative system in Judea. Five districts (*pelek*) are named: Jerusalem
(v. 9), Beth-Haccherem (v. 14), Mizpah (vv. 15, 19), Beth-zur (v.
16), and Keilah (vv. 17f.). Most, if not all, districts were divided
into two sub-districts, as is clear from the references to half-districts.
Intelligent guesses at the capitals of the unnamed half-districts may
also be made (Avi-Yonah, *Holy Land*, p. 20; Aharoni, *Land*, p. 364).
Whether Nehemiah's official status enabled him to exert pressure on
his subordinates, or whether the co-operation of so many provincial
officials is a mark of popular enthusiasm for his project is hard to
say; but in any case we are to understand these 'rulers' as leading
officials, and not merely foremen of gangs, as some would have it
(also *RSV* mg on 9, 11 etc.).

## THE NORTH WALL

### 3:1–7

Gates and wall on the north side are mainly said to be **built**, which
implies they had suffered considerably more damage than those
sections which were only 'repaired' (cf. also on v. 16). This was
probably the case, since the northern wall, fronting the main access
route to Jerusalem, would have had to bear the brunt of enemy
attacks.

1. Whether the rebuilding of the **Sheep Gate** was assigned to
the high priest's family because of some special importance attaching
to it—it is the gate with which this list begins and ends and the gate
of entry for one of Nehemiah's dedicatory processions (12:39)—or
whether the list begins at this point because this happened to be
the task assigned to the leading family in the city, the high priest's,
is impossible to say. Certainly it speaks well for Nehemiah's diplo-
macy that he was able to persuade **Eliashib the high priest** (cf. on
Ezr. 10:6) and **Meshullam** (cf. v. 4), both related by marriage to
Nehemiah's opponents (13:28), to co-operate with him. The **Sheep
Gate** (elsewhere only 12:39; Jn. 5:2), may reasonably be located in
the eastern half of the north wall, perhaps giving entry from the
Jericho road; its name doubtless arose from a market there for
sacrificial sheep (cf. on Fish Gate, v. 3). It is likely to be identical
with the pre-exilic Benjamin Gate (Jer. 17:19, emended; 20:2; 37:13;

38:7), the easternmost gate of the city (Zech. 14:10). It is strange that the builders should be said here to have **consecrated** it when it is only in 12:27–30 that we read of the consecration of the wall; but perhaps they are different ceremonies (here *qdš*, 'to set apart as holy', whereas in 12:27–30, *ḥnk*, 'to dedicate', and *ṭhr*, 'to purify'). If we can suppose that this section of wall also formed part of the temple enclosure, a double consecration may be intelligible; elsewhere, priests did not 'consecrate' their work (vv. 21f.). **Tower of the Hundred** (also 12:39); probably the headquarters of a centurion with 100 men (cf. such in monarchic times, e.g. 2 Sam. 18:1, and in Roman times, e.g. Mt. 8:5, as well in the Persian empire, cf. *AP* 2.11; 22.19f.). **Tower of Hananel** (cf. 12:39; Jer. 31:38): Marking the northernmost point of the wall (Zech. 14:10), it is probably to be identified with 'the fortress of the temple' (Neh. 2:8) and the 'castle' (7:2). Herod's Antonia fortress on essentially the same site had towers at its four corners (Josephus, *War* 5.5.8), and it is possible therefore that the two towers mentioned here similarly formed part of one structure, designed to protect the north-west approach to the temple mount.

**2.** The phrase **next to him** or **next to them**, lit. 'at his, their, hand', is used consistently in vv. 1–12, while in vv. 16–31 'after him, them' is used (except in vv. 17, 19). Some have thought that this stylistic difference, together with more substantial differences of presentation in vv. 1–15 and vv. 16–32, points to difference of authorship. But the major differences can now be accounted for otherwise, as shown above (on Ch. 3), so that little weight can be put on the minor differences. **men of Jericho**: cf. on Ezr. 2:34. Other gangs from localities are mentioned in vv. 5, 7, 13, 27. **Zaccur b. Imri** (= Amariah) is to be distinguished from Zaccur b. Bigvai (Ezr. 8:14), the Levite Zaccur (Neh. 10:12), and Zaccur b. Mattaniah (13:13).

**3. Hassenaah**, 'the Senaah': cf. on Ezr. 2:35. **Fish Gate**: presumably so called from a fish-market there, and naturally located towards the west of the city, closest to the sea; it was perhaps the north-west corner gate of the city. It is associated in Zeph. 1:10 with the Second Quarter (*mišneh*) (2 Kg. 22:14), probably an extension of the city on the north-west, bounded by Hezekiah's 'other wall' (2 Chr. 32:5). The Fish Gate is probably identical with the Ephraim Gate (8:16; 12:39; 2 Kg. 14:13), and was perhaps also known in pre-exilic times as the Middle Gate (Jer. 39:3). The description of the building of a gate is repeated in v. 6, with variations in vv. 1 13, 14, 15. **bolts**: the metal brackets into which the wooden or bronze bars were dropped.

**4.** The family of **Hakkoz** or Koz to which **Meremoth** b. **Uriah**

belonged was one of those unable to prove its priestly ancestry at
the time of its return under Zerubbabel (Ezr. 2:61), but it had
obviously been legitimated by the time of Ezra (Ezr. 8:33). The fact
that **Meremoth** is not called a priest here does not indicate that he
has not yet achieved priestly status; so this cannot be used as an
argument for dating Nehemiah before Ezra. Meremoth repaired
another section too (v. 21). **Meshullam b. Berechiah**, who likewise
repaired two sections (cf. v. 30), was the father-in-law of Tobiah
the Ammonite (6:18). **Baana** was one of the leaders in Zerubbabel's
company (Ezr. 2:2); the name is possibly the family name Baana
found among the signatories to the pledge (Neh. 10:27). **Meshezabel**: cf. on 11:24.

5. The non-co-operation of the **nobles** of Tekoa (Am. 1:1), c. 10
m. south of Jerusalem, is the one positive sign of resistance to
Nehemiah within the Jewish community; it may be significant that
in the lists of returning exiles Tekoa is not mentioned. The citizens
of Tekoa compensated, however, for their leaders' indolence by
being the only locality-team to undertake two wall-sections (cf. v.
27). The unexpectedly picturesque language of the ox being yoked
to pull a heavy load (cf. Jer. 27:11f.), and the use of a different
word for nobles (*'addîr*) to that otherwise used by Nehemiah (*ḥôr*)
suggests another author to some. Their **Lord**, rather 'lord' or ox-
driver, if the metaphor is being continued, is Nehemiah (cf. Ezr.
10:3); would Nehemiah himself have used such an autocratic image?
*NEB* removes the metaphor entirely.

6. **Joiada b. Paseah** is perhaps a descendant of a temple-slave
(Ezr. 2:49). **Old Gate** (also 12:39): an impossible translation. The
Hebrew could mean 'Gate of the Old (city?; wall?)', perhaps a gate
in the original western wall which had been made redundant when
the Mishneh quarter was enclosed. A small emendation (*yšnh*, 'old',
to *mšnh*, 'second') would make its connection with the Mishneh
quarter explicit, and would enable it to be identified with the Corner
Gate (2 Chr. 26:9; Jer. 21:37; Zech. 14:10, emended), which is to
be located at least 400 cubits (c. 200 yds south of the Ephraim Gate
(2 Kg. 14:13). Less probable is the view that *yᵉšānâ*, 'old', is the
village name Jeshanah (2 Chr. 13:19), c. 15 m. north of Jerusalem
and apparently a frontier post between the provinces of Samaria and
Judah, the gate giving access to the Jeshanah road being named the
Jeshanah gate (so *NEB*). Such a gate would have to be in the north
wall, and there does not appear to be room in Nehemiah's north
wall for another gate.

THE WEST WALL

**3:7–14**

If the location of the Jeshanah Gate at the north-west corner is correct, vv. 7–14 describe the west wall, which unfortunately cannot be associated with any archaeological remains.

**7. Gibeon** is *c.* 6 m. north-west of Jerusalem, Meronoth (also 1 Chr. 27:30) is unidentified, and **Mizpah** is usually identified as Tell en-Nasbeh, *c.* 8 m. north of Jerusalem. **Melatiah** and **Jadon** would seem to be officials of some kind in their towns. The last phrase, lit. 'at, to, belonging to, *or* namely, the throne, *or*, seat of the governor (i.e. satrap) of Abar-nahara' is enigmatic. The best solution is to translate 'Mizpah, namely, the seat of the satrap'. We know that after 587 BC Gedaliah, appointed governor of Judea by the Babylonians, resided at Mizpah (2 Kg. 25:23, 25; Jer. 40–41), and it is entirely probable that the Persian satrap should have used the same official residence when visiting the area to hold court or conduct investigations (cf. Ezr. 5:8).

**8. Harhaiah** is unintelligible as a personal name, and the emendation to 'the guild, or guildsmen' (*ḥbr* or *ḥbry*, for *ḥrhyh*) is attractive, since it also accounts for the plural **goldsmiths**, lit. 'refiners', jewellers and, at times, idol-makers (e.g. Isa. 40:19). On guilds, see I. Mendelsohn, *BASOR* 80 (1940), pp. 17–21. The goldsmiths' guild is also represented on the last section of wall (v. 32). **perfumers**: another guild, whose products were used for hygienic and religious purposes as well as for pleasure. These guildsmen may have been allocated to this stretch of the wall because their bazaars were set up in the valley outside. **they restored Jerusalem**: *RSV*, *NEB* use a postulated verb '*zb*, 'repair'; but '*zb* usually means 'abandon', and what is probably referred to is the abandonment of part of the western or Mishneh quarter of pre-exilic Jerusalem. **Broad Wall**: It lay between the Ephraim Gate and the Tower of the Ovens (12:38f.). It may have been a retaining wall for a fill which broadened the narrow neck of land joining the city of David to the temple mount.

**9. Hur**, perhaps originally a Hurrian name meaning 'child', is well attested in this period. **ruler of half the district**: a title probably to be connected with the Assyrian title *rab pilkani*, 'ruler of the districts'. For the other half-district of Jerusalem, see v. 12.

**10. Harumaph** is a nickname, 'cleft nose' (cf. Lev. 21:18). **Hattush** is not the Davidite of Ezr. 8:2, but may be the covenant-signatory (Neh. 10:4), with whom stands Shebaniah, perhaps equivalent to **Hashabneiah** here.

**11.** If **Malchijah b. Harim** is identical with the Malchijah b. Harim in Ezra's mixed-marriage list (Ezr. 10:31), the 398 BC date for Ezra is improbable. But little weight can be placed on the name, Malchijah being a common name, and Harim in Ezr. 10:31 of course being a distant ancestor, who may have had more than one descendant named Malchijah. But at face value the name would harmonise well with a 458 date for Ezra. **Pahath-moab**: an old pratry name, cf. on Ezr. 2:6. Seven gangs (vv. 11, 19, 20, 21, 24, 27, 30) repaired **another**, lit. 'second', **section**, though in only one case (v. 27), perhaps two others (vv. 24, 30), has the gang been mentioned previously. The list must be textually defective; if we know that six names are missing, we can only speculate how many others we do not know of have also been accidentally dropped. **Tower of the** (bakers') **Ovens**: named also in 12:38 as south of the Broad Wall, but otherwise unknown, though we do hear of the bakers' street in pre-exilic Jerusalem (Jer. 37:21), situated near the royal palace, and thus in the right locality.

**12. Hallohesh**, also in 10:14 as a family name, bears the curious name 'the whisperer', i.e. the snake charmer (cf. *lḥš* in Ps. 58:5; Ec. 10:11; Jer. 8:17; and cf. N. L. Corkill, *Iraq* 6 [1939], pp. 45–52). Shallum's **daughters** are mentioned presumably only because he had no sons; on all parts of the wall the women would have done their share of the work. The other sub-district of Jerusalem may be Gibeon.

**13. Zanoah** (also 11:30) lies 14 m. south-west of Jerusalem in the Shephelah, probably in the district of Keilah. **Valley Gate**: cf. on 2:13. The **thousand cubits** from there to the **Dung Gate** is *c.* 500 yds, probably the longest stretch of wall without a gate; the whole city from north to south was only 1,200 yds.

**14. Beth-haccherem** ('House of the Vineyard'): now identified as Ramat Rachel, a lofty village (cf. Jer. 6:1) 2 m. south of Jerusalem. **Dung Gate**: cf. on 2:13.

THE EAST WALL

3:15–32

Especially in the southern half of this wall, the wall-builders appear to have been working from scratch. This will explain the large number of gangs that worked between the Fountain Gate and the Water Gate. Inexplicably, none of the gates on this side, except the Fountain Gate (v. 15), is said to have been built or repaired, or named as terminus of a section.

**15. Colhozeh**, 'the all-seeing one', seems to be an ancestral name (in a genealogy, 11:5) rather than a patronym. Since **the ruler of the district of Mizpah** is mentioned here and a different 'ruler of Mizpah' in v. 19, we should suppose the latter to be the ruler of the city. **Fountain Gate**: cf. on 2:14. **Pool of Shelah**: The name is almost certainly identical with Shiloah (Isa. 8:6), implying that the pool was fed by the waters of Shiloah, very likely a canal running from the spring Gihon along the west slope of the Kidron valley and, after a brief underground passage, into a pool at the southern tip of the city (modern Birket el-Hamra); see Simons, *Jerusalem*, pp. 176ff. This may be identical with the King's Pool (2:14), which watered the King's Garden (also 2 Kg. 25:4) in the lower Kidron valley south of the city. The wall of the Shelah pool was at the same time a city wall. The **stairs that go down from the City of David**, i.e. Zion (2 Sam. 5:7), the original Jebusite town on the south-east hill, are identified with remains of a staircase near the Fountain Gate, possibly a postern gate through which the stairs continued down to the floor of the Kidron valley (Simons, *Jerusalem*, pp. 94–98, 102f.). Thus the stairs are essentially the same point on the wall as the Fountain Gate (cf. 12:37).

**16.** **Azbuk** appears to be a pagan name, '(The god) Buk is mighty'; this may be an ancestral name, like Azgad (Ezr. 2:12, *q.v.*), so it proves little about his descendant, a namesake of Nehemiah's. **Beth-zur**, modern Kh. et-Tubeiqah, *c.* 4 m. north of Hebron, is another district capital; the other half of the district is not named, but may be Tekoa (v. 5). Mention of the **sepulchres of David**, i.e. of the Davidic kings, directly after the stairs of the city of David corresponds well with the frequent references to the burial of kings in 'the city of David' (1 Kg. 2:10; 11:43; etc.). In this area R. Weill discovered several tombs cut in the rock, but since the tombs were severely damaged in antiquity by quarrying in that area, identification remains uncertain. On the archaeological problem, see Simons, *Jerusalem*, pp. 198–225; Kenyon, *Jerusalem*, p. 70; S. Yeivin, *JNES* 7 (1948), pp. 30–45; D. Ussishkin, *BA* 33 (1970), p. 46. The location of **the house of the mighty men**, which sounds like an army barracks (*NEB* mg; cf. David's 'mighty men', *gibbôrim*, 2 Sam. 10:7; etc.), is unidentifiable.

**17.** **Bani** and his family are known to be among the Levite singers (11:22; cf. 8:7; 9:5); they are not the lay family of Ezr. 2:10. **Hashabiah** is presumably the Levite of 10:11. If he is the Levite Hashabiah of Ezr. 8:19 who returned with Ezra, Ezra must have preceded Nehemiah; but not too much weight may be laid on the identification, since Hashabiah is a common Levite name. His half-district, of which the other half (v. 18) has been thought to be Adullam or Zanoah, is centred on **Keilah**, 17 m. south-west of Jerusalem, already in Saul's time a 'town with gates and bars' (1 Sam. 23:7). Being only a Levite was no barrier to high administrative office (cf. vv. 18f.).

18, 19. Among their **brethren**, i.e. fellow-Levites, are descendants of **Henadad** (cf. Ezr. 3:9) and of **Jeshua** (Ezr. 2:40; 3:9). On **Mizpah**, cf. on v. 15. **Bavvai** should probably be emended to Binnui (so *NEB;* cf. v. 24). The topographical details here are obscure; the **armoury** was apparently located in the old Davidic city, the **Angle** being a notable feature in the line of the wall, though obviously different from the angle of vv. 24f.

20–21. **Baruch b. Zabbai** (perhaps = Zaccai, Ezr. 2:9) seems to be a layman (Ezr. 10:28). Unless we assume that the Water Gate lay much further north than the old Water Gate above Gihon (cf. on v. 26), **the house of Eliashib the high priest** will have lain a remarkably long way south of the temple. The wall-section built by **Meremoth** is very short, only the length of a house, albeit the high priest's house; this is perhaps because he had undertaken another section also (v. 4).

22. The **Plain** (*kikkār*) is usually the Jordan valley (e.g. Gen. 13:10ff.; Dt. 34:3), but more probably here means rather the 'district' of Jerusalem (cf. on 12:28f.), where there would have been priests' villages like Anathoth (Jer. 1:1).

23. We cannot tell if **Benjamin** and **Hasshub** who apparently shared a house (cf. Ps. 133:1!), were priests; there is a lay Benjamin in Ezr. 10:32, and a lay Hasshub earlier in this list (v. 11); but there is also a Levite Hasshub in 11:15. **Azariah b. Maaseiah b. Ananiah** bears three names presumably because his own and his father's are among the commonest Hebrew names; even so his identity eludes us.

24–27. The topographical details are very obscure, and even their general identification depends on the location of **the Water Gate** (v. 26; cf. 12:37). The Water Gate of the pre-exilic city was doubtless located just above the spring Gihon; K. Kenyon discovered what she believed to be the northern tower of this gate (*Jerusalem*, pp. 30f.; pl. 11). Nehemiah's city wall, being built on the crest of the Kidron slope, will of course have left the old Water Gate outside the city, and whether Nehemiah incorporated a new water gate we do not know (Hezekiah's tunnel had led the waters of Gihon to the southern tip of the city but there must still have been some access to the spring from the northern quarter where the temple was located). Since nothing is said here of the building of a Water Gate in the city wall, but the wall is said to be built **to a point opposite** it and **on the east** of it, the gate is best understood as situated in the enclosure wall of the temple or palace (like the Muster Gate, v. 31). If so, the **Angle** and the **corner** (v. 24) may be the point at which the wall bends northwards, just south of the Herodian temple platform, while the **Angle** and the **tower** (v. 25) will be features inside the wall, part of the palace compound. **the upper house of the king**: the Solomonic palace which would have been higher up the Ophel hill than David's original palace. Some evidence for the location of Solomon's palace just north of the Davidic north wall is the existence in that area of an Israelite-type casemate wall which may have enclosed the royal quarters; a proto-Ionic pilaster capital such as adorned Omri's Samaria and some well-dressed stone blocks, which have been found fallen down the slope, suggest that an important building stood on the crest in monarchic times. **Ophel**, lit. 'swelling, bulge', though often loosely used for the whole southeast hill, is used here in the proper sense of the slight eminence which today protrudes into the Kidron valley just south of the temple area. The Ophel **wall** is probably an east-west wall separating the Ophel from the royal quarter.

The former **section** of **Binnui** (v. 24) is probably mentioned in v. 18 (*q.v.*). Parosh (v. 25) is elsewhere a lay name (Ezr. 2:3; Neh. 10:14; etc.), so **Pedaiah** b. **Parosh** is probably not the Levite of 13:13, but the lay leader of 8:4, even though we would expect to find a Levite supervising Nethinim. The **temple servants** (Nethinim; cf. on Ezr. 2:43) are here said as a group to live on Ophel, though in v. 31 their 'house' is further north; rather than omit the phrase as a gloss (so *NEB*), we may either adopt with *RSV* a small emendation (*hywšbym* for *hyw yšbym*), 'who were living on Ophel' (i.e. only some lived there), or, preferably, suppose that their 'house' (v. 31) is their workplace.

**28. Horse Gate**: another city gate, mentioned in Jer. 31:40 as the easternmost point of the city; but some identify it with an internal 'entrance of the horses to the palace' (2 Kg. 11:16) or 'horse gate of the palace' (2 Chr. 23:15), giving access from the temple to the palace. We are certainly nearing the temple area, beside which the priests' quarters would naturally have been situated.

**29. Zadok** belongs to the priestly family of **Immer** (Ezr. 2:37), while the gatekeeper **Shemaiah** will have been a Levite (cf. Ezr. 2:42; Ezek. 44:11). The **East Gate** is generally agreed to have been a gate of the temple court (as in Ezek. 40:6), not of the city wall.

**30.** We are perhaps meant to attribute this 'second section' to the Hananiah of v. 8 and the Hanun of v. 13. If the translation **the sixth son** is correct, we have an unparalleled detail, which is rather suspicious. Perhaps **the sixth** (*hššy*) conceals the name of the place from which Zalaph originated; a small change to *hšmšy* would yield 'the man of Beth-Shemesh'. This is the second section repaired by **Meshullam** b. **Berechiah** (cf. v. 4), so some suggest **another section** should belong to this, not the previous, sentence. His **chamber**

means (cf. 12:44; 13:7) not his house, but one of the priests' apartments in the temple building (cf. on Ezr. 10:6).

**31–32.** On the **goldsmiths**, see on v. 8. The **house of the temple
servants** (Nethinim) will probably be not their dwellings (cf. on v.
26) but their quarters in the temple, a further indication that we
have now reached a point in the east wall opposite to the temple.
**Muster** (*mip̄ḵād̲*) **Gate**, alternatively Inspection Gate (cf. the
perhaps identical Gate of the Guard, 12:39; or Gate of the Appointed
Place; cf. Ezek. 43:21). Some regard it as a city-gate at the north-
eastern corner of the city, identifying it with the Benjamin Gate
(Jer. 37:12; but see on v. 1 above); but it is more probably a gate
of the temple court. A business quarter centred on the Sheep Gate
(v. 1) will have lain in the triangle between the temple area and the
north city wall; this will explain the presence of the shops of
goldsmiths and merchants. We need not imagine that the commer-
cial quarter had encroached on the temple area, as in later times (Mt.
21:12; Jn 2:14). **the upper chamber of the corner**: a watchtower at
the point where east and north walls meet. The last section (v. 32)
completes the 1½ m. circuit of the walls, returning us to the **Sheep
Gate**.

## OPPOSITION FROM THE SAMARIANS

### ch. 4

Nehemiah's narrative resumes from 2:20 with his account of how
news of the building of the wall quickly provoked the wrath of the
governor of Samaria and his officials. Already in ch. 2 we observed
how every forward step produced opposition (2:10, 19), and the
same pattern prevails here. The successful organisation of the building as a co-operative effort by all the citizens of Judea (ch. 3) is
followed by the mocking anger of Sanballat (4:1ff.), and likewise,
the notice of the completion of the wall to half its planned height
(v. 6) is followed by a more serious threat of attack (vv. 7f.). It does
not appear that the Jews' enemies ever marched upon Jerusalem,
and of course had they done so they would sooner or later have
been called to account by the Persian government. But Nehemiah
clearly judged them capable of using their might against his right,
Persian government or no, and in any case repeated rumours were
sapping the people's morale (vv. 10f.). Nehemiah's defensive measures (vv. 13–23) both ensured instant readiness for any surprise
attack and strengthened the Judeans' confidence and enthusiasm.

SANBALLAT'S MOCKERY

4:1–3

1. On **Sanballat** and the reason for his anger, see on 2:10.

2. While at first Sanballat may hardly have believed that Nehemiah's efforts would amount to anything, his speech sounds like one designed for home consumption by a politician non-plussed by an awkward situation. His audience are his **brethren**, i.e. his fellow-officials, including Tobiah (v. 3), and the **army of Samaria**, the troops he would have had as governor.

The exact point of Sanballat's witticisms sometimes eludes us. **these feeble**, or 'impotent' (there may be a sexual undertone; cf. 1 Sam. 2:5; Jer. 15:9), **Jews**: There is no implication that Sanballat is within sight of Jerusalem; **these** is not in the MT and we should envisage a conference in Samaria. He seems to be sneering at their ability to build a strong defensive city-wall, since his yes-man Tobiah chimes in with **Yes . . . if a fox goes up on it he will break down their stone wall**, or rather 'wall of stones', which sounds, as it was meant to, less stable. So **Will they restore things?** (*RSV*), or 'fortify themselves' (*AV*), should be replaced by a more literal translation 'Will they repair (*'zb;* see on 3:8) for themselves?', i.e. 'Is this a do-it-yourself job?' (city-walls built to last are made of dressed stone by professional masons). We may note that Samaria itself, since the time of its foundation an elegantly built city, was after its destruction rebuilt by Sargon II 'better than it was before', according to his claim (*ANET*, p. 284). **Will they sacrifice?**, possibly referring to a foundation sacrifice (but see R. S. Ellis, *Foundation Deposits in Ancient Mesopotamia* [1968], pp. 35–45), and **Will they finish up in a day?**, i.e. Do they think this is a one-day job?, are sneers at the naive enthusiasm of the Jews, who have no conception of the magnitude of their undertaking. And where do they expect to find wall-stones? Will they retrieve broken, chipped, and damaged stones from the rubbish heaps which are all that remain of Jerusalem?; **revive** is sometimes used of restoring a city (1 Chr. 11:8). Such a wall would indeed be inelegant, but the Jews had no time to quarry fresh stones. For a photograph of part of Nehemiah's wall, with its rough, irregularly shaped, undressed stones, and indeed inferior in quality to the excavators' own retaining wall, see Kenyon, *Jerusalem*, pl. 54. Contrast Zerubbabel's wall (see on Ezr. 5:16), erected under royal patronage.

## NEHEMIAH'S PRAYER
### 4:4-5

Other prayers of Nehemiah that lack a time setting (like 1:4f.) belong to the time of writing his memoirs (e.g. 5:19), but here presumably we have his prayer upon hearing of Sanballat's taunt. His prayer that God should **give** his enemies **up to be plundered**, and should **not cover their sin**, may seem reprehensibly violent to the modern reader, as do the 'imprecatory Psalms' (e.g. Ps. 79:12; 109:6–20; cf. Jer. 18:21ff.). Yet without assuming that every attitude of Nehemiah's was justifiable, we may judge this prayer more positively than that. If God had by the prophetic word and the events of history made plain his purpose that Israel should be restored to its land, Nehemiah was right in regarding the enemies of the restoration as God's enemies; in praying for their punishment he proves himself an orthodox believer in the doctrine of retribution, and prays for nothing which God has not already promised to do. But the situation has a dialectic significance; that is to say, it is fatally easy for the religious mind, with its vast capacity for self-deception, to identify its own ambitions with the will of God when the two do not really correspond. Was Nehemiah right to see Sanballat's hostility as hostility to God's intentions? Events seem to have proved Nehemiah in the right, but at the time who could have affirmed unhesitatingly that even an attack by Sanballat and further devastation of Jerusalem could not have lain within God's plans? Perhaps only a saint or a prophet can justifiably pray an imprecatory prayer, making 'His will as if it were thy will, so that He may do thy will as if it were His will' (*Ethics of the Fathers* [*Pirqe Aboth*], 2.4). What we should not do is bluntly to juxtapose Nehemiah's words and Christ's words of forgiveness from the cross; however fundamental forgiveness is to the personal Christian ethic, the 'Christian magistrate', to whom Nehemiah corresponds, may not always be called upon to exercise forgiveness to law-breakers and invaders. See further, C. S. Lewis, *Reflections on the Psalms* (1958), pp. 20–33; C. Barth, *Introduction to the Psalms* (1966), pp. 46ff.; J. Bright, *The Authority of the Old Testament* (1967), pp. 234–41.

**4.** However we judge the morality of Nehemiah's prayer, the pathos of his wish that they should be driven into a 'land of captivity' (*AV*) is very striking, for of all the curses current in the ancient world, he chooses that under which his people had already suffered. He himself had not suffered too badly from his captivity, we would say, but it is plain that he strongly identified himself with the shame of his people, and was for that reason impelled to journey to Judea (1:3).

The reversal of the **taunt** is marked by a play on words: **we are despised** (*bûzâ*); therefore **give them up to be plundered** (*bizzâ*, lit. 'for a prey', *AV*). The image of the wicked man finding his evil deeds returning 'upon his own head' is a traditional one (e.g. Ps. 7:16; Jl 3:4; Ezek. 9:10).

5. These words are borrowed from Jer. 18:23. To **cover** and to **blot out**, strictly 'to wipe out' (from God's reckoning-book; cf. on 13:14), both mean to forgive (cf. the parallelism in Ps. 32:1; 51:1). **they have provoked thee to anger before the builders**: a dubious translation, since the Hebrew has no word for 'thee'; perhaps it is better to translate 'they have insulted', or 'openly provoked' (*NEB*), 'the builders' (cf. v. 1).

### WALL-BUILDING CONTINUES

### 4:6

Soon after the taunts of their opponents had been reported, so it is implied, an important milestone in the work was reached: the circuit of the wall was completed, even though repairs had reached only half the necessary height. Jerusalem was now a defensible unity, a fact that gave the workers fresh determination (**for the people had a mind to work** should be translated 'and the people got determination, or the mind [lit. heart] to work').

### THE SAMARIANS' PLOT AND THE JUDEANS' RESPONSE

### 4:7–23

With the change of scene to Samaria, we are taken back a little in time to the moment when it is reported there that the Jews are in earnest and have actually started building the wall by filling in the breaches, the natural points at which to begin.

7. **repairing**: lit. 'healing (of a wound)'. Along with **Sanballat and Tobiah** are named **the Arabs**, under their king Geshem (cf. on 2:19), their territory lying to the south of Judah, **the Ammonites**, inhabitants of the Persian province on Judah's eastern border, and **the Ashdodites**, inhabitants of Philistia, which had become after 711 BC an Assyrian province on Judah's western boundaries. On all sides, Judah is surrounded by enemies.

8. Now that it is plain that the Jews mean business, Sanballat holds a council of war with the other provincial governors, and they plan to attack Jerusalem and, if our text is right, to **cause confusion in it**, i.e. presumably, to spread disruptive and frightening propaganda in the city (cf. v. 12). **it** (masculine in Hebrew) is odd, since

cities are feminine; many think **in it** (*lô*) is a scribal error for *lî*, 'to me'.

**9.** Nothing seems to have come of the plans for attack, but Nehemiah naturally had to take the threat seriously, so once more, as Rudolph says (p. 124), he obeys his motto *ora et labora*, praying, but also setting a guard (cf. on 2:1–8, 17f.).

**10.** The contrasts between advance in the work and dangers of failure follow now in quick succession. Nehemiah can cope with Sanballat's threat, but now he hears among the workmen a popular song which, if not the composition of a fifth columnist, would certainly have pleased the opposition right well. The Judeans generally (**Judah**), were singing, in the *qînâ* rhythm, three beats followed by two, often used in laments:

> *kāšal kōaḥ hassabbāl / wᵉheʿāp̄ār harbēh*
> *waʾᵃnaḥnû lōʾ nûk̲al / libnôt bahômâ*
> 'Failing is the strength of the carrier / and the rubbish is great
> And we are not able / to build the wall.'

Note the internal rhyme (*hassabbāl*, *nûk̲al*). Myers, translating the second line 'And we are unable by ourselves to rebuild . . .' (there is an emphasis on **we**), thinks that the song contains a hopeful note, that 'the assistance of Yahweh and the resourcefulness of Nehemiah were ample cause for confidence ' (p. 126); but that does not seem to be the point. It is not followed by appeal to Yahweh, which communal prayers employing such language would contain (e.g. Ps. 44).

**11–12.** 'The opposition's reaction, although not here in verse, is a kind of proverb put here artistically as an antiphon' (North, p. 435). They were apparently planning a surprise attack, presumably by night. **the Jews who lived by them**, i.e. in the country near the various borders of Judea, may be Nehemiah's informants. The **ten times**, i.e. frequently (cf. Gen. 31:7), repeated report is unfortunately unintelligible, lit. 'From all places which you shall return to us.' This could perhaps mean that the Jews 'from all the places' warned, 'Come back to us', i.e. flee from Jerusalem and take refuge in the country; but 'from all places' should accompany **came**, not **said**. *RSV* (cf. *NEB*) emends 'you shall return' (*tšwbw*) to **they live** (*yšbw*), and taking a hint from the LXX, inserts **they will come up** (*yʿlw*) before **against us** ('*lynw*). This reading suggests a concerted attack from all points of the compass, which would explain Nehemiah's posting defenders all around the city (v. 13), a measure he later abandoned when the surprise attack was given up (vv. 15–20). Another attractive emendation, involving only three letters, is *kl-*

*hmzmwt 'šr ḥšbw 'lynw*, 'all the plans which they had devised against us' (Rudolph, p. 124), for MT, *mkl-hmqmwt 'šr tšwbw 'lynw*.

**13.** Nehemiah responds to the threat of attack by halting the work and mobilising the population as a show of strength to the enemies' scouts (implied in v. 15). His tactic is to arm the citizens and station them at all points where the walls could be overlooked from outside the city; i.e. **the lowest parts of the space behind the walls**, especially in open places where denser concentrations of forces could be drawn up; this will give the impression that similar masses of defenders lie behind the whole circuit of the wall. The massing of the inhabitants would also increase their own confidence. This interpretation of a difficult verse, following Schneider (p. 185) in part, is preferable to the emendation of **in the lowest parts** (*mthtywt*) to 'spearmen' (*mty ḥnyt* or *ḥnytwt*) (Rudolph, p. 126), in order to provide an object for the first 'I set' (cf. *AV*). It is easier to delete the second 'I set' (cf. *RSV*). *NEB*, 'they would station themselves on the lowest levels below the wall', is tactically incredible. By this time, even if he had not been officially appointed governor before leaving Persia (cf. on 2:1–8), Nehemiah was plainly acting as governor (cf. also on v. 16; 5:7). **families**: the phratries (*mišpāḥâ;* cf. on Ezr. 2:1) which form the natural fighting units (*'elep*, 'thousand').

**14. looked**: i.e. reviewed the mustering; though the term *r'h*, 'see', is strange in this context, an emendation to 'I saw that you were afraid' (*w'r* to *w'r ky yr'w*) is unjustifiable. Nehemiah then delivers the usual pre-battle speech of encouragement (cf. 2 Sam. 10:12; 2 Chr. 20:20). The **great and terrible** God (cf. 1:5; Dt. 7:21) will help them as they help themselves (cf. on v. 9).

**15.** It appears that Nehemiah's ruse succeeded, and that his opponents, having realised that their planned attack would be no surprise to the Jews, called the attack off; thereupon work on the walls resumed. Of course it is always possible that the Samarians were only bluffing from start to finish.

**16.** After the false alarm, a more prepared state of alert is maintained. Three groups are variously armed: first, Nehemiah's **servants**, lit. 'lads' (5:10, 16; 13:19; cf. 2:12), his police force or private army which was his right as governor (cf. on v. 2). Previously they had all doubtless been assigned to construction work, but now half of them were armed and stationed behind the wall-builders, **the house of Judah** (cf. v. 10; Zech. 10:3); **the leaders** (*hśrym*) should be omitted as a dittograph of **coats of mail** (*hśrynym*). Nehemiah has to maintain morale as well as security, and the sight of even a few dozen fully-armed soldiers surrounding bands of workers outside the walls, for example, may have played a useful part. The soldiers' equipment is that of the Persian soldier, the short **spear**, wicker **shield**, the long **bow**, and **coats of** iron **mail** (see Olmstead, *History*, p. 239; Herodotus, *Hist.* 7.61). Missing is the short sword slung at the right hip, but since the list curiously begins with 'and' (*AV*, 'both'), we may suspect that the word has dropped out; alternatively, the sword is not mentioned because, as the commonest weapon, its use is taken for granted.

**17.** There cannot have been many soldiers, so all the wall-builders were armed as well. The second group mentioned are the labourers, or rather 'basket carriers' (M. Held, *JAOS* 88 [1968], pp. 94f.), who as they carried their loads on their heads or shoulders would have had one hand free for a **weapon**, lit. 'missile', of what kind we cannot tell. There may be some idealisation here; it is hard to imagine men working day after day under such a handicap when no enemy was in sight.

**18a.** The third group are the builders proper, who would of course need both hands free for their work, but could gird their short **sword** on out of the way.

**18b-20.** The workers were spread along the one and a half mile circuit of the walls, so a system of signals in case of attack on one isolated working-party was essential. The system here described is not very efficient, since any danger would first have to be reported to Nehemiah, providing he could be found, and then success in rallying everyone to the threatened spot (itself a dubious strategy) would depend on the lungs of one trumpeter. Josephus, *Ant.* 11.5.8, sensing the same difficulty, adds: 'he stationed trumpeters at intervals of 500 feet'. Perhaps Nehemiah was not a very good general, or perhaps his system was more foolproof than appears here. It never seems to have been put to the test! The theme of **God** as Israel's warrior is one of the nation's oldest traditions (Exod. 15:3; cf. 1 Sam. 17:47), and is especially drawn on by the Chronicler.

**21.** To hasten on the building, the working day was extended from its apparently usual length of sunrise to sunset (cf. Dt. 24:15), to last 'from the rising up of the dawn until the coming out of the stars'. **and half of them held the spears** is to be deleted as intrusive from v. 16.

**22.** Most of the wall-builders lived in the country villages and presumably returned home each evening. Nehemiah puts a stop to this commuting, ostensibly to increase the supply of night-watchmen and to get a full day's work from everyone, but also possibly for the workers' own safety and to prevent contacts with the enemy. Each worker can hardly have had his own **servant**, but the instruction perhaps implies 'where applicable'.

**23.** Nehemiah set a good example of thorough dedication, and

plainly inspired the loyalty of those around him. **brethren**: in the
narrower sense of close kinsmen (cf. 1:2; 5:10; 7:2). **men of the
guard**: distinct from Nehemiah's **servants**, and thus the citizens
rostered for the night watches, who patrolled the city with him
(**followed me**). **in his hand**: an emendation of *mym*, 'water' (cf.
*RSV* mg), to *b(y)mynw*, 'in his right hand'; in the square Hebrew
script a final *nw* can easily be mistaken for *m*.

As we have noted above (on 2:9–20; 4:1–23), every advance in
the work Nehemiah has set his heart on meets with some kind of
opposition. His reaction is interesting: instead of diverting resources
to meet the threats of the Samarians, he actually turns their threats
to good advantage by extracting a longer working day out of his
wall-builders and improving their morale by redeploying his 'lads'.
The work prospers because the main business is attended to and
energies are not drained by the opposition. The positive work of
building will itself in no long time achieve a more permanent 'wall'
against the opposition than any amount of temporary defensive
measures.

### ECONOMIC DIFFICULTIES AND NEHEMIAH'S SOLUTION

### 5:1–13

No sooner had adequate defensive measures against external
opponents been taken when an internal crisis broke that threatened
to delay the wall-building. The building project can hardly have
been responsible for the poverty and debt depicted here (the whole
work took only 52 days, 6:15), but Nehemiah's order against leaving
the city (4:22) may have exacerbated the distress of some peasants.
Some scholars, recognising that this crisis could not have been
provoked by the wall-building, have sought to date it later in
Nehemiah's career, perhaps at the time of 13:5; but why then should
Nehemiah recount it here? It is unlikely that it is simply for the
dramatic reason of heightening the seriousness of the crisis
Nehemiah faced.

A food shortage because of famine (v. 3) had inflated prices, and
many citizens had been forced to mortgage their land (v. 3) or their
children (v. 2) to borrow money for food. Some, who might otherwise have managed, got into debt to pay the royal taxes (v. 4). A
Jew had little wish to sell his ancestral land-holding (cf. 1 Kg.
21:1–16), and it would indeed have been foolish for him to turn his
only assets into cash for day to day existence. But to borrow money
one needed to give a pledge (cf. Dt. 24:10), an article of clothing
perhaps for a small loan (Exod. 22:26), but for a larger loan one's
property could be mortgaged, with the produce being applied to

pay off interest and loan; in extreme need the law recognised a mortgage of one's children (Exod. 21:7; cf. 2 Kg. 4:1; Isa. 50:1) or oneself (Lev. 25:39), whose labour would clear the debt (see further, de Vaux, *Ancient Israel*, pp. 170–7, 532). The laws of the remission-year (Dt. 15:1–18; cf. Exod. 21:2) and the jubilee (Lev. 25) were intended to mitigate the evils of the mortgage of persons, but it is dubious how far these laws were implemented. In the one known instance (Jer. 34:8–16) the law was readily circumvented (cf. on v. 12).

The lending of money was itself no evil; better that a man should be in debt than that he should have to beg his bread. Nehemiah shows no remorse for having been a moneylender (v. 10). But the present situation is critical, since many personal mortgages have apparently been taken, the supply of wall-builders threatens to diminish as fewer can afford to leave their own farms and businesses, and above all, a powerful protest is being raised by the debtors. Are they not, equally with the rich, members of the same Jewish family (v. 5; cf. Lev. 25:39–46)? Why then should some brothers be slaves and others masters? It is something of a novelty in the *OT* that their demand for social justice is based directly on the kinship of the nation and the mutual responsibility of kinsmen, which is not just a matter of blood being thicker than water, but is also a divine ordinance (cf. **the fear of God**, v. 9b); for a parallel, cf. Porten, *Elephantine*, pp. 270f.

Nehemiah has to admit the force of their claim, and adopting their argument (notice his use of **brother**, vv. 1, 7, 8) persuades the creditors to follow his example by immediately restoring to the debtors their pledges and perhaps remitting the debts entirely. Doubting their sincerity to forgo both capital and security, he exacts an oath of them and curses any who may break their word. His measures here are obviously dictated by the pressing need of the moment, and a less impetuous system is later established, presumably at his direction, in the pledge of ch. 10 (see especially on v. 31).

**1. outcry** (*şeʿāqā*): the technical term for the poor's cry of distress (e.g. Job 34:28; cf. 9:4); here exceptionally, it is made by the women also.

**2.** The first group of debtors are landless people who for want of other assets are having to mortgage their children; we should translate 'We are mortgaging our sons and our daughters' (emending *rbym*, **many**, to *ʿrbym*, 'are giving in pledge'; similarly *NEB*) since MT, 'our sons, our daughters, we are many', is strange syntax, and having a large family is no ground of complaint against one's fellow countrymen (v. 1)!

**3.** A second group are peasants who are having to mortgage their land and property. The failure of the crops (barley harvest in April/May, wheat in May/June) must have been disastrous for **famine** already to be felt in August/September, the months of the wall-building (6:15).

**4.** The third group have mortgaged their fields and vineyards to pay the **king's tax** (cf. on Ezr. 4:13; 6:8), which of course has first claim upon their income. 'From the satrapies a constant stream of silver flowed in . . . Little of this vast sum was ever restored to the satrapies . . . Only a small portion was ever coined . . . Thus, despite the precious metals newly mined, the empire was rapidly drained of its gold and silver. For a time, credit made possible a continuance of business, but the insensate demand for actual silver in the payment of taxes drove the landlords in increasing numbers to the loan sharks, who gave money in exchange for the pledge' (Olmstead, *History*, pp. 297f.).

**5.** Those who have mortgaged their property to pay their taxes are now being impelled, like the first group, to mortgage their children, **forcing** them **to be slaves.** Possibly their argument is meant to represent that of all the poor. Their appeal is not to some theoretical 'equality of man' but to their common brotherhood (**flesh,** cf. 2 Sam. 5:1; Jg. 9:2; cf. also 2 Chr. 28:8–11). Special reference to **our daughters . . . already . . . enslaved** suggests that the verb here (*kābaš*) has a sexual significance (cf. Est. 7:8); slave girls, as so often, were expected to submit to their masters' advances (cf. also Exod. 21:7–11). It may, however, simply be that daughters were regarded as less productive than sons, and so were the first to be sold into service (and a different legal status for sons and daughters may be reflected; cf. Exod. 21:7–11, and B. Cohen, *Jewish and Roman Law*, I [1966], pp. 172f.). Whatever the nature of the children's slavery, the parents obviously can do nothing about it, because **other men have** (own) **our fields . . .** ; i.e. they cannot save enough to redeem their children because all their produce from the land goes straight to the creditors. We need not assume that the creditors have already moved in and taken possession of the property.

**6.** A fine city wall is a prerequisite for peace, but built in vain if the citizens are at enmity (cf. Isa. 58:9*b*-12). Nehemiah is **very angry** (cf. 4:4f.; 13:8, 21, 25) that Jerusalem harbours a cause for just complaint—which is as shaming to the city (v. 9*b*) as its physical desolation (1:3; 2:17). The **outcry** is perhaps the wailing of the women (v. 1), as distinct from the **words,** the actual complaints (vv. 2–5).

**7. nobles and officials** (cf. 2:16): the lenders of money. **took counsel with myself:** understanding *mlk*, 'rule' (cf. *NEB* 'mastered

my feelings'), in the Aramaic sense 'consider'; this is the self-reliant,
secretive facet of Nehemiah's personality. L. Kopf's translation, 'I
was beside myself' (*VT* 9 [1959], pp. 261f.), using an Arabic
cognate, is less probable, though not out of character for Nehemiah!
**brought charges:** The translation is too formal (before whom would
he bring the charges?), and 'rebuked' (*AV*) or 'reasoned with'
(*NEB*) is preferable. The reason for his rebuke is apparently not
because they were charging interest, but because of the evils which
arose from the demand for pledges. **exacting interest** (*AV*, 'usury')
is not implied by the Heb. *nāśâ*, 'to lend,' or 'to lend against pledge'.
*NEB*, 'You are holding your fellow Jews as pledges for debt',
unjustifiably restricts *nāśâ* to personal mortgages. Taking interest
(*nešek*) from a fellow-Israelite was illegal (Lev. 25:36f.; Dt. 23:19f.),
but nevertheless not unknown (Ps. 15:5; Prov. 28:8; cf. Ezek. 18:8,
13, 17; and the closely contemporary contract for a loan at 60 per
cent p.a. interest from a Jewish lender at Elephantine in 456 BC,
*AP* 10). There were ways of circumventing the law, e.g., the loan
could be made free of interest, but on failure to repay within a
specified time interest would be charged (cf. S. W. Baron, *A Social
and Religious History of the Jews*, I [1952], p. 409 n. 150). Taking
pledges, however, was sanctioned by the law (Dt. 24:10), though
certain safeguards were specified (Dt. 24:6, 10–13; Exod. 22:26f.);
consequently Nehemiah cannot charge the moneylenders (of whom
he also is one!) with breaking the law, but can only argue that what
they are doing is 'not good' (v. 9; cf. Exod. 18:17; I Sam. 26:16;
and contrast Neh. 13:17, 27). The point of Nehemiah's rebuke is
that it is from their **brothers** that they are demanding pledges. **I
held a great assembly against them,** or rather, 'to deal with them'
(Myers). *NEB*, translating 'I rebuked them severely', perhaps
correctly identifies the rare word *qᵉhillâ*, usually translated
'assembly', with an Arabic root 'to rebuke' (cf. Brockington, p.
151), though there certainly was an assembly (*qāhāl;* v. 13). Appeal
to the nobles' sense of brotherhood proving fruitless, Nehemiah
calls a formal assembly of the people, even though precious time
for wall-building will be wasted.

**8.** His argument is: 'We have, whenever possible, paid out
ransom money for our Jewish brethren who had got into the clutches
of Gentile moneylenders (cf. Lev. 25:47ff.). Now the moneylenders
are Jewish, so ransom money will have to be paid by Jews to Jews!'
The last clause, **that they may be sold to us** really means 'so that
they will have to be bought back (if by anyone at all) by us'. The
implication is: What a waste of Jewish money, which is in such
short supply!

**9.** The **fear of God,** i.e. piety, is a more pervasive influence on a man's life than is mere desire to stay on the right side of the law; it demands a whole-hearted concern for the underprivileged (cf. v. 15; Lev. 25:36). Ultimately the moneylenders' adherence to their legal rights will bring disgrace on Israel which has claimed to be a kin-group ('*am*, 'people') and not one of the nations (*gôy*), whose members like T. S. Eliot's Londoners simply 'huddle close together . . . to make money from each other' (*Choruses from 'The Rock'*, iii).

**10.** Nehemiah himself, **his brethren,** i.e. close kinsmen (cf. on 4:23), and his **servants** (cf. on 4:16), all wealthy men, have likewise been **lending** against pledges **money and grain.** It is not a question of charging interest. Had he been illegally charging interest he would hardly have said simply **Let us leave off this interest;** the last word (*maśśā'*) is in fact the noun from *nāśā'* (=*nāśâ*, v. 7), and means 'loan against pledge'. Many think he is proposing to write off all loans as gifts, and in the crisis this would have been an admirable thing to do, though unrealistic as a general rule. But it is more likely that he is simply urging that all pledges should be returned (so v. 11); thus the moneylenders agree to restore what they have taken in pledge and **require nothing** (by way of pledge) from their debtors (v. 12). The cancellation of certain types of debts (e.g. arrears of payment) may be paralleled in second millennium Babylonia (see J. Bottéro, *JESHO* 4 [1961], pp. 113–64, esp. 143ff., 147ff.), but that seems a more consciously economic decision than Nehemiah's.

**11.** To **return** pledges to debtors means to return the equivalent of mortgage deeds so that there is no fear of the creditor distraining upon unpaid debts, nor any compulsion, for example, for all the proceeds of the year's crop to be applied to clearing a mortgage. The creditor is of course left without legal guarantees for his money and Nehemiah would have to be trusted to apply moral and social pressures on unjustifiably defaulting debtors. **olive orchards:** not mentioned in vv. 2–5, but often associated with **vineyards** (e.g. Exod. 23:11; Dt. 6:11). No mention is made, oddly, of the return of mortgaged sons and daughters, but that is to be presumed. **the hundredth:** emend *m't*, 'hundred of', to *mš't*, 'pledge of'. The normal word for 'hundred' (*mē'â*) is meaningless in the context; 'interest' is not in question, and in any case 1 per cent interest would make no difference to the situation—even a monthly interest rate of 1 per cent would be regarded as a bargain in the Persian empire (cf. Olmstead, *History*, pp. 83ff., 299; Porten, *Elephantine*, pp. 76–9. For an example of a *monthly* interest rate of 100 per cent on grain, see *BMAP* 11.3). **grain, wine, and oil:** traditionally the three chief products of Palestine (cf., e.g., Dt. 7:13). It may have been the angry mood of the popular assembly which so quickly persuaded the moneylenders to bid farewell to their financial security and cheap labour; certainly Nehemiah was not prepared to trust the moneylenders further than he could see them.

**12.** Perhaps with the episode of Jer. 34 in mind, Nehemiah has the priests administer an oath, of some such form as 'May the Lord do so to me and more also, if I do not return . . .' (cf., e.g., 1 Sam. 3:17).

**13.** Not satisfied with that, Nehemiah adds his own symbolic action (like those of the prophets; cf., e.g., Ezek. 12:3–7) and his curse. Taking his sash or girdle or 'fold of my robe' (*NEB; not* **lap,** *RSV*), the ancient equivalent of pockets (cf. 2 Sam. 20:8), he shook it empty, calling down the same fate of being **shaken out and emptied** upon any who might break his promise. Traditionally, the power of a curse depended on the psychic strength of the curser; the people adding their **Amen** (cf. on 8:6) to Nehemiah's curse strengthened its potency. S. Talmon saw the **Amen** as the introduction to an oath which is not recorded (*Textus* 7 [1967], pp. 124–9). The taking of the oath is really an expression of social solidarity which is given a religious expression (note the solemn use of the name 'Yahweh', **the LORD**; cf. on 1:5). The **people** who **promised** must be the nobles and moneylenders, not the 'people' of v. 1.

NEHEMIAH'S UNSELFISHNESS AS GOVERNOR

5:14–19

The story of how Nehemiah eased financial burdens in Judea by forgoing his own rights as a creditor and compelling others to follow his example is supplemented now by an account of how for the common good he forwent some of his rights as governor.

**14.** Nehemiah's term as **governor** of Judea ran **twelve years,** from 445 to 433/2 BC. If he was not already officially governor when he left Susa, as some maintain, he was certainly appointed to the position during his first year in Jerusalem (cf. on 2:1–8). As governor he was entitled to levy a tax on his province to cover his considerable hospitality expenses. Because the obligatory provincial tax ('the servitude', v. 19) for the central government was already heavy, he paid his expenses out of his own pocket. He was plainly entitled to use the **food allowance** for the support of his family (**brethren**) as well as himself.

**15.** The generous food allowance of the governor is **forty shekels of silver** 'per day for food' (cf. *NEB*), as we should translate the Hebrew. *'aḥar* cannot mean **besides,** and the phrase *wyyn 'ḥr,* 'and wine besides', should probably be emended to *lywm 'ḥd,* 'for one day'; in any case, the allowance is clearly a daily one. **shekel:** Whether the Median shekel coin of 5.6 grams or the shekel weight (c. 11.4 grams) is referred to cannot be decided, since coinage, introduced into Persia by Darius I, seems to have been slow in reaching Judea. Nevertheless, gold coins figure in the homecomer list (Ezr. 2:69), and probably are also implied in Hag. 1:6 (R. Loewe, 'The Earliest Biblical Allusion to Coined Money?', *PEQ* 87 [1955], pp. 141–50). On the supposition that the shekel weight is meant, Nehemiah's daily income was 1 lb. of silver, worth today *c.* £700, though such comparisons are inevitably misleading. The tax may have been raised in kind (cf. Mal. 1:8). **former governors** of Judea: their identity has been much debated. Some, following Alt (*KS*, II, pp. 316–37), have regarded Nehemiah as the first Judean governor, Judea previously having been subordinate to Samaria; in that case the former governors would have been the governors of Samaria. But the view is taken here that Zerubbabel at least was 'governor of Judea' in the full sense (cf. Hag. 1:1), and that we may therefore assume a succession—not necessarily unbroken, however—of governors between his time and Nehemiah's. Nehemiah is sometimes maligned for his quick temper and supposed self-righteousness (already in the Talmud, TB *Sanh.* 93b), but it should also be observed how he regards the forgoing of one's rights as a part of true religion (**fear of God**; cf. v. 9; 1 Cor. 9:12). **their servants** are their armed force (cf. on 4:16), not their officials.

16. A further example of his generosity, though it applies only to the early weeks of his governorship, is his undertaking of the wall-building (*RSV* **held to** wrongly suggests his perseverence is in mind here), probably at considerable personal expense; that seems the implication of **and acquired no land.** Nehemiah's **servants** had no particular allotment on the wall, according to ch. 3, so they apparently worked where needed (cf. 4:16). **this wall** suggests that he wrote these 'memoirs' in Jerusalem.

17–18. Some details, doubtless far from exhaustive, of the cost to himself of relieving his people of the governor's food allowance tax (v. 15) are now given. His regular establishment numbered some 150 officials, both Jewish and Persian (**Jews** means Jewish officials; **officials** means probably Persian officials; cf. on 2:16); incessant visits of imperial and satrapy officials (**from the nations which were about us**) added a fluctuating number of guests to Nehemiah's table. Modest though his provisions were by comparison with Solomon's daily requirements (1 Kg. 4:22f.; and for examples of food consumption at courts, see K. A. Kitchen, *NBD*, pp. 431f.), the expense must have eaten quite a hole in his personal fortune. Batten calculates that enough meat for 600 or 800 people a day was provided

(p. 246). **fowls** (also 1 Kg. 4:23) would have included both game birds and fatted birds; though cocks and hens are not mentioned in the *OT*, a seal from Tell en-Nasbeh *c.* 600 BC, showing a cock, attests their existence (W. F. Badè, *ZAW* 10 [1933], pp. 150–6; cf. *IDB*, II, p. 777; *DOTT*, p. 222 with pl. 13). A. Kahan thinks Nehemiah's menu did not include birds (*sipporîm*) but he-goats (*šepîrîm*) (*BM* 12 [1966f.], pp. 139f.). **prepared for me:** i.e. at my expense. **skins of wine:** *RSV*, *NEB* reasonably adopt the reading of a few MSS, *nbly-yyn*, for MT *bkl-yyn*, 'in all kinds of wine'. **the servitude:** not simply the wall-building, since Nehemiah is speaking of the whole period of his governorship; he uses of the heavy imperial taxes a word which is reminiscent of bondage in Egypt (e.g. Exod. 1:14).

**19.** This prayer (cf. also 13:14, 22, 31) is a committal of his expectation of reward to God, in the knowledge that only the just Judge, and not man, can be relied on to give credit where credit is due. His prayer that God should 'remember' Tobiah and Sanballat (6:14) is likewise a plea for just retribution. For parallels, see *ANET*, p. 307 (Nebuchadrezzar II); p. 316 (Cyrus). On the significance of the prayer in determining the literary character of Nehemiah's memoirs, see Introduction, II.1.

In the earlier part of this chapter (vv. 1–13), we have seen Nehemiah in confrontation with economic difficulties. An economist might remark how unrealistic and ultimately counter-productive were the measures Nehemiah took; for had Nehemiah's policy of returning pledges to debtors (v. 11) been perpetuated, those with capital would eventually have given up lending money, and the poor who needed loans would in the end have been no better off. Yet there are occasions when the 'fear of God' (v. 9) sets aside long-term prudential considerations, and demands an immediate demonstration or gesture to establish which side of a controversy one is on. The same applies to Nehemiah's payment of the expenses of his office out of his own pocket (vv. 14–19). What an unfortunate and unwelcome precedent he was setting for later incumbents! But how creditably he was expressing that 'fear of God' (v. 15) which compelled him to see the over-taxed Jews as his brothers and not as people who owed him a living.

IN SPITE OF TRAPS FOR NEHEMIAH, THE WALL IS FINISHED

### ch. 6

Chapter 5 has marked the passage of some weeks of wall-building, and now the stage has been reached when the walls stand complete, without as yet the doors being hung in the gates (v. 1). Nehemiah's enemies can hardly prevent the complete fortification of the city now, but they make a desperate attempt. Their plan (vv. 2–9) is to lure him away from Jerusalem and do him some unspecified harm. But both a simple invitation (vv. 2–4) and the threat of a frame-up (vv. 5–9) fail to entice him. All they can hope for now is to discredit him, and accordingly, if Nehemiah's suspicions are correct, they pay a Jewish prophet to inveigle him into disgracing himself (vv. 10–14). Though that ploy fails, attempts, especially by Tobiah, to make him lose his nerve continue (vv. 17–19); note the theme-word 'frighten', used in all the three sections of this chapter (vv. 9, 13f., 19). But by this time (if vv. 17–19 are not out of place), the wall and its gates are finished, and Nehemiah's city and his status are equally secure.

1. For Nehemiah's enemies, cf. on 2:10, 19. 'To' ($l^e$) is missing before **Tobiah** because as Sanballat's henchman he plays no independent role; his absence from vv. 2 and 5f. may be similarly explained (less easily if he were the Ammonite governor).

2. **one of the villages:** or possibly, an unknown town Kephirim (or Hakkephirim, *NEB*) **in the plain of Ono,** *c.* 20 m. north-west of Jerusalem. The Heb. *bkpyrym* could mean 'with the lions', metaphorical for 'princes' (R. Schiemann, *VT* 17 [1967], pp. 367ff.), but this is unlikely in the present context. The place was presumably suggested as a neutral spot; the area, though some Judeans had settled there (Ezr. 2:33), belonged to neither Judea, Samaria, nor Ashdod, but directly to the satrapy, an arrangement perhaps dating back to Assyrian times. Sanballat can hardly have dared to suggest a conference at Jerusalem or Samaria after the distinctly violent turn his intentions, or at least his propaganda, had taken (4:8–11). But the alternative, a neutral site, sounded suspicious to Nehemiah. Did he just imagine that Sanballat **intended to do** him **harm?** (presumably, in the context, personal injury, even murder). 'What else could [Sanballat] do', asks R. North, 'except try to come to an understanding that would avert complete breakdown in co-operation and subsequent cracking together of heads from above?' (p. 436). But it is hard to see what Sanballat hoped to achieve just at this time, and his unimaginative importunity (v. 4) is not the mark of a constructive statesman.

3–4. Nehemiah shows a nice wit in making his work his excuse for not coming when he knows quite well that the intention of the invitation is to stop his work. It is part of his subtlety (cf. on 2:1–8) that he does not directly reject the invitation: **Why should the work stop . . . ,** could be a question of reproof (cf. on 13:11), implying 'You make a mistake to ask me to stop the work', or it could sound like a genuine question, viz. 'Is it really important?'

5. Sanballat, in a classic example of gamesmanship, writes a letter which professes concern for Nehemiah but which passes on a piece of gossip to the effect that Nehemiah is plotting rebellion against the empire; and he sends it as an **open letter**! An open letter would be an unsealed sheet of papyrus, or an ostracon, a piece of pottery, as used for example for the Lachish letters (*DOTT*, pl. 12). Nehemiah was of course intended to see that Sanballat planned to spread this rumour, and Sanballat hoped that Nehemiah would be sufficiently alarmed to hurry to Ono and plead with him to scotch it.

6. **Geshem:** more correctly Gashmu (*RSV* mg); cf. on 2:19. This report was lent a fair show of plausibility by the 'Gaullist grandeur and separatist assurance' (North, p. 436) of Nehemiah, but it would have been profoundly damaging to Nehemiah if it had reached the king's ears; see the threats against traitors in Darius' Behistun inscription (Kent, *Old Persian*, pp. 116–34; *AP*, pp. 257ff.). On Jerusalem's reputation as a rebellious city, cf. Ezr. 4:12. Royal pretensions on Nehemiah's part would seem all the more probable if, as some suggest, he was of Davidic descent (cf. on 1:6; 2:3).

7. It is not at all improbable that **prophets** were hailing Nehemiah as a messiah; they need only have been a little more explicit than Haggai (2:21ff.) and Zechariah (3:8; 4:6–10; 6:10–14) were about Zerubbabel (and Joshua?) for Sanballat's charge to have some foundation.

8. Nehemiah replies with assurance that the accusation itself and even the very idea of a rumour are figments of Sanballat's hostile imagination. **mind,** lit. heart: cf. on Ezr. 6:22.

9. Sanballat alone had written the letters, but Nehemiah, undoubtedly correctly, believed there was a conspiracy (**they all;** cf. v. 1) to demoralise the Jews (lit. 'let their hands be weakened'; cf. on Ezr. 4:4). The last clause is made a prayer in most modern versions by the conjectural addition of **O God;** this would be an ejaculatory prayer on the occasion (like 4:4f.), since it does not suit the time of composition. *NEB*, following LXX, has 'I applied myself to it with greater energy', but '*attâ*, 'now', cannot refer to the past.

10. Attempts to entice Nehemiah out of Jerusalem having failed, a more subtle attempt to destroy his reputation (v. 12) in Jerusalem is made. It is risible that Sanballat's grandiose schemes for preventing the building of the wall (4:11) have now been whittled down by Nehemiah's persistence to this desperate effort to discredit him. Visiting, presumably by invitation, the otherwise unknown prophet **Shemaiah,** Nehemiah finds him **shut up,** an obscure term. In 1 Sam. 21:7 and 36:5 it apparently refers to ritual defilement, but if that were the case here Shemaiah could hardly have suggested

going into the temple—unless perhaps his ritual impurity would be cleansed by the evening (cf., e.g., Lev. 11:24, 27). An ingenious but unlikely interpretation is that Shemaiah had shut himself up as a symbolic prophecy of the necessity for enclosure in the temple (cf. 5:13). An alternative view is that Shemaiah was one who himself had sought asylum in the temple by pledging life-long dedication to its service; as an adoptive temple servant (as *'aṣûr*, 'shut up', could well mean), he would have had the right of access to the temple at night (see L. Delekat, *Asylie und Schutzorakel am Zionheiligtum* [1967], pp. 320–5). Shemaiah's prophecy, which like many prophetic oracles, is in poetic form, urges Nehemiah to seek asylum from assassins that night in the temple. Now the right of asylum attached to the altar (1 Kg. 1:50–53; 2:28–34), but that was in the temple courtyard, not in the temple, for laymen were not permitted to enter the temple (Num. 18:7; see H. C. Thomson, 'The Right of Entry to the Temple in the Old Testament', *TGUOS* 21 [1965f.], pp. 25–34). Had Nehemiah taken the prophet's advice and entered the temple itself, he could have been accused of both cowardice and impiety.

11. Nehemiah's indignant reply shows what a feeble plot it is. He resents the suggestion that he, as governor of a Persian province, should flee for his life (**should such a man as I flee?**), and moreover, he has obviously judged Shemaiah to be a false prophet because his message does not accord with previous revelation (cf. Dt. 13:1–5); it is not God's will that a **man such as I am**, i.e. a layman, should enter the temple. His horror of profaning the sanctuary would be all the stronger if he were a eunuch (cf. on 1:10f.; cf. Lev. 21:17–20, 23; Dt. 23:1).

12. Like Jeremiah (23:21), Nehemiah calls the false prophet one **not sent** by God. As a false prophet, his prophecy was not for Nehemiah's good, as it appeared, but really against him. Nehemiah must have had some reason, no longer known, for connecting Shemaiah specifically with **Tobiah** who, exceptionally, appears before **Sanballat** (also in v. 14). Nehemiah can only suppose that any compatriot who acted against him must have been bribed to do so; but the possibility is that Shemaiah acted on his own initiative. It was no crime to pay a prophet (cf. 1 Sam. 9:7f.), but obviously prophets were as open to corruption as other people (cf. Mic. 3:5).

13. Here it seems that the greatest risk Nehemiah would have run if he had acceded to Shemaiah's proposal was that he would acquire **an evil name,** presumably among the Jews, with resultant loss of prestige and possible loss of status altogether; thus he would become discredited (cf. *NEB*). The law (Num. 18:7) however seems to prescribe death for trespassers into the temple, and Nehemiah

himself believed he was in danger of death (v. 11*b*). The significance of the episode thus remains obscure.

**14. remember:** i.e. reward; cf. on 5:19. **according to these things that they did:** MT 'according to these *his* works'—which suggests that **Sanballat** is a secondary insertion both here and in v. 12. Reference to the otherwise unmentioned **prophetess Noadiah** (was she Shemaiah's wife?) and **the rest of the prophets** only shows how little we know of what was happening in these critical days.

**15.** The climax of Nehemiah's work is reached with the completion of the wall on the 25th of the sixth month **Elul**, i.e. 2 October 445 BC, fifty-two days after it was begun, on August 11 if sabbaths were included in the total (these dates assume the correctness of the emendation of 1:1). Nehemiah, who received permission to leave Susa in the first month (2:1), can hardly have taken more than 100 days from his arrival in Jerusalem for this prestigious achievement. Josephus' statement that the building took two years and four months (*Ant.* 11.5.8) may be discounted, possibly as due to textual corruption (J. Bewer, *JBL* 43 [1924], pp. 224f.). There would be nothing remarkable in building, or rather, repairing, a 1½ m. wall in 28 months, despite J. Bright's view that Josephus' figure refers to the 'actual completion' of the wall with reinforcements, gates, and battlements (*History*, p. 381). For the dedication of the wall, see 12:27–43.

**16. our enemies:** presumably, the personal opponents of Nehemiah; **the nations round about:** the provinces adjoining Judea. **were afraid:** better, 'saw' (*RSV* mg, *NEB*), adopting a small revocalisation of MT (*wayyîr'û* for *wayyēr'û*). **fell greatly in their own esteem** (lit. 'in their eyes'): Alternatively the phrase could mean that Sanballat and his colleagues fell in the esteem of their subjects (**the nations**). A small emendation (*wyplw* to *wypl'*) offers an attractive reading; 'and it was very marvellous in their eyes' (similarly *NEB*; cf. Ps. 118:23, also in connection with building). In any case, the rapidity of the work seemed to others (or so Nehemiah believed) sure proof that the Jews had enjoyed divine assistance.

**17–19.** Instead of an account of the dedication of the walls, which we expect now (or at least after 7:3), but which follows only at 12:27–43, we have an appended account (note **moreover**, v. 17) of contacts between Jewish **nobles** and **Tobiah,** which many think must have originally occurred before the completion of the walls. But correspondence between Tobiah and his relatives and business associates in Jerusalem is perfectly probable even after the completion of the walls, and Nehemiah is clearly using these circumstances as a foil to the account of the successful completion of the wall (cf. on 2:19). Nehemiah apparently regarded any interest of Tobiah's in

Jerusalem as an intrusion, and any direct approach as a threat
(v. 19b). But it is hard to see what Tobiah was hoping to achieve
by threatening Nehemiah and at the same time arranging for his
friends to speak of his **good deeds** in Nehemiah's presence (but cf.
on v. 19). More likely than not, Tobiah was now less interested in
removing Nehemiah from the scene than in keeping open lines of
communication with his Jerusalem associates.

18. Tobiah's relationship by marriage to **Shecaniah** b. **Arah**
(perhaps cf Ezr. 2:5) and **Meshullam** b. **Berechiah** (3:4) gave him
an *entrée* into Judean society (cf. also 13:4), from which **many** were
**bound by oath** to him, presumably as business associates.

19. **good deeds,** lit. 'good things', i.e. presumably benefits to
Judah's economy through Tobiah's trading interests. But the Heb.
word *ṭôḇōṭāyw* may be revocalised as *ṭibbōṭāyw*, 'his rumours',
cognate with Aramaic *ṭibbâ* (so *NEB* mg). R. Gordis, *VT* 5 (1955),
pp. 88ff., following LXX, suggested 'his words', on the basis of a
new Hebrew word *ṭôḇ*, 'word, speech'.

In these episodes, Nehemiah finds that opposition to a 'great
work' (v. 3) done in the name of God does not always come by
force, but often enough by stealth. Nehemiah does not need to
respond to the ruses of his enemies with deceit; he is as wise as a
serpent and harmless as a dove (Mt. 10:16). He replies first with a
cleverly phrased, but none the less blunt, refusal to Sanballat and
Geshem's invitation to parley (v. 3), secondly by calling Sanballat's
bluff (v. 8), and thirdly by a stubborn refusal to transgress the
known will of God (v. 11). His only weapons are his confidence in
the work to which God has called him (v. 3), which is not a self-
confidence, but a reliance upon God's 'strengthening' (v. 9).

PREPARATIONS FOR THE PEOPLING OF JERUSALEM

7:1–73a

Now that the fortifications of the city are complete, Nehemiah
prepares for an expansion of the population to a number worthy of
a capital city. First he takes a census of the whole people (v.5) as a
preliminary to resettling some of the inhabitants of country towns
in the city (as narrated in 11:1f.); this census was accomplished with
the help of the genealogical list (vv. 6–73a), which is also reproduced
in Ezr. 2.

SECURITY ARRANGEMENTS

7:1–3

These would have been made directly after the completion of the
wall (6:15); they are probably only temporary measures.

1. The setting up of the **doors** must be implied in 6:15 since it is expressly excluded in 6:1. **the singers and the Levites:** Since they have nothing to do with the security of the city, most commentators (and *NEB*) delete these words as a scribal, or more probably, editorial, gloss (cf. vv. 43ff., where in any case the **gatekeepers** guard the temple, not the city, gates).

2. Though still governor of the province, Nehemiah needed now to appoint a governor of the capital city (cf. on Mizpah, 3:15). It is unlikely that he should have appointed two men to the same post, and even more unlikely that they should bear almost identical names; so we may take **and** (i.e. 'namely') **Hananiah** to be explicative (cf. on Ezr. 8:18) of **Hanani,** of which Hananiah is simply a longer form. This also removes the oddity that while reasons are given for Hananiah's appointment, Hanani's only qualification is that he is Nehemiah's brother! Hanani has already been mentioned at 1:1, and the **castle,** or fortress, of the temple at 2:8; 3:1. Hanani owed his promotion to his faithfulness, i.e. loyalty to Nehemiah and to the Persian government, and to his piety (cf. 5:9).

3. **And I said to them,** viz. to Hanani and the official gatekeepers (so Qere, oral tradition); alternatively we may read 'And he (Hanani) said to them' (so Kethib, written tradition). Usually city **gates** were opened before or at sunrise, but when **the sun is hot,** though a vague mark of time, must be considerably later. **while they are still standing guard:** The translation is a rather improbable guess, following LXX, at a very obscure phrase. Some reference to sunset is expected; but even the best emendation, *w'wd hw' 'md,* 'while yet it (the sun) is standing (in the sky)', is not entirely convincing. *NEB,* following G. R. Driver, *ZAW* 78 (1966), pp. 4ff., takes it that the gates are not to be left open *during* the heat of the day, the midday siesta time; but 'let them not be opened' is a curious way of saying 'Let the doors, already open, be shut', and 'during' is a rare meaning of *'ad,* 'until'. And *'āmad,* 'stand', can hardly mean 'stand at ease'. With so many ambiguities it is remarkable that the gatekeepers knew what to do! All we can be sure of is that some unusual security precautions were to be taken. **guards from among the inhabitants:** an emergency force of vigilantes additional to the regular gatekeepers; apparently each was stationed at a point on the wall close to his own house, though the Hebrew is far from clear.

REGISTERING POTENTIAL INHABITANTS OF JERUSALEM

7:4–5

4. This sentence may serve as a reason for the extraordinary security measures: the city was so sparsely inhabited that a night attack in

a lonely quarter could allow invaders into the city unnoticed. Such a state of affairs must not continue; Nehemiah clearly had big ideas for Jerusalem. While Jebusite Jerusalem had occupied 11 acres, and Herodian Jerusalem was later to occupy 140 acres (K. Kenyon, *Jerusalem*, p. 155), Nehemiah's Jerusalem extended to about 30 or 40 acres, and even a population of a couple of thousand in such an extensive walled city would have seemed **few,** especially by comparison with its population at the end of Nehemiah's governorship. That **no houses had been built** can only mean that no new buildings had yet been erected; both the preceding verse and the list of wallbuilders presuppose the existence of houses before this time (e.g. 3:20, 29; cf. also Hag. 1:4). Little weight therefore can be placed on this verse as evidence that Nehemiah's city-building activity preceded Ezra (cf. Introduction, IV; U. Kellermann, *ZAW* 80 [1968], p. 66).

**5.** The problem of populating newly founded cities was well known in the ancient world, and a proved method had been the practice of *synoikismos*, as the Greeks called it, by which, in one of its forms, inhabitants of surrounding country areas were more or less forcibly removed to the new city. This method was, as far as we know, a novelty in Israel, so Nehemiah is concerned to state its divine origin: **God put it into my mind** (cf. on 3:12). **mind:** lit. 'heart' (cf. on Ezr. 6:22). In order to carry out his plan to bring ten per cent of the country population into the city, Nehemiah had to have an accurate census of the province by villages. But why he should need to summon a general assembly to produce such a census is unclear; perhaps people gathered in their own villages to be enrolled (cf. Lk. 2:1–4). The significance of an enrolment according to genealogy must be that only those who could prove pure Jewish descent could be transferred to Jerusalem. The **book of the genealogy of those who came up at the first,** viz. 7:6–73, is the same list as in Ezr. 2. The labour of the census could be minimised if genealogies needed to be traced back less than a century (we may assume that the register contained the names of all returning heads of fathers' houses, as in Ezr. 8:1–14, and not just the total numbers, as here). Nehemiah cannot have used only this register, since the names of other returning Jews would have been listed, for example, only by Ezra (Ezr. 8:1–14).

**7:6– 73a The register of returned exiles.** On the question of the original setting of this list, cf. on Ezr. 2:1–70, where it is argued that its place in Nehemiah is original, and that it was later copied from the Nehemiah memoirs to the historically appropriate place in Ezr. 2. The details of the list, including variations between its two forms, have already been discussed there.

**73a.** As in Ezr. 2:70, the inexplicable mention both of **some of the people** and of **all Israel** calls for an emendation distinguishing between inhabitants of Jerusalem and country dwellers (1 Esd. 9:37 mentions Jerusalem). But if, as in Ezr. 2:70, we insert 'lived in Jerusalem' after **some of the people,** we have the curious result that only the Nethinim and (the rest of) **all** (lay) **Israel** are said to have lived in the country. Rudolph suggests that the verse is a conflation of two similar sentences (pp. 11–15). The first, the proper conclusion to the list, was exactly the same as Ezr. 2:70; the second, which originally was the conclusion to the narrative of the return under Ezra (Ezr. 8), read something like 'And the priests and the Levites and some of the people dwelt in Jerusalem, and the Nethinim and the rest of the people in the cities of Judah' (cf. *NEB*). This may help to explain how the continuation of the Ezra story (Neh. 8) came to be transferred from its original place following Ezr. 8 to its present setting.

## II. EZRA'S ACTIVITY (continued) 7:73b–9:37

Nehemiah's memoirs have temporarily ceased at 7:73a, and in the section that follows the principal figure is plainly Ezra; it is doubtful whether Nehemiah plays any part here at all (cf. on 8:9). These chapters, whether a light revision by the Chronicler of Ezra's own memoirs, or an independent account by the Chronicler on the basis of a narrative about Ezra, were clearly associated at an earlier stage with the Ezra narratives of Ezr. 7–10. Here the dates given in the text are of great value. In Ezr. 7–10 we find that Ezra left Babylonia on 1.I.7 (i.e. on the first day of the first month of the seventh regnal year) of an Artaxerxes and arrived in Jerusalem on 1.V.7 (Ezr. 7:9), and that during his dealings with the mixed marriages the dates 20.IX.(7) (Ezr. 10:9), 1.X.(7) (Ezr. 10:16), and 1.I.(8) (Ezr. 10:17) occur. Two questions arise: What was Ezra doing between 1.V.7 and about 20.IX.7?; and, Was the setting up of the mixed marriages commission really his first public action after arriving in Judea?

If we turn to the dates in the book of Nehemiah, we find that Nehemiah obtained permission to visit Jerusalem on (1).I.20 of Artaxerxes, 445 BC (2:1), and that he completed the building of the walls on 25.VI.(20) (6:15). If we follow the natural course of the narrative, it appears that in the same year, the events of Ch. 7–9 took place: the law-reading assembly on 1.VII (8:2), the subsequent instruction on 2.VII (8:13), the festival of booths on 15–22.VII (8:18), and the penitential assembly on 24.VII (9:1). A further question arises here: Why did Ezra not hold an assembly for the reading of the law until 1.VII.20 of Artaxerxes, although he had been commissioned by the king thirteen years previously to establish the Jewish law as state law in Judea (Ezr. 7:7ff.)?

It may be that we simply do not know the answers to these questions, and most of those scholars who accept the view taken in this commentary, that Ezra's activity preceded that of Nehemiah (see Introduction, IV), are content to leave these problems unsolved. But the suggestion which is adopted here is that the events of these chapters actually occurred in the year of *Ezra's* arrival in Jerusalem (458 BC), the seventh year of Artaxerxes I, and not in the year of *Nehemiah's* arrival (445 BC), the twentieth year of Artaxerxes. If that were so, all three of the questions raised above would be satisfactorily answered: the first months after Ezra's arrival were spent in teaching the law, his first concern was with the law as a whole and not with the relatively minor matter of one hundred or so marriages, and he carried out promptly the commission with which he had been charged by the Persian king.

There are, admittedly, two objections to this reconstruction of events. One is that Nehemiah appears in Ezra's law-reading ceremony at 8:9, which he can hardly have done in 458 BC (since he did not arrive until 445). The other is that this reconstruction supposes that the events of the book of Nehemiah are not in chronological sequence. To the first it may be replied that a close inspection of 8:9–10 makes it doubtful whether Nehemiah's name originally appeared in this narrative, and to the second that this would not be the first time that the narrative of these books has been recounted out of chronological sequence. For in Ezr. 4:6–23 the Chronicler has introduced material which is not relevant chronologically, in order to illustrate the theme which he is developing. In a similar way, it may be suggested, the Chronicler told the story of Ezra's reading of the law and the penitential ceremony at this place, between the list of those entitled by birth to live in Jerusalem (ch. 7) and the actual repopulation of the city (ch. 11), in order to make the point that it was a community faithful to the law which Nehemiah brought to people the 'holy city' (11:1; see also on 12:27–43).

## EZRA'S READING OF THE LAW
### 7:73b–8:12

The two months since Ezra's arrival in Jerusalem (Ezr. 7:9) had not been wasted: he had been privately preparing for the public reading of the law. He would have had to choose suitable portions (cf. on v. 3) and, more importantly, to instruct his Levite assistants in the meaning and application of the law (cf. on vv. 7f.). Similar careful private preparations for dealing with the mixed marriages are hinted at in Ezr. 10:3 (cf. on 9:1–2).

The day he chose for the law-reading was **the first day of the seventh month** (v. 2), the holy day at the beginning of Israel's most important festival month. At a special assembly the reading of portions of the law caused dismay among the people, presumably because they realised how far short of the divine will they fell. This was not a new law that Ezra was propagating; the attentiveness and concern of the people is due to the fact that this traditional law is now to be rigorously applied with the full authority of the Persian government.

**73b.** The **seventh month,** on the view adopted here, is in the seventh year of Artaxerxes, i.e. 458 BC if Artaxerxes I is meant, 398 if Artaxerxes II. (It is 445 BC, however, if the activity of Ezra and Nehemiah overlapped.)

**8:1. the square before the Water Gate** (cf. on 3:24–27): perhaps the same as the 'temple square' of Ezr. 10:9 (cf. the 'eastern square', 2 Chr. 29:4). But some have thought that this ceremony was designedly held outside the temple area in a non-sacral place so that even those who were ritually unclean could attend. As we have elsewhere observed (cf. on Ezr. 10:7–17), Ezra takes great care not to assert his authority, but organises the occasion in such a way as to make the reading of the law the responsibility of the people: **they told Ezra the scribe to bring the book;** who **they** are precisely is not important, since their function is to represent the people. **the book of the law of Moses** was brought by Ezra from Babylonia (cf. Ezr. 7:6, 14), its identity has been much debated, but it is very likely the Pentateuch as a whole in more or less its present form. So Wellhausen, *Prolegomena,* pp. 405–8; Schaeder, *Esra,* pp. 68f.; Rudolph, p. 169; Eissfeldt, p. 557. The priestly code alone is thought of by e.g. Meyer, *Entstehung,* pp. 206–16; Oesterley, *History,* II, p. 135; and Deuteronomy alone by e.g. Bowman, pp. 627, 734; U. Kellermann, *ZAW* 80 (1968), pp. 373–85. Ezra did not of course read all of the law-book (cf. v. 3), and if the closest parallels exist between Ezra's law and Deuteronomy, that does not mean that Ezra propagated only the Deuteronomic law, but only signifies that the style of Deuteronomy was most suited for public reading (cf. G. von Rad's view of Deuteronomy as a homiletic presentation of older cultic and legal material; *Studies in Deuteronomy* [1953]; *IDB,* I, pp. 831–8). There is little doubt that the Chronicler himself would have intended 'the book of the law of Moses' to refer to the whole Pentateuch.

**2.** Ezra (as in Ezr. 7:6, 11, 21) is both **scribe** and **priest. the**

**assembly:** Though the formal cultic term is used of the gathering, the place of meeting is itself enough to show that this was not a regular festival celebration. **the first day of the seventh month** (Tishri): Though later celebrated as new year's day, it was probably still only one of the new moon days, albeit perhaps the most important, being the seventh (cf. Num. 29:1–6; 10:10; Lev. 23:24f.). The hypothesis of a pre-exilic new year festival on Tishri 1 is widely held, especially due to the influence of S. Mowinckel (cf., e.g., *The Psalms in Israel's Worship* [1962]), but lacks concrete attestation (cf., e.g., de Vaux, *Ancient Israel*, pp. 502ff.; D. J. A. Clines, 'New Year', *IDBS*, pp. 626–8). The date, if in 458 BC, was October 2; if in 398, September 28. **women** and children (**all who could hear with understanding,** obviously the sons and daughters of 10:28) are specifically mentioned because their presence at religious gatherings was perhaps unusual, though they attended such readings of the law (Dt. 31:12; Jos. 8:35; and cf. 2 Chr. 20:13). See also C. J. Vos, *Woman in Old Testament Worship* (1968), pp. 133–67.

**3.** The attentiveness of the people was remarkable, considering the five or six hours' duration of the assembly, from **early morning,** lit. 'the light', to midday. This is a summarising verse; the details follow in vv. 4–8.

**4–8.** As may be expected, this ceremony is parallel at several points with the Chronicler's account of the reading of the 'book of the law' under Josiah (2 Chr. 34:14–32) and especially with the account of Solomon's assembly (2 Chr. 5–7). Here the occasion is the seventh month (v. 2; cf. 1 Chr. 5:3), the reader stood on a platform (v. 4; cf. 2 Chr. 6:13), the people stood at the blessing (v. 5; cf. 2 Chr. 6:3), and dispersed with joy (v. 12; cf. 2 Chr. 7:10). These parallels need not imply that one account was the literary prototype of the other; sufficient causes for the details of each ceremony arise from the historical situations. But we cannot know to what extent the details of such ceremonies were traditional in the Chronicler's day or to what extent he projected the customs of his own time back on to earlier occasions.

**4. pulpit** (*miḡdāl*, lit. 'tower'), or rather 'platform' (*NEB*): It enabled Ezra to be seen and heard, and as well seated thirteen dignitaries. Their seat of honour facing the congregation was probably the prototype of the 'best seats in the synagogue' hankered after by scribes of Jesus' day (Mt. 23:6). 'How sat the elders in the synagogue? Their face was toward the people, and their back to the holy (i.e. the Torah-cupboard)' (Tosefta, *Meg.* 4.21 [227]). We might expect the same number of persons on either hand; perhaps the name **Meshullam** (*mšlm*), missing in LXX (1 Esd. 9:44), should be removed as a scribal corruption of **on his left hand** (*mśm'lw*);

there would have thus been a representative body of twelve men. But, oddly, there are thirteen Levites also (v. 7). Ezra's council of reference, whose presence lent weight to the occasion, probably included laymen and priests; though none can be certainly identified without his patronym, **Anaiah** and **Hashum** could be lay family heads (cf. lay ancestors with those names in 10:22 and 7:22). **Hilkiah** occurs elsewhere (12:7, 21; Ezr. 7:1) as a priestly name.

**5.** When Ezra **opened the book,** or rather, 'unrolled the scroll', the people stood up, probably following an already established custom of standing for the reading of scripture (cf. 9:3; and the standing before a king, e.g. Dan. 1:19), and apparently remained standing throughout the ceremony.

**6.** The blessing would probably be a brief thanksgiving for the law, such as are given in the Talmud for use before reading scripture (TB, *Berakot* 11b). The rather unusual title **the great God** (cf. 9:32; Dt. 10:17; Jer. 32:18; perhaps Ezr. 5:8) may preserve some of Ezra's blessing formula. **Amen,** lit. 'it is firm, established', signifies the assent of the listener to what has just been said (e.g. 1 Kg. 1:36; Jer. 11:5); liturgically, it marks the congregation's assent to the utterance of its leader (e.g. Dt. 27:15). The double **Amen, Amen** (e.g. Num. 5:22; Ps. 41:14), the *NT* 'verily, verily' (there, however, at the beginning of a speech), is a strengthening. **lifting up their hands:** cf. on Ezr. 9:5. **bowed:** the first stage of prostration, i.e. **faces to the ground,** a more submissive posture than Ezra's (Ezr. 9:5; 10:1). **worshipped** (*hištaḥᵃwâ*) here refers simply to the physical act of prostration.

**7–8.** Most of the thirteen men named here bear the names of Levites known from elsewhere in Neh. (seven in 10:9–13, four in 9:4f., two in 11:16). **helped the people to understand the law:** The traditional interpretation has been that they translated or paraphrased the Hebrew text into Aramaic, which would have been more easily understood by the ex-Babylonian Jews. The rabbis therefore saw here the first reference to the Targums; see TB, *Megillah* 18b; *Genesis Rabbah* 36.8 (and cf. K. Hruby, 'La survivance de la langue hébraïque pendant la période post-exilienne', in *Ecole des Langues Orientales Anciennes de l'Institut Catholique de Paris. Mémorial du Cinquantenaire 1914–1964* [1964], pp. 109–20). This may well have been the case, though the text says nothing directly about translation, and some have thought that the Levites' task was not translation but explanation (for their teaching function, cf. v. 9; 1 Chr. 17:7ff.; 35:13). The key word is *mᵉpōrāš* (v. 8), **clearly,** which literally signifies 'separated, split up', i.e. with distinct pronunciation, or, more probably, with pauses between each verse. Certainly the Hebrew text was read this way in the later

synagogue practice in order to give time for an Aramaic translation
to be made (P. Billerbeck, *ZNW* 55 [1964], p. 155); and sentence
by sentence translation is also implied by the equivalent Aramaic
term *mᵉp̄āraš* (Ezr. 4:18). But it is equally possible that only explanatory interpretation is involved in the present context. It is strange
that Ezra himself is not said to have read the law; some have
suggested that before the Chronicler edited the narrative the first
verb of v. 8 was 'he read'—which would certainly be a natural
division of labour. Even so, the mechanics of the operation are
unclear. Did the thirteen Levites, each with a copy of Ezra's Pentateuchal selections, move among the people (**the people remained
in their places**), expounding and/or translating to various groups of
people? Or did perhaps all the Levites stand on 'the stairs of the
Levites' (9:4) and cantillate Ezra's text in unison? (cf. M. Gertner,
*VT* 10 [1960], pp. 244–8; S. Levin, *JBL* 87 [1968], p. 70; A. Cody,
*A History of Old Testament Priesthood* [1969], p. 189 n. 39). Such a
form of recitation may have been necessary to enable the sound to
carry throughout the large and probably noisy assembly; for if all
those of an age of understanding were there (v. 2), the young
children can hardly have been left at home.

**9.** The weeping which accompanied the reading of the law is
reminiscent of Josiah's reaction on hearing **the words of the law** (2
Chr. 34:19); the reason is probably similar: 'Great is the wrath of
the LORD that is poured out on us, because our fathers have not
kept the word of the LORD' (34:20). Ezra can hardly have been
propounding a new law, but reminding the people of a law which
they already recognised as authoritative, though it was no doubt
imperfectly known and obeyed. **Nehemiah:** Mention of him here is
the only evidence (together with 12:36 and perhaps 12:26) that
the activities of Ezra and Nehemiah were contemporaneous. But
circumstances and text are both questionable. Nehemiah appears
nowhere else in ch. 8–9, and there is no particular reason for an
intervention by him at this point. Further, the verb **said** is singular
(as also in v. 10), which suggests that only Ezra was originally
mentioned here. The word for **governor** (*tiršāṯā'; cf. on Ezr. 2:63)
is never used elsewhere for Nehemiah; but that proves little. It is
not unreasonable to regard the reference to Nehemiah as due to the
editor or scribe who removed ch. 8–9 to the present position. The
only alternatives are to emend the date in Ezr. 7:7–8, or to suppose
that Ezra, having arrived in 458 BC, did not read the law until 445,
when Nehemiah appeared on the scene (see further, Introduction,
IV). **and the Levites who taught the people:** This phrase should
probably also be regarded as a gloss, though their action here makes
good sense (cf. v. 11 where the reference to them is more probably

original). **do not mourn or weep:** Though repentance is a fitting response, this is not the time for a public demonstration of grief, for it is a day **holy to the LORD,** and therefore shares, as it is able, his character, which is not grim or vengeful, but joyous (on **holy,** cf. on Ezr. 8:28). So much for the supposedly baleful God of the *OT* and the sombre religion of the post-exilic age! The joy of festive occasions is strongly marked in Deuteronomy (e.g. 12:12; 14:26; 16:11, 15; cf. 2 Chr. 29:36: 30:25), from which Ezra had principally drawn his readings.

**10.** It is not clear whether the people have been expecting to celebrate a festival. Those **for whom nothing is prepared** can hardly mean those caught out by the short notice, for everyone must have known it was a festival day; they must be the poor and foreigners, who are to be provided for at festival times (Dt. 14:29; 26:12f.). **portions** were usually sent as well to one's friends at festivals (cf. 1 Sam. 1:4; Est. 9:19, 22). **fat:** regarded in the east as the choicest part of the meat, which was in any case eaten only on special occasions. **the joy of the LORD is your strength:** i.e. 'joy in Yahweh, the great and gracious God, is the best defence against his wrath, for "there is no refuge against God except in him" ' (Rudolph, p. 149, quoting *Quran* 9.118).

**11.** As in v. 8, the Levites transmit Ezra's instructions to the people.

**12.** Superfluous to say that the people **understood** the instructions to make holiday; rather, they understood (*bîn*, lit. 'discerned') the inner connection between holy-day and holiday (v. 9).

CELEBRATION OF THE FESTIVAL OF BOOTHS

8:13–18

The law-reading continued next day with a smaller audience, the family heads and temple officials, who lived in Jerusalem (cf. 11.1), and had not like most people gone home to the country (v. 12). Ezra, who was here acting as 'scribe' in the Jewish sense of student and teacher of the law (cf. on Ezr. 7:6), saw to it that the prescriptions of the law for the current month were perfectly understood by the leaders. Most important was the observance of the week-long festival of booths (tabernacles) beginning on the 15th. It is quite mistaken to suppose that 'the narrative assumes that the people were absolutely ignorant of the law prescribing the Feast of Booths' (as Batten, p. 363). The Chronicler has already recorded an observance of it (Ezr. 3:4); the only novelty about it lay in the manner of its performance (cf. on v. 17).

The absence of reference to the Day of Atonement, prescribed for the 10th of this month (Lev. 16:29–34; 23:26–32; Num. 29:7–11), is surprising; some conclude that in Ezra's law-book the date was not fixed, others that Ezra transferred its celebration to the 24th (ch. 9; but does this describe a day of atonement?), and others that it was observed in the customary manner and so called for no special mention. (See respectively, Rudolph, p. 153; M. Kegel, *Die Kultus-reformation des Esra* [1921], p. 123; F. Ahlemann, *ZAW* 59 [1942f.], pp. 88, 92.)

**13. heads of fathers' houses:** a term not found in the Nehemiah memoirs; cf. on Ezr. 1:5.

**14–15.** The festival law (**written** in Exod. 23:16; 34:22; Lev. 23:33–36, 39–43; Num. 29:12–38; Dt. 16:13–15; cf. Ezek. 45:25) specifies the **seventh month** only in Lev. 23 and Num. 29, while the commands to **dwell in booths** and to cut down tree **branches** occur only in Lev. 23, and the conclusion of the festival with 'a solemn assembly' 'on the eighth day' (v. 18) is prescribed only in Lev. 23 and Num. 29. The presumption is therefore that it was Lev. 23 that was being studied. Nevertheless, it is not said there, or anywhere else, that the leaders should **publish and proclaim** the festival in all their towns, nor do the trees prescribed there coincide with those here, nor does the Leviticus passage say what is to be done with the boughs. All this may mean that Ezra's copy of Levit-icus differed in minor points from our own, but the last item leads us to think that we are dealing here not with variant texts, but with a contemporary reinterpretation of the law. Ezra would doubtless have argued that what the law implied it also commanded. Why else would boughs have been gathered at the festival of booths except to make booths? How else could the people learn their duty if the leaders did not publish it? And as for the names of the trees, the present list may reflect Ezra's interpretation of the law (cf. Ezr. 9:1) in the light of which types of trees were now available. Mentioned both here and in Lev. 23:40 are the **palm**, not common in the highlands (though growing in the valleys about Jerusalem; cf. also Jn 12:13), and **leafy trees**, not a specific type. The types mentioned here and not in Leviticus are the **olive**, the pine (not **wild olive**, *RSV*, *NEB*), probably Aleppo pine (*pinus halepensis*), one of the common Palestinian evergreens (*IDB*, II, pp. 293f.), and **myrtle**, an evergreen shrub, whereas Leviticus mentions also 'goodly trees', lit. 'trees of splendour', and 'willows of the brook', i.e. poplars. The Leviticus passage may have been interpreted by Ezra as referring to categories of trees.

**16–17.** What was so novel about this celebration? We know that the festival was held in Solomon's time (2 Chr. 7:8ff.; 8:13), appar-ently in Hosea's (Hos. 12:9), and plainly in Zerubbabel's (Ezr. 3:4).

Yet **from the days of Jeshua** b. **Nun** (Jeshua being a variant of Joshua) **the people of Israel had not done so** (cf. 2 Kg. 23:22; 2 Chr. 35:18); this Jeshua can hardly be a mistake for Jeshua b. Jozadak, high priest in Zerubbabel's time (Ezr. 3:2). Most think the text must be referring to a centralised celebration both of sacrifices and living in booths, such as would have last been possible when Israel was encamped at Gilgal in Joshua's time. On this view, the reference in v. 16 to the erection of booths only in Jerusalem would make sense. Mention of house rooftops, a cool sleeping-place for family or guests (cf. 1 Sam. 9:25) in summer, and courtyards (see H. K. Beebe, 'Ancient Palestinian Dwellings', *BA* 31 [1968], pp. 38–58), shows that Jerusalem was not entirely desolate (cf. on 7:4). **Water Gate, Gate of Ephraim:** in east and north walls respectively; cf. on 3:26, 6. **all the assembly . . . those who had returned:** As so often, the Chronicler regards all Judeans as returned exiles (cf., e.g., Ezr. 4:1, 4); the two phrases are in apposition. The rejoicing associated with this festival later produced a miniature festival called 'Rejoicing in the Law' (Simḥat Torah).

**18.** The daily reading of the law is not prescribed for the festival, though in Dt. 31:10–13 the law is to be read in every sabbatical year at the festival, and some have thought 458/7 BC was such a sabbatical year (so J. Morgenstern, 'Studies in Calendars', *HUCA* 10 [1935], p. 70 n. 107; F. Mezzacasa, 'Esdras, Nehemias y el Año Sabatico', *Rev. Bibl.* 23 [1961], pp. 1–8, 82–96). In any case, an extraordinary reading in a non-sabbatical year would have been perfectly legitimate—even if there had not been a custom of annual law-reading in pre-exilic times (as supposed, for example, by A. Weiser, *The Psalms* [1962], pp. 35–52). The text may in fact indicate a replacement of the sabbatical law-reading by an annual ceremony (Ackroyd, pp. 297f.).

What a strange outcome there has been to the grand commission of Ezra by the Persian king to propagate the law of Moses among the Jewish people! All that has happened, it seems, is that the Jews have been reminded to celebrate a national festival; the reading of the law has accomplished nothing but the promotion of a ritual observance. Was it for this that Ezra was sent to Judea? And yet we must ask whether this is all that has really happened. Is it not that Ezra has been teaching the people to obey the law in all its particulars even when it goes against their own best feelings of what is appropriate for such an occasion? Their inclination, a perfectly proper and natural one, is to respond to the reading of the law with penitence and sorrow (v. 9). But overriding this inclination is the fact that the law prescribes rejoicing for this day (vv. 10f.), so rejoicing there must be. Here is a clamp on spontaneity, to be sure,

but at the same time there is an admirable earnestness to be faithful
to the letter of God's law.

## A DAY OF REPENTANCE AND ITS PENITENTIAL PSALM

### 9:1–37

It is unfortunately impossible to determine with certainty the historical setting of this chapter. In its present context, the day of repentance was the 24th of the seventh month (v. 1), but it seems very
strange that an eight-day festival of joy should be followed, after an
interval of only one day, by a special day for national mourning.

Perhaps the simplest solution to the difficulty is that on this, the
first free day after the joyful festival of booths, an opportunity is
given for the public manifestation of that grief which the people
had felt as they heard the law read (8:9, 11) (so, e.g., Kellermann,
pp. 33f.). The sequence probably seems odd to us only because we
do not fully understand Hebrew psychology; and in any case the
definitive pattern of festivals for the seventh month had the sequence
joyful (new year), penitential (atonement), joyful (tabernacles), all
within a period of three weeks. Whether this setting puts the episode
in 458, 445, or 398 BC must depend upon the decision made about
ch. 8, with which, on this view, it is closely linked.

Many scholars, however, have found the key to the setting of the
chapter in the statement: **the Israelites separated themselves from
all foreigners** (v. 2). This may seem to refer to the dissolution of
the mixed marriages (Ezr. 9–10), in which case the day of repentance
may be regarded as the sequel to Ezr. 10. If so, the month is not
the seventh month of Ezra's first year in Jerusalem, as in ch. 8,
but the first month of his second year, since the mixed marriages
commission sat until the first day of that month. The three-week
interval between the conclusion of their work and the national day
of penitence on the 24th (19 April 457 or 16 May 397, in two of
the possible years) would give time for the divorces to be made.

The difficulties with this view are that it lays too much weight
on v. 2a, that the prayer has no specific relation to the episode of
the mixed marriages, and that one of the leading Levites here,
Pethahiah (v. 5), seems to be one of those who had contracted a
mixed marriage (Ezr. 10:23); he could hardly have taken such a
prominent part if he had been found guilty only a few months
previously.

In sum, fewest problems are raised if we connect this chapter
with ch. 8, and locate both after the events of Ezr. 9. But why, if
this chapter belongs to the Ezra material, is Ezra not mentioned?
It must be because this ceremony is represented as a popular reaction

to the reading of the law, not a service conducted by Ezra; there is no prescription of such an occasion in Ezra's law-book. The Levites naturally figure as the religious leaders of the people, while Ezra remains in the background.

## THE ASSEMBLY

### 9:1–4

**1.** Several of the usual rituals of mourning were also used to express penitence; here we find **fasting** (cf. on Ezr. 8:21), a stylised starving to death, and the wearing of **sackcloth**, a coarse dark cloth, which probably represented the nakedness of death (cf. Job 1:21), though again in a stylised fashion for decency's sake (at one time it was apparently used as an undergarment, perhaps a loincloth; cf., e.g., Gen. 37:34). Putting **earth** upon one's head (cf. Jos. 7:6; Job 2:12) probably indicates that one regards oneself as dead and buried. See further, E. F. de Ward, 'Mourning Customs in 1, 2 Samuel', *JSS* 23 (1972), pp. 1–27, 145–66; E. Lipiński, *La liturgie pénitentielle dans la Bible* (1969).

**2. the Israelites separated themselves from all foreigners:** It seems difficult to restrict the reference to the divorcing of foreign wives, and strange that if their penitence was for the mixed marriages that their confession should be of their **sins** in general, and of the **iniquity of their forefathers,** especially when there is no hint that marriage with foreign women had been practised by previous generations. It is strange too that the prayer of confession should say nothing either of the mixed marriages themselves or of offences in the past against the purity and separateness of Israel. It seems better therefore to regard this separation simply as a preparation for a ceremony involving those fully Jewish. If the connection between this chapter and ch. 8 is preserved, it is plain why this separation is mentioned: at the previous assembly, the festival of booths, all inhabitants (theoretically) were present (8:1f.), whether Jews, half-Jews, or sojourners (resident aliens), who while obliged to keep the law (cf. Num. 15:15f.; Dt. 29:10–13) were not in every respect equal to native Israelites (cf., e.g., Dt. 14:21; Exod. 12:48; Lev. 25:47–55), and had no need to confess the sins of Israel as their own. As R. North comments: 'It is not really separatist to exclude others from our acknowledgement of faults whose guilt we do not wish to imply extends to them' (p. 437).

**3–4.** The course of this service is far from clear. Did **they** (the people) stand in their place while others (perhaps the Levites) **read from the book of the law?** And was there an act of confession both before (v. 2) and after (vv. 3, 6–37) the law-reading? What did the first group of Levites say (v. 4), and how are the two Levitical groups, which have several names in common, related? Rudolph frankly excises v. 3 as the work of an editor who wanted to represent the assembly of ch. 9 (originally unrelated to ch. 8 on Rudolph's view) as similar to the law-reading assembly of ch. 8. However, the reading of the law, with its divine commands and threatened punishments, is one of the more intelligible elements in a service of confession, and must be allowed to stand.

What is depicted is a service of the same duration as that in 8:3, the six hours or so being divided into law-reading and confession. Ezra and the Levites together are represented in 8:3, 8 as reading the law, so presumably that is what is intended here. The confession of sins in v. 2 is probably just an anticipatory generalisation of the confession itself (vv. 3*b*, 4*b*, 6–37). The 'worship' accompanying confession refers to the posture of prostration (cf. 8:6). The mournful appeal (**cried:** z*ʿq* = ṣʿ*q*), the technical term of the cry of the oppressed for deliverance; cf. on 5:1) is the 'confession' contained in vv. 6–37. **the stairs of the Levites:** These are otherwise unknown, but they may be the wooden platform of 8:4 (though here it is occupied by laymen and priests as well).

<br>

SUMMONS TO PRAYER

9:5a

Following the summarising account of the 'confession' comes a fuller account. The public confession is prefaced by a summons to stand and to **bless the LORD** (cf. Ps. 106:1). Since in the two Levite lists (vv. 4, 5), each with eight names, five Levites appear twice, it is reasonable to assume that the same group is referred to, and that the repetition of the names, and the differences between the lists, should be accounted for as scribal errors. **Jeshua, Bani,** or Binnui, and **Kadmiel** usually head lists of Levites (10:9; 12:8; cf. 8:7; perhaps also 7:43; 12:24; Ezr. 3:9). **Shebaniah** and **Sherebiah** (cf. 10:12) change places. The other six names, which appear only once, are all attested elsewhere as Levite names.

**Bless the LORD from everlasting to everlasting** is an unparalleled summons, and strictly illogical, since commands cannot refer to the past; we might expect 'from now and for evermore' (cf. Ps. 115:18). Moreover, the first half of the exhortation is addressed to the people, whereas the second half suddenly turns to address God. *NEB* neatly solves the problem by adding 'saying' after **the LORD your God,** by reading 'is blessed' (*brwk*) instead of 'and let them bless' (*wybrkw*), and by linking **from everlasting to everlasting** with 'thy glorious

name is blessed'. Verses 5b–37 are thus the prayer in which the
Levites lead the people.

## THE LEVITICAL PRAYER

### 9:5b–37

There seems no good reason to reject the clear implication of the
Hebrew text that this was a prayer by Levites (cf. on v. 6). This is
implied in the view taken here that this prayer is identical with the
confession (v. 3) and levitical cry for deliverance (v. 4) already
mentioned.

The prayer draws so widely on older literature that it is impossible
to pinpoint its authorship. Its style is unlike that of Ezra's prayer
(Ezr. 9) and it does not show much evidence of the distinctive
phraseology of the Chronicler. Its attribution to Levites, however,
may point to the role of Levites in preserving the prophetic and
Deuteronomic traditions, which form the bulk of the prayer. Cf.
G. von Rad, 'The Levitical Sermon in I and II Chronicles' (1934),
in *The Problem of the Hexateuch* (1966), pp. 267–80; O. Plöger,
'Reden und Gebete im deuteronomistischen und chronistischen
Geschichtswerk', *Aus der Spätzeit des Alten Testaments* (1971),
pp. 50–66.

The subject of the prayer, as of the book of Judges, Ps. 78 and
106, and Ac. 7, is the history of Israel viewed as a story of apostasy.
The structure is (i) divine blessing (vv. 6–15), (ii) blessing continued
in spite of rebellion (vv. 16–25), (iii) rebellion in spite of blessing
(vv. 26–31), (iv) appeal for deliverance (vv. 32–37). The centre of
gravity is v. 32: **let not all the hardship seem little to thee**, i.e.
release us from the evil of foreign domination. The reading of the
law has thus provoked both repentance for national sin (vv. 6–31)
and appeal that the promises of the covenant (v. 32) may be fulfilled
(vv. 32–37); the prayer has thus been a confession (v. 3) and a 'cry'
(v. 4).

The prayer is a patchwork of citations from earlier Hebrew literature. The author, whether the Chronicler himself or a Levite, draws
upon a wide range of texts to elaborate his themes, many of which
are not treated elsewhere in the Chronicler's work (e.g. creation,
the patriarchs, exodus, the wilderness journeys).

We are impressed in these books with the professional equanimity
of Ezra and Nehemiah towards the Persian government, but in this
prayer, if in any sense it belongs to the period, we have another
insight into the mood of the time when, in spite of all the blessings
of the restoration, it could never be forgotten that Israel was still a
subject people. Ezra himself lets slip a phrase or two which shows

he shared this feeling (Ezr. 9:9f.: 'our bondage'; 'we are bondmen'), though he may not have been so tactless as to imply, as the present prayer does, that Persian kings are no less tyrannical than the notorious Assyrians (vv. 32, 37).

The rhythmic character of the prayer is apparent even in translation and it is not surprising that some have analysed it as a metrical psalm, complete with strophic structure. Rudolph discovers in vv. 9–37 (omitting v. 22) a psalm of 71 lines, consisting of three strophes of 16 + 8 + 8 (= 32) lines preceding, and four strophes of 8 + 8 + 8 + 8 (= 32) lines following, a central seven-line strophe (vv. 24f.). This may be correct, but it would be unwise in our present state of knowledge about Hebrew poetry to conclude that the centre of the strophic structure is also the centre of the thought of the poem.

### DIVINE BLESSING FROM CREATION TO SINAI
### 9:6–15

Verses 6–11 now form part of the Jewish morning liturgy; the whole prayer had a considerable influence on the synagogue liturgy (see L. J. Liebreich, *HUCA* 32 [1961], pp. 227–37).

**6. And Ezra said:** added by *RSV* from LXX, but without warrant; LXX equally gratuitously added the same phrase in 8:15. **Thou art the LORD** (Yahweh), **thou alone:** an impossible translation, since no other god ever claimed to be Yahweh; translate 'Thou, O Yahweh, art the only (God),' a reference to the incomparability of Yahweh. Probably *'lhym*, 'God', should be inserted after 'Yahweh' (as in 2 Kg. 19:19; 1QIs. 37:20), or else *'lyhm* should be read for *yhwh* (as in 2 Kg. 19:15; Is. 37:16). On the idea, see C. J. Labuschagne, *The Incomparability of Yahweh in the Old Testament* (1966). **heaven . . . earth . . . seas:** The threefold cosmos is a psalmic image (Ps. 69:34; 96:11; 146:6). **the heaven of heavens** (also Dt. 10:14; 2 Chr. 2:5; 6:18), probably a superlative (cf. *NEB*). Used together with **heaven** by itself, it seems to envisage a plurality of heavens as in later Jewish thought (1 Enoch 3–19; cf. 2 Cor. 12:2). **their host:** The heavenly bodies, often themselves objects of worship (Dt. 4:19), here are worshippers of Yahweh (cf. Ps. 148:2ff.). **preserved:** lit. 'keepest alive' (cf. 1 Sam. 2:6; Ps. 104:24–30). Reference to the creation in such summary histories of Israel is unique. It presupposes the completion of the Pentateuch. Its function here seems to be to stress God's faithfulness to his creation (**preservest**) as also to his chosen Abraham, himself also faithful (v. 8).

**7–8.** Important here is the promise of the land, and God's faithful (**thou art righteous**) fulfilment of his promise. The faithfulness of

Abraham (Gen. 15:6; 22:18*b*) as the other party to the covenant is also stressed, as a foil to the subsequent theme of the infidelity of Israel. The change of Abraham's name signalises the promise (Gen. 17:5–8).

**9–15.** From Abraham to the conquest the goal is the fulfilment of the promise of the land, achieved in v. 15*b*. Even the bondage in Egypt, the gravest threat to the fulfilment of the promise, does not spell disaster for God's plans; his part in those events is remembered only with praise. The wonders of the desert journey are viewed here simply as the divine means by which safe arrival in the land was assured. Even the law-giving at Sinai (vv. 13f.), sandwiched here—out of chronological order!—between divine provisions for Israel's physical survival (vv. 12, 15), appears as a gracious gift to preserve Israel's life. The law is viewed not as some heavy obligation but as a gift for the well-being of the people.

**9.** Cf. Exod. 3:7; 14:10. **cry:** cf. on v. 4.

**10. signs and wonders,** especially against the Egyptians, is typically Deuteronomic language (e.g. Dt. 4:34; 6:22; closest to v. 10*a* is Dt. 29:2f.; 34:11). The reason for the destruction of the Egyptians, that they **acted insolently,** is given uniquely by Jethro (Exod. 18:11). **thou didst get thee a name:** cf. Exod. 9:16; but more relevantly, Jer. 32:20 (cf. Is. 63:12, 14; Dan. 9:15; Rom. 9:17).

**11.** Phrases are combined from Ps. 78:13 (cf. Exod. 14:21; Isa. 63:12); Exod. 14:22, 23; 15:5, 10 (**mighty** (*'az*) seems to come from Isa. 43:16).

**12.** Mostly derived from Exod. 13:21, but **the way in which they should go** is Deuteronomic (Dt. 1:33; cf. Ps. 32:8).

**13.** The order of the law-giving (Exod. 19–23) and the manna and water from the rock (Exod. 16, 17) is reversed—possibly to set the law within the framework of divine gifts (vv. 12, 15). Verse 13*a* is from Exod. 19:18, 20; **from heaven** recalls 20:22; Dt. 4:36. **right ordinances . . . :** most reminiscent of Ps. 119 (cf. vv. 137, 142, 68); cf. also Rom. 7:12.

**14. thy holy sabbath:** specifically mentioned because of its importance in the post-exilic period (cf. on 13:15, 22). The closest parallel in language is Ezek. 20:11f., where also the life-giving purpose of the law is stressed.

**15.** The reference is to Exod. 16:4; 17:6 (cf. Num. 20:8; Ps. 105:40). **to go in to possess the land:** a Deuteronomic expression (e.g. Dt. 11:31). **the land which thou hast sworn:** lit. 'lifted up the hand', the gesture of an oath. **to give them:** the language of Exod. 6:8; Ezek. 20:6, 28, 42 (with a different verb, cf. Gen. 24:7; 26:3). Now 'the gifts and the call of God are irrevocable' (Rom.

11:29), and throughout this prayer we must recognise the contemporary political implications for the post-exilic period of this rehearsal of ancient history.

### BLESSING CONTINUED IN SPITE OF REBELLION
### 9:16–25

This section, like vv. 9–15, has as its goal the fulfilment of the promise, the settlement of the land. Here the theme is how God's promise is not thwarted even by Israel's unfaithfulness (cf. Rom. 3:3). And how remarkable that unfaithfulness was! They even made plans, clean against God's plan, to return to their bondage in Egypt (v. 17). God's response was simply to renew the gifts already given: pillar and cloud, manna and water, and the instructing Spirit to complement the law (vv. 19f.). God's patience proved more durable than their impatience (v. 21), and even before they entered the promised land, he gave them lands as a bonus (v. 22) and many children (v. 23), as a sign that the promise to Abraham (Gen. 12:2; 15:5; 17:4ff.) was already beginning to take effect.

**16.** Just like the Egyptians (v. 10), they **acted presumptuously** (*RSV* obscures the repetition of the verb; but cf. *NEB*), but how different were the consequences (v. 11, contrast vv. 17, 19–25); **they and our fathers**: rather, 'they, that is, our fathers' (cf. *NEB*). The language of vv. 16f. is largely Deuteronomic; for **presumptuously** cf. Dt. 1:43; 17:13; **stiffened their neck,** like the ox who resists the guidance of the yoke, cf. Dt. 9:6, 13; 10:16.

**17.** Phrases are borrowed from Jer. 11:10 (cf. 1 Sam. 8:19); Ps. 105:5 (cf. 78:11, 32; 106:21f.); Num. 14:4, where the thought is as good as the deed; Exod. 34:6 (cf. Ps. 86:15; 103:8). **in Egypt:** *RSV, NEB* emend *bmrym*, 'in their rebellion', to *bmṣrym*, following LXX and some MSS. **forsake:** cf. on Ezr. 9:9.

**18.** Reference is to Exod. 32, especially v. 4. **great blasphemies** (*ne'āṣâ*) refer to the faithless murmuring for a leader to take them back to Egypt (Num. 14:11; *nā'aṣ*, *RSV* 'despise').

**19–20.** The other wonders of the desert journeys were repeated (**cloud** and **pillar,** cf. Num. 10:34; 14:14; **manna,** Num. 11:6–9; **water,** Num. 20:7–11), but the law-giving was unrepeatable, so in the place of that *torah* (instruction) stands the **Spirit to instruct them** (Num. 11:17, 25). On the relation between spirit and wisdom, cf. P. van Imschoot, 'Sagesse et esprit dans l'AT', *RB* 47 (1938), pp. 23–49. **thy good spirit** (cf. Ps. 143:10): the holy Spirit (Ps. 51:11; Is. 63:10). The importance of this 'higher gift than grace' is marked by its position, parallel to the law in vv. 13f. There is a play on the words **didst . . . withold** (*māna'tā*) and **thy manna** (*man<sup>e</sup>kā*).

**21.** Dt. 2:7 and 8:4 (cf. 29:5) are drawn upon. A pleasant Jewish fancy of later times had it that 'the clouds of Divine Glory used to rub the dirt off their clothes and bleach them so that they looked like new white articles, and, also, their children, as they grew, their clothes grew with them, just like the clothes (shell) of a snail which grows with it' (Rashi on Dt. 8:4).

**22. Heshbon:** a city of Moab (Num. 21: 21–31; Dt. 2:24–35). **Bashan:** cf. Num. 21:32–35; Dt. 3:1–11. Reference to these conquests is not intrusive, since these wars east of the Jordan occurred before the conquest of Canaan proper. **didst allot to them every corner:** an obscure phrase, lit. 'didst divide them into corners' (*AV*); curiously, the troublesome word 'corner' (*pē'â*) occurs elsewhere in reference to Heshbon and Moab (Num. 24:17; Jer. 48:45) apparently as a term for a city (Ar) or cities ('*ārê*) of Moab (cf. the similar Num. 21:28.) Thus the allusion may be to Israel's settlement of Moab in Num. 21:24f. *NEB* connects *pē'â* with an Arabic cognate, and translates 'spoils of war'.

**23.** The language recalls Gen. 22:17 (cf. Dt. 1:10); the reference is to the census of the people in Num. 26.

**24.** The climax of this section of the prayer is also (as in vv. 8*b*, 15*b*) the possession of the land. That it was only the **descendants,** not those who had left Egypt (cf. Num. 14:30ff.), who **went in and possessed the land,** is glossed over, since the author is stressing the fulfilment of promise. There is a play on the words **subdue** (*kn'*) and **Canaanites** (*kn'nym*) (cf. on 'manna', v. 20). **as they would:** lit. 'according to their pleasure', a post-exilic phrase (cf. v. 37; Est. 9:5; Dan. 8:4; 11:3, 16, 36), usually with a bad sense.

**25.** The language is largely Deuteronomic (cf. Dt. 3:5; 6:11); see F. C. Fensham, 'An Ancient Tradition of the Fertility of Palestine', *PEQ* 98 (1966), pp. 166f. **became fat** has a derogatory sense (Dt. 32:15) connected with apostasy. **thy great goodness:** Even that can prove a 'springboard' for sin (cf. Rom. 7:11); already the theme of vv. 26–31 is hinted at.

### REBELLION IN SPITE OF BLESSING

### 9:26–31

Israel's history from conquest to exile is briefly sketched: it was a series of apostasies followed by deliverance, an understanding familiar to us from Deuteronomy and the Deuteronomistic history (Joshua—2 Kings).

**26. Nevertheless** (Heb. 'and') creates too strong a disjunction

between vv. 25 and 26; apostasy was already germinating in v. 25
**were disobedient and rebelled:** These verbs, not elsewhere linked,
form a further play on words (*wayyamᵉrû, wayyimrᵉḏû*). Elsewhere
it is said that Israel **cast** *Yahweh* **behind their back** (1 Kg. 14:9;
Ezek. 23:35); the **law** may here be a surrogate for Yahweh. The
conception of Israel (or Jerusalem) as prophet-murderers, and thus
of prophets as typically martyrs, so significant in the *NT* (cf. Mt.
23:29–37; Lk. 11:47–51; 13:13f.; Ac. 7:52; Rom. 11:3; Rev. 16:6;
18:24) is first expressed here (but cf. 1 Kg. 19:10, 14; Jer. 2:30).
The factual basis for this generalisation is slender, as far as our
evidence goes (1 Kg. 18:4; Jer. 26:20–23; 2 Chr. 24:20ff.), and it
may be a rhetorical heightening of Israel's rejection of the prophetic
word. See O. H. Steck, *Israel und das gewaltsame Geschick der
Propheten* (1967), esp. pp. 60–4. **warned,** lit. 'testified', belongs to
the Deuteronomic picture of God's lawsuit with his people (Dt.
4:26; 8:19; 30:19; 31:28). **great blasphemies:** Here (contrast v. 18)
they refer to the despising of God's word spoken through the
prophets (cf. *nāʾaṣ*, Ps. 107:11; Is. 5:24; Jer. 23:17; 2 Sam. 12:14;
cf. v. 9).

**27.** The history of the judges period is here regarded as typical
of Israel's history as a whole (cf. Jg. 2:11–18). **enemies . . . suffer:**
The words are from the same root; thus we could render: 'Thou
didst give them into the land of their oppressors, who oppressed
them; and in the time of their oppression . . .'. **hear . . . from
heaven** recalls especially Solomon's prayer (2 Chr. 6:21, 23, etc.;
7:14).

**28. had rest** refers again to the time of the judges (Jg. 3:11, 30;
etc.).

**29. by the observance of which a man shall live:** The life-
giving quality of the law (cf. on v. 14; Rom. 10:5) is a specially
Deuteronomic thought (e.g. 4:1; 5:33), but Lev. 18:5 offers the
closest verbal parallel. **acted presumptuously:** cf. on v. 16. **stiffened
their neck:** like a recalcitrant ox (cf. on v. 16). **turned a stubborn
shoulder,** lit. 'offered a withdrawing shoulder', i.e. refused to accept
the yoke.

**30. bear with** translates *mšq*, 'draw, extend', to whi.h we should
add *ḥeseḏ*, 'mercy' (as in Ps. 36:10; 109:12; Jer. 31:3), translating
'extend, or continue, mercy'. **by thy Spirit through thy prophets**
may reflect Zech. 7:12. **many years** carry us down to Israel's
captivity by **the peoples of the lands** (cf. on Ezr. 9:1), here the
Assyrians and Babylonians.

**31. didst not make an end of them:** The continued existence of
the nation, though only as a remnant (cf. 1:2; Ezr. 9:8), as a sign

of God's mercy is especially a theme in Jeremiah (4:7; 5:18; 30:11; 46:28).

APPEAL FOR DELIVERANCE

9:32-37

This 'confession' (vv. 6–31) has not been without a more practical motive; it is an appeal to the known character of God that he should once again deliver Israel from their overlords, and restore the promised land to them. Thus God is addressed as the one who **keepest covenant and steadfast love** (v. 32). But Israel has broken the covenant, and logically can have no claims upon it (whether the covenant *exists* any longer is beside the point); so they can only hope for God's uncovenanted mercy. It is with the recognition of this ambivalence of the covenant that this prayer will ask no more than that Israel's oppression should **not . . . seem little** to God. To some readers the ending of the prayer has seemed abrupt: **we are in great distress.** But the abruptness is really a mark of the delicacy of the author's spirituality (cf. the very similar stance of Ezra's prayer, Ezr. 9:6–15). It may be that any more explicit appeal was precluded as politically dangerous, but the desire for national independence is already quite clear in the prayer as it stands.

**32.** The address to **God** is reminiscent of Nehemiah's (1:5). The term for hardship ($t^el\bar{a}'\hat{a}$) recalls the bondage in Egypt and the privations of the wilderness (Exod. 18:8; Num. 20:14), and is specifically used here of foreign domination, which has persisted since **the time of the kings of Assyria.**

**33.** The author takes care that his lament should not sound like criticism of Yahweh's behaviour; God has been **just** (cf. v. 8*b*; Ezr. 9:15), he has **dealt faithfully.**

**34.** Prophets are missing, by comparison with v. 32, from the list of classes that have sinned, since the prophets are here regarded as God's faithful messengers (cf. v. 26); the merits of the true prophets seem to have cancelled out the memory of the false prophets.

**35–37.** The contrast between **they,** their pre-exilic ancestors (**in their kingdom**), and **we** is not felt as an injustice, but the natural consequence of sin (cf. Exod. 34:7*b*). The important contrast is between the fathers' refusal to **serve,** i.e. worship (*'āḇaḏ*), Yahweh, and the present generation's status as servants (*'aḇāḏîm*) (*RSV*, **slaves**) to the Persian kings. Though release from exile in a foreign land was a great blessing (cf. Ezr. 9:9; Neh. 1:2), there was a bitter irony in being slaves in their own land, and in being compelled to hand over its traditionally rich yield (Dt. 6:3) to their masters. The weight of the royal tax is exemplified by 5:4. **power . . . over our bodies:** probably *corvée* duty (cf. on Ezr. 4:13). **our cattle:** They could be requisitioned for Persian officials (cf. 5:16). **at their pleasure** (cf. on v. 24) reflects a subject people's resentment at the apparently arbitrary rule of their masters.

What in this prayer does God not know already? What is the point of rehearsing before God the all too well known history of Israel's apostasy? It is that there is more than one way of telling the history of Israel (cf. Pss. 105 and 106). It can be recited as a story of salvation or of apostasy; it can be recounted with praise or with penitence. God needs no reminder of the tragic history; but the congregation in praying thus is confessing how it understands itself. Prayer is here shown to be not simply a matter of speaking to God, but also of critical self-reflection in the light of God's demands and his grace. Hence this prayer cannot conclude with a superficial appeal for deliverance from misery, but must end simply on a note of confession (vv. 33ff.) and distress (vv. 36f.). It does not jog God's elbow, but leaves him entirely free to act according to his own will.

## III. NEHEMIAH'S COMMUNITY 9:38–13:31

### THE PLEDGE OF REFORM
### 9:38–10:39

In the present form of the book, ch. 10 seems firmly attached (cf. **because of all this,** 9:38) to ch. 9 as the sequel to the day of penitence. A pledge to keep God's law would be a fitting conclusion to a ceremony in which national disobedience to the covenant had been lamented. However, it is more than strange that Ezra's name does not appear among the signatories, but that Nehemiah's does; and the activity of the two men, on the view taken in this commentary, did not overlap. Even more telling is the close correspondence of the particular pledge made here with the laws which Nehemiah found disregarded in ch. 13. There can be little doubt therefore, as most scholars agree, that this chapter belongs chronologically after Neh. 13, and has nothing to do with Ezra.

How then does it come to be in its present position? W. Rudolph believes that the Chronicler deliberately concluded his account of Ezra (i.e. Ezr. 7–8; Neh. 8; Ezr. 9–10; Neh. 9–10) with this pledge document, in order to present a successful conclusion to Ezra's work, instead of the final fiasco, as Rudolph considers it, of the mixed marriage reform. But quite apart from the possibility that the document bore a date (as did many of the Elephantine papyri)

which the Chronicler would have recognised as too late for Ezra,
Neh. 9 should probably be attached to Neh. 8 (cf. on 9:1–37) and
not with Rudolph to Ezr. 10. If then the link between Neh. 9 and
10 (9:38) were the Chronicler's own, Neh. 10 would have in the
Chronicler's book preceded Ezr. 9–10—which is impossible since
Neh. 10 includes a pledge not to contract mixed marriages while in
Ezr. 9 the question of mixed marriages is plainly raised for the first
time. It therefore seems that the present position of Neh. 10, along
with the link verse (9:38), is due to the post-Chronicler editor's
sense that the pledge document formed an appropriate conclusion
to a ceremony of national repentance.

What then was the origin of Neh. 10? Though it is related to the
work of Nehemiah, it is not integrated into his memoirs (as the
wall-builders list of Neh. 3 is), and it bears no signs of his authorship. Neither is it the Chronicler's handiwork, and we can only
suppose that the document came from some other source, possibly
the temple archives.

THE HEADING

9:38

The Hebrew Bible rightly takes this verse, contrary to the modern
versions, as the first verse of ch. 10. In spite of **because of all this**
a connection with the prayer of ch. 9 is not at all plain. Literary
connection with the end of Neh. 13 is not possible either, and we
must either suppose that the chapter once formed part of a longer
document recording the events leading up to the pledge-making,
or, more probably, that **because of all this** is a linking phrase added
by the editor who put ch. 10 after ch. 9. **covenant:** This pledge
made by Israel is obviously not of the same character or significance
as the Sinai covenant, which overwhelmingly comes from God's side
(cf. on Ezr. 10:3); even the usual word for covenant (*berît*) is not
used, and it would be best to translate the term *'amānâ*, lit. 'firm,
faithful (agreement)', by 'pledge'. **our princes . . . set their seal
to it:** lit. 'upon the sealed (document) are (the names of) our princes
. . .'. A seal was used, among other purposes, as a form of legal
assent to a written document. Possibly, however, the word 'sealed'
(*ḥātûm*) had come to mean any document, and the 'seals' may have
been signatures (cf. the later Hebrew *ḥittûm*, 'signature'). Only the
leading priests, Levites, and laymen signed or sealed their names;
the others swore an oath (vv. 28f.).

## THE SIGNATORIES
### 10:1–27

Inexplicably, the order in the heading (9:38) is princes, Levites, and priests (Levites preceding priests is unusual, but paralleled in 2 Chr. 19:8; 30:21), while in the list itself the order is governor (and secretary?), priests, Levites, princes. Some have doubted that the list of names originally stood at this point, partly because of the varying order of signatories, partly because in the contemporary Elephantine papyri names are usually listed at the end, and partly (on Rudolph's view) because the Chronicler would not have used a list in which Ezra's name was lacking to supplement his Ezra material. But some such list must have accompanied the document (vv. 28–39) for it to be meaningful; 9:38 is very probably editorial, linking either with ch. 9 or with an account of the prelude to the pledge-making; in the Elephantine papyri the names of witnesses are at the end, but these names in 10:1–27 are not of witnesses, but of signatories, whose names naturally begin a document (cf. *AP* 20.2; 28.2); and it is not accepted here that the Chronicler related this chapter to Ezra's work.

## STATE OFFICIALS
### 10:1

**Those who set their seal:** A revocalisation of MT is implied, from *'al haḥᵃṭûmîm*, 'upon the sealed (ones), documents', to *haḥᵃṭōmîm*, 'the signers, sealers', omitting *'al*, 'upon', or perhaps emending it to *'ēleh*, 'these (are)'. **governor:** On this term, cf. on Ezr. 2:63. **Zedekiah:** Not known as a priest of this time (and in any case Seraiah seems to be the high priest); he could be Nehemiah's chief official, his scribe (cf. Ezr. 4:8f., where the 'scribe's' name stands second in a letter), and may be 'Zadok the scribe' of 13:13.

## THE PRIESTS
### 10:2–8

The 21 names are virtually identical with the 22 said to have returned with Zerubbabel (12:1–7) and the 21 listed as heads of priestly phratries in the next generation (12:12–21). Since the same men cannot be involved (Zerubbabel, *c.* 520; Neh. 11, *c.* 430 BC), these must be family, or rather course, names, exemplifying the post-exilic arrangement of the priesthood according to courses, each course being responsible for temple services for a fortnight. In 1 Chr. 24:7–18 are listed 22 or 23 course names; while a pre-exilic date cannot be ruled out, the prevalence of that list in later times, both at Qumran and after the destruction of the temple, has suggested to many that it was drawn up later than the present list. See further, J. Milik, *VTS* 4 (1957), p. 25; P. Winter, *VT* 6 (1956), pp. 216f.; M. Avi-Yonah, in *The Teacher's Yoke* (H. Trantham volume), ed. E. J. Vardaman and J. L. Garrett (1964), pp. 46–57. For a recent analysis, ascribing the origin of the course system to David, see H. G. M. Williamson, *VTS* 30 (1979), pp. 251–68.

**2. Azariah:** the long form of the name Ezra (12:1, 13). We do not know which course Ezra the scribe belonged to, but as he had two Azariahs among his ancestors, this may have been his course.

**3. Pashhur:** one of the four priestly families of Ezr. 2:36–39 (*q.v.*). **Amariah:** probably a long form of Immer (11:13; Ezr. 2:37). **Malchijah:** a long form of Malluch (v. 4); only Malluch appears in other lists, so perhaps one name is superfluous here.

**4. Shebaniah** (also 12:14) appears as Shecaniah in 12:3, obviously a scribal error in the square script where *b* is very like *k*.

**5. Harim** (also 12:15; Ezr. 2:39; I Chr. 24:8) is by scribal error (*rḥm* for *ḥrm*) Rehum in 12:3. **Meremoth** (12:3; Ezr. 8:33) is preferable to Meraioth (12:15). **Obadiah:** probably a scribal error for Iddo as in 12:4, 16.

**6. Daniel,** not in the other lists, is the name of a priestly phratry head who accompanied Ezra (Ezr. 8:2); his family has apparently by this time attained the status of a course. **Ginnethon:** corrupted to Ginnethoi in 12:4.

**7. Mijamin** (also 12:5, a lay name in Ezr. 10:25) is a variant of Miniamin (12:17, 41).

**8. Maaziah,** also a priestly course name in I Chr. 24:18, is probably a preferable form to Maadiah (12:5), or Moadiah (12:17). **Bilgai:** Bilgah elsewhere (12:5, 18; I Chr. 24:14).

THE LEVITES

10:9–13

The names of the **Levites** in these books are in great confusion, and one cannot be sure even whether the names here are ancestral or personal names. The first three names at least; **Jeshua, Binnui** (or Banni, Bunni), and **Kadmiel,** seem to be ancestral names, since they occur in the lists of Zerubbabel's return (Ezr. 2:40, Neh. 12:8) and in the temple building account (Ezr. 3:9), and head all lists of Levites except Neh. 12:24. The primacy of these three is indicated by the phrase **and their brethren** (v. 10). Among personal names will probably be **Hodiah, Kelita, Pelaiah, Hanan, Sherebiah,** all of whom are named at Ezra's law-reading (Neh. 8:7). The repetition of the sequence **Shebaniah, Hodiah** (vv. 10, 12f.) looks suspicious; **Beninu** (v. 13), an improbable Hebrew name, may well be a mistake for Chenani (9:4). **Hashabiah** and **Sherebiah** (vv. 11f.) are presumably the Levites of those names who returned with Ezra (Ezr. 8:18f.).

THE LAYMEN
10:14–27

The first half of the list is very similar to the great return list of Ezr. 2 and Neh. 7, but is slightly fuller than either, which would fit the supposition that the present list comes from the document of Neh. 10, and is not related literarily to either form of the return list. Thus it includes **Magpiash** (v. 20; Ezr. 2:30; not in Neh. 7), and **Hariph** (v. 19; Neh. 7:24, not in Ezr. 2). Curiously, however, Shephatiah, Arah, and Zaccai, which occur near the head of the return list in both its forms are missing here; it is improbable that these families had died out since Zerubbabel's time, so the omission of the names may be merely a scribal accident, or else due to the adoption of new names by sectors of a large phratry. Other variations are: **Hashum, Bezai** (v. 18, as in 7:22f., vice versa in Ezr. 2:17, 19); **Bani** and **Bunni** (vv. 14f., like Ezr. 10:29, 38 (Bani and Bunni), whereas Ezr. 2 has only Bani, Neh. 7 only Binnui). **Azzur** and **Hodiah** (not in Ezr. 2 or Neh. 7, though 1 Esd. 5:15 has Azzur) appear after **Hezekiah**. **Adonijah** (v. 16) before **Bigvai** must be the Adonikam of Ezr. 2:13 par., **Nebai** (v. 19) the Nebo of Ezr. 2:29 par., and **Magpiash** (v. 20) the Magbish of Ezr. 2:30. **Anathoth** (v. 19) appears here among family names, not place names (as in Ezr. 2:23), showing the possibility of adoption of a place name as an ancestral name (similarly with **Nebai** and **Magpiash** if town names in Ezr. 2). The fairly constant order of names in all the lists is due to a recognised ranking of the families according to some criterion unknown to us.

As might be expected, new phratries had developed in the century since the first return, most probably as the older phratries grew too large. The new phratry names extend from **Meshullam** (v. 20) to the end of the list. Perhaps six of these names appear as ancestral names of Nehemiah's wall-builders: **Meshezabel** (v. 21; 3:4), **Hashabnah** (v. 25; =? Hashabneiah, 3:10), **Hallohesh** (v. 24; 3:12), **Maaseiah** (v. 25; 3:23), **Harim** (v. 27; 3:11), **Baanah** (v. 27; 3–4). Perhaps five of the new phratry names are to be found among Ezra's lay 'council of reference' (8:4), **Meshullam, Anaiah, Hashabnah** (=? Hashbaddanah), **Maaseiah**, and **Malluk** (probably = Malchijah), but most of these names are very common, and little can be deduced from this. The names seem to be family, not personal, names, throughout the whole list.

## THE PLEDGE

### 10:28–39

The people bind themselves not only to observance of the Pentateuchal law in general, but to particular interpretations of that law. The stipulations of the pledge thus arise not only from Nehemiah's experiences as narrated in ch. 13, but from the necessity of establishing a definitive interpretation of the law. We gain here therefore an insight into the beginnings of that process of legal elaboration and definition which resulted ultimately in the vast Mishnaic and Talmudic literature. See further, D. J. A. Clines, 'Nehemiah 10 as an Example of Early Jewish Biblical Exegesis', *JSOT* 21 (1981), pp. 111–17.

## INTRODUCTORY SUMMARY

### 10:28–29

Many see in v. 28 the work of the Chronicler, finding genuine only **the rest of the people. separated themselves from the peoples of the lands** is very like the Chronicler's language in Ezr. 6:21, while **all who have knowledge and understanding** recalls Neh. 8:2, possibly also the Chronicler's. **the gatekeepers, the singers, the temple servants** must however derive from an editor other than the Chronicler, since the Chronicler himself included these groups with the Levites (1 Chr. 15:22f.; 23:3–6).

But the context demands a reference to the ordinary members of the priestly and Levite class; it would be incredible that while of laymen only the nobles signed, every priest and Levite signed his own name; given a division of the people into princes, Levites, and priests (9:38), **people** (*'am*) (v. 28) can only mean the laymen. Further, an even closer parallel to **separated themselves** . . . may be found in Ezr. 9:1, which is probably from the Ezra memoir, and not from the Chronicler; and **all who have knowledge** . . . is not so similar to 8:2 as to demand common authorship. It is reasonable therefore to see v. 28 as part of the original document.

The fivefold division of Judah into **people** (laymen), **priests, Levites, gatekeepers, singers, temple servants,** is probably a traditional scheme, reflected in Ezr. 2 par., though the order **gatekeepers, singers** occurs only in Neh. 7:73 (not Ezr. 2:41f., 70; Neh. 7:44f.). While the leaders (**nobles**) of the lay, priestly, and Levite classes signed their names to the document, the rank and file signified their assent only by the **oath**, in which all joined. **all who have separated themselves from the peoples of the lands to the law of God**: not a way of describing the people as a whole, but a sixth group of proselytes or 'sojourners' who had taken upon themselves the full obligation of the law, including circumcision, and had thus joined themselves to Israel (cf. on Ezr. 6:21). The phrase has no relationship to the question of mixed marriages, whether in Ezra's day or Nehemiah's. The Deuteronomic tone of v. 29 is unmistakable: for **to walk in God's law**, cf. Dt. 8:6 (also 2 Kg. 10:31); for **to observe and do all the commandments**, cf. 28:15; for **the LORD our Lord**, cf. 1:6.

## MARRIAGE WITH GENTILES

### 10:30

Highest priority is given to the question of mixed marriages, since the community of Nehemiah obviously felt that only a strict policy here could preserve national identity. This stipulation, based on the law, especially of Exod. 34:11–16 and Dt. 7:1–4 (cf. on Ezr. 9–10), was prompted by Nehemiah's experience of the results of mixed marriages (13:23–27), but also by the need to define that Ashdodite, Ammonite, and Moabite, for example, are included by implication among the list of foreign nations in the law (cf. also on Ezr. 9:1). It is noteworthy that the pledge says nothing of any dissolution of existing marriages. Since we do not know what Nehemiah thought should be done about marriages already contracted, we cannot say that his attitude was more tolerant than Ezra's (cf. on 13:23–29).

## THE SABBATH

### 10:31a, b

Observance of the Jewish calendar, **the sabbath** being its most distinctive feature, was a natural way to promote the sense of national identity. Inclusion of this item was prompted by the incidents of 13:15–18; the correspondence of language between this verse and 13:15f. is the best confirmation that the pledge is to be related to Neh. 13. Nehemiah's blanket prohibition of entry to Jerusalem on the sabbath (13:19) could only have been tolerated as a temporary measure, and the present oath would have hopefully made it unnecessary. The sabbath law, which in each of its formulations specifically enjoins rest from work (Exod. 20:8–11; 23:12; 31:13–17; 34:21; 35:2f.; Lev. 23:3; Dt. 5:12–15), nowhere defines buying food as work, and though Am. 8:5 shows that pre-exilic Israelites did not trade on the sabbath (cf. also Exod 16:22–30; Num. 15:32–35), the presence of Gentile merchants in Nehemiah's Jerusalem raised the legal question whether simply to **buy** was breaking the law. No 'God-fearer' (in the sense of Mal. 3:16; cf. Ezr. 9:4; 10:3) would have had much doubt about the answer, but a public definition was desirable. (Cf. also J. Weingreen, 'Oral Torah and Written Records', in *Holy Book and Holy Tradition*, ed. F. F. Bruce and E. G. Rupp [1968], pp. 54–67, esp. 63f.) At the same time the status of the **holy day** also (e.g. Num. 28:18, 26; 29:1, 7, 12) is fixed. We note that sabbath observance in general, including the prohibition of trading of Israelite with Israelite, is taken for granted by the pledge.

## THE SABBATICAL YEAR

### 10:31c

Naturally attached to the pledge on sabbath observance is one about the sabbatical (**seventh**) **year**. A novelty in this item is that the fallow year law (Exod. 23:10f.; cf. Lev. 25:2–7, 20f.) and the remission (*šᵉmiṭṭâ*) year law (Dt. 15:1–18; cf. Exod. 21:2–6), originally diverse in origin, are combined, creating an explicit undertaking that both will be equally observed. For the fallow law works to the disadvantage of the farmer, and the remission law to the disadvantage of the merchant or employer; it would be an injustice if one sector of the community were to profit from another's sacrificial observance of the law. Obedience to God's law has social as well as religious values, as is already clear in Exod. 23:11 (cf. Lev. 25:6f.) where only a humanitarian reason for the fallow year law is offered.

But even more novel than this balancing of the law's demands is the pledge to put into practice these laws which had never, so far as we know, been more than a dead letter. The only recorded attempt to follow the remission law (Jer. 34:8–16) had proved abortive. In fact we do not know that the signatories of the present document ever obeyed these extremely idealistic laws; our earliest testimony to their observance is from the second century BC (1 Mac. 6:49, 53 [163–162 BC]; cf. Josephus, *Ant.* 13.8.1).

This item is not related to any incident in Neh. 13, but plainly reflects the episode in 5:1–13, where only temporary measures were taken. **forego**, lit. 'release, drop', **the exaction of every debt** probably means not only that the repayment due that year will be remitted, but that the whole debt will be written off.

THE TEMPLE TAX

10:32–33

That this is a pledge additional to the obligations of the law is specified by **We also lay upon ourselves the obligation**. A half-shekel tax is said to have been levied on one occasion on males twenty years and upwards for the work of the tabernacle (Exod. 30:11–16; 38:25), and in a nostalgic appeal to old-time generosity Joash had temporarily revived the tax for urgent repairs to the temple (2 Kg. 12:4–15; 2 Chr. 24:4–14), but at no time was an annual levy ever raised. Under the monarchy, the official cult had been largely maintained from the royal exchequer. At the time of the restoration a certain provision for the temple was made by Darius (cf. on Ezr. 6:9f.), and in Ezra's time an apparently annual temple grant was approved by Artaxerxes (Ezr. 7:21f.). The present pledge may reflect economies in the imperial budget, or perhaps the sheer difficulty of extracting money from the satrapy treasurers (Ezr. 7:21) when three other provincial governors were determined to thwart Nehemiah in every way possible (cf. 4:7). Alternatively, this could be a sign of a reviving sense of national independence. Certainly, by making support of the temple everyone's responsibility rather than the concern simply of the local or imperial government, Nehemiah gave his community a focus and a sense of solidarity. The conception of this pledge, which plainly derives from Nehemiah (cf. 13:30f.), is thus all of a piece with his other great achievement, the building of the wall, the military significance of which was overshadowed by its function as a monument to national unity. The tabernacle tax was a half-shekel, as also the temple tax in New Testament times (Mt. 17:24; cf. Josephus, *War* 7.6.6). Mention of a third-shekel tax here may be due solely to contemporary use of a heavier shekel (on the value, see on 5:15). For a near contemporary list of contributions to a Jewish temple tax, see *AP* 22 (Porten, *Elephantine*, pp. 160–4, 320–7).

The uses of the temple tax are now specified. **showbread**, lit. 'bread of piling, *or*, row', i.e. loaves piled up or laid out in rows on a table in the sanctuary; also called 'bread of the presence of Yahweh' (e.g. Exod. 25:23–30). The twelve loaves prescribed (Lev. 24:5–9) are a thank offering from the twelve tribes. **continual burnt offering**: a lamb each morning and evening (Exod. 29:38–42; Num. 28:3f.). **continual cereal offering**: an adjunct to the burnt offering (Exod. 29:40f.; Num. 28:5). Num. 28–29f. prescribes the offerings for **sabbaths** (two additional lambs), **new moons** (two bulls, one ram, seven lambs) and **appointed feasts**, the heaviest expenditure, Unleavened Bread and Tabernacles together requiring 296 animals.

Up to this point the regular offerings are arranged in order of cost; there follow two irregularly occurring expenses for sacrifices not prescribed in the law. The **holy things**, set as they are between two types of offerings, must themselves be public offerings (cf., e.g., 2 2 Chr. 29:33; 35:13). **sin offerings to make atonement**: hardly those of the Day of Atonement, which is among the **appointed feasts**, but offerings for special occasions like days of national penitence or purification (cf. Ezr. 6:17; 8:35; 2 Chr. 29:21–24). **the work of the house of our God**: repair to the fabric; another term (*'aḇôḏâ*, not *mᵉlā'ḵâ*) is used in v. 32 for the cultic work or 'service'.

Verse 33 contains many typical expressions of the Chronicler, which may suggest the verse is his insertion, but may simply mean that he too used the usual post-exilic cultic vocabulary, which he certainly did not invent.

## THE WOOD OFFERING

### 10:34

The fire on the altar was to burn perpetually, **as it is written in the law** (Lev. 6:8–13), but the law prescribed no arrangements to ensure a supply of wood. Nehemiah persuaded his countrymen to organise the collection and transport of wood (cf. 13:31), the families (**fathers' houses**) responsible on each occasion being determined by lot (hardly Urim and Thummim). **the priests, the Levites and the people:** The odd position of this phrase suggests it is a glossator's addition, but it probably reflects ancient practice, since the Talmud too mentions the priests' wood-offerings (TB *Ta'anit* 28a). This item in the pledge also reflects ch. 13 (v. 31).

## FIRST FRUITS, PRIME PRODUCE, AND TITHES

### 10:35–39

Most of these contributions in kind by the laity for sacrifice and for the support of temple personnel are prescribed in the Pentateuch; the chief novelty here seems to be that the laws of temple gifts are to be observed in their entirety. Nehemiah suggests (13:31) that the first-fruits law had fallen into abeyance, and plainly narrates how the tithe law had been neglected (13:10f.), and it is very probable that the full Pentateuchal requirements, which cumulatively are exceedingly onerous, had never been met previously in Israel. Also novel is the organisation of the collection of the tithes (vv. 38f.).

**35.** The annual offering, generally at the Festival of Weeks (called 'First Fruits Day' in Num. 28:26), of some of the **first fruits** of the fields for the use of the priests (Num. 18:12f.) followed an ancient

law (Exod. 23:19; 34:26; Dt. 26:1–4). 'Their purpose was probably
not to consecrate the rest of the crop, but to deconsecrate it. All
was God's until the first portion had been offered and accepted in
lieu of the whole. Only then was the restriction on the human use
of the remainder removed (Lv. xxiii. 14, *cf.* xix. 23–25)' (R. J.
Thompson, *NBD*, p. 1117). Specification of **the first fruits of all
fruit of every tree** is a novelty; the Pentateuch speaks only of the
'first-fruits of your land' or 'the first of all the fruit [i.e. produce]
of the ground' (Dt. 26:2), which may or may not include the fruit
of trees (for further development of the first-fruits law, see the
Mishnah tractate *Bikkurim*).

**36.** Offering of male **first born** of humans and animals is also
Pentateuchal law (Exod. 22:29f.; 34:19f.; cf. 13:2, 12–15; Num.
18:15ff.; Dt. 15:19f.). It is implied of course that the first-born of
men and of unclean animals will, as those laws prescribe (cf. also
Lev. 27:27), be redeemed with money or a substitute animal, and
not actually be sacrificed. While all male first-born, whether **our
sons** or **our cattle** (preferably 'our animals', since the word could
include asses, for example), are to be offered to God, only the clean
animals, of **herds** and **flocks**, are destined for priestly consumption.

**37.** A further category of offerings intended for priestly use
(Num. 18:12; Dt. 18:4; cf. Ezek. 44:30) consists of prime or choice
(*rē'šît*, RSV **first**) food, distinguished from the first fruits in that it
is not raw like first fruits, but manufactured in some way. The
products mentioned here are **coarse meal**, hulled grain, or, less
probably, dough, or, if Num. 15:20 is being alluded to, some kind
of bread or cake, **wine**, and olive **oil**, the three chief products of
Palestine (cf. Dt. 7:13). **our contributions**: an explanatory gloss,
awkwardly placed, on **the first. the fruit of every tree**, even if not
an erroneous scribal repetition of the phrase in v. 35, is not meant
to include raw fruit, but only the products of trees, principally wine
and oil.

**the tithes** ('tenths'), which perhaps originated as a royal tax (cf.
1 Sam. 8:15, 17; de Vaux, *Ancient Israel*, pp. 380ff., 403ff.), were
in Pentateuchal law the perquisite of the Levites (Num. 18:26–32).
They were levied on the produce of the **ground**, and so apparently
included wine and oil as well as corn (cf. v. 39; Num. 18:27; Dt.
14:23). A tithe of herds and flocks also is occasionally mentioned
(Lev. 27:32; 2 Chr. 31:6), but may have been little practised.
Deuteronomy depicts a variant system of tithing (14:22–29;
26:12–14). Nehemiah's discovery on his return to Jerusalem that
the tithes had not been paid to the Levites (13:10–13) is clearly the
background to this item of the pledge.

**for it is the Levites who collect . . .**: Possibly this is a gloss reflecting a later system of collecting tithes at levitical depots in provincial towns (**rural towns**). However, it may well be that it is just this system which is being agreed to in this pledge; it would be a more accurate method of raising the revenue than the old system of placing the responsibility upon the taxed to bring their taxes to the temple (cf. 12:44; 13:5; Dt. 14:23f.; Am. 4:4; Mal. 3:10).

**38.** A novelty in the pledge is the requirement that **the priest, the son of Aaron**, apparently any priest, though the phrase suggests the high priest, should be present at the receipt of the levitical tithe. The reason is doubtless that the priests were legally entitled (Num. 18:26ff.) to a tenth of the Levites' income (i.e. a **tithe of the tithes**) and thus had an interest in checking the amount of the levitical tithes. The priestly dues were to be brought by the Levites to the temple **chambers** (cf. on Ezr. 8:29), i.e. the storehouse, where also the 'prime produce' of the laity was brought (v. 37). The tithe due to the Levites, on the other hand, need not under this new arrangement be brought to the temple, but only to the provincial depots.

**39.** Summarising, the verse points to the destination of the **contribution** of laity and Levites towards maintainance of the priests. The **contribution** (*terûmâ*) of the laity (**people of Israel**) is strictly the 'prime produce' (*rē'šît*) tax (v. 37), which is distinct from the tithe, while the Levites' **contribution** is their 'tithe of the tithe' (called *terûmâ* in Num. 18:26–29). **the vessels of the sanctuary**: presumably specified as the containers of the produce (cf. Jer. 40:10), though of course other sacred vessels also were stored in the temple chambers. **the priests that minister**, i.e. who are currently rostered for temple duties and living on the premises, together with **gatekeepers** and **singers** (cf. on Ezr. 2:41f.), are mentioned as the cultic officials who will receive and consume the *terûmâ*.

**We will not neglect the house of our God**: This concluding pledge summarises all the obligations of vv. 32–39, and presents a gratifying public response to Nehemiah's charge 'Why is the house of God forsaken?' (13:11; the same verb (*'zb*) is used).

With the signing of this pledge by the members of Nehemiah's community, a seal is put upon the work of Ezra. He was commissioned to teach the Pentateuchal law to all the Jewish people, and now we find those people taking the detailed stipulations of the law to heart and even pledging themselves to further observances not laid down in the law. Though it may have seemed at the end of ch. 8 that Ezra's law-reading had had only a superficial effect, the judges and law-administrators appointed and instructed by Ezra have obviously done their work, so that we find here, from a period only a few decades after Ezra, a commitment to the law which would have gratified him immensely. What was new about this pledge by the community was that the keeping of the law was plainly made the responsibility of everyone, not just of kings and princes. No one could any longer plead that his neglect of the law was of no consequence, nor could anyone doubt that his personal response to the will of God would in some way contribute to the welfare of his society as a whole.

### THE POPULATION OF JERUSALEM AND JUDAH
### 11:1–36

Chapters 8–10 have intruded into Nehemiah's account of his governorship in Jerusalem, chs. 8 and 9 from the Ezra material, and ch. 10 from a temple archive document relating to the second governorship of Nehemiah (ch. 13). Now, in ch. 11, Nehemiah's memoirs resume from the point reached in 7:73a, but they are soon interrupted once more by a number of lists (11:3–12:26). Thereafter, with the exception of 12:44–13:3, the rest of the book is occupied by the memoirs.

In spite of the different materials in the present chapter, it is intelligible as a whole, for it first recounts how more citizens were brought to live in Jerusalem (for Nehemiah's preparations, cf. on 7:1–73a), and then presents lists of the expanded population of the city.

### INCREASING JERUSALEM'S POPULATION
### 11:1–2

It is by no means certain that these verses are from Nehemiah's memoirs: they are not in the first person form, and they do not mention Nehemiah. But since 7:1–5 is intelligible as Nehemiah's preparations for this synoecism, 7:4 especially demanding a sequel like 11:1f., it is not unreasonable to suppose that Nehemiah's memoirs recounted some such incident, even if the present wording is not Nehemiah's.

1. The leaders (*śārîm*, 'princes') already lived in Jerusalem. This cannot mean that all leaders, family-heads, 'chiefs of the people', lived there, for rulers (*śārîm*) of provincial districts, for example, must have resided in provincial capitals. All that can be meant is that Jerusalem as the administrative centre of Judea had attracted to itself sufficient members of the ruling class (cf. the many Jewish officials who dined at Nehemiah's table, 5:17), and that what was needed to swell Jerusalem's population were ordinary folk, the rest of the people. A forced removal of population is rightly offensive to the modern libertarian conscience. Yet we should note that the

financial burden may not have been so severe as it would be today (Porten, *Elephantine*, pp. 75f., reckons that a house of this period could be built for the equivalent of six weeks' basic wage); and there was no question of splitting up families, for the lots would doubtless have been cast by families rather than individuals. Ecclesiasticus (49:13) and Josephus (*Ant.* 11.5.8) report that Nehemiah built houses in Jerusalem; even if this tradition is not reliable, it is unlikely that Nehemiah as governor would have no interest in the housing problem of the new settlers. **the holy city**: a rarely used name for Jerusalem in the *OT* (see Isa. 48:2; 52:1; cf. also Mt. 4:5, and its modern Arabic name *al-quds*, 'the sanctuary'). The use of the term here possibly reflects part of the inducement to settle in Jerusalem: it is to become the holy city of prophetic aspiration (cf. e.g. Jl 4:17; Isa. 65:25; Zech. 8:3ff.).

**2. willingly offered** (lit. 'volunteered'): The same root (*ndb*) is used in Jg. 5:2; Ps. 110:3 of volunteering for military service; and more relevantly, of volunteering to constitute a religious community, in the Qumran *Manual of Discipline*, 1QS 1.7; 5.1. Possibly this is how the compulsorily resettled inhabitants of Jerusalem came to regard themselves, putting a brave face on things and recognising, for this was no secularist age, that when **lots** are **cast** 'the decision is wholly from the Lord' (Prov. 16:33). It is possible of course that the 'volunteers' were additional to those chosen by lot, but one would have naturally thought it would have been fairer to praise those who went, even though unwillingly, rather than those who did not mind going!

### LIST OF FAMILY HEADS RESIDENT IN JERUSALEM
#### 11:3–19

It is not impossible that Nehemiah himself may have incorporated such a list into his memoirs at this point in order to provide statistical evidence of the success of his plans for the peopling of Jerusalem. But most scholars prefer to regard this list, like those which follow, as an editorial insertion; the preface (v. 4) at least can hardly come from Nehemiah's pen, since it is not to his purpose to refer to what went on in **the towns of Judah**. Fairly clearly, however, the list does belong more or less to Nehemiah's time, as inclusion of **Shabbethai** and **Jozabad** (v. 16), actually mentioned elsewhere as Levite contemporaries of Ezra (Neh. 8:7; Ezr. 8:33; 10:15), will show (cf. also on **Jedaiah** v. 10). A different view is held by U. Kellermann, 'Die Listen in Nehemia 11 eine Dokumentation aus den letzten Jahren des Reiches Juda?', *ZPDV* 82 (1966), pp. 209–27, who regards both the family and the town lists here as pre-exilic.

The present list appears also, in vastly different form, in 1 Chr. 9, where likewise it purports to derive from the post-exilic period (9:2), though there it is suggested that it reflects the situation immediately after Zerubbabel's return ('the first to dwell again in their possessions'). Comparison of the two lists shows both to have been badly mutilated, so that even after amalgamating them we are still probably far from the original form of the list. Like the home-comer list of Ezr. 2, this list follows the order of laymen, priests, Levites, singers, gatekeepers, temple servants; but unlike that list the laymen are arranged not according to phratry name (Parosh, Shephatiah, etc.) but according to tribe and to the names of the larger clans which were the principal subdivisions of the tribe (e.g. in the case of Judah: Perez, Shelah, and Zerah). Why this classific-ation is used here we cannot tell; we might have expected at this point the names of the family heads who had brought their families to live in Jerusalem.

### THE HEADING

### 11:3

**in the towns of Judah . . . in their towns**: One clause can hardly contain both phrases; we should translate: 'These are the chiefs of the province who lived in Jerusalem and in the towns of Judah; in their towns every man lived on his own property, laymen (**Israel**), priests, etc.'. However, since the chapter does not list **chiefs** who lived in the towns, and only the towns in which Judahites and Benjamites lived (vv. 25–35), we must assume that everything after **Jerusalem** is a secondary addition to the heading. The heading here was presumably written on the basis of v. 20 by the editor respon-sible for inserting the lists 11:25–12:25, which are not really relevant in their present position. Further, this secondary title has been reproduced from this place to 1 Chr. 9:2 where it is likewise not totally appropriate (though sons of Solomon's servants are rightly omitted from the title, the Nethinim are still mentioned in the title, though unmentioned in the list).

### LAY POPULATION

### 11:4a

Only two lay tribes, **Judah** and **Benjamin**, returned from the exile, according to the view of these books (cf. on Ezr. 1:5), though the parallel heading in 1 Chr. 9:3 adds Ephraim and Manasseh. Some think that members of these northern tribes were included in the original list, any reference to them being omitted here because it

would suggest that Nehemiah settled Samaritans in his city! But no
Ephraimites or Manassehites are listed in 1 Chr. 9 either, and
mention of these tribes there may be simply a scribal insertion.

## JUDAHITES

### 11:4b-6

Such an introduction as we have in v. 4a presages a massive list,
but what follows is only a fragment of the original document.
Supplementing these verses by 1 Chr. 9:6, we find the names of the
three leading family heads of the three branches or clans of the
**Judah** tribe: Perez, Shelah (cf. on v. 5), and Zerah (1 Chr. 9:6).
Gen. 38 recounts the origin of the threefold division of the Judah
tribe: Judah had five sons, of which the first two died (cf. also 1
Chr. 2:3f.). The status of the contemporary clan representatives,
Athaiah, Maaseiah, and Jeuel, is indicated by their lengthy genealogies. The list would probably have originally included the names
of all family heads, and the listing of each clan would have concluded
with totals such as that given in v. 6.

**4b.** 1 Chr. 9:4 offers for **Athaiah**, whom it calls by the short
form Uthai, an almost entirely different line of ancestry back to
Perez, which suggests that the original of both our present forms
of the list was considerably fuller. **Amariah**: the long form of Imri
(1 Chr. 9:4).

**5. Maaseiah** (Asaiah in 1 Chr. 9:5, but both names mean
'Yahweh's work') is called **son of the Shilonite** (also in 1 Chr. 9:5),
a minor misvocalisation of the 'Shelanite' (cf. *NEB;* Num. 26:20),
i.e. the descendant of Shelah (Gen. 38:5; 1 Chr. 3:2). 1 Chr. 9 omits
his ancestry, **Baruch** (*brwk*) being altered by a scribal error into
'first-born' (*bkwr*). At this point 1 Chr. 9 preserves the name of a
third clan head: Jeuel of the sons of Zerah (on Zerah, cf. also on
v. 24).

**6.** This total logically belongs after v. 4, to where *NEB* transfers
it. 1 Chr. 9:6 gives 690 for the clan of Zerah, comparable with the
468 of **Perez**. **valiant men** probably means 'men capable of military
service', which may point to the original purpose of this list as a
reckoning of Jerusalem's military strength.

## BENJAMITES

### 11:7–9

Only one Benjamite clan head is mentioned here, **Sallu** a descendant
of Jeshaiah (of Hassenuah in 1 Chr. 9:7), but 1 Chr. 9:8 has also
Ibneiah b. Michri, Elah b. Uzzi and Meshullam b. Ibnijah; oddly,

of the ancestral names only Uzzi occurs elsewhere in Benjamite genealogies (1 Chr. 7.7).

**8. and after him Gabbai, Sallai**: this obscure phrase should be emended to 'and his brothers [so *NEB*], men of valour' (cf. v. 14). The 928 is probably a variant of the 956 given in 1 Chr. 9:9 for all four Benjamite clans; adding the figures for Judah (cf. on v. 6), we may suppose a citizen army of *c.* 2,500, plus priests and Levites.

**9.** In the context, the **overseer Joel** b. **Zichri** (a common Benjamite ancestral name; cf. 1 Chr. 8:19, 23, 27), was probably the military commander (as *pāqîd* may mean) responsible for Jerusalem's lay reservists (cf. the priestly commander Zabdiel, v. 14). **Judah** b. **Hassenuah** (a Benjamite clan in 1 Chr. 9:7; cf. also Hassenaah, Neh. 3:3; Ezr. 2:35) is his second-in-command.

PRIESTS

**11:10–14**

Three leading priests are mentioned, one from each of three priestly phratries listed among Zerubbabel's company, **Jedaiah, Immer**, and **Pashhur** (Ezr. 2:36–39). The total of the three phratries is 1,192, whereas 1 Chr. 9:10–13, which has not given the individual sums, has a total of 1,760, which perhaps includes the figure for the Harim phratry, which is missing from here and 1 Chr. 9, probably by accident. Comparisons with the figures of Zerubbabel's list suggests that most of the high-priestly family lived in Jerusalem (973 there, 822 here) while only a fraction of the other priestly phratries did so (1,247 and 1,017 there, 128 and 242 here respectively). Why are no other priestly phratries (such as those in 10:1–7) mentioned? The list is probably much abbreviated (as are the lists of laymen), and naturally begins with the names of those phratries which first returned from exile. For this reason, little weight can be placed on the argument (e.g. by Rudolph, pp. 69, 185) that because neither of the priests of Ezra's company (Ezr. 8:2) are mentioned here the list, and therewith Nehemiah's first governorship, must antedate Ezra. Nor is the Daniel b. Ithamar of Ezr. 8:2 necessarily to be identified with the family name Daniel in the list of priestly courses (Neh. 10:6) from Nehemiah's second governorship; though even if it were, that would not challenge the priority of Ezra.

**10–11. Jediah** b. **Joiarib, Jachin**: these names appear in 1 Chr. 9:10 as Jedaiah, Jehoiarib, Jachin, three priests. Rudolph, followed by *NEB*, thinks **Jachin** (*ykyn*) is a scribal error for 'son of' (*bn*), and would thus find in these verses a lengthy genealogy of only one priest, **Jedaiah, ruler of the house of God**, probably a title of the high priest (cf. 2 Chr. 31:10 with 31:13); we should certainly expect the high priest's name to stand first in the list. (However, the *nāḡōḏā'*, a term cognate with *nāḡîḏ*, 'ruler' here, of the Elephantine temple was apparently the chief administrator, not the high priest; cf. Porten, *Elephantine*, p. 201.) Jedaiah would be a brother of Eliashib (12:10), and Joiarib would have to be corrected to the name of some other former high priest, probably Joiakim (12:10). The genealogy from **Seraiah** (= Azariah) backwards is plainly that of the high priestly line. But who is this high priest **Jedaiah**? We know the high-priestly family of Zerubbabel's time called itself 'sons of Jedaiah' (Ezr. 2:36), a pre-exilic high priest not otherwise heard of, but we know of no post-exilic high priest named Jedaiah. So probably the name is simply a variant of Joiada or Jehoiada (all three meaning 'Yahweh knows'), and this Jedaiah is the high priest Joiada (12:22), successor of Eliashib, and a contemporary of Nehemiah (13:28). A minor difficulty which remains is that none of the high priestly genealogies we have (e.g. 1 Chr. 6:1–14; Ezr. 8:1–5) mentions a Meraioth between Ahitub and Zadok; the name may here be misplaced, or else be derived from a fuller high-priestly list. The present genealogy is carried back to **Ahitub** (of 1 Chr. 6:11f.); why no further we cannot tell.

12. If vv. 10f. give the name of only one priest, **their brethren** must be corrected to 'his brethren' (so *NEB*). **Adaiah** belongs to the **Pashhur** phratry, one of the four priestly phratries returning with Zerubbabel (Ezr. 2:38); his genealogy is abbreviated in 1 Chr. 9:12.

13. **his brethren**: the other 'extended family' heads of the Pashhur phratry. **Amashsai**, better spelled Amasai (*NEB*), has been corrupted in scribal transmission in 1 Chr. 9:12 to Maasai by the transposition of the first two letters. His phratry is **Immer** (see Ezr. 2:37). Comparison of his genealogy with that given in 1 Chr. 9:12 well illustrates the extent of scribal corruption in these names.

14. **their brethren** should be 'his brethren' (as LXX, *NEB*; cf. 1 Chr. 9:13). The **overseer** (*pāqîḏ*) **Zabdiel** is probably, like the *pāqîḏ* in v. 9, a military official. 1 Chr. omits any reference to a *pāqîḏ*, and transforms the **mighty men of valor** into 'very able men for the work of the service of the house of God' (v. 13). **Haggedolim** means 'the great men' (cf. *AV*) and can hardly have been anyone's personal name; it may be a scribal error for *haggāḏôl*, 'the high (priest)'.

LEVITES

11:15-18

Six leading **Levites** are named, corresponding roughly to the first six in 1 Chr. 9:14ff.; the final name there, Berechiah, is doubtless omitted because his family 'dwelt in the villages of the Neto-phathites', not in Jerusalem. As is usual (cf. on Ezr. 2:41f.), the singers of the **Asaph** and **Jeduthun** lineages are included with the Levites. As elsewhere (Ezr. 2:40; cf. 8:15-20) there are considerably fewer Levites than priests (28 as against perhaps 1,760; cf. on vv. 10-14 above).

**15.** **Shemaiah's** distant ancestor is here **Bunni**, but in 1 Chr. 9:14 Merari; Bunni may be simply a scribal error for 'sons of' (*bwny* for *bny*). Merari was one of the three branches of the Levi tribe.

**16.** Following the leading Levite name come not military officers this time (contrast vv. 9, 14), but two men, **Shabbethai** and **Jozabad**, contemporaries also of Ezra (cf. Neh. 8:7), who are direc-tors of temple works. **outside work**: the physical aspect of temple business, as distinct from the more directly cultic 'work of the house' (v. 12); thus Jozabad appears as one of the temple treasurers (Ezr. 8:33). In 1 Chr. 9:15 the names of Heresh and Galal, directors of works in a later period, are substituted.

**17.** Of the three guilds of singers (1 Chr. 25:1), **Asaph** and **Jeduthun** appear here, though only Asaph in Ezr. 2:41 (*q.v.*). An awkward MT may be restored by a minimal emendation (*hattᵉhillâ*, 'the psalm', for *hattᵉhillâ*, 'the beginning') to 'psalm-reader (who) praises (i.e. leads the song of praise) at prayer (time)', as Asaph had been appointed to do (1 Chr. 16:7). Mention of the choir-leader **Bakbukiah** (possibly the singer Bukkiah in 1 Chr. 25:13) as Mattan-iah's **second** suggests twin choirs which sang antiphonally (12:8-9, 27-42; Ezr. 3:11). Mattaniah's ancestors include a **Zabdi** or, rather, Zichri (1 Chr. 9:15) (*b* and *d* closely resemble *k* [ch] and *r* respecti-vely in the square Heb. script). **Abda, Shammua** appear in variant forms in 1 Chr. 9:16.

GATEKEEPERS

11:19

Cf. Ezr. 2:42. As in the parallel, 1 Chr. 9:17-32, which contains much more detail, and a higher total (212, as against 72) the **gate-keepers** are listed after the Levites, though at least the four chief gatekeepers were Levites (9:26; cf. on Ezr. 2:41f.). Curiously, only the second and third of these are mentioned here, **Akkub** and **Talmon** (but cf. Neh. 12:25). Since gatekeepers with these names were also in Zerubbabel's caravan (Ezr. 2:42), the names here will probably be, unlike the rest of the list (though cf. v. 21), family names.

## MISPLACED HEADING
### 11:20

This verse, from which the inapposite elements of v. 3 were derived, probably originally headed the list found in vv. 25–36. Verses 21–24 still concern Jerusalem.

## SUPPLEMENTARY NOTES
### 11:21–24

These notes, missing from the parallel list in 1 Chr. 9, are possibly a later addition to the list; but there is no reason to doubt their accuracy.

## THE TEMPLE SERVANTS
### 11:21

The Nethinim (cf. on Ezr. 2:43) are usually listed after the gatekeepers. **Ophel**: cf. on 3:25ff. **Ziha** and **Gishpa**, if a corruption of Hasupha (the second Nethinim name in the Ezr. 2 list), are family names already in Zerubbabel's time (Ezr. 2:43); so they are very likely family names here too (cf. on v. 19).

## THE OVERSEER
### 11:22

No *pāqîd* (cf. vv. 9, 14) of the Levites has been mentioned above, perhaps through scribal omission (neither Shabbethai, Jozabad, nor Mattaniah [vv. 16f.] are called *pāqîd*, and their functions were certainly not military). The supplementer adds the name of the Levite *pāqîd* **Uzzi**, apparently the great-grandson of the choir-leader Mattaniah (v. 17); thus the present note is some generations later than the rest of the list. **over**, or rather 'for', **the work**, i.e. 'divine service' (not 'business', *AV, NEB*), **of the house of God**, probably denotes the singers' function, not Uzzi's.

## THE SINGERS
### 11:23

The royal command for the performance of music and the maintenance (*'amānâ*, settled provision, 'pledge' in 9:38) of the singers must in view of the word 'king' in v. 24 refer to the Persian government's sponsorship of sacred music (though a similar reference in 12:24, perhaps from the same supplementer, is to David's institution of sacred music; and cf. on 12:47). None of the imperial decrees preserved in Ezr. makes such a stipulation, though 7:20, 23 may authorise such expense in principle; so we must think of a later decree, like that of Darius II to the Jews at Elephantine (*AP* 21).

## THE GOVERNOR
### 11:24

**Pethahiah**, an official **at the king's hand in all matters concerning the people** was obviously someone so important that he could not be left out of any list of Jerusalem's population. He may be conjectured to be the Persian governor at the time of the supplementer (author of vv. 21 [?], 22–24), about two generations after Nehemiah; as such, his period of office would fall between Bagoas (Nehemiah's successor) and Jehezkiah *c.* 330 (for the chronology, see S. Talmon, *IDBS*, pp. 327f.). **at the king's hand** need not imply physical proximity to the Persian court. **in all matters concerning the people**: The phrase indicates a wider authority than Ezra's, for example, and suggests an office of similar, if not identical, rank to that of governor. The Judahite clan of **Zerah**, to which Pethahiah belonged, is accidentally missing from the list in vv. 4*b*-6, but may be supplied from 1 Chr. 9:6; he may also belong to the **Meshezabel** family mentioned among the wall-builders (3:4).

## COUNTRY TOWNS WITH JEWISH POPULATIONS
### 11:25–36

Some account of the Jewish settlements outside Jerusalem was thought appropriate at this point by an editor. This list of towns, however, hardly furthers Nehemiah's narrative, and its literary form—as a catalogue of towns—marks it off as quite distinct in origin from the preceding list of families and leading citizens. It has been seriously doubted whether the list has anything to do with the Judea of Nehemiah's time (e.g. Kellermann, p. 104). Many towns mentioned elsewhere in Neh. have no place here: Tekoa (3:5), Meronoth, Gibeon, Mizpah (3:7), Beth-haccherem (3:14), Beth-zur (3:16), Keilah (3:17), Bethlehem, Netophah (7:26), Beth-azmaveth (7:28), Kiriath-jearim, Chephirah, Beeroth (7:29), Jericho (7:36), Beth-gilgal (12:29). And on the other hand, those towns that are mentioned are relatively far from Jerusalem, in the Negeb, the Shephelah, the central hills to the north and west, and the coastal plain, where—on the whole—returning exiles did not settle, so far as we know.

The Judah list (vv. 25–30) shows close affinity with the much fuller list of towns of Judah in Jos. 15:20–62, which has been variously dated to the time of Josiah (A. Alt, *KS*, II, pp. 282ff.) and to the ninth century BC (F. M. Cross and G. E. Wright, *JBL* 75 [1956], pp. 202–26). The disposition of the towns mentioned in the present list suggests strongly that we have here a list of forts and garrison towns on the borders of Judah. At least four of the Negeb places are known to have been forts in pre-exilic times: Jekabzeel, Beersheba, Tell el-Milḥ, Kh. el-Meshâsh (Y. Aharoni, *IEJ* 17 [1967], pp. 10f.); and the last group of places (Zorah to Azekah) seem to have had a military significance also; note the term **encamped** (v. 30*b*). An alternative view is that these are the names of towns which had not been sacked by the Babylonians, and which had been inhabited by the 'residue of the people' that had not been deported (cf. Aharoni, *Land*, pp. 355f.). Though they had come into the Arabian sphere of influence (cf. on 2:19), they perhaps still retained their Jewish populations in Nehemiah's time and later, and so were included by an editor in this list of the post-exilic community.

## TOWNS OF JUDAH

### 11:25–30

The original heading of this section was v. 20 plus **and the villages with their fields**. It is 'towns' (v. 20), not **villages**, unwalled settlements (cf. Lev. 25:31), lit. 'daughters', that are here listed. All these Judahite towns except **Dibon, Jeshua**, and **Meconah**, figure in the list of Jos. 15; and **Dibon** may be Debir (Jos. 15:49) or Dimonah (15:22), while **Jeshua** could be Shema (15:26). The list begins with Hebron, called unaccountably by its ancient name (Jg. 1:10) **Kiriath-arba**, and proceeds southward in a roughly clockwise direction (identifications are those of Aharoni, *Land*, and Aharoni and Avi-Yonah, *Atlas*, except where otherwise indicated). To the area of the Negeb belong the ten towns following Hebron: **Dibon**, possibly the Dimonah of Jos. 15:22, and perhaps to be identified with el-Qebab, 22 m. east of Beersheba (Abel, *Géographie*, II, p. 89); **Jekabzeel** or preferably Kabzeel (Jos. 15:21), Tel 'Ira (Kh. Ḥōra), 12 m. east of Beersheba, and capital of the Negeb district (see Aharoni, *IEJ* 8 [1958], pp. 36ff.; 17 [1967], p. 11); **Jeshua**, if Shema, possibly Tel Jeshu'a (Tell es-Sa'aweh), 15 m. east of Beersheba; **Moladah**, possibly Khereibet el-Waten (Ḥorvat Yittan), 2 m. east of Beersheba; **Beth-pelet**, perhaps Tell es-Saqati (Tel Shoqet),

6 m. north-east of Beersheba; **Hazar-shual**, 'Jackal settlement', unidentified; **Beersheba**, not on the site of the modern city, but 2 m. east, at Tell es-Saba' (Tel Beer-Sheva); **Ziklag**, possibly Tell esh-Shari'ah (Tel Ser'a), 13 m. north-west of Beersheba; **Meconah**, possibly erroneous for Meronah (Kh. Marrân) (Albright, *JPOS* 4 [1924], p. 152) or for Madmannah (Kh. Umm ed-Deimneh), 10 m. north-east of Beersheba; **En-rimmon**, 'Pomegranate Spring' (cf. Zech. 14:10), possibly Kh. Umm er-Ramamim (Abel, *Géographie*, 11, p. 89), 12 m. north-east of Beersheba.

This group of Negeb towns is followed by an easily identified group in the Shephelah, beginning with Zorah, and again proceeding clockwise toward the south. **Zorah**, a Danite town in some lists (e.g. Jos. 19:41) but elsewhere part of the lowland district of Judah (e.g. Jos. 15:33), lies 17 m. west of Jerusalem; it is well known as Samson's home-town (Jg. 13:2). **Jarmuth**, Kh. Yarmuk, is 5 m. south; **Zanoah**, 3 m. south; **Adullam**, 9 m. south; **Lachish**, 20 m. south-west; **Azekah**, 6 m. south-east.

The summary, **so they camped from Beersheba**, the traditionally southernmost point in Judah (and in Israel as a whole, as in 'from Dan to Beersheba'), **to the valley of Hinnom**, the northernmost point on the boundaries of Judah (Jos. 15:8), does not seem to correspond to the foregoing list, unless perhaps it is a way of saying 'these are the fortified places in Judah, from south to north'.

### TOWNS OF BENJAMIN
### 11:31–36

These settlements, partly in the hill-country north of Jerusalem, and partly on the coastal plain, are listed in four groups. **Geba, Michmash, Aija** (= Ai) and **Bethel**, lying between 6 and 11 m. north of Jerusalem, are listed from south to north; then **Anathoth, Nob** and **Ananiah** are a more southerly group, within 3 m. of Jerusalem, and listed from north to south. These two groups lie along the main approach route to Jerusalem from the north. **Hazor** and **Ramah** lie slightly west of this line, while the remaining group of six towns lies far to the west, in the coastal plain. As with Judah, a number of Benjamite towns (cf. Jos. 18:21–28) known to have been inhabited after the exile are not mentioned here (cf. on vv. 25–36). Once again, the list is perhaps to be understood as a list of fortified towns. This is not a complete list of Benjamite towns at any period, and may therefore record towns of strategic importance. Many of the places lay outside the post-exilic province of Judea, which suggests that the list belongs to the late pre-exilic period, but it is well known (cf. Ezr. 2:33) that returning exiles settled in towns outside the province, a situation not without its military significance (cf. on 4:12).

**31.** The verse should begin: 'Some of the people of Benjamin lived at Geba, Michmash . . .' (transferring **from** [*m*], i.e. 'some of', to the beginning of the verse, as in v. 25). The towns are mentioned in Ezr. 2:26ff. **Aija** was probably a settlement at Kh. Ḥaiyān, a mile south-west of Kh. et-Tell, possibly the original Ai, from which it derived its name.

**32. Anathoth** and **Nob** (= Nebo) appear in Ezr. 2:23, 29. **Ananiah** is most probably *NT* Bethany (el-'Azariyeh).

**33a,b.** The name of Benjamite **Hazor**, not to be confused with the well-known city in Naphtali, may be preserved in Kh. Ḥazzûr, 5 m. north-west of Jerusalem, though the site must lie elsewhere; alternatively we may identify it with Baal-hazor (2 Sam. 13:23), Tel Aṣur, 15 m. north of Jerusalem, though this lay some miles outside Benjamite territory. For **Ramah**, cf. Ezr. 2:26.

**33c-35. Hadid, Lod,** and **Ono** (cf. on Ezr. 2:33) are securely identified places in the coastal plain, *c.* 30 m. north-west of Jerusalem. **Gittaim** is probably to be identified with Tell Râs Abū Ḥamîd, near Ramleh. **Neballat** is Beit Nabala (Ḥorvat Nevallat), a little north-east of Lod, and **Zeboim** may be Kh. Sabieh, north of Lod. **the valley of craftsmen**, more probably 'the valley of woods' (*NEB* mg), possibly a wooded region near Lod.

**36.** The text apparently means that some **Levites** who had previously lived in Judahite cities removed to Benjamite territory, but the significance of this eludes us. Perhaps we should emend slightly to read 'And certain levitical divisions (i.e. groups of families) lived in Judah and Benjamin', as distinct from those who lived in Jerusalem (v. 22).

#### THE CLERGY OF THE POST-EXILIC COMMUNITY

#### 12:1-26

Appended to the skeleton lists of inhabitants of post-exilic Jerusalem and Judea in ch. 11 are these fuller lists of post-exilic priests and Levites. There are: (i) a list of priests and Levites purportedly of the time of Zerubbabel and Jeshua, *c.* 520 BC (vv. 1–9; (ii) a list of high priests from Jeshua to Jaddua, i.e. down to 323 BC (vv. 10f.); (iii) a list of priests and Levites from the time of Joiakim, i.e. some time between 520 and 445 BC (vv. 12–21, 24ff.). An inserted note (vv. 22f.) gives some information about the registration of these clergy.

These lists can hardly have belonged to Nehemiah's memoirs, nor even to the work of the Chronicler whose narrative resuming at 12:27 seems to refer back to 11:20 (with v. 25*a*, *q.v.*) and perhaps 11:36. Most probably their inclusion is due to a post-Chronicler editor, who wished to give as comprehensive a picture of the post-exilic community as possible, and therefore inserted other lists of clergy (cf. 11:10–18) which were known to him.

### PRIESTS AND LEVITES IN JESHUA'S TIME

#### 12:1–9

##### PRIESTS

##### 12:1–7

Ezr. 2, our most clearly authentic source for the names of home-comers under Zerubbabel, speaks of only four priestly families (vv. 36–39), so the present list of 22 priestly families is usually thought an unhistorical retrojection of the classification existing in the time of Joiakim in the mid fifth century BC (12:12–21) and in the time of Nehemiah (10:2–8). Nevertheless, the evidence of Ezr. 2 itself is that in the time of Zerubbabel or shortly afterwards the four priestly families provided 4,289 priests. Sub-grouping of these large phratries must have existed, and it is natural that from the very beginning of renewed temple worship the priests should have been arranged in courses and their duties rostered. In principle therefore the names here listed could be course names from Zerub-babel's time; the total of 22 names here, like that of 21 in 10:2–8 and 12:12–21, probably results from faulty copying of lists that originally had 24 names (2 courses for each month).

Problems remain, however. It is hard to believe that the whole structure of the priestly classification was developed in the first few years after the return and that consequently those priests who returned later, e.g. with Ezra (Ezr. 8:2), were totally assimilated to the existing priestly courses and families. Also, there is a possibility that the names from **Joiarib** onwards are later additions to the list: for 'and' appears before Joiarib in both v. 6 and v. 19, which can hardly be accidental, and these names are missing altogether from the priestly pledge signatories in Nehemiah's time.

A hypothetical reconstruction is that the supplementer possessed a list of personal names of heads of father's houses from the time of Joiakim (12:12–21), and aligned these with the course names current in his own day. Since he believed, and probably correctly, that the course system was reinstituted in the time of Zerubbabel and Jeshua, he inferred that the course names must have been borne by individuals of that era; hence the list 12:1–9. This list is thus an artificial construction, but it presents the essentially correct view of the supplementer that the religious institutions of his age (perhaps the second century BC; so Kellerman, p. 105) were founded by the earliest leaders of the restored community, and bore the stamp of their authority.

On the names as far as **Shemaiah** (v. 8), cf. on 10:2–8. **Joiarib** was an ancestor of the Maccabees (1 Mac. 2:1), so some think the addition of this and the other names may be of Maccabean date. But Joiarib appears in 1 Chr. 24 as the priestly course Jehoiarib (v. 7), so the name may be pre-exilic. The double occurrence of **Jedaiah** (vv. 6, 7) is suspicious, though not entirely impossible. A Septuagintal reading suggests Hodaviah for the second Jedaiah, though that is not elsewhere attested as a priestly name. **and of their brethren**: a meaningless phrase, and due to careless copying; the **brethren** cannot be the Levites, who are sometimes so called elsewhere, since the priests are not their 'heads'.

## LEVITES

### 12:8–9

The three Levite leaders of Zerubbabel's caravan were **Jeshua, Binnui** (or Bani), and **Kadmiel** (Ezr. 2:40, emended). **Sherebiah** and **Judah** can hardly have been further family heads of that era, since only 74 Levites returned with Zerubbabel. **Sherebiah** seems to have been erroneously introduced into that period from the time of Ezra (Neh. 8:7; 9:4f.) and Nehemiah (10:12; 12:24), and **Judah** similarly (9:5; 10:10, 13, where Hodiah = Judah). The choir leader **Mattaniah** and his deputy **Bakbukiah** also belong to Nehemiah's time (11:17; cf. on 12:25), not Zerubbabel's. Their colleague **Unni** is otherwise unheard of, though he bears the name of a singer in David's time (1 Chr. 15:18, 20); the name may be an error for Abda (11:17; = Obadiah, 12:24). These singers are reckoned Levites here (as 11:15–18), and not separately categorised. **stood opposite** suggests antiphonal singing (cf. 11:17).

## HIGH-PRIESTLY GENEALOGY

### 12:10–11

The official high-priestly genealogy in 1 Chr. 6:3–15 carries the line down to Jozadak, high priest at the time of the exile. **Jeshua**, c. 520 BC, was son of Jozadak (Ezr. 3:2), so the six names here may be intended as a supplement to the Chronicles list. **Joiakim** spans the period between the return and the time of Ezra and Nehemiah (c.

458, 445), while his successor **Eliashib** appears several times as a contemporary of Nehemiah (3:1, 20, 21; 13:4, 7; cf. Ezr. 10:6). Eliashib's son **Joiada** is mentioned in 13:28, but it is not clear whether he is at that time (?*c.* 430) already high priest. His successor's name is evidently not **Jonathan** but Johanan (as in vv. 22f.; so also Josephus, *Ant.* 11.7.1); he is called 'son of Eliashib' in v. 23 (cf. also on Ezr. 10:6), which suggests to some that he was Joiada's brother, not his son, and thus that the present list has erroneously been transformed from a succession-list into a genealogy. Though v. 23 could mean that Johanan was the grandson of Eliashib (so *NEB*), it is curious that he is not called son of Joiada, if that is what he was. Josephus reports that this Johanan, provoked by his brother Jeshua who wanted to gain the high-priesthood for himself, slew his brother in the temple (*Ant.* 11.7.1ff.). Josephus may be confused (he tells in 11.8.2 of a fraternal dispute over the high-priesthood in the next generation also), but even if his facts are correct it is not impossible that Johanan's action may have been regarded as 'an act of self-defence against an attack by a godless would-be usurper' (J. A. Emerton, *JTS* 17 [1966], p. 12). Thus the questions of Johanan's character and of whether Ezra on the 398 BC date would have consorted with the perpetrator of such a deed must remain open, though the balance of probability favours an earlier date for Ezra. **Jaddua** is presented by Josephus (*Ant.* 11.8.3–5) as the high priest contemporary with Alexander the Great (332 BC); if he was, he must have been nearly 100 years old by that time. It is more likely that there were two fourth-century Jadduas (so Bright, *History*, p. 409 n. 8; Cross, *JBL* 94 [1975], p. 6). On the whole subject of the high-priestly succession in the fifth and fourth centuries BC, see F. M. Cross, 'A Reconstruction of the Judean Restoration', *JBL* 94 (1975), pp. 4–18.

### PRIESTS AND LEVITES IN JOIAKIM'S TIME
### 12:12–26

#### PRIESTS
#### 12:12–21

The authenticity of the list of priestly course names, which is largely identical with that in vv. 1–7, has been discussed there. The present list contains besides course names the personal names of the family heads in charge of each course. These personal names are all unknown to us, with the possible exception of **Zechariah** of the **Iddo** family (v. 16), who may well be the prophet Zechariah (cf. Zech. 1:1; Ezr. 5:1).

The name Hattush (12:2; 10:4) following **Malluchi** (v. 14) has accidentally fallen out, as has also the name of the head of the **Miniamin** family (v. 17). Other slight variations between the lists have been noted at 10:2–8.

## SOURCE OF THE LISTS

### 12:22–23

In its present form this note is difficult to understand. A small emendation (*m'l* for *'l*, 'from' for **until**) helps a little, enabling the **Darius** to be identified as Darius I (so W. F. Albright, *JBL* 40 [1921], p. 113). But problems still remain, notably the conflict between the *terminus ante quem* of the time of **Jaddua** (v. 22) and the time of **Johanan** (v. 23). Plainly the editor is quoting his source for these lists, which can only be **the Book of the Chronicles** (not, however, our canonical book) in the case of both priests and Levites. So Rudolph's reconstruction is very reasonable: '(22) The family heads of the priests in the time of Eliashib, Joiada, Johanan, and Jaddua were registered in the Chronicles until the reign of Darius the Persian. (23) The sons of Levi: The family heads were registered in the Chronicles but [only] down to the time of Johanan, the son of Eliashib' (similarly *NEB*). This reconstruction supposes that **the Levites** (v. 22) was originally a marginal heading alongside v. 23, and that reference to the Chronicles in v. 22 was accidentally omitted because of the similarity with v. 23.

If **Darius** marks the terminal date of the lists, as seems probable, he could be Darius II Nothus (423–404 BC) or Darius III Codomannus (336–331). If Jaddua survived as long as Josephus believed (or if there was a second fourth-century Jaddua; cf. on vv. 10f. above), Darius III could be intended, but Darius II is on the whole more probable. The title **Darius the Persian** is no mark of a late date; cf. R. D. Wilson, 'Titles of the Persian Kings', *Festschrift E. Sachau* (1915), p. 193. **Jaddua** may in any case be a later editorial addition to the high priestly list (both **Jonathan** and **Jaddua** are prefaced by **and**).

## LEVITES

### 12:24–26

These Levite names are taken from the records of the time of the high priest **Joiakim** (v. 26), which is also said to be the time of Nehemiah and Ezra. While the high priest contemporary with Ezra may well have been Joiakim, if we date Ezra to 458 BC, the only high priest mentioned in Nehemiah's time is Eliashib (cf. 3:1),

Joiakim's successor. This may mean simply that the same levitical office-bearers survived into Nehemiah's day, or it may be a hint that the reference to Nehemiah is not original at this point. Or it may be that v. 26*b* was a marginal heading to the narrative which follows, in which both Nehemiah and Ezra (v. 36) participate, Nehemiah playing the major part, and thus naturally mentioned before Ezra here (as in 8:9; cf. 3:8; 4:3). Certainly this verse cannot be used as evidence that Nehemiah preceded Ezra.

The three Levite family heads **Hashabiah, Sherebiah**, and **Jeshua** b. **Kadmiel** are probably, as the text stands, to be taken as the leading representatives of the three post-exilic Levite phratries often attested, Jeshua, Bani (or Binnui), and Kadmiel (cf. on Ezr. 2:40). If Ezra's arrival is dated to 458 BC, **Hashabiah** and **Sherebiah** could be the companions of Ezra (Ezr. 8:18f., 24 *q.v.*). But the name **Jeshua** b. **Kadmiel** arouses suspicion: Why should he alone be recorded with his family name? Are there not perhaps hidden in his name the three Levitical phratry names, Jeshua, Bani (easily misread as *ben*, 'the son of'), and Kadmiel (cf. *NEB*)? Sherebiah certainly appears several times in lists beginning with Jeshua, Bani, and Kadmiel (9:4f.; 10:9–13; 12:8; cf. 8:7), and Hashabiah likewise once (10:9–13), but never do they precede the leading trio; so the list remains enigmatic. **their brethren over against them**: obviously the Asaphite singers (11:17), whose duties and courses (*RSV*, **watch**) had been traditionally established by David (1 Chr. 25; cf. 2 Chr. 8:14) as the divinely authorised institutor of Israelite worship (**man of God**; cf. on Ezr. 3:2). The family heads of the singers have already in vv. 8f. and 11:17 been noted as **Mattaniah, Bakbukiah** and **Obadiah** (Abda in 11:17; Unno in 12:9), so these three names are to be attached to v. 24*b*, not v. 25. **Meshullam** (or Shallum), **Talmon**, and **Akkub** are listed elsewhere also as names of gatekeeper families (11:19; Ezr. 10:23; 1 Chr. 9:17). Elsewhere in Ezra-Nehemiah the door-keepers are not included with Levites, but the supplementer here takes his cue from the impeccable levitical genealogy of Shallum provided in 1 Chr. 9:19 (cf. on Ezr. 2:41f.).

THE DEDICATION OF THE WALL

12:27–43

The story of Nehemiah, which has since ch. 7 been interrupted by the Ezran material (ch. 8–9), a chronologically displaced document relating to Nehemiah (ch. 10), and seemingly interminable lists (ch. 11–12), is now resumed. However awkward a literary and historical problem they have left us, the Chronicler and the editor responsible for this rearrangement of the Chronicler's work (on the view taken in this commentary; cf. Introduction, III) were not irrational in their working. The dedication of the walls of the city is plainly the climax of the Nehemiah story; and the Chronicler has delayed this climax not so much for dramatic reasons as to convey a rounded impression of the Jewish community enclosed (symbolically if not actually) by that wall. Thus he has pictured a community dedicated to the law of Moses (ch. 8), weighed down by the consciousness of its national heritage of sin, but daring to hope for a greater deliverance than it has hitherto experienced (ch. 9). To that the later editor has added a glimpse of a community creatively resolving to transform the written law into a way of life for the whole community (ch. 10). To complete the picture, the names of the founders of this new community, the ancestor of the editor's own, are recorded in detail, along with the furthest limits of the community's settlement (ch. 11, 12). The Ezra story has ended with the shutting in of the Jewish people.

The significance of dedication is that by making over the work of human hands to God's ownership, that work is put under divine protection. Not only religious buildings were so dedicated, but also private houses (Dt. 20:5). It is hard to say if the dedication ceremony at Jerusalem would have been delayed for the several months needed to accomplish the peopling of the city. Certainly the fact that the dedication is narrated only after the notice of repeopling proves little, but the chronological order may well have been correctly preserved: just as the dedication of a house marked (presumably) the moment when it began to be lived in, the dedication of the wall may have marked the completion of Nehemiah's programme of resettlement.

This narrative clearly derives from Nehemiah's memoirs: the 'I' form (vv. 31, 38, 40) indicates that. But fairly clearly also the Chronicler has expanded Nehemiah's account, and the opening and concluding paragraphs (vv. 27–30, 44–47) may be attributed to him; we may observe throughout these verses the special role given to the Levites, a characteristic interest of the Chronicler.

### GATHERING OF THE LEVITES

### 12:27–30

Indispensable for a service of thanksgiving is the presence of singers and musicians, so the Chronicler is not exceeding the bounds of historical probability is giving first place to the organisation of the levitical music for the ceremony.

**27.** The Levites had to be sought **in all their places** because many of them had settled in country villages (cf. 3:17; 11:20, 36;

and on 10:37, 38) and came to Jerusalem for temple duties only when rostered. This, however, was a special occasion, when all Levites, or at least, all the levitical singers (cf. on 11:15–18), would be needed. By correcting a slight disarray in the Hebrew particles, we can reconstruct a better text: 'to celebrate a joyous dedication festival (lit. to make celebration and joy) with songs of praise and music of cymbals, harps, and zithers' ('and' before **with thanksgiving** is to be omitted, unless perhaps it means **both**, as *AV*; **singing** is to be translated 'music', since vocal music is already implied in **thanksgivings**; and **with** before **harps** is to be deleted). The beginning of temple rebuilding had been celebrated with priestly trumpets and levitical cymbals (Ezr. 3:10, *q.v.*); now, as also at Hezekiah's rededication of the temple (2 Chr. 29:25), levitical harps and zithers join the orchestra. Both **harps** (*nebel*) and zithers (*kinnôr: RSV,* **lyres**) were stringed instruments, the one played with the fingers, the other with a plectrum. Instrumental music seems to have been a 'backing' for the vocal music, rather than following the line of the sung melody. The phrase **And at the dedication of the wall of Jerusalem** is thought by Rudolph to have been taken by the Chronicler from Nehemiah's introduction to this narrative; but perhaps Nehemiah would not have thought to say **of Jerusalem**.

**28–29.** Some **singers** of course lived in Jerusalem (cf. 11:17, 22), but others had created their own villages (v. 29*b*), mostly on the fringes of the settled land, since the Levites had no ancestral holdings (Num. 18:24; Dt. 14:29; Jos. 14:3), and even in the levitical cities only their houses and the associated pasture-lands (unfit for agriculture) had been their own possession (Num. 35:2–8; Lev. 25:32ff.). See B. Mazar, 'The Cities of the Priests and Levites', *VTS* 7 (1960), pp. 193–205. **circuit** (*kikkār*, 'a district', translated 'plain' at 3:22, though probably incorrectly): villages close to Jerusalem in contrast to the more distant levitical settlements, **the villages**, unwalled hamlets, **of the Netophathites**, i.e. surrounding Netophah (cf. on Ezr. 2:21f.), 8 m. south of Jerusalem, **Beth-gilgal**, probably 8 m. north-east of Jerusalem, **Geba** (11:31; Ezr. 2:26) and **Azmaveth** (Ezr. 2:24), 7 m. and 5 m. north of Jerusalem. Of these, only Geba appears in the lists of levitical cities in Jos. 21.

**30.** The purification of clergy, people, and wall before the dedication service was a ritual deriving originally from ancient magical conceptions of 'cleanness'. Cf. W. Eichrodt, *Theology of the Old Testament*, I (1961), pp. 133–7; de Vaux, *Ancient Israel*, pp. 460f. That such rites persisted in Israel can be explained only by their reinterpretation as expressions of the moral purity of Yahweh and of human sinfulness. The rituals employed here are unspecified: the purification of the clergy (cf. Ezr. 6:20) may have involved personal observances such as fasting (cf. Lev. 16:31), abstinence from sexual intercourse, and washing of garments (cf. Exod. 19:14f.; Num. 8:7), as well as public sacrifices (cf. Num. 8:8). The laity would have likewise washed themselves and their clothes, or have been sprinkled with water (Ezek. 36:25) shaken from a hyssop branch (cf. Ps. 51:7; Lev. 14:4–7). A similar sprinkling would accomplish the purification of the wall (cf. Num. 19:18), which may have been regarded as defiled through its contact with the bodies of those killed in defending it at the fall of Jerusalem and with many kinds of unclean objects, persons, and animals since that time. The theocratic ideal is very prominent here: even the gates and wallstones of the 'holy city' (11:1) are sacralised (cf. Ezek. 48:35; Zech. 14:20).

### CIRCUMAMBULATION OF THE WALLS
### 12:31–39

The purification ceremonies had been concerned with the removal of harmful impurity incurred in the past, and now the dedication, to ensure security for the future, may take place. The dedication includes a ritual procession about the walls, such as is reflected in some Psalms (e.g. 48:12ff.; for musicians accompanying processions, cf. 68:24ff.), and is attested in many cultures and periods. Cf. G. d'Alviella, in *Encyclopaedia of Religion and Ethics*, ed. J. Hastings, III (1910), pp. 657ff.; M. Eliade, *Patterns in Comparative Religion* (1958), p. 371. Nehemiah's procession however was unusual: two separate processions, setting off from the same point, each completed half the circuit of the city, and reunited at the temple square. Each procession was arranged thus: a choir (vv. 31, 38a), a lay group of princes (vv. 32, 38b), seven priests (vv. 33f., 41), eight Levite musicians (vv. 35–36a, 42). With vocal music from the front of the procession, and instrumental music from the rear (cf. 'singers in front, minstrels last', Ps. 68:25), the whole procession must have been enveloped in stereophonic sound.

**31.** Both processions seem to have walked along the top of the walls wherever possible. The 8 ft width of the eastern wall (Kenyon, *Jerusalem*, p. 111) would at least have permitted a single file procession. **companies which gave thanks** translates 'praises' (*tôḏôt*), used here concretely for 'choirs'. **went in procession** guesses at an unknown word which is probably a scribal error (*thlkt* for *h'ht hlkt*) for 'the one went' (so *NEB*; cf. v. 38), which *RSV* inserts anyway, since the phrase is needed. The assembly point for the processions must have been roughly equidistant from the temple square via either the east or west walls of the city, for otherwise one group would have to stand about waiting after reaching their goal. A

suitable assembly point would be the Valley Gate (2:13), not otherwise mentioned in the course of the processions. The eastbound
group **went to the right** (*i.e.*, obviously, right hand as one faces
towards the city).

**32.** Following the levitical choir came a leading layman
**Hoshaiah**, otherwise unknown, accompanied by half the lay **princes
of Judah**, i.e. heads of the families listed for example in 10:14–27.

**33–35. a.** Fairly clearly these seven names are of priests: **Azariah,
Meshullam, Shemaiah**, and **Jeremiah** are priests of Nehemiah's
time in 10:2–8, while **Ezra** (not of course Ezra the scribe), a short
form of Azariah, may here be simply a scribal alternative to Azariah
(note absence of 'and' before **Ezra**). **Benjamin** is unknown as a
priestly name, and is probably a minor corruption of Miniamin
(vv. 5, 17), which LXX actually reads; **Judah**, though known as a
Levite name (v. 36), is not a priestly name, and may be a scribal
addition to accompany Benjamin (note no 'and' before **Judah**). The
**priests' sons** (v. 35) are those just named, and certainly not, as
*RSV* and *NEB* imply, the names which follow, which are levitical
(**and** should be deleted). **trumpets** are the priestly musical instru-
ment (cf. Ezr. 3:10); already in David's time, according to the
Chronicler (1 Chr. 15:24), seven trumpet-blowing priests were
employed in a procession.

**35b–36.** Next come the nine Levite musicians headed by **Zechariah** who is supplied with a five-member genealogy, a clue that the
Levite-minded Chronicler has here been expanding Nehemiah's
terse account. As the text stands, Zechariah is great-grandson of the
**Mattaniah** who was choir-leader in Nehemiah's time (11:17), which
is hardly possible. Rudolph suggests that **son of Micaiah, son of
Zaccur** (= Zichri) has been added (though incorrectly, since Zechariah was contemporary with Mattaniah) in order to identify Zechariah's ancestor Mattaniah with the Mattaniah of 11:17. This is not
entirely satisfactory, for if Zechariah was not Mattaniah's descendant
but his contemporary, one wonders why Mattaniah himself is not
leading the levitical contingent. The post-Chronicler editor, the
compiler of 1 Chr. 9, is perhaps responsible, since he believed that
the Jerusalem inhabitants list (1 Chr. 9 = Neh. 11), which includes
Mattaniah, came from the days of Zerubbabel's return (1 Chr. 9:2),
and thus perhaps reasoned that the leading musician contemporary
with Nehemiah must have been the next but two in a genealogical
list he had. The other musicians' names are not listed elsewhere,
though **Shemaiah** (= Shammua, 11:17), **Gilalai** (= Galul, 11:17),
**Nethanel** (2 Chr. 35:9), **Judah** (Neh. 11:8), and **Hanani** (1 Chr.
25:4) are Levite names elsewhere, though of varying dates. **Milalai**
looks suspiciously like a corrupt doublet of Gilalai, but we need

nine Levites to balance the other procession (v. 42). **Azarel** is in one Septuagint tradition Uzziel, elsewhere a levitical musician's name (1 Chr. 25:4). On **David the man of God**, cf. on v. 24.

Reference to **Ezra the scribe** is surprising, since apart from two other textually doubtful passages (8:9; 12:26) there is no evidence of his activity in Nehemiah's time. It is not clear whom he is said to have preceded; if he marched in front of the Levites, he would, reasonably enough, have been with his brother-priests. But, it is argued, that position would have destroyed the symmetrical arrangement of the two processions, and moreover, why should Ezra be last of all the priests? The text in fact suggests that Ezra's place, corresponding to Nehemiah's in the other procession (v. 38), was after the singers and thus at the head of the procession proper. But it seems curious, though not perhaps impossible, that the leader should be mentioned at the end, and the view of most scholars that the reference to Ezra is an editorial addition is very plausible. The intention of this addition is however not mistaken: it represents the foundation of the post-exilic community as the joint work of Nehemiah and Ezra. Moreover it cannot be proved that Ezra's participation is unhistorical; it is not impossible that Ezra should have been brought from retirement or from Babylonia specifically to engage in this ceremony.

**37.** The MT has 'At/to the Fountain Gate and before them they went up'; either 'and' is erroneous, or some verb like 'they walked' has dropped out. The difficulty is obscured by the versions. This procession perhaps temporarily abandoned the course of the wall at **the Fountain Gate** (cf. on 3:15) and climbed the **stairs** (cf. on 3:15) which led up into **the city** from that gate, **the ascent of the wall** itself being too steep. They were doubtless back on the wall by the time they passed **above the house of David** (actually Solomon's palace, cf. on 3:24–27), and left it finally at a point (probably the Horse Gate, 3:28) east of the temple enclosure's **Water Gate** (cf. on 3:24–27).

**38.** The westbound procession, arranged like the other one, contained an advance choir, the leader, and half the laymen, priests, and Levites. Their direction from the Valley Gate is in MT said to be 'in front of them', but this is obviously a scribal error for **to the left** (*RSV, NEB*) (reading *lśmw'l* for *lmw'l*), i.e. northwards. The processions do not involve all the inhabitants of the city, but only some leading representatives, so **half the people** must mean half the lay 'princes' (cf. v. 32); *NEB* inserts 'the leading men'.

**39.** On these landmarks, cf. on 3:1, 3. The **Gate of Ephraim** must be in the north wall and so is out of place here; it is probably a gloss on **Fish Gate** (see M. Avi-Yonah, *IEJ* 4 [1954], p. 242; C.

G. Tuland, *AUSS* 5 [1967], p. 175). The **Gate of the Guard** will be a temple gate, giving access to the 'court of the guard' (3:25).

## THE TEMPLE SERVICE
### 12:40–43

The two processions join forces in the temple court, the first having entered it by the Water Gate (v. 37) and the second by the Gate of the Guard (v. 39; probably the Muster Gate of 3:31). The two choirs apparently took up their position in the temple, but Nehemiah, the lay leaders and the instrumentalists must have stood outside (cf. on 6:11).

**41–42.** The priests and Levites of Nehemiah's procession are now named. Most of the seven trumpet-blowing **priests** (as in v. 35) bear names elsewhere attested as priestly names, though identification of the individuals is uncertain; priests named **Maaseiah, Elioenai, Zechariah**, and **Hananiah** are contemporary with Nehemiah (Ezr. 10:18, 22; Neh. 12:1*b*, 12).

The group in v. 42 is, by comparison with vv. 35f., levitical. Though **Eleazar, Jehohanan**, and **Malchijah** are not elsewhere in Ezra-Nehemiah Levite names, **Maaseiah, Shemaiah, Uzzi** and **Ezer** are levitical contemporaries of Nehemiah (Neh. 8:7; 11:15, 22; 3:19) These lists of names, which seem intrusive into Nehemiah's account and are usually reckoned the work of the Chronicler, may nevertheless be authentic; the juxtaposition of names both attested and unattested elsewhere in his material suggests that he was neither inventing names nor drawing upon irrelevant lists. **Jezrahiah, leader** of the levitical musicians, corresponds to Zechariah (v. 35); his musicians are instrumentalists, not vocalists, and we should translate 'the musicians played loudly', on cymbals especially (cf. the same verb, 1 Chr. 15:16, 19).

**43.** The **great**, that is to say, many, **sacrifices** by which this day was marked were of course thank-offerings, one of the types of 'peace-offering' (Lev. 3), in which the choicest part, the fat, was offered to God, part was given to the priest, and the rest of the sacrificial animal was eaten by the worshipper and his family (cf. **women and children**) in a joyful and noisy celebration. The festivity of the occasion is almost overemphasised by the five times repeated 'joy, rejoice'; as at the celebration of the beginning of temple restoration (Ezr. 3:13) **the joy of Jerusalem was heard afar off**, without however the dark ambiguity that the rejoicing held there.

## AN IDEAL COMMUNITY
### 12:44–13:3

At first sight it appears that these verses narrate further events of the day of dedication of the walls (cf. **on that day**, v. 44; 13:1). But it becomes plain from v. 47 that we are being presented with an overview of the whole age of Nehemiah; **that day** includes the whole period from Zerubbabel to Nehemiah!

This idealistic picture of the post-exilic community, in which levitical concerns figure prominently, clearly comes from the pen of the Chronicler. Its principal purpose is undoubtedly to warn the reader that the abuses mentioned in the closing pages of Nehemiah's memoirs (13:6–29) are not to be regarded as typical of those times, but as shocking exceptions in a well-adjusted and law-abiding community. Maybe the Chronicler saw the past through rose-tinted spectacles, but to give him his due, he did not suppress Nehemiah's trenchant narratives of the scandals of his age (ch. 13), and his own bland assessment may in the end be a reasonably fair verdict.

This passage from the Chronicler also serves the purpose of filling the gap of twelve years or more between the completion of the wall and Nehemiah's second governorship (cf. 13:6). Nehemiah's memoirs seem to have been predominantly concerned with the first few months of his first governorship: he refers to his twelve years of office only incidentally (5:14–18), and even his return to the Persian court and appointment to a second term of duty is mentioned parenthetically (13:6f.).

### PROVISION FOR THE CLERGY
### 12:44–47

**44.** It seems that the Chronicler, in his enthusiasm, speaks as if the vast quantity of offerings made at the dedication festival prompted the institution of storehouse officials: **on that day men were appointed . . . for Judah rejoiced over the priests and the Levites**. This is unrealistic, of course, because what is actually referred to are the regular, stated contributions towards maintenance of the clergy, and not the occasional and voluntary offerings of this joyful family festival; and in any case the appointment of temple treasurers to receive the 'contributions' may well be the episode from Nehemiah's second governorship narrated in 13:13. But this is the Chronicler's way of illustrating the harmony in Nehemiah's community: even obligatory taxes were paid joyfully, he says. **On that day** may of course have a wider reference period (cf. *AV*, 'at that time'), although the Chronicler may have had the day of dedication particularly in mind. On the temple **chambers**, cf. on Ezr. 10:6. The **contributions** are specified as the 'prime produce' dues (not **first fruits**, *RSV*) and the tithes, the former required by the law to be paid to the priests, the latter to the Levites (cf. on 10:37); the first-fruits obligation is not mentioned presumably because it yielded only a small income, and that in raw produce, most of which would have to be consumed and not stored. The taxes were collected **according to the fields of the towns**, i.e. the dues of each town were assessed on the area of its tillage (cf. *NEB*).

**45.** The zeal of the laity was matched by the devotion of the clergy, manifested by their adherence to the anciently formulated liturgies and rituals (cf. 1 Chr. 23–26; 2 Chr. 8:14). Priests and Levites both performed the cultic **service** and the **service of purification**, though the latter was especially the Levites' responsibility (cf. 1 Chr. 23:28). Reference to **singers** and **gatekeepers**, which comes somewhat awkwardly in the Hebrew, may be the addition of the post-Chronicler editor who thought that they also should have been mentioned specifically, and added a note (v. 46) to confirm the ancient institution of the service of song.

**46.** All the clergy performed their duties 'according to the command of David and his son Solomon' (v. 45), so why the institution of only the service of *song* by David is specifically referred to is inexplicable. It is odd too that **Asaph** should be spoken of as if he were not himself a **chief of the singers**, and strange that the existence of three chiefs of the singers (1 Chr. 15:16f., 19) should be overlooked (as by *NEB*, translating 'Asaph took the lead as chief of the singers'). We should perhaps read with Q^ere, 'there were chiefs' (cf. *AV*).

**47.** The ideal state of provision for the clergy is summarised: Israel gave to the **singers** and **gatekeepers** their daily portions (contrast 11:23 where their support seems to come from an imperial grant), and **set apart** (i.e. dedicated, hallowed, removed from secular use) the tithes of the Levites, who, as a matter of course in such a harmonious community, **set apart** the tithe of the tithe for the priests (cf. on 10:38). That all these arrangements operated effectively throughout the first century of the restored community, from the first governor **Zerubbabel** to **Nehemiah** the governor is hardly likely, but it would be unwise to deny that some rudimentary system of maintenance for the clergy must have been in existence from the earliest days of the return.

## EXCLUSION OF FOREIGNERS
### 13:1–3

The Chronicler continues, as in 12:44–47, to warn the reader that what is about to be narrated in the Nehemiah memoirs must not be thought typical of those times. In particular, the continued existence of foreigners in the new community (Tobiah, vv. 4f.; foreign women, vv. 23f.; Sanballat, v. 28) is shown to have been altogether contrary to the will of the people, which had deliberately excluded all foreigners from 'Israel' (v. 3). Such exclusion was of course not Ezra's dissolution of the mixed marriages (Ezr. 9–10), for here it is a question of debarring all foreigners from temple worship (cf. on 'assembly', v.1). Nevertheless, the motive is similar: separation from foreign influence is but the other side of the coin to an increasingly intense adherence to the law, and insistence on purity of worship. The occasion of this application of the law is unknown, but it would obviously have appealed to Nehemiah (cf. vv. 8, 25, 28). It is uncertain whether the Chronicler had definite knowledge of such an assembly, or whether he simply inferred that the law of Dt. 23:3ff. must at some time have been read publicly and acted upon by the exclusive and strict community of those days (cf. also 10:28f.).

1. **On that day**, as in 12:44, refers quite generally to the period of Ezra and Nehemiah. An assembly like that described in ch. 8 is envisaged. And as in that case, what is expressed is the united will of the whole people to follow the law in its details (cf. on 8:1); it is not a matter of a narrow-minded group of scholars imposing their opinions on the people. The law quoted (Dt. 23:3ff.) from the **book of Moses** (a phrase of the Chronicler's; cf. 2 Chr. 25:4; 35:12; cf. also Neh. 8:1), excluding Ammonites and Moabites from the **assembly** (*qāhāl*, the worshipping community; similarly 'Israel', v. 3) **unto the tenth generation**, is patient of a more liberal and a more rigid interpretation. The more liberal, which was perhaps originally intended, would allow their entry after the tenth generation (cf. the case of Edomites, who are acceptable in the third generation, Dt. 23:7f.), which time had of course been reached centuries earlier; not surprisingly, however, Nehemiah's community opted for the stricter, though not improper, interpretation that the law imposed a perpetual ban on these races, even in the tenth generation.

2. The first incident referred to is narrated in Num. 21:21ff., though there it is the Amorites of Heshbon, not the Ammonites, who refuse Israel passage through their territory. But the two kingdoms adjoined one another, and Ammonites were probably closely related originally to the Amorites. Up to this point, Israel had been

sold **bread and water** by the Edomites and Moabites (Dt. 2:28f.) who had no objection to making an easy profit from the Israelites as long as they kept their distance and travelled up the eastern borders of their territories. However, to enter Canaan from the fringes of Moab, Israel had to pass through Amorite territory; the Amorites proved to be as uncooperative as the Edomites had earlier been when Israel had proposed to travel through, and not alongside, their territory (Num. 20:14–21). Hence Israelite hostility to Amorites and Ammonites.

The second episode referred to, the 'hiring' of **Balaam**, concerns the Moabites principally, though a tradition that Balaam himself was an Ammonite, or at least resident in Ammon, may lie behind the present association of Moab with Ammon (taking Pethor [Num. 22:5] not as the place-name Pitru, but as 'dream-interpreter'; so L. Yaure, 'Elymas-Nehelamite-Pethor', *JBL* 79 [1960], pp. 297–314). The narrative (Num. 22–24) does not explicitly mention a 'hiring' of the prophet Balaam, though it may naturally be inferred (cf. 22:18; explicit in Dt. 23:4). Payment of prophets was a perfectly respectable practice in the ancient world, and it was only later that Balaam's acceptance of money came to be regarded as indicative of his avaricious character (so Philo, *De vita Mosis* 1.48; 2 Pet. 2:15; Jude 11) and that he became the stock example of one who perverts the truth, and seduces the people of God; cf. also Num. 31:8, 16; Jos. 13:22; Rev. 2:14; *Pirqê Abôt* 5.19; and see G. Vermes, *Scripture and Tradition in Judaism* (1961), pp. 175ff.

The **curse** (cf. also on 5:13) against Israel was of course never uttered; Balaam, whose curses were always effective (Num. 22:6), found it impossible to curse those whom God had blessed (23:8; cf. 22:12). In the Balaam story, the prophetic quality of the curse, which removes it from the level of witchcraft and makes it the expression of the divine will, is particularly emphasised: Balaam can speak only what is put in his mouth by God (22:18, 35, 38; etc.). Far from merely evading a curse, Israel is positively blessed by Balaam; 'surely the wrath of men shall praise thee' (Ps. 76:10; and cf. Gen. 50:20).

**3. those of foreign descent** might include those with any non-Israelite ancestors (thus *NEB*, 'all who were of mixed blood'), but the Heb. 'ere*b*, probably at root 'immigrants' (so W. A. van der Weiden, *VD* 44 [1966], pp. 97–104) rather than 'mixture', refers most naturally to aliens without any Jewish ancestor. Exclusion of **all** such from the cult reflects an interpretation of Dt. 23:3–6 on a *pars pro toto* basis, but it is contrary to the intention of Dt. 23 itself (cf. vv. 7f.), and conflicts with the inclusion of non-Jews among those who bound themselves to the pledge in Neh. 10 (cf. on v. 28). The Chronicler must be speaking rather generally.

## REFORMS DURING NEHEMIAH'S SECOND GOVERNORSHIP
### 13:4-31

After the Chronicler's glowing pictures of the community of the restoration, we now read Nehemiah's account of the somewhat less rosy reality. The period described in this section, almost universally ascribed to the Nehemiah memoirs, is the second phase of his governorship, from c. 432 BC onward. He had served as governor for an unbroken period of twelve years (445–433 BC; cf. 5:14), and had then paid a visit to Babylon (v. 6). Had his term of office expired, or was this merely a routine visit to the king, long delayed because of the pressure of work in Jerusalem? (Cf. the absence of the Persian governor Arsames from his post at Elephantine; AP 30.4f.) It is not at all clear, but certainly Nehemiah returned to Jerusalem as governor, not as a private citizen (cf. vv. 11, 13, 19).

Rudolph and others have wished to locate the activity of Ezra in the interval between Nehemiah's two tours of duty. Since Nehemiah's journey to and fro would have taken some six months (cf. on Ezr. 7:8f.), and it is not unreasonable to suppose a six-month residence by Nehemiah at the Persian court, Ezra's work, which could have been completed within twelve months, could in principle have occupied the interval. But other factors have also to be taken into account; cf. Introduction, IV.

In this second phase of his governorship, Nehemiah's interest has shifted quite markedly from the physical and political problems of Jerusalem to more religious matters.

## PURIFICATION OF THE TEMPLE PRECINCT
### 13:4-9

Nehemiah is not done with his old enemy **Tobiah** (cf. 2:10; 6:17ff.) yet! Awed by Nehemiah's autocratic spirit, so long as the governor resides in Jerusalem, Tobiah takes advantage of his absence to get himself installed in a temple apartment. Tobiah's effrontery and the complaisance of **Eliashib** the temple dean are remarkable, since both must have realised how Nehemiah was likely to react when he discovered an Ammonite living in the temple chambers. Perhaps they had not expected Nehemiah to return to the governorship of Judea.

**4. Now before this** is the editorial linking phrase of the Chronicler, to indicate that the installation of **Tobiah** preceded the

assembly depicted in vv. 1ff.; naturally it must have preceded the
decision of the community to exclude foreigners from worship,
otherwise the people would be represented as having gone back on
their decision. The phrase cannot be from Nehemiah's memoirs,
which last narrated the dedication of the wall (12:31–43); for
Nehemiah cannot have visited the Persian court before the dedication of the walls. Nor can we assume that some episode, perhaps in
connection with his trip to Persia (so Bowman), has been omitted
from the Nehemiah memoirs, since vv. 6f. seem to be mentioning
Nehemiah's furlough for the first time. **Eliashib the priest** can
hardly be the contemporary high priest of that name (3:1; 12:10f.),
not because he is not called high priest (for that could be a derogatory omission of his title by Nehemiah or an editor), but because
the high priest is not likely to be called the one **appointed over the
chambers** (cf. on Ezr. 8:29) of the temple—clearly a managerial
office. Nevertheless, it would be strange that **Tobiah** was able to
make this gesture of defiance to Nehemiah's politico-religious policies if he did not have the support of a number of priests, and
perhaps also of the high priest himself, who presumably was not
entirely in sympathy with the direction obedience to the law had
taken (cf. 13:28). It is not impossible that Tobiah had simply intimi-
dated the Jerusalem priesthood, inconfident now that they had lost,
for the first time in twelve years, an authoritative leader. Tobiah's
connection with Eliashib was very likely by marriage (cf. also 6:18),
though the Hebrew is not explicit.

5. To turn a temple room into a *pied-à-terre* for a layman, let
alone a foreigner, was an act of sacrilege; Tobiah was taking his
revenge on Nehemiah. On the **cereal offering**, cf. on 10:33. The
principal use of **frankincense** (*lᵉbōnâ*, 'the white [substance]'), a
resin from terebinth-like trees from S. Arabia, the genus *Boswellia*,
was as a supplement to the cereal offering (Lev. 2:1f.); a different
term (*qᵉtōret*) is usually employed for the incense offered as an
independent sacrifice (e.g. Exod. 30:1–10). See further, G. W. Van
Beek, 'Frankincense and Myrrh', *BA* 23 (1960), pp. 70–94; M.
Haran, 'The uses of incense in the ancient Israelite ritual', *VT* 10
(1960), pp. 113–29. For the **vessels**, both for storage and for cultic
use, cf. on 10:29. The **tithes** for the Levites and the **contributions**
(*tᵉrûmâ*) for the priests have already been discussed at 10:37, 39.
**given by commandment to** probably mistranslates the Hebrew
*miṣwat*, 'commandment', here used in a derived sense 'alms,
charity', as in later Hebrew (see S. Lieberman, *JBL* 65 [1946], pp.
69–72).

6. Nehemiah hastens to add that of course he bore no responsibility for Tobiah's invasion of the sanctity of the temple; in similar

vein the Jewish priests at Elephantine excuse their governor Arsames from responsibility for the sacrilegious destruction of their temple which had occurred during his absence at the Persian court (*AP* 30.4f., 30). There is no particular reason why Nehemiah should refer to **Artaxerxes** by his title, **king of Babylon** (cf. on Ezr. 1:1); elsewhere he says only 'the king' (1:11; 2:1; 5:14). But it is not necessary to see an editorial hand here, still less to reject the report of Nehemiah's visit to the court and second governorship as an attempt by the post-Chronicler editor to exonerate Nehemiah from responsibility for what was happening in Jerusalem (Kellermann, pp. 49ff.).

**7. a chamber in the courts**: one opening on to the courts of the temple (cf. 8:16).

**8.** Nehemiah was obviously **very angry**, but the Hebrew rather means 'it was very displeasing to me' (cf. *RV*). While his violence must have been prompted to some extent by Tobiah's assault on his authority, there was no doubt also a more noble motivation in his temple cleansing. The use of sacred things for purposes of self-advancement is no mere ritual defilement, but a real attack upon God and his rights. At least in his zeal for the house of God Nehemiah is not sub-Christian (cf. Jn 2:14–18)! As governor of a province bound by Pentateuchal law (cf. on Ezr. 7:25), Nehemiah apparently had official jurisdiction over temple affairs, and he does not seem to have been acting simply on his own personal and moral authority. The picture is a vivid one: the irate governor himself throws Tobiah's household effects out into the temple court. We may presume that Tobiah himself was conveniently absent. An interesting parallel to the Tobiah episode is Cambyses' cleansing of the Egyptian temple of Neith, involving the expulsion of foreigners who had installed themselves in the precincts (cf. *The Cambridge Ancient History*, ed. J. B. Bury *et al.*, IV [1926], pp. 22f., 188).

**9.** The priests seem to obey Nehemiah's orders to perform a ritual purification (cf. 2 Chr. 29:15–19) of the contaminated area as meekly as they had acquiesced in Tobiah's tenancy. (For a ritual of temple purification at Babylon, cf. *ANET*, p. 333b.) Not only the room itself but the **chambers** adjoining, or perhaps the whole block of temple rooms, are regarded as deconsecrated by the presence of a non-Jew, who is in a state of permanent ritual uncleanness. When the stores traditionally housed in Tobiah's large chamber are returned to their place, the tithes for the Levites are conspicuous by their absence. There thus comes to Nehemiah's attention a second scandal, which he proceeds to deal with.

RESTORATION OF TITHES FOR THE LEVITES

13:10–14

While the income of other temple clergy has apparently not dimin-
ished, the **portions**, i.e. tithes (cf. on 10:37), the sole source of
income for the Levites, do not seem to have been paid at all (a
similar situation is reflected in Mal. 3:8ff.). There had consequently
been a mass exodus of Levites from Jerusalem together with refusal
by country Levites to come up to Jerusalem for their rostered duty;
temple worship must have been brought virtually to a standstill.
Nehemiah's concern was not primarily humanitarian but religious:
the **house of God** was **forsaken** (v. 11). His measures, here recounted, for ensuring regular delivery of levitical tithes were to be super-
seded by the arrangements agreed in the community's pledge
(10:37ff.): establishment of levitical depots throughout the country
would prove more effective than expecting **all Judah** to bring **the
tithe . . . into the storehouses** (v. 12) by themselves.

**10. And I also found out** obscures, especially by the gratuitous
insertion of **also**, the close connection between the returning of
stores to Tobiah's room and Nehemiah's discovery about the tithes;
it would be better to translate 'and I realised'. How could the
Levites have fled **each to his field** when according to the law (Dt.
14:29; 18:1f.; Num. 18:20–24) they have no landed property in
Israel? It is true that the Pentateuch allows them no agricultural
land, but the priestly legislation establishes 48 levitical cities (see
M. Haran, *JBL* 80 [1961], pp. 45–54, 156–65) with associated
pastures (Num. 35:1–8; Jos. 21), and some such cities (cf. on
12:28f.) may be referred to. The fact that all levitical cities in the
territories of Benjamin and Judah had belonged only to Aaronite
Levites is no real problem; for there must have been a redistribution
after the exile. It is also possible that Levites had been (illegally)
buying fields, both during the exile and thereafter. The **work** of
**Levites and singers** is of course the cultic service of the temple;
gatekeepers are strangely not mentioned.

**11.** Once more Nehemiah intervenes in religious matters, and the
justice of his reproof cannot be gainsaid. He takes it for granted
that the lay leaders (**officials**, cf. on Ezr. 9:2), and not just the
clergy, have a responsibility for the maintenance of worship, a
viewpoint which underlies the reform pledge of ch. 10 (cf. on
10:32f.). The **why** question is one of the conventional forms of an
accusation (cf. on 2:19). The Levites themselves are not guiltless;
their duty was to remain at their sacred posts, whether they were
paid or not. So Nehemiah begins by haling them back to their
**stations** or workplaces; only then is their **tithe** paid.

13. The appointment of **treasurers**, referred to already (12:44) by the Chronicler in his generalising introduction to this last chapter of Nehemiah's memoirs, is not necessarily the institution of that office; therefore the fact that Ezra found a similar body in existence upon his arrival in Jerusalem (Ezr. 8:33) cannot be used as evidence that Nehemiah preceded Ezra. While the temple treasurers in Ezra's time consisted of two priests and two Levites, Nehemiah's appointees numbered: a priest, **Shelemiah**; a scribe, **Zadok**, possibly identical with Nehemiah's personal secretary Zedekiah (10:1, *q.v.*); a Levite, **Pedaiah** (cf. on Ezr. 3:25); and, apparently, a singer, **Hanan** b. **Zaccur** b. **Mattaniah**, very possibly the grandson of the choir-leader Mattaniah (11:17; **Zaccur** would thus have been named after a family ancestor, Zaccur or Zichri; cf. on 12:35; 11:17). Priests are represented on this board since their interests also are involved (cf. on 10:38); if our identification of Zadok is correct, the governor himself is represented, to ensure justice.

14. Each episode in this chapter (vv. 4–13 counting as a single incident) concludes with a brief prayer (vv. 14, 22, 29) that God will **remember** Nehemiah for good. This he would do by entering and not erasing the record of Nehemiah's deeds in his heavenly account book (cf. Isa. 65:6; Dan. 7:10; Rev. 20:12). The book of deeds is a somewhat different image from the book of life (Exod. 32:32f.; Ps. 69:28; Dan. 12:1), from which names may be erased, but it serves a similar function. The word for **good deeds** (*ḥesed*) is that usually translated by *RSV* 'steadfast love'; it refers to deeds, whether God's or man's, motivated by loyalty to the covenant, and is here best translated 'my pious deeds'; the *ḥāsîd* is the pious man, who feels himself bound to Yahweh. Nehemiah's piety has, in the preceding narrative, moved him to act on behalf of **the house of his God** (vv. 4–9, the cleansing of the temple) and the **service** (vv. 10–13, arrangements for the Levites).

### PREVENTION OF PROFANATION OF THE SABBATH

### 13:15–22

The previous abuses were due in the first case to the influence of one individual, Tobiah, and in the second case possibly to a break-down in the machinery of government during Nehemiah's absence. The guilt of sabbath-breaking, however, lay more squarely on the common people. If Ezra did precede Nehemiah, and had already established Pentateuchal law as state law (Ezr. 7:26), it is remarkable that disobedience, especially to one of the Ten Commandments, could go unchecked. In itself, this is an argument for the priority of Nehemiah. But it should be recalled that Ezra's work now lay thirty years in the past, and it is perfectly credible that a new generation should not display the same enthusiasm for the law as the community of Ezra's day had. It is incorrect to label Ezra's reforms a fiasco, as do most supporters of the priority of Ezra, since Nehemiah's account implies a high standard of legal obedience throughout the fourteen years of his first governorship. What is inconceivable in the light of this neglect of the sabbath is that Ezra's reforms, together with the national assemblies depicted in Ezr. 10 and Neh. 8, should have taken place during Nehemiah's absence from Jerusalem.

Nehemiah's reform again involves intervention in religious matters. The pledge later signed by the people (Neh. 10) represents a certain relaxation of Nehemiah's emergency measures (cf. on 10:31). For emphasis on the sabbath in post-exilic times, cf. also Isa. 56:2, 4, 6; 58:13.

**15.** It is not made clear whether the profaners of the sabbath were returned exiles or 'the people of the land' (cf. on Ezr. 3:3). In either case, Nehemiah holds the 'nobles' responsible (v. 17), though they may not personally have been guilty. The season of this narrative is fixed by the date of the grape-harvest, September-October. The **grain** cannot be sheaves (*AV*), since the grain-harvest takes place some three months earlier, and the Nehemiah of v. 8 is hardly likely to have postponed action three months. The **figs** of that season would be the late, or autumn, figs (cf. Jer. 8:13).

As well as the general law of sabbath rest (Exod. 20:8–11), harvesting on the sabbath is explicitly prohibited (Exod. 34:21), and the resting of one's beasts is demanded (Exod. 23:12). Whether the restriction of travel on the sabbath (cf. Ac. 1:12; *IDB*, IV, p. 141) applied already at this time is unknown (but cf. the precedent in Exod. 16:29). Nehemiah warned them off **on the very day when they sold food**, though the clause may mean 'I warned (them) (*or*, I protested) because of the day on which they were selling food'; he does not of course mean that it was only or chiefly the selling that was reprehensible.

**16.** It is not clear whether the Tyrian fishmongers and merchants were settled **in the city** or simply in the province of Judea (the Heb. is lit. 'in it'). For evidence of Phoenician trading colonies, see S. Moscati, *The World of the Phoenicians* (1968), especially pp. 82–7. Nehemiah's complaint is not against the presence of foreigners in the holy city or holy land, but against their encouragement to the Jews to disregard the sabbath. **and in Jerusalem** may mean 'and that in Jerusalem' (*NEB*, 'even in Jerusalem'); that they should choose Jerusalem for their wrongdoing compounds the sin. Alternatively, the phrase has been misplaced from the beginning of the verse, where it formed a counterpart to 'in Judah' (v. 15).

**17.** Nehemiah has taken direct action against the law-breakers, but now, to greater effect, he turns to the **nobles**, the Jerusalem-based family heads (11:1), who have not themselves necessarily been involved in commerce on the sabbath, but who are apparently responsible for good behaviour in the city. To refrain from exercising their authority to check disobedience to the law is itself a crime (**this evil thing**), itself a profanation of the sabbath (the phrase is pre-eminently Ezekiel's, e.g. 20:16). **What is this evil thing which you are doing?**: a standard way of beginning an accusation (cf. on v. 11).

**18.** Nehemiah takes his cue from the prophets, especially Jer. 17:19–27 (cf. also Ezek. 20:12–24), where the carrying of loads into Jerusalem on the sabbath is expressly said to be a profanation of the sabbath (v. 22), and the destruction of Jerusalem is threatened if the practice does not cease (v. 27). Nehemiah does not mean of course that it was infringement of the sabbath law alone that had brought upon Israel **this evil** of exile and upon the city the **evil** of destruction, but obviously he took that specific prophetic reference very seriously (cf. v. 19*b*). In speaking of **your fathers** but of **our God**, he is at this moment refusing to identify himself with his nation (contrast 1:6f.): there is no point in joining in collective repentance for sins which one has not committed, nor ever would commit. For the fear that the Jewish community may yet earn for itself an even more devastating experience than the exile, cf. Ezr. 9:14.

**19.** It is preferable to translate 'when the gates (i.e. market-places at the gates) of Jerusalem began to empty', or 'had been closed' (*NEB*, following G. R. Driver, *VTS* 16 [1967], pp. 62f.), at nightfall on the Friday. The **gates**, or more precisely, the wooden **doors** set in the gates, would have been shut at nightfall in any case (cf. 7:3); Nehemiah orders that they should remain shut until the Sunday morning. He was not prohibiting movement in and out of the city: people could still presumably use small postern gates, and, indeed, do their shopping outside the city, bringing their provisions back with them. Doubtless it was to prevent this evasion that Nehemiah posted his own **servants** (cf. on 4:16) at the gates.

**20.** Finding their entry to Jerusalem barred, the traders settled down outside the walls to wait the sabbath out. Nehemiah can hardly have objected to that, and one may suspect that they were selling their produce to any citizens who cared to come out to them, or at least that their presence was a standing temptation.

**21.** He gives them a chance to realise that it is not worth their while coming on the sabbath; they apparently still hope to do business, so he threatens them with violence.

**22.** The transference of guard-duty to **the Levites** is no desperate attempt by the Chronicler to introduce Levites wherever possible, but plainly designed to relieve Nehemiah's personal servants, probably disgruntled by having to work overtime on the sabbath. The Levite gatekeepers hitherto had been responsible for the temple gates only, but now the keeping of the city gates on the sabbath (they are not replacing the regular gatekeepers) is made a religious duty, requiring like other divine service (cf. 12:30; Ezr. 6:20) ritual purification.

Nehemiah's measure is an excellent example of the Jewish tendency to make 'a hedge about the Torah': lest the sabbath law of burden-carrying should be broken, with fearful consequences (v. 18), he removes as far as possible any opportunity for breaking the law. But to forcibly prevent one's fellows from disobeying God's law is not usually the best way of encouraging their willing obedience, and we may be relieved to find in the pledge of ch. 10 (precipitated by the events of ch. 13), that the show of force in the shape of Levite guards has been dropped, the possibility of food being brought into Jerusalem for sale on the sabbath is envisaged—*and* the community pledges itself not to buy (10:31).

The paragraph concludes with Nehemiah's reiterated prayer (cf. v. 14) that God will **remember** and reward him; if previously he prayed that God would not 'wipe out' his 'deeds of loyalty' (*ḥeseḏ*), here he acknowledges that any reward will necessarily be according to the greatness of God's covenanted 'loyalty' (*ḥeseḏ*) (cf. 1:5). To **spare** means to 'spare the life' (cf. e.g. Dt. 13:8f.; Ezek. 5:11f.); this is therefore a prayer for long life or continuing vitality.

### ACTION AGAINST MIXED MARRIAGES

### 13:23-29

If Ezra has already brought about the dissolution of mixed marriages (Ezr. 9-10), how can Nehemiah have found **Jews who had married** women of **Ashdod, Ammon and Moab**? Advocates of the priority of Nehemiah naturally use this text as evidence for their case, sometimes arguing besides that a tightening up by Ezra is more probable than a relaxation of an Ezran decision by Nehemiah. This latter argument is in my judgment entirely without foundation; as for the former, while the most natural inference is that Ezra's reforms had not yet taken place, that is by no means a necessary inference. Above all the length of time between Ezra and Nehemiah should be taken into account: it is now at least thirty years since

Ezra's reforms in 458 BC; there has been enough time for a completely new generation to grow up, mixed marriages to be contracted, and children of those marriages to have learned to talk. Ezra himself may well have been dead by c. 430 BC. If his reforms were wholly effective for only one generation, he cannot be counted a failure.

Was Nehemiah's attitude to mixed marriages more tolerant than Ezra's? It is often assumed to have been so, but he does not say directly what he did about existing marriages, and there are some hints that he may have demanded that they should be dissolved (vv. 25, 27). The question must remain open. As for the propriety of their methods, some may find it hard to choose between the massive exertion of moral pressure by Ezra and the direct physical violence of Nehemiah!

**23. In those days** is a very vague marker of time, but it may link Nehemiah's discovery here reported with his previously mentioned observations in Judea (**I saw**; cf. v. 15). These Jews with Gentile wives must have lived on the fringes of Judea, otherwise their children would have been bilingual in their mother's and father's languages. On **Ashdod** and **Ammon**, cf. on 4:7; on **Moab**, cf. on 13:1, 2.

**24.** Why are only those who spoke Ashdodite mentioned? Most commentators think that Nehemiah spoke only of Ashdodite-Jewish marriages, and that 'Ammon and Moab' in v. 23 is a later gloss. This involves deleting as well **but the language of each people**, a phrase lacking also in the Septuagint; once 'Ammon and Moab' had crept into the text from the margin, this could have been added to avoid the impression that Ashdodite was spoken also by children of Jewish-Ammonite and Jewish-Moabite parents. But a case may be made for retaining 'Ammon and Moab' in v. 23. As far as we know, both Ammonite and Moabite were mutually intelligible with Hebrew; thus the other **half** of the children of mixed marriages did not arouse Nehemiah's wrath, since they would have been able to speak the language of Judah. What the Ashdodite language was we do not know; recent excavations at and near Ashdod have produced inscriptions in Aramaic and Hebrew, but Nehemiah can hardly have become so angry if the children spoke only Aramaic, not Hebrew: it had already proved necessary, it seems, for the law to be orally interpreted into Aramaic for returned exiles (cf. on 8:8f.). Only a quite different language, whether the old Philistine language, or the language of Assyrian settlers, would suit the account.

One thing certain is that the older idea of a hybrid Hebrew-Ashdodite language (cf. *AV*, 'half in the speech of Ashdod') cannot be correct; this is clearly not a case of patois developed over several

generations, but of children speaking their mother's language. The
**Jew's language** (*yᵉhûḏît*, lit. 'Jewish') is the only Hebrew term we
know for the Hebrew language (elsewhere only 1 Kg. 18:26, 28 and
parallels). The inability to speak Hebrew will of course result in a
loosening of attachment to the nation and the religion.

**25.** The rather trivial matter of children unable to speak Hebrew
is not the full cause of Nehemiah's wrath: he sees the perpetuation
of mixed marriages as endangering the existence of the community
(cf. v. 18) and as an act of disloyalty to God (v. 27). Against
Nehemiah's fears we may set the fact that the Jewish community
at Elephantine managed to preserve its individuality for some ten
generations in spite of intermarriage with non-Jews, wholesale adoption of Aramaic, and the borrowing of Aramaic and Egyptian legal
and economic customs (see Porten, *Elephantine*, p. 299). **contended
with** means 'reproached' (cf. vv. 26f.). Nehemiah obviously does
not feel that he demeans himself by resorting to personal abuse and
assault (cf. vv. 8, 21); it is hardly 'correct' official behaviour, but it
has the desired effect. 'In Egypt, Palestine, etc., persons are
whipped with the Koorbash and struck with the hand in a way that
would be firmly resented in the West by the most menial' (Witton
Davies). To pull out (some of) the hair is a conventional sign of
grief (cf. on Ezr. 9:3), and also a humiliating punishment (Is. 50:6);
though some see in Nehemiah's act a symbolic meaning, as if to
say: 'It is you who should be pulling out your own hair in repentance
for your misdeeds', it is more likely that this was just an attack
made in the anger of the moment. The Syriac version makes
Nehemiah even more violent by identifying *'mrtm*, 'I plucked', with
the Syriac verb *tmr* 'to bury', and expanding the sentence to 'I killed
some of them and buried them'! The oath would of course be in
the form 'I will not give' (lit. '[May Yahweh do so to me and more
also] if I give'); Nehemiah reports the words he demanded of them.
They promise, as does the whole community later (10:30), that in
future the law of Dt. 7:3 will be kept; specific reference to this
verse explains why he makes them swear **not** to **give your daughters
to their sons** although that is not entirely relevant to the present
situation where Jewish men are married to heathen women. But
why should they swear that they themselves will not marry foreign
women, when they have already done so? **for yourselves** is not in
the Deuteronomic law, and is in fact omitted here by the Septuagint,
probably because of this very difficulty of interpretation. It is
possible that such an oath demands the divorce of wives married
contrary to the law, and that Nehemiah's attitude to mixed marriages was not so very different from Ezra's.

**26.** It is no use thinking that the faith of a Jewish husband will triumph over that of his pagan wife: even Solomon **beloved by his God** as he was (his other name Jedidiah means 'beloved of Yahweh'; 2 Sam. 12:24f.) and incomparably wise (for **no king like him**, cf. 1 Kg. 3:12) was led astray by his foreign wives (1 Kg. 11:1–8).

**27. Shall we then listen to you and do** . . . is a possible translation, but who are **we**, and how can 'we' listen, since Nehemiah seems to be doing all the talking himself? **listen** (*šāma'*) can mean 'obey'; the sense could be: 'Not even Solomon is to be "obeyed" (i.e. followed) in this matter of foreign wives; how much less should you be "obeyed" who have no authority?' (cf. *NEB*, 'are we to follow your example?'); this would be a typical rabbinic argument 'from greater to less'. Or we could understand: 'Shall we (the authorities) listen to you, i.e. allow you, to do this great evil?' This suggests that Nehemiah intends to break up the mixed marriages (cf. on 'for yourselves', v. 25). Less probable is the translation which takes the verb as a passive: 'Is it heard concerning you that you do . . .', since it was a scandal uncovered by Nehemiah himself, not reported to him. To contract marriages with foreign women is to **act treacherously** (*mā'al*), i.e. in breach of covenant (cf. 1:8; Ezr. 9:2; 10:2, 10).

**28.** Here was a far more blatant case of 'treachery' than those half-Jewish ménages on the fringes of Judah (cf. on v. 23): the grandson or son of the high priest (**high priest** could refer to **Jehoiada** or **Eliashib**) had married a daughter of Nehemiah's arch-enemy Sanballat (cf. 2:10). The Samaria papyri (discovered in 1962) make it likely that this marriage was not that of Manasseh, brother of Jaddua, with Nikaso, daughter of Sanballat, mentioned by Josephus (*Ant.* 11.7.2) who traces the origin of the Samaritan temple to Manasseh's exile to Samaria; cf. F. M. Cross, *BA* 26 (1963), pp. 120f. While the law about foreign marriages for Israelites generally was open to variant interpretations (cf. on Ezr. 9–10), the law for a high priest (and by implication, for potential high priests) was plain: 'he shall take to wife a virgin of his own people' (Lev. 21:14). In a dramatic exercise of authority Nehemiah exiled (cf. on Ezr. 7:26) the nameless priest from Judah (**chased him from me**); relations with the governor of Samaria were already so bad that they could not be damaged by this.

**29.** Nehemiah's memoirs will end with a twofold **remember**: a plea for vengeance (cf. 6:14) on priestly wrongdoers (v. 29), and for blessing for himself (v. 30; cf. vv. 14, 22). **them** must refer to the high-priestly family who have allowed an alliance with Sanballat's family. The best commentary on **the covenant of the priesthood** (or preferably, with some versions, 'the priests') **and the Levites** is Mal. 2:1–8: God's 'covenant with Levi' (i.e. with the whole tribe,

priests included) was 'a covenant of life and peace' from God's side
(cf. Num. 25:12f.) and a responsibility on the clergy's side that 'the
lips of a priest should guard knowledge, and men should seek
instruction from his mouth' (cf. Dt. 33:8ff.). But here one case of
practical disobedience to the law has called in question the whole
teaching ministry of the priests (cf. Mal. 2:8f.).

## SUMMARY OF OTHER REFORMS IN NEHEMIAH'S SECOND GOVERNORSHIP

### 13:30–31

**Thus** is misleading (and not in the Hebrew), since what follows has
no direct reference to what precedes, but itemises further cultic
reforms. **I cleansed them**, presumably the priests and Levites,
**from everything foreign** is a more far-reaching reform than the
banishment of Jehoiada's son (v. 28) or the ejection of Tobiah (vv.
4–9), but precisely what it involved we cannot tell. Establishment
of **the duties of the priests and Levites, each in his work** again,
unless Nehemiah is exaggerating his own importance, must mean
more than the appointment of four treasurers (v. 13); that the lay
governor could overhaul the temple administration speaks volumes
for the state of the clergy. Provision for the **wood offering** and **first
fruits** also lie outside the scope of ch. 13, though these reforms are
plainly enough reflected in the national pledge at 10:34f.

Nehemiah's preoccupation in this account with cultic affairs does
not mark him out as a priest *manqué*, but displays a zeal to bring
his community into subjection to the law of God. Here at last is
something he has in common with Ezra. For him obedience to the
law was not an end in itself, however: he saw it as simply the
indispensable condition for the continuance of the community; just
as he knew his own personal faithfulness to the law to be the
prerequisite for the fulfilment of his prayer: **Remember me, O my
God, for good.**

# ESTHER

# INTRODUCTION
## to
## Esther

# INTRODUCTION TO ESTHER

## I. CONTENTS OF THE BOOK OF ESTHER

This commentary deals only with the Book of Esther as it appears in the Hebrew Bible and Protestant versions of the Bible in modern languages. The book itself, however, exists in three major forms, of which the standard Hebrew text is only one. Of the two ancient Greek versions, one (the A-text) probably translated fairly closely a variant Hebrew edition of the book which at first apparently did not extend beyond Est. 8:5, but which was later supplemented by a conclusion composed in Greek to link the story of Esther with the festival of Purim (see C. A. Moore, 'A Greek Witness to a Different Hebrew Text of Esther', *ZAW* 79 [1967], pp. 351–8 [= Moore, *Studies*, pp. 521–8]; H. J. Cook, 'The A-Text of the Greek Versions of the Book of Esther', *ZAW* 81 [1969], pp. 369–76). The A-text now contains all the additions found in the B-text, but it probably did not contain them originally but borrowed them from the B-text. The A-text is printed as a separate text in the larger Cambridge Septuagint and the Göttingen Septuagint; the text and the only complete translation of it is printed in D. J. A. Clines, *The Esther Scroll* (1984).

The other Greek version (the B-text) was made from yet another recension of the Hebrew text and had several lengthy additions (some composed in Hebrew, some in Greek) inserted into it; it also omits many words or phrases found in the Masoretic Hebrew text. The importance of this Greek version, normally printed as part of the Septuagint translation of the Old Testament, is that it formed the original of the Latin Vulgate and all modern language versions descended from the Vulgate. This longer version of Esther, with the Hebrew text and Greek additions, is to be seen in English in Catholic translations like the *Jerusalem Bible* and the *New American Bible*, while in the *Authorised Version (KJV)* and Protestant versions the additions appear in a separate place, forming the book of the Apocrypha called 'The Additions to the Book of Esther' (so in *RSV*, for example). In the *NEB* Apocrypha, though there is a book entitled 'The Rest of the Chapters of the Book of Esther which are found neither in the Hebrew nor in the Syriac', what is printed is a translation of the *complete* Septuagint text of Esther with the Additions in their appropriate places, the sections corresponding to the Hebrew book being set in square brackets with the chapter and verse numbers in italics. This is a most helpful way of presenting the variant recensions of Esther. On the question of the original language of the Additions, see C. A. Moore, 'On the Origin of the LXX Additions to the Book of Esther', *JBL* 92 (1973), pp. 382–93 (= Moore, *Studies*, pp. 583–94); R. A. Martin, 'Syntax Criticism of the LXX Additions to the Book of Esther', *JBL* 94 (1975), pp. 65–72 (= Moore, *Studies*, pp. 595–602).

The six major additions to Esther are counted as Est. 10:14 – 16:24, and are now usually lettered as Additions A–F. Their contents are:

A. (11:2–12:6) A dream of Mordecai concerning coming destruction, and his discovery of the chamberlains' conspiracy [A is prefixed to 1:1].

B. (13:1–7) The contents of the edict against the Jews sent out by Ahasuerus at Haman's instigation [B follows 3:13].

C. (13:8–14:19) Prayers of Mordecai and Esther for deliverance [C follows 4:17].

D. (15:1–16) An account of Esther's appearance before the king in anxiety for her own safety (an alternative account to 5:1–2) [D follows C].

E. (16:1–24) The contents of the edict on behalf of the Jews sent out by Ahasuerus at Mordecai's instigation [E follows 8:12].

F. (10:4–11:1) The interpretation of Mordecai's dream as relating to the events of the narrative [E follows 10:3].

A translation of and commentary on these additions is provided by C. A. Moore, *Daniel, Esther and Jeremiah: The Additions* (Anchor Bible, 44; 1977). Various reasons for the existence of the additions have been offered: clearly C adds an explicitly religious note so conspicuously lacking in the Hebrew text; the other additions are typical of narrative expansions in Jewish literature designed to satisfy the reader's curiosity and to impart an air of mystery and divine design to the events of history.

The variety of forms in which the essential core of the Esther story has come down to us entitles us to consider whether the Masoretic Hebrew text itself is a wholly unified work or whether perhaps it also has been subject to certain secondary additions. Est. 9:29–32, which has Esther writing a 'second letter' covering mainly the same ground as Mordecai's previous letter, seems likely to be such an addition (cf. S. E. Loewenstamm, 'Esther 9:29–32: The Genesis of a Late Addition', *HUCA* 42 [1971], pp. 117–24 [= Moore, *Studies*, pp. 227–34]), and indeed many scholars regard as secondary the whole of 9:20–32 (viz. both Mordecai's and Esther's letters requiring a memorial observance which 9:19 has already said was customarily performed; see e.g. Paton, pp. 57–60). Est. 10:1–3 also bears all the marks of an addition, since its vague generalities contribute nothing to the concrete narrative of the book. In this commentary it will be suggested that the whole of ch. 9, recounting the vengeance taken on their enemies by the Jews, is not of a piece—either linguistically or in story line—with the preceding chapters. On this view, the narrative in an earlier form ended with the issuance of the two mutually contradictory but unalterable royal decrees, the one against the Jews and the other in their favour (for a similar conclusion reached by different arguments, see C. C. Torrey, 'The Older Book of Esther', *HTR* 38 [1944], pp. 1–40 [= Moore, *Studies* pp. 448–87]); the story thus reflected the irony of diaspora Judaism's position, both protected and threatened by the imperial powers to which it was subject. Est. 9, on any view of the book's origins, owes its existence to the endeavour to establish (or, maintain) a link between the story of Esther and the festival of Purim (see below, section V).

## II. CANONICITY

Both among Jews and Christians the book of Esther did not enjoy for several centuries after the formation of the canon the same secure position as the majority of Old Testament books.

On the Jewish side, it may be significant that Esther is the one *OT* book not found among the Dead Sea Scrolls of the Qumran community (2nd cent. BC to 1st cent. AD); but Qumran was not representative of mainstream Judaism, and the absence of Esther from its library may be an accident of the preservation of manuscripts or may be due to Qumranic opinions about the celebration of the Purim festival (but for the view that Esther was not unknown at Qumram, see J. Finkel, 'The Author of the Genesis Apocryphon Knew the Book of Esther' [Heb.], in *Festschrift E. Sukenik*, ed. Y. Yadin, pp. 163–82; on this, see Bardtke, *Ex Oriente Lux* 19 [1965f.], pp. 523f. [= Moore, *Studies*, pp. 95f.]). More substantive are the incidental remarks made in two places in the Talmud (*Megillah* 7a; *Sanhedrin* 100a) by rabbis of the third or fourth century AD calling into question the canonicity of the book. But here again, these opinions are clearly unrepresentative, and are mentioned only in order to be refuted. The fact that the book of Esther gave the authorisation for a popular Jewish festival must have outweighed any doubts about its suitability as a sacred book. Its place in the list of twenty-four books of the Jewish canon given in the Baraitha of *Baba Bathra* 14b-15a (a second-century AD portion of the Talmud) is a definitive statement of its status in Jewish scripture.

Among Christians, more serious doubts have been expressed in

many centuries. The book of Esther is never cited in the New
Testament, it is absent from some of the earliest lists of canonical
books, and it was even slower in gaining acceptance in the east than
in the west. Thus, in the list of Melito, bishop of Sardis (c. AD 170),
Esther is the only book of the Hebrew Bible not mentioned, and by
Athanasius of Alexandria (fourth century AD) it was denied canonical
status and grouped with books like Judith and Tobit purely as
'edifying reading'. Some uncertainty about its status is reflected by
its position as the *last* of the *OT* books in the lists given by Origen
(third century AD), Epiphanius (fourth century AD). In the west, on
the other hand, though there is no unambiguous evidence of its
canonicity until the fourth century AD, several fathers of that century
(e.g. Hilary, Augustine) as well as the church councils of Hippo (AD
393) and Carthage (AD 397), plainly regarded it as canonical

The reasons for doubt over its canonicity cannot always be
pinpointed, but the following factors must have played a greater or
lesser part: (i) The manifestly secular spirit of its narrative, and the
absence of the name of God from the Hebrew text (though of course
the book was known to most Christians only in its Greek or Latin
versions, with the 'religious' additions); (ii) its association in theme
with the Book of Judith, never considered by the Jews as canonical;
(iii) the morality of the book. Christian lack of enthusiasm about
the book is reflected in the absence of any commentary upon it until
that of Rhabanus Maurus in AD 831, by Luther's remark, 'I am so
hostile to it that I wish it did not exist, for it Judaises too much
and displays too much pagan behaviour' (*Table Talk* = *WA*
XXII.2080), and by the comment of L. B. Paton in his *ICC*
commentary (1908), 'The book is so conspicuously lacking in religion that it should never have been included in the Canon of the
OT., but should have been left with Judith and Tobit among the
apocryphal writings' (p. 97). It should be added that despite O.
Eissfeldt's laconic comment in his *The Old Testament. An Introduction* that 'for Christianity Luther's remark should be determinative'
(p. 512), H. Bardtke has shown how untypical this casual remark
of Luther's was of his quite positive use of the book in his sermons
and writings (*Luther und das Buch Esther*); cf. his remarks in *Ex
Oriente Lux* 19 (1965f.), pp. 545–46 (= Moore, *Studies*, pp. 117f.).

These negative opinions are worth recording as typical of many
readers' initial impressions of the book; but it does not need a very
subtle reading of the book to see that, though God is not explicitly
mentioned, the many coincidences that lead to the salvation of the
Jewish people cannot be depicted as mere chance, but must be
intended to portray the hidden care of God for his people and his
manipulation of seemingly trivial events of history for the sake of

Israel's preservation. The undoubted 'Jewishness' of the book is something it shares with the whole of the Old Testament; if that is an 'offence' in Christian eyes, it is a stumbling-block that must be surmounted before any part of the Old Testament is appropriated for Christian use. Esther may thus perform a valuable critical function for the Christian reader as a test case for whether one truly accepts the Old Testament as a legitimate and necessary part of the Christian Scriptures. (See also B. W. Anderson, 'The Place of the Book of Esther in the Christian Bible', *JR* 30 [1950], pp. 32–43 [= Moore, *Studies*, pp. 130–41].)

## III. HISTORICITY

The current consensus of opinion on the question of the historicity of the Esther narrative is that it is a 'historical novel' (so, e.g., O. Eissfeldt, *The Old Testament. An Introduction*, p. 507), by which is meant an essentially fictional story with probably a foundation in some historical event. This view appears to have emerged as a compromise between the common scholarly position of the last hundred years, that the work is entirely fictional, and the position shared by pre-critical scholars and conservatives that the work is an authentic historical report (see B. S. Childs, *Introduction to the Old Testament as Scripture*, p. 601).

The history of scholarship on the question was amply documented by Paton in his *ICC* commentary (1908), pp. 111–18. The earliest systematic critique of the book's historicity appears to have been that of J. S. Semler in his writings of 1773. Paton's commentary itself is a classic exposition of the then prevailing opinion that 'the Book of Esther is not historical, and . . . it is doubtful whether even a historical kernel underlies its narrative' (p. 75). The contrary view has been supported by fragments of evidence from the ancient historians and from archaeological discovery (cf., e.g., J. Hoschander, *The Book of Esther in the Light of History*, and R. Gordis, 'Religion, Wisdom and History in the Book of Esther—A New Solution to an Ancient Crux', *JBL* 100 [1981], pp. 359–88). J. M. Myers' compromising formulation that the book should be viewed as a historical novel with greater emphasis on the adjective than on the noun has become an influential statement of present opinion (J. M. Myers, *The World of the Restoration*, p. 92).

The term 'historical novel' is a misleading one, however. No matter how authentic the period detail of a historical novel may be, if its central plot or narrative is fictional, it belongs on the fiction shelves and not among histories—good, bad or indifferent. To call

Esther a historical novel with emphasis on the adjective can only properly mean that while its story-line is quite fictional its circumstantial detail is rather accurate. If one wishes to affirm the essential historicity of the story it presents, while allowing that some elements of the narrative have been fabricated, one is obliged to describe the book with some such term as novelistic history or romantic history. Or, if one judges only that it 'probably' has a foundation in some historical event, it would be better to term it 'probably a novelistic history' than a 'historical novel with emphasis on the adjective', since adjectives can only *qualify* nouns, and cannot transform them into different entities.

Paton was correct in noting that 'most of the statements of Esther are unconfirmed by external evidence' (p. 65). The question of its historicity therefore becomes one of balancing probabilities.

## (I) Evidence against the historicity of the book

Here we should distinguish (as has infrequently been done) between evidence damaging to an essentially historical kernel of the book and fiction-like traits (e.g. exaggerations) that do not affect the question seriously.

1. The central historical claim of the book, that the Persian king Xerxes authorised the extermination of the Jewish people, seems implausible. But we do know of a massacre of 'all who were of Italic race' carried out by Mithridates VI Pontus in 88 BC, in which, according to Cicero, between 80,000 and 150,000 Romans were slaughtered in a single day (*de lege Manilia* 3.7). Large-scale massacres of Scythians and Magi by Persians are also noted by Herodotus (1.106; 3.79).

2. The co-ordinated slaughter of 75,000 Persians on one day by the Jews can likewise be paralleled by the above examples. It must be remembered, however, that parallels are not positive evidence for the historicity of the story, but only evidence against any initial impression of implausibility.

3. The announcement of the massacre eleven months before its execution seems a further historical implausibility (cf. on 3:13–14). A parallel time-lag (though admittedly only of four months) can, however, be found in the case of a decree issued by Antiochus III of Syria in 193 BC (R. Gordis, *JBL* 100 [1981], p. 383).

4. The elevation of the Jewess Esther to the throne is said to contradict Herodotus' statement (3.84) that Persian kings could choose their queens only from the members of seven noble families (Herodotus 1.135 and 7.61, sometimes quoted in this connection, are irrelevant). The passage in Herodotus 3.84, however, is the narrative of a pledge made by Darius with his fellow-conspirators

against Pseudo-Smerdis that they would take wives only from one another's families; Herodotus himself does not indicate that this pledge became formal imperial policy. Hoschander remarked that 'History shows that kings hardly ever faithfully observe agreements made by distant ancestors with their subjects' (p. 34); but more to the point is the evidence of marriages by Persian kings to wives from outside the families of the seven (concubinage is not relevant here). According to Herodotus 3.87, Darius married three wives who were not from any of the seven families—in addition to a wife who was a daughter of Otanes, a co-conspirator. His son Xerxes (himself not the offspring of a daughter of one of the co-conspirators) married Amestris, daughter of an Otanes (Herodotus 7.61) who is not to be identified with the conspirator Otanes (cf. Ph.-E. Legrand, *Herodote. Index Analytique* [1954], p. 60; A. D. Godley, *Herodotus*, vol. 4 [1925], pp. 367f.). These facts, which were pointed to by J. S. Wright, 'The Historicity of the Book of Esther', in *New Perspectives on the Old Testament*, ed. J. B. Payne, pp. 37–47 (pp. 38f.) are more impressive evidentially than Gordis' supposition that Esther may not have been Xerxes' principal queen, or, more improbably still, that she may have been by birth a Persian but later converted to Judaism (*JBL* 100 [1981], pp. 385f.). See also on 3:4.

4. The name of Xerxes' queen is known to us as Amestris (Herodotus 7.61, 114; 9.109; Ctesias 13.51) whereas in Esther Xerxes' queens are Vashti and Esther. Moreover, 2:16 and 3:7 show Esther as queen in the seventh and twelfth years of Xerxes' reign (480/79 and 475/4 BC) whereas Herodotus tells a story of Amestris as queen that is set in 479 after the battle of Mycale (9.109–113). On the latter point, Herodotus' story of Amestris' mutilation of a supposed mistress of her husband's cannot easily be preferred as a historical source to the Esther story. If all the dates are to be accepted as firm, it could be argued that Amestris and Esther are the same person, the name Esther being a shorter form of Amestris (so Gordis, *JBL* 100 [1981], p. 384); but the difficulty would remain that Amestris, unlike Esther, seems clearly to have Persian ancestry. J. S. Wright argues that Amestris is actually Vashti; Amestris certainly does not appear in accounts of Xerxes' life after 479 BC (the evidence is very sparse, so that may not be surprising), though she does reappear as queen-mother in the reign of her son Artaxerxes (465–425 BC). The difficulty with Wright's view is that the Amestris/Vashti who in Esther is deposed in Xerxes' third year (484/3) is according to Herodotus accompanying Xerxes during part at least of his campaign against Greece (481–479 BC). Wright is compelled to argue unconvincingly that Vashti's deposition was not actually carried out until Xerxes' return to Persia.

It seems better to acknowledge that Esther is unknown to extra-biblical historians, and at the same time to allow that Amestris may not have been Xerxes' only queen. We in fact know the names of three wives of the earlier Persian emperor Darius, which would be unlikely if they did not have regal status or something approaching it; and the story of Esther makes reference to 'the house of the women' (or, 'wives') and tells us that Esther was preferred to all Xerxes' 'women' or 'wives' (2:14, 17). None of this proves that there was a queen Esther, but the existence of a queen Amestris does not make the existence of Esther improbable.

5. Mordecai is apparently said in 2:5f. to have been deported from Judah with Jehoiachin in 596 BC, whereas in 8:2 he becomes grand vizier of Persia in the twelfth year of Xerxes (cf. 3:7), viz. 474 BC, 122 years later. However, 2:5f. may be read (admittedly not in its most natural sense) to mean that it was Kish, Mordecai's great-grandfather, who was taken captive, not Mordecai himself.

6. A rather considerable number of elements in the story appear fanciful or exaggerated. Principal among them are the improbable coincidences with which the story abounds: e.g. that there should be a Jewish queen of Persia at the very time when genocide of the Jewish people is plotted; that the signal service rendered by Mordecai to the king (2:21–23) should not be immediately rewarded, but that the record of his service should be read before the king on the very night after Esther had decided to plead for her people (6:1–2). Other elements of a more fanciful kind are: the decree sent throughout the empire instructing wives to obey their husbands (1:19f.); the process of selection and preparation of maidens for the king (2:8–14); the casual acquiescence of the king in a plan to destroy a vast number of his subjects (3:8–15). The incidence of so many implausibilities is cumulatively weighty evidence against the historicity of much of the detail of the narrative.

7. A number of other improbabilities alleged against the narrative must, on the other hand, be rejected as of slight significance. So, for example, the 'contradiction' between 1:1 which speaks of 127 provinces of the Persian empire and Herodotus 3.89 which notes 20 provinces or satrapies is more apparent than real: satrapies are larger units than provinces (Dan. 6:2 speaks of 120 satrapies, by which must be meant the 'provinces' of Est. 1:1). Again, it is commonly noted that the theory of the irrevocability of the laws of the Medes and Persians (1:19; 8:8; similarly Dan. 6:8) is unattested outside the OT and is inherently implausible; a possible rejoinder is that, on the contrary, such a rule is presupposed by any imperial dictatorship, and that in any case the emphasis (in 1:19 at least) may be more on the obligation to execute royal decrees to the letter

rather than on any question of their alterability. Again, the danger Esther ran by entering the presence of the king (4:11) is often thought 'contrary to all that we know of old Persian court life' (Paton, p. 72); but the issue in 4:11 is one of coming before the king *unsummoned*—which Herodotus confirms (3.84) was (at one time at least) a privilege reserved to Darius' six co-conspirators against Pseudo-Smerdis.

Moore appropriately summarises the evidence against the historicity of Esther when he writes: 'Taken individually, few, if any, of these improbabilities and contradictions are sufficiently serious to undermine the essential historicity of Esther, since errors in detail can easily occur in an essentially true historical account' (p. xlvi). Robert Gordis more confidently writes: 'There is nothing intrinsically impossible or improbable in the central incident . . . the book is to be regarded as a basically historical account of an anti-Semitic attempt at genocide which was foiled during the reign of Xerxes' (*JBL* 100 [1981], p. 388). Against such conclusions must be set the fact that the story as we have it is for the most part a series of unlikely coincidences. We may indeed regard these as mere tokens of the story-teller's art and therefore as peripheral to the question of the book's central historicity. But if we do, we must realise that we are then left with a very tiny historical core, however sound that core may be.

*(II) Evidence in favour of the historicity of the book*
It is acknowledged on all sides that the author captures many details of Persian life aptly and accurately. Paton was right in asserting that 'they do not prove that this story is historical any more than the local colour of the *Arabian Nights* proves them to be historical' (p. 65); the authentic colouring is what we would expect of a 'historical' *novel*. Nevertheless, the presence of many authentic details and the absence of any that can be proved inauthentic must raise the question, What more would we expect of a true *history*? The presence, therefore, of such details is not a negligible factor in assessing the historicity of the book, however much we may feel instinctively that its story is in essence a romance. Some of the most pertinent points of evidence in favour of its historicity are the following:

1. The king Ahasuerus can be readily identified with Xerxes (though the Greek version calls him Artaxerxes and some modern scholars like J. Hoschander have identified him with Artaxerxes II), who is a historical personage well known to us from the pages of Herodotus' *History of the Persian Wars*, especially Books 7–9.

2. The dates in Ahasuerus' reign given in Esther coincide with what we know of Xerxes' life. The banquet in his third year (1:3),

with which the book opens, would fit into the period before he left for the war against Greece (483–479 BC); some would even identify it with the council of war called by Xerxes in his third year (Herodotus 7.8) after his campaign in Egypt and before the invasion of Greece. The four years between the deposition of Vashti and the installation of Esther as queen (in the seventh year, 2:1*b*) coincide with the four years Xerxes was absent from Persia on the expedition against the Greeks (it can be assumed that Xerxes' years are reckoned on the accession year system, with the first year beginning on the first new year's day of his reign). The latest date in Esther is at the end of his twelfth year (cf. 3:7 and 9:1), which fits comfortably within his reign of twenty years.

3. Other details of Persian life confirmed by extra-biblical sources include: the extent of the empire under Xerxes from India to Ethiopia (1:1); the council of seven nobles (1:14); the efficient postal system (3:13; 8:10); the keeping of official diaries including records of the king's benefactors (2:23; 6:8); the use of impalement as a form of capital punishment (2:23; 5:14; 7:10); the practice of obeisance to kings and nobles (3:2); belief in lucky days (3:7); setting crowns on the heads of royal horses (6:8); reclining on couches at meals (7:8). See the commentary on the passages mentioned.

4. The author makes use of a number of Persian terms for specifically Persian objects: *part$^e$mîm*, 'officials' (1:3); *karpas*, 'cotton' (1:6); *dāt* 'decree, law' (1:8 and 19 other occurrences); *pitgām*, 'decree' (1:20); *'$^a$ḥašdarp$^e$nîm*, 'satraps' (3:12); *patšeḡen*, 'copy' (3:14); *'$^a$ḥašt$^e$rānîm*, 'couriers' (8:10); *rammāḵîm*, (?) 'post-stations' (8:10).

5. There are 35 Persian proper names in the book. Not all can be understood as authentically Persian names, but most can be satisfactorily so interpreted, revealing the author's further familiarity with things Persian. See Paton, pp. 66–71; H. S. Gehman, 'Notes on the Persian words in the Book of Esther', *JBL* 43 (1924), pp. 321–8 (= Moore, *Studies*, pp. 235–42; A. R. Millard, 'The Persian Names in Esther and the Reliability of the Hebrew Text', *JBL* 96 (1977), pp. 481–8.

No clear conclusion emerges from this survey of the evidence, but there can be little doubt that the evidence should be thoroughly reviewed before any decision by a reader is reached.


## IV. THE FUNCTION OF THE BOOK OF ESTHER

Since the story of Esther confronts us as a not wholly unified literary work it betrays several different functions, depending on where its climax is thought to fall.

In the final shape of the book, the last word is given to the summary statement of the greatness of Ahasuerus *and* of Mordecai (10:1–3). Rounded off by this notice, the story functions as an affirmation of the mutually beneficial roles of the Persian administration and of the Jewish people, and as a reassurance to diaspora Jewry that collaboration with the authorities is no sin against Jewish identity. For it is possible for Mordecai *the Jew* to stand next in rank to the king, *and* at the same time to be popular with his co-religionists (10:3). The story has given the lie to Haman's initial charge that 'it is not for the king's profit to tolerate' the Jews (3:8). As the use of the book in Jewish society throughout the centuries shows, it undoubtedly serves to boost Jewish self-esteem; but, less simplistically, it also presents an implicit critique of the ghetto-mentality and portrays a Judaism that—despite occasional threats to its national survival—can for the most part contentedly enjoy the security offered by a super-power.

A different—though not dissimilar—function is served by the story when it is viewed as effectively concluding with the letters of Mordecai and Esther instituting and enjoining observance of the festival of Purim (9:20–32). In this context this story gives content to a day of national festivity—which can very easily become nothing but an occasion for high spirits—by insisting that what is being celebrated is the survival of the Jewish people; at the same time the letters of Mordecai and Esther perform a critical function upon the nature of that celebration by insisting that survival is properly a matter of 'rest' or relief from danger and not of victory over enemies. Read without the ponderous phrases of 9:20–32 the story of Esther could well seem merely a celebration of Israel's diplomatic cunning and its military prowess. Read with the solemn injunctions of 9:20–32, the story as a whole comes to a climax not with the Jewish massacre of their enemies (which is virtually written out of the record) but with the domestic details of merrymaking and the giving of gifts. Furthermore, the apparently secular story of Esther is brought within the framework of Jewish religious life, Purim being numbered among the 'appointed seasons' (9:31), to be 'remembered and kept throughout every generation' (9:28), like the ancient festivals prescribed in the law. See further, B. S. Childs, *Introduction to the Old Testament as Scripture*, pp. 603ff.

A third function is served by what may be supposed to have been the original story of Esther (ending with ch. 8 of our book). This will have been a story with the primary purpose of entertainment. Skilful though its narrative is in every scene, it reaches its climax with an act of consummate diplomatic invention which demonstrates the triumph of brain over brawn, of Jewish flair over Persian

bureaucracy, of Jewish cunning over Persian cunning (and stup-
idity), of Jewish resoluteness over foreign pliability, indeed of Jewish
charm (Esther) over Jewish gaucherie (Mordecai). It is self-congratu-
latory in every way that an ethnic minority is obliged to be in
preserving its own identity. Subtler questions of the twin loyalties
of diaspora Jews to nation and state may be adumbrated in the tale
(as in 7:4), but chiefly its function is to entertain its audience by
assuring them of their superiority. The last sentence of the postulated original tale (8:17) depicts a scene of mass proselytism to
Judaism, an ultimate symbol of the supreme value of Jewishness.
This function is by no means subverted by the additions made to
the tale: the book remains a work of serious entertainment in the
cause of Jewish national fervour, but in its final form embodies
more discriminating concerns as well.

## V. THE BOOK OF ESTHER AND THE FESTIVAL OF PURIM

The book of Esther ostensibly recounts the origin of the Jewish
festival of Purim. Few students of the book, however, are
completely convinced that the narrative account is plausible. The
primary problem lies in the explanation given for the name Purim:
according to 9:26 the festival was called Purim ('lots') after the term
*pûr*, 'lot', since the date of the planned annihilation had been fixed
by Haman's casting the 'lot' (9:24, referring back to 3:7). No one
now doubts, since the article of J. Lewy, that the biblical writer
was correct in interpreting *pûr* as 'lot' (see his 'Old Assyrian *puru'um*
and *pūrum*', *RHA* 5 [1939], pp. 117–24). The difficulty in the
connection of Purim and *pûr* is twofold: first, in the story it is only
*one* lot (*pûr*) that is significant whereas the festival is called 'lots'
(*pûrîm*) (in Hebrew one casts 'a lot'—not 'lots', as we say in English);
secondly, and perhaps more importantly, the lot-casting plays a very
minor role in the narrative—and, we may suppose, in any event
that lay behind the narrative. Compared with the central concern
of the story with national danger and escape, with the machinations
of the evil Haman abetted by the soulless imperial bureaucracy and
with the ultimate salvation of the Jewish people through human
cleverness and divine providence combined, the particular means
chosen by Haman to determine the precise date seems a trivial
matter indeed.

The former difficulty, rarely remarked upon, is a real one, and
cannot be alleviated by supposing that Purim is a plural noun
because there are two days of festival. The second difficulty has

recently received a new explanation by G. Gerleman (pp. 25ff.). He suggests that *pûrîm* means not only the lot that is cast, but—like *gôrāl*, 'lot', the term with which it is explained in 4:7 and 9:24—also means the thing that is apportioned by lot. Purim is therefore named after the custom of exchanging 'portions' (*mānôt*, 9:12, 22) as a token of rejoicing for national deliverance. The sending of portions (*mānôt*) is also attested in Neh. 8:10, 12 as a festive custom, though there it is linked with a unique ceremony of reading the law, which may or may not reflect the customs of a new year's day. On Gerleman's view the connection of *pûr*, 'lot', with Haman in 3:7 and 9:24 is entirely secondary, though he cannot explain why if *pûrîm* originally meant 'portions' its meaning was ever forgotten. A more important objection is that 'lot' (*gôrāl*) always retains at least an allusion to the act of allotting by 'chance', whereas the 'portions' exchanged as gifts have no such significance.

Another explanation was put forward by A. D. Cohen (' "Hu Ha-goral": The Religious Significance of Esther', *Judaism* 23 [1974], pp. 87–94 [= Moore, *Studies*, pp. 122–29]), who saw the *pûr* as the symbol of pagan chance-fate. 'All the events are "cast" to give the appearance of chance-occurrences, or, *purim*' (p. 89). But the coincidences of the tale are only apparently chance; in reality they are an interwoven mesh of divine providence. 'Haman rests his hopes on chance, but providence prevails . . . The day he plans for the destruction of the Jews becomes their day of rejoicing' (p. 94). We could see it somewhat differently by regarding the 'lots' as the *double* fates decreed for the Jews by Haman and by God. On one level, Haman's plan is made void by an equally valid but countervailing imperial decree; on another level Haman's plan is not just counterbalanced but positively overturned (cf. the verb *hāpak*, 'change, turn', in 9:1, 22) and thus destroyed by another destiny or 'lot' ordained by God. On such a view, Purim would derive its name not from Haman's act of lot-casting, but from the two contradictory fates or 'lots' cast for the Jews in the days of Esther. The plural of Purim would be thus explained and the importance of Haman's lot-casting would be minimised. Against this attractive theory is the fact that it supposes that a popular festival took its name from an essentially conceptual construction of events (historical or fictional) rather than some concrete event, ritual or custom.

This difficulty directs us towards the type of solution preferred by most scholars to the enigma of the origin of Purim, namely, that it has a non-Jewish origin. It should be immediately admitted that no non-Jewish festival (whether Persian, Babylonian or Greek) can in fact be identified with Purim either in name, date, or ritual. Nevertheless, if Purim means 'lots' and if its origin is to be sought outside the Esther narrative or the events told therein, it could reasonably be supposed to be a festival of the time of fixing the destinies for the coming year, as at the Babylonian new year festivals. Its location in the last month of the year (Adar), immediately before the normal Babylonian spring new year, is a further pointer to such a significance. On this view, the festival would be older than the story (or, events) of Esther but would be given specifically Jewish meaning by a narrative about Jewish destiny.

Many scholars have offered more ambitious explanations than the foregoing, however. In most cases they have tried to relate the events of the book of Esther and/or the names of its leading characters to non-Jewish festival rituals or mythology. Thus, for example, H. Zimmern ('Zur Frage nach dem Ursprunge des Purimfestes', *ZAW* 11 [1891], pp. 157–69 [= Moore, *Studies*, pp. 147–69] and P. Jensen, 'Elamitische Eigennamen. Ein Beitrag zur Erklärung der elamitischen Inschriften', *WZKM* 6 [1892], pp. 47–70, 209–26) saw in the names Mordecai and Esther the Babylonian deities Marduk and Ishtar, and in Haman and Vashti the Elamite deities Humman and Mashti; the story of the victory of Mordecai and Esther over Haman and Vashti would thus have been a myth of a conflict of deities (for details, see Paton, pp. 89–94). More commonly now a Persian background for Purim has been postulated. J. Lewy ('The Feast of the 14th Day of Adar', *HUCA* 14 [1939], pp. 127–51 [= Moore, *Studies*, pp. 160–84]) saw in Purim the Persian festival of Farvardīgān, a kind of All Souls celebration; he claimed that the festival was held on Adar 11–15 and that the narrative of Esther reflects a persecution by Mithras worshippers in Susa against Marduk worshippers who attributed their deliverance to the Babylonian goddess Ishtar (Esther). Lewy's tortuous argument has found less acceptance than T. H. Gaster's claim that the Esther narrative portrays typical new year rituals in Persia and other Near Eastern cultures (*Purim and Hanukkah in Custom and Tradition* [1950]). Elements of such rituals are the choosing of a new queen, the parading of a commoner in the garb of the king, the execution of a criminal as a scapegoat, a dramatised fight, and the exchange of gifts. Gaster's parallels, however, come from widely scattered areas and periods, and therefore do not constitute a significant explanation for either Purim or the biblical narrative. H. Ringgren's more discriminating selection of parallels ('Esther and Purim', *SEA* 20 [1956], pp. 5–24 [= Moore, *Studies*, pp. 185–204]) leads him to the more modest conclusion that Purim is derived from some form of Persian new year ceremonies, the Esther story having perhaps some historical nucleus in a persecution of Jews on the occasion of a Persian religious festival (pp. 23f.).

That the festival of Purim had an origin outside Judaism is not implausible; that the story of Esther had such an origin is a view that has little to commend it. Firmer conclusions cannot be justified.

## VI. LITERARY INFLUENCES ON THE BOOK OF ESTHER

Irrespective of the connection between historical actuality and the narrative of Esther, the story has evidently been shaped—to some extent—according to pre-existing literary models. Some of these literary influences may have been hypothetical source documents, others may have been other biblical or non-biblical writings of a similar character.

The story of Vashti (ch. 1) has often been thought to be derived from a harem tale of the kind richly represented in the *Thousand and One Nights* (see E. Cosquin, 'Le prologue-cadre des Mille et une Nuits. Les légendes perses et le livre d'Esther', *RB* 18 [1909], pp. 7–49, 161–97; cf. also Bardtke, pp. 249f.). It is certainly detachable from the Esther story proper, and could well have had an independent existence before it was used by the author to account for the king's search for a wife.

Some scholars have found evidence of two sources behind the present story. H. Cazelles, 'Note sur la composition du rouleau d'Esther' (in *Lex tua veritas. Festschrift H. Junker*, ed. H. Gross and F. Mussner, 1961, pp. 17–29 [= Moore, *Studies*, pp. 424–36]) presented the case thoroughly. One source, according to Cazelles, revolved about Esther and had a liturgical aim; the other had Mordecai as its principal character and derived from a historical event of a persecution of Jews in Susa. Various inconsistencies in the narrative (e.g. the two letters of 9:23–32) can be explained by the theory, but at no point in the body of the main narrative is recourse to the theory desirable; that does not, however, amount to a disproof of it. H. Bardtke independently put forward a similar view in his commentary (1963), seeing in Esther a combination of three originally unrelated tales, of Vashti, Esther and Mordecai (pp. 248–52). (For Bardtke's comments on Cazelles' view, see Bardtke, 'Neuere Arbeiten zum Estherbuch. Eine kritische Würdigung', *Ex Oriente Lux* 19 [1965f.], pp. 519–49 [533–41 = Moore, *Studies*, pp. 105–113]). A more precise definition of the configuration of the Esther and Mordecai tales has been attempted by J. C. H. Lebram, who argues on the basis of 9:20–28 that the Mordecai tale concluded with a celebration of Purim by Palestinian Jews on the fourteenth of Adar, while the tale of Esther issued in a celebration on the fifteenth by Jews of the diaspora ('Purimfest und

Estherbuch', *VT* 22 [1972], pp. 208–22 [= Moore, *Studies*, pp. 205–19]). But since the two major sources cannot be disentangled mechanically (Ringgren, p. 374), it is preferable to view the book as essentially a unity, the work of a single author who no doubt drew upon various motifs and traditions (Dommershausen, p. 15)—whether complete, self-contained Esther and Mordecai stories or not. A full examination of the evidence for distinct narrative sources behind the book of Esther is undertaken in my monograph, *The Esther Scroll. The Story of the Story* (1984).

As for the influence of other literature upon the Esther story, the Joseph story has long been noted as a possible source of influence (see L. A. Rosenthal, 'Die Josephsgeschichte, mit den Büchern Ester und Daniel verglichen', *ZAW* 15 [1895], pp. 278–84 [= Moore, *Studies*, pp. 277–83]; cf. M. Gan, 'The Book of Esther in the Light of the Story of Joseph in Egypt' [Heb.], *Tarbiz* 31 [1961f.], pp. 144–9; H. Bardtke, *Ex Oriente Lux* 19 [1965f.], pp. 529–33 [= Moore, *Studies*, pp. 101–5]; Berg, *Esther*, ch. 5, pp. 123–65). In both cases, the locale is a foreign court, the principal personages attain high position and are able to deliver their people at a time of danger; the fortunes of the hero are similar (advancement from a lowly status, being forgotten at a crucial moment); there are very many parallels also of phraseology and minor episodes (cf. Est. 4:16 and Gen. 43:14). W. L. Humphreys has investigated the motifs shared by Esther not only with the Joseph story but also with the stories of Daniel and Ahiqar as examples of 'tales of the wise courtier' ('A Life-Style for Diaspora: A Study of the Tales of Esther and Daniel', *JBL* 92 [1973], pp. 211–23; *id.*, 'Esther, Book of', *IDBS*, pp. 279–81). A. Meinhold has more recently reaffirmed the common diaspora background of both tales, especially emphasising the significant differences between them both in story-line and in theological outlook ('Die Gattung der Josephsgeschichte und des Estherbuches: Diasporanovelle II', *ZAW* 88 [1976], pp. 72–93 [= Moore, *Studies*, pp. 284–305]).

A different source of influence has been proposed by G. Gerleman, who sees the story of Esther as patterned on the exodus and passover narrative of Exodus (*Studien zu Esther. Stoff–Struktur–Stil–Sinn* [Biblische Studien, 48], 1966 [= Moore, *Studies*, pp. 308–49]; *Esther* [BKAT 21; 1973], esp. pp. 11–23). The book of Exodus also is a deliverance story; Esther plays in many details a similar role to Moses; many striking parallels of language occur. Primarily, however, the significance of the parallels is that Esther represents 'a deliberate and thorough desacralisation and de-theologisation' of a basic narrative of Israel's sacred history (*Esther*, p. 23). Gerleman's claim is too exclusive, but he has rightly shown how diverse the literary influences upon the book of Esther have been, and how Esther must be viewed as commentary upon analogous biblical narratives; whether or not the author designedly intended to make such commentary, the collection of Exodus and Esther in the Hebrew canon constitutes an invitation to read each in the light of the other.

Recently, R. Gordis has suggested that Esther should be regarded as unique in its literary genre within the Bible in that it purports to be written 'in the form of a chronicle of the Persian court, written by a Gentile scribe' ('Religion, Wisdom and History in the Book of Esther—A New Solution to an Ancient Crux', *JBL* 100 [1981], pp. 359–88; quotation from p. 375). This stance adopted by the narrator may explain the absence of the name of God from his narrative and the six times repeated description of Mordecai as 'the Jew'; but the author's interest in things Persian seems more appropriate in an author who shares with his audience an outsider's position *vis-à-vis* the Persian court; and it is hard to see how a Gentile authorial stance would—for Jews—'buttress confidence in the veracity of his narrative' (Gordis, p. 375). And especially because we have no knowledge of what Persian court chronicles may have been like (though there are plenty of Israelite narratives which could as easily have formed his exemplars, as we have seen), this suggestion contributes little to our understanding of the book.

## VII. THE THEOLOGY OF THE BOOK OF ESTHER

The absence of the name of God from the book of Esther can hardly be accidental; but its absence is no sign of lack of interest in theological issues.

Two primary theological themes may be identified in the book: (i) the activity of God in human history reverses the fortunes of Israel and brings it salvation; (ii) human initiatives and divine action can be complementary.

(i) The reversal of fortunes is one of the most elemental narrative plots in world literature. In the Old Testament, however, the reversal of fortunes is typically ascribed to Yahweh; a classic exposition of this theology appears, for example, in the song of Hannah (1 Sam. 2:7–8):

> The LORD makes poor and makes rich;
>   he brings low, and also exalts.
> He raises up the poor from the dust;
>   he lifts the needy from the ash heap.

Cf. also the Song of Mary (Luke 1:51–53).

The whole of the book of Esther can readily be seen as one grand reversal (cf. the verb *hāp̄ak̲*, 'overturn, change', in 9:1, 22), as H. Striedl observed in his literary study. 'Untersuchung zur Syntax und Stilistik des hebräischen Buches Esther', *ZAW* 14 (1937), pp. 73–108. Y. T. Radday indeed finds a formal chiastic structure to the whole book ('Chiasm in Joshua, Judges and Others', *Linguistica Biblica* 3 [1973], pp. 6–13); S. B. Berg finds especially noteworthy a series of 'theses' and 'antitheses' in chs. 3–8 which lead her similarly to conclude that the book 'is ordered according to the theme of reversal' (*Esther*, p. 106). The narrator had no need to enlighten his audience about the origin of this reversal: with resonances of the Joseph and Exodus stories throughout the book, the activity of God will have been entirely plain. The greater the number of 'coincidences' necessary for the salvation of the Jewish people, and the more implausible they seem, the more directly the role of God is pointed to. God, as a character of the story, becomes more conspicuous the more he is absent.

The author of Esther is, like his audience, totally familiar with the sacred traditions of his people; in them deliverance from danger is always deliverance by God, the 'rest' that Israel attains (9:16) is always God's rest (cf. Ps. 95:11; Deut. 12:9; 1 Kg. 8:56). Whether it is theologically sophisticated or religiously naive to adopt those national traditions so wholeheartedly as to take them for granted is hard to say (C. H. Miller, 'Esther's Levels of Meaning', *ZAW* 92 [1980], pp. 145–8, using a model from developmental psychology, finds it rather naive); but the author has something of a precedent in the story of Joseph where also, by comparison with other narratives of Genesis, God is largely absent from the events of human history.

The absence of God from the pages of Esther is no problem for either theology or faith. Such a problem *is* known in the Old Testament, whether when it is the nation that experiences that absence (e.g. at the death of the righteous king Josiah, or at the fall of Jerusalem, the city of God) or when the individual suffers from God's absence (as in the psalmists' experience of abandonment by God). But the story of the institution of a festival of rejoicing must be, for Israel, a story of a mighty deed of its God. It would be going too far to speak of a deliberate 'concealment' of God or of a 'hidden causality' (cf. Berg, *Esther*, pp. 178f.; J. A. Loader, 'Esther as a Novel with Different Levels of Meaning', *ZAW* 90 [1978], pp. 417–21); the causality is patent to any reader who approaches the story by way of the core narratives of Israel's history.

In that framework, the allusions to divine activity ('signals of transcendence') fall into their proper place: they are not the only or even the primary expression of the book's religious outlook, but almost accidental evidences of a world-view that cannot be suppressed. Mordecai's famous line, 'If you keep silence at such time as this, relief and deliverance will rise for the Jews from another quarter' (4:14), does not indeed mean that if Esther refuses to act then God will (see the comment on 4:14), but that the deliverance of the people is unquestionably assured (by whom the author does not need to say). Again, the statement that 'the very day when the enemies of the Jews hoped to get the mastery over them . . . had been changed to a day when the Jews should get the mastery over their foes' (9:1) provokes the question 'changed by whom?'—which is no sooner asked than answered. In the same category we should put every one of those narrative coincidences that trouble the historian (see section III above) and at the same moment point the reader beyond the implausibilities of natural causality to a higher 'grand design'.

(ii) These observations make it impossible to read the story as merely a tale of human wisdom and cunning. W. L. Humphreys has rightly characterised the story as a court tale of a contest of courtiers for position and power ('A Life-Style for Diaspora: A Study of the Tales of Esther and Daniel', *JBL* 92 [1973], pp. 211–23). Less convincingly, but attractively nevertheless, S. Talmon has called it a 'historicized wisdom-tale', a portrayal of wisdom in action 'with the covert, but nevertheless obvious implication that . . . ultimate success derives from the proper execution of wisdom maxims, as set forth, e.g. in Proverbs' (' "Wisdom" in the Book of Esther', *VT* 13 [1963], pp. 419–55; followed by Moore, pp. xxxiiif.); the linkage with wisdom is open to doubt principally because of the difficulties of giving the concept of 'wisdom' meaningful content if it is found pervasively in Old Testament literature (cf. J. L. Crenshaw, 'Methods in Determining Wisdom Influence upon "Historical" Literature', *JBL* 88 [1969], pp. 129–42 [esp. pp. 140ff.]; on Talmon's essay, see also H. Bardtke, *Ex Oriente Lux* 19 [1965f.], pp. 541–5 [= Moore, *Studies*, pp. 113–17]). The tendency of both these essays is to obscure any supernatural dimension in the narrative. Talmon explicitly relates the absence of the name of God and of cultic acts like prayer to the humanistic wisdom ideology infusing the book. J. A. Loader is led by such views to postulate two distinct *levels* of meaning, according to one of which the story is one of God's intervention on behalf of his people, and according to the other a story of human initiative, action and success, with *humans* appearing as the saviours ('Esther as a Novel with Different Levels of Meaning', *ZAW* 90 [1978], pp. 417–21). Certainly (with Loader and against Humphreys and Talmon), both traits are present in the narrative, but the question is, How are they connected?

There is in reality no tension or conflict between the divine and human roles in the narrative. Mordecai's remonstration with Esther (ch. 4) is skilful rhetoric, Esther's plan for bending the king to her will (chs. 5–8) is native cunning, the letter devised by Mordecai for reversing the imperial edict (ch. 8) is astute statesmanship. Without the craft and courage of the Jewish characters the divinely inspired coincidences would have fallen to the ground; and without the coincidences, all the wit in the world would not have saved the Jewish people.

Again, there is no theological problem or religious tension here. For the story-teller divine-human co-operation is the most natural thing in the world (see also on Ezr. 6:22). He does not see the world, like the author(s) of Gen. 1–11, as a place where human initiatives always lead to disaster and where God acts principally by way of reaction to the human initiatives. Nor does he see the world, like the author(s) of the Genesis patriarchal stories, in process of working out a divine destiny willed upon the Abrahamic family by a God who cannot be thwarted by human failure or downright sinfulness. For him, God and Israel have an equal stake in the survival of Israel; their interests coincide, and they each contribute their best talents to achieving that end. 'The preservation of the Jewish people', writes Robert Gordis, 'is itself a religious obligation of the first magnitude . . . Jewish survival is not merely an expression of the human instinct of self-preservation, but a Divine commandment' (*Megillat Esther*, p. 13)—which God himself, we might add, also feels bound by.

It is perhaps not surprising that a writing that so energetically commends Jewish-Persian co-operation (see Section IV above) should take for granted a divine-human synergism. Despite the grisly fate of Haman and his sons and the massacre of the 'enemies', the book is not primarily *against* anyone, but 'pro-existence'; theologically, its author recks nothing of original sin or Israelite waywardness but is comfortably assured that God too regards Israel's survival as *his* religious obligation. It might be more sophisticated to be wracked with theological doubt, but it is hard to beat taking God for granted as an expression of genuine faith.

## VIII. DATE OF COMPOSITION

The facts about the date of composition are few and simple. For obvious reasons, the book of Esther cannot have been written earlier than the time in which it is set (fifth century BC). Nor can it have been later than the first century BC, since the colophon appended to the Septuagint translation (11:1 = F 11) refers to its translation into Greek in the reign of 'Ptolemy and Cleopatra'; and that probably dates the translation to 114 BC or else to 77 BC. The first external evidence for the existence of the Book of Esther is the use made of it by Josephus in his *Antiquities of the Jews* (c. AD 90).

Within that range of possibilities for its date of composition, the current tendency is to place the Hebrew Esther earlier rather than later. It is true that no mention is made of Mordecai or Esther in ben Sira's 'Praise of the Ancestors' (Ecclus 44–49), c. 190 BC, but then Ezra was not mentioned by ben Sira either. So no inference about the existence of the book can be drawn from ben Sira's silence. The best clue to its date may lie in the relatively favourable attitude it displays towards the Persian emperor and the Jewish-Gentile co-operation it commends. Such an attitude towards overlords and foreigners is most likely to have been adopted by a Jewish author of the Persian period (i.e. before 31 BC), but perhaps also in the early Hellenistic period (late fourth to third centuries) before relationships with non-Jewish rulers must have ruled out the likelihood of an author adopting such a stance.

The rather complex redactional history of the book which I have analysed in my study, *The Esther Scroll. The Story of the Story*, would also suggest an earlier rather than a later date. The issue is discussed more fully by C. A. Moore in his Anchor Bible commentary, pp. lvii–lx.


## IX. ANALYSIS OF THE BOOK OF ESTHER

1:1–22   A vacancy occurs in the Court of Ahasuerus
2:1–18   Esther becomes Queen
2:19–23  Mordecai saves the King's life
3:1–15   Haman's promotion and plot against the Jews
4:1–17   Mordecai's counter-measures
5:1–8    Esther's first audience
5:9–14   Haman's pride a threat to Mordecai
6:1–14   Mordecai is rewarded by the King
7:1–10   The fall of Haman
8:1–17   Haman is replaced and his plot overturned
9:1–32   How Adar 14–15 became the Purim Festival
10:1–3   A footnote about Mordecai

# ESTHER

## 1:1–22

The episode in this chapter is not part of the Esther story proper, but serves to introduce the character of the king, to offer a reason for Esther's rise to a place of importance, and to set the tone of the narrative as a whole. This Persian emperor, who lives in unparalleled wealth and exercises well-nigh universal dominion is at bottom a vain man, easily enraged and—most to the point for the story—an utterly unselfconscious male chauvinist who is astonished to be worsted in the battle of the sexes when on every other front he is masterfully supreme. The deposition of Vashti is of course necessary for the plot; space must be made for Esther who will behave obediently (2:8, 10, 20; etc.) as a foil to Vashti the disobedient (1:15). The tone of the narrative is lightly satirical: the emperor cannot command his wife's obedience; the authority of every husband in the kingdom is threatened by one wife's disobedience; men are exposed as timid while Vashti conceals with dignity her reasons for not complying with her husband's command. The king who exerts his authority over his queen will in the end be thoroughly manipulated by her successor under guise of duty and obedience. And a Persian king will promote a Jewish exile above all his nobles and princes (2:5f.; 10:3), overturning all tradition and custom.

This initial episode has three movements: (i) a setting of the scene (vv. 1–9); (ii) the exchange between Ahasuerus and Vashti (vv. 10–12); (iii) the consequences (vv. 13–22). Movement (i) is description, movement (ii) narrative, movement (iii) dialogue.

### THE FEAST OF AHASUERUS

## 1:1–9

The book opens with the depiction of two splendid feasts that demonstrated the wealth and magnificence of the Persian king. Since the narrative as a whole functions as the occasion for the institution of the Purim festival, these opening festivals and the several others which follow them may be seen as foreshadowings of the concluding festival (9:17–19). See further, Berg, *Esther*, pp. 31–57, on banquets as an important motif in the book.

**1. Ahasuerus** is better known as Xerxes (485–465 BC), the Persian king who conducted war against Greece from 480 to 470—the subject of Books 7–9 of Herodotus' history and of Aeschylus' drama *The Persians*. On the name, Heb. *'ᵃhašwērôš*, see on Ezr. 4:6–7. In

speaking of **the Ahasuerus who reigned** . . . the narrator suggests
that he knows another Ahasuerus, perhaps the father of Darius the
Mede (Dan. 9:1); but equally **the Ahasuerus** may mean 'the famous
Ahasuerus' (as the phrase is taken to mean in one of the targums;
translation in Paton, p. 122). Certainly, the extent of his reign **from
India to Ethiopia** cannot specify which Persian king is meant; for
the Persian empire had been given its essential shape already by
Cyrus (539–529 BC), Egypt being added to its possessions by
Cambyses (529–522) (Herodotus 3.97), and north-west India as far
as the river Indus by Darius (521–486). (Herodotus 3.94–106).
Xerxes himself made the same claim on a foundation tablet from
his palace at Persepolis (*ANET*, pp. 316f.). A division of the empire
into **one hundred and twenty-seven provinces** is not attested in
Persian sources, though Dan. 6:1 speaks of 120 provinces. The
Persians generally reckoned between twenty and thirty-one satrapies
(cf. Herodotus 3.89; Olmstead, *History*, p. 59), and the figure of
120 or 127 must refer to the provincial subdivisions like Judea and
Samaria in the satrapy of Beyond the River-cum-Babylon (cf. on
Ezr. 2:1); these are technically *mᵉdînôt*, 'provinces', the term used
here. It is not clear that Persian lists of subject peoples and of
administrative districts can be successfully correlated with the
satrapal list of Herodotus (see G. G. Cameron, 'The Persian
Satrapies and Related Matters', *JNES* 32 [1973], pp. 46–56), so
rejection of the datum here may well be premature.

**2. In those days**: Movement toward the crucial event of the
(double) feast is indicated by the triple note of time: 'in the days
of' (v. 1), 'in those days when he sat in Susa' (v. 2), 'in the third
year of his reign' (v. 3).

**sat on his royal throne**: Some have seen here an allusion to the
campaigns of Xerxes in Egypt and Babylon in the first two years of
his reign, and have translated 'sat securely . . .'. The great feast,
whose occasion is not otherwise mentioned, could be understood as
a victory celebration. LXX has 'to celebrate his marriage'. But it is
more likely that the phrase points primarily to the location of the
story in Susa. **Susa**, the former capital of Elam, became one of the
three capitals of the Persian kings; according to Xenophon (*Anabasis*
3.5.15; *Cyropaedia* 8.6.22), they spent the winters in Babylon, the
spring in Susa and the summer in Ecbatana (cf. on Ezr. 6:2; Neh.
1:1; 2:1). **Susa the capital**: rather, the acropolis (*bîrâ*) of Susa, as
distinct from the city (as in 3:15, 8:15). Its site has been excavated
several times since 1851; see R. Ghirshman, *Cinq campagnes de
fouilles à Suse, 1946–1951* (1952); *id.*, *Iran* (1963); E. M. Yamauchi,
*Near Eastern Archaeological Society Bulletin* 8 (1976), pp. 5–14.

**3. the third year**: 483 BC. **a banquet**: This 180-day banquet for officials and army chiefs preceded the seven-day banquet for all the citizens of Susa (v. 5). Though Heb. *mišteh* literally means 'drinking bout', we may regard this banquet as essentially a 'reception' (as LXX, *dochē*). M. Heltzer, 'A propos des banquets des rois achéménides et du retour d'exil sous Zorobabel', *RB* 86 (1979), pp. 102–6, has recently offered some cuneiform evidence of types of food prepared for such banquets. **princes**: rather, officials, not the Persian aristocracy. **servants** may be specifically 'courtiers' (*NEB*), though both 'officials' and 'servants' may be generalising expressions. **army chiefs**: *RSV* translates Heb. *ḥayil*, 'army', thus, perhaps supposing that the whole army of 14,000 men (cf. Herodotus 7.40–41) was too numerous to entertain. Others find in LXX's *kai tois loipois* (Heb. *wšʾr*) evidence that MT originally had *wšry*, 'and the officers of' (so Moore). Even if the depiction is not somewhat exaggerated, feasts at Persian courts for vast numbers can be paralleled: Ctesias (fragm. 39) tells of 15,000 guests at a feast given by Artaxerxes Mnemon (405–359 BC). Another quite likely suggestion is that the term *ḥayil* refers to the class of high-ranking noble families **of Persia and Media** (so Gerleman); the term **the nobles** (Pers. *fratama*, 'first') would then be in apposition to *ḥayil;* cf. also on Ezr. 7:14. Such nobles are pictured on reliefs at Persepolis (*ANEP*, pls. 28, 29).

**4.** Two elegant phrases for the object of the celebration portray the royal pomp: **the riches** of 'the glory of his kingdom', and **the splendour** of the **pomp of his majesty**—both triple phrases exactly parallel in the Heb. The wealth of Persian kings is frequently referred to by classical writers (e.g. Herodotus 3.95f.). A feast of **a hundred and eighty days** either belongs to the world of fantasy (like the 120-day feast in Jdt. 1:16) or else implies successive visits by groups of officials; in reality the administration of the Persian empire can hardly have been suspended for six months. This stagey portrait is in any case only the backcloth for a more intimate episode more carefully depicted on a much smaller scale. Possibly what was on display in Susa were the completed refinements to the royal palace, mainly the work of Darius but finished by Xerxes (F. S. König, *Der Burgbau zu Susa nach dem Bauberichte des Königs Dareios I*, *MVÄG* 35.1 [1930]; R. G. Kent, 'The Record of Darius' Palace at Susa', *JAOS* 53 [1933], pp. 1–23).

**5.** After the imperial celebration comes the citizens' festival, the garden court of the royal palace being open to the (male) public from the acropolis (*bîrâ;* cf. on v. 2) of Susa. The **court** is a paved area (v. 6) between the **garden** or park, and the royal **palace** or rather summer house or pavilion (Heb. *bîtan*); see A. L. Oppenheim, 'On Royal Gardens in Mesopotamia', *JNES* 24 (1965), pp. 328–33 (Moore, *Studies*, pp. 350–5). Xenophon (*Cyropaedia* 1.3.14) refers to such parks (or 'paradises') surrounding Persian palaces. Some archaeologists have identified the site of this pavilion as in the northern sector of the acropolis of Susa (e.g. M. Pillet, *Le Palais de Darius I<sup>er</sup> à Suse* [1914], pp. 101ff.; R. Ghirshman, *Cinq campagnes de fouilles à Suse, 1946–1951*, pp. 1–18), but all the remains are considerably later than the time of Darius and Xerxes.

**6.** Difficult though the interpretation of various terms here are, and unconnected though the whole sentence is syntactically with what precedes, the impression of extravagant luxury is unmistakably conveyed. The use of foreign and rare words may even be a deliberate striving for an exotic effect (Dommershausen, p. 146). **white** and **blue** (or 'violet', *NEB*) were the royal colours (cf. also 8:15; Quintus Curtius, *History of Alexander* 6.6.4). The **hangings** served as awnings for shade; they were **caught up . . . to silver rings**, themselves attached to **pillars**, the **marble pillars** of an open-air hall of pillars ('alabaster' in *NEB* is not the English or Italian alabaster, a variety of gypsum, but oriental alabaster, a true marble which is a calcium carbonate). **couches of gold and silver:** Solid gold and silver is no doubt meant (cf. Herodotus 9.82); the couches were for reclining on during the banquet. The tesselated **pavement** was apparently a mosaic of four types of stone of different colours: **porphyry,** or malachite (*NEB*), both red stone (though the meaning is uncertain); **marble,** probably a white stone; probably some silvery stone like shell-marble, a marble containing fossil shells (cf. P. Haupt, 'Critical Notes on Esther', *AJSL* 24 [1907f.], p. 106 [= Moore, *Studies*, p. 10]), **mother-of-pearl** (*RSV, NEB*) being used for delicate inlays and hardly suitable for a pavement (Heb. *dar* probably cognate with Arab. *durr*, 'pearl'; LXX also had *pinninos*, 'pearl'); and finally a green stone (cf. *NEB*, 'turquoise'), **precious stones** also being inappropriate in a pavement. For ancient testimony to the magnificence of Persian banquets, see Herodotus 1.126; Athenaeus 12.512; Horace, *Odes* 1.38).

**7. drinking** rather than eating is, not surprisingly, specially mentioned, the Persians being famous for their feats of drinking (Herodotus 1.133; 9.80; Xenophon, *Cyropaedia* 8.8.10; Strabo 15.3.20). The variety of drinking vessels, **goblets of different kinds,** is probably referred to in order to highlight the royal ostentation; F. W. König noted the admiration here evinced for the individual work of art, so contrary in spirit to the bureaucratic and mechanistic tendency he found typical of the Achaemenian empire (*MVÄG* 35.1 [1930], p. 16). More prosaically, the point may be the quantity, not the quality of the vessels—smaller banquets depicted on the monuments show drinking vessels uniform in size, shape and material (Witton Davies). **according to the bounty of the king**, lit. 'according to the king's hand'. Alternatively, the sense may be 'of the quality drunk by the king himself' (Bardtke; similarly LXX), or 'according to the king's personal decree' (Gerleman), or 'as befitted a king' (Moore; similarly Vulg.).

**8.** That **drinking was according to the law** seems to mean that whenever the king drank all the guests drank (cf. Josephus, *Ant.* 11.188), but that is contradictory to **no one was compelled**. Translate rather: 'The law of the drinking was that there should be no restraint' (cf. *NAB*, 'By ordinance of the king the drinking was unstinted'), the root *'ns* meaning 'restrain' rather than 'compel' (Haupt, *AJSL* 24 [1907f.], p. 106 [= Moore, *Studies*, p. 10]). In an autocracy, even the absence of a rule requires a decree! The unstinted liberality with wine, allowing **every man to do** as he **desired**, spotlights the (insignificant) area of male power by way of foil to the immediately subsequent scene in which Vashti wins a (significant) moral victory against the king.

**9.** There appears to have been no compulsory segregation of the sexes at Persian meals (cf. Neh. 2:6; Herodotus 5.18; 9.110; Plutarch, *Artaxerxes* 5; *Praecepta Coniugalia*, 16. Plutarch, *Symposium* 1.1, and Macrobius, *Satires* 1.1, do not assert the opposite, as is often claimed); here, however, it is a necessity for the narrative. The absence of reference to ostentation and inebriation at the women's banquet (though both are quite probable among Persian women) further evidences the tendency of the narrative: women are put in a favourable light.

The name **Vashti** is unattested in extra-biblical sources, where Xerxes' queen is known only as Amestris (Herodotus 7.61; 9.109–113). Vashti may represent Avestan *Vahishta*, 'the best' (Haupt), or *uas*, 'the beloved' (H. S. Gehman, *JBL* 43 [1924], p. 322 [= Moore, *Studies*, p. 236]). See also J. Duchesne-Guillemin, *Le Muséon* 66 (1953), p. 106 (= Moore, *Studies*, p. 274); R. Stiehl in F. Altheim and R. Stiehl, *Die aramäische Sprache unter den Achaimeniden*, I, p. 203. The name could be an honorific title applicable to any Persian queen. The historicity of the story is neither supported nor negated by the use of the name Vashti. The location of her **banquet** is noted as **the palace which belonged to King Ahasuerus**, not simply 'the palace' (Heb. *bêt hammal⁽e⁾kût*) or 'the house of the women' (Heb. *bêt hannāšîm*, 2:9); the king's proprietary rights are insisted on in preparation for Vashti's act of defiance.

### VASHTI'S REFUSAL TO OBEY AHASUERUS

#### 1:10–12

The central scene in the narrative of ch. 1 is told briefly, almost cryptically. The grounds for Vashti's refusal to appear before Ahasuerus and his guests are only hinted at. The sequel to her defiance shows that it is connected with what may be reasonably expected by any husband of any wife, and the narrator's observations in v. 10 that the king was tipsy and that Vashti was commanded to 'show the peoples and the princes her beauty' make it clear enough that there was a conflict between the royal command and women's rights—at least as understood by Vashti. It is not correct therefore to regard Vashti's refusal as a whim (Paton), or as merely a dramatic necessity (Moore).

**10. when the heart of the king was merry with wine**: lit. 'was good with wine'. 'The remark that he did this when he was heated with wine indicates the opinion of the author that he would not have acted so if he had been in his right mind' (Paton).

It is a feature of this narrator's style to mention the names of characters incidental to the story. His purpose is not to give a greater air of historical verisimilitude to his story (as Bardtke)—which is not an issue that concerned him, whether he believed he was recounting historical actuality or consciously composing fiction. It belongs to the same impulse to decorative handling of his story that led him to the portrayal of the hangings and pavement in v. 6.

The **seven eunuchs** belong to a numerous class of Persian palace officials, mostly personal attendants or dignitaries of either sex, but also bureaucrats, military officials or governors. See E. F. Weidner, *AfO* 17 (1956), pp. 264ff. The names are apparently all Persian, though they cannot all be certainly equated with known Persian names or words. See H. S. Gehman, 'Notes on the Persian Words in Esther', *JBL* 43 (1924), pp. 321–8 (= Moore, *Studies*, pp. 235–42); J. Duchesne-Guillemin, 'Les noms des eunuques d'Assuérus', *Le Muséon* 66 (1953), pp. 105–8 (= Moore, *Studies*, pp. 273–6); A. R. Millard, 'The Persian Names in Esther and the Reliability of the Hebrew Text', *JBL* 96 (1977), pp. 481–8.

**11.** Vashti's **beauty** is for Ahasuerus an object for display or **show**, just like his wealth spoken of in v. 4 (the verb *hir'â*, 'show', is the same); it is indeed the chief treasure he possesses and has been saved up for the seventh and final day of the second banquet. The targums inferred from reference to the **crown** that she was to wear nothing but that, but the biblical text does not suggest that. The **crown** was probably the tall stiff cap, with jewels inset, that is depicted on the monuments. See H. W. Ritter, 'Diadem und

Königstracht. Untersuchungen zu Zeremonien und Rechtsgrund-
lage der Herrschaftsantritts bei den Persern, bei Alexander dem
Grossen und im Hellenismus', *Vestigia* 7 (1965), pp. 14ff. Herodotus' story (*Hist.* 1.8–13) of how the Lydian king Candaules
arranged to display the naked beauty of his wife to his bodyguard
Gyges is frequently cited as a parallel to this narrative. However,
beyond the common feature of a king wishing to display his wife's
beauty there is no further resemblance between the tales.

**12. the king's command conveyed by the eunuchs:** The wording
emphasises the *formal* propriety of the **command**, however improper
or insulting its content may have been.

### THE PERSONAL AND NATIONAL CONSEQUENCES OF VASHTI'S REFUSAL

#### 1:13–22

Vashti's simple and unelaborated refusal forms an amusing contrast
to the histrionic reaction of the king and his counsellors. While the
outcome is (perhaps) tragic for Vashti, it is in other respects pure
farce, involving the full panoply of Persian law and
administration—to say nothing of the postal service—in asserting
the right of every man to be master in his own house. It is implied
that the story of Vashti's independence will spread like wildfire
throughout the empire, with no need of assistance from the famed
Persian communications system, and that every wife in the empire
waits only for a sign from the empress to break out in long-stifled
rebellion against her husband.

**13.** At some unspecified time—though the text suggests a deliber-
ation while the participants are still in their cups (cf. 'next to him',
v. 14; 'this very day', v. 18)—the king consults **the wise men who
knew the times.** These sound like astrologers such as those of Dan.
2:27; 5:15; etc. (cf. Herodotus 1.107; 7.19, for the consultation of
magi by Astyages and Xerxes). But since their reply (vv. 16–20)
does not hang on technical astrological lore (nor even upon any
expertise with law or precedent), we should perhaps compare a
similar phrase in 1 Chr. 12:33 where the tribesmen of Issachar are
said to 'have understanding of the times, to know what Israel ought
to do'. The point is essentially a satirical one: it takes the legal
experts and the flower of Persia's aristocracy to formulate a response
which any self-respecting male chauvinist could easily dream up for
himself. On this view, those who knew the times will be identical
with **all who were versed in law and judgment.** For the view
that two overlapping groups are involved and that Ahasuerus first
consulted the legal experts and then the 'wise men' including his
seven princes, see O. Eissfeldt, 'Rechtskundige und Richter in

Esther 1,13–22', *Festschrift W. Eilers* (1967), pp. 164–7. The emendation of 'the times' (*ha'ittîm*) to 'the laws' (*haddātîm*) (Haller, Moore) is unconvincing, as is the suggestion followed by *NEB* that *'ittîm* is cognate with Arab. *'anat*, 'caused trouble', and means 'misdemeanours'.

**14. the seven princes:** A similar group of seven counsellors is mentioned in Ezr. 7:14. See also Herodotus 3.31, 84, 118: Xenophon, *Anabasis* 1.6.4; Josephus, *Ant.* 11.31. **saw the king's face:** i.e. had easy access to him (cf. *NEB;* Mt. 18:10), and (probably) rendered him personal service (cf. *NAB*); Herodotus says they had access to him at any time except when he was with one of his wives (3.84). **sat first in the kingdom:** a metaphorical phrase reflecting their place on ceremonial occasions, probably three on either side of the king, and one in front of him.

**15. According to the law:** Strikingly, though the phrase is in emphatic position, **law** plays no part in the response; it is purely pragmatic advice that is delivered, under guise of legal formality. The use of the titles **Queen . . . King** continues the note of formality.

**16. Memucan,** spokesman for the counsellors (cf. on v. 21), takes a hint from the king's style of speech and represents that Vashti's disobedience is a state matter, though he cannot foresee any greater damage to the state than 'contempt and wrath in plenty' (v. 18)—on the purely domestic front.

**17.** It is a simple matter of marital disagreement, even though **King** and **Queen** are concerned; Vashti is not fomenting political rebellion (as some have conjectured). **their husbands:** The narrator naturally prefers *ba'al*, 'lord', to *'iš*, 'man', in this context. The autocratic mind can only construe disobedience as **contempt.** On obedience/disobedience as an important motif in Esther, see Berg, pp. 71–82. Vashti's disobedience both contrasts with Esther's obedience (cf. 2:10) and parallels Esther's acts of disobedience (in ch. 5, by appearing before Ahasuerus without being summoned, and by refusing to give the reason for so doing).

**18.** The principal rebels against their husbands' authority, says Memucan, will be the aristocratic **ladies** (among them his own wife!), as distinct from 'all women' (v. 17) of the empire. **telling it:** Because the verb 'will say' (*to'marnâ*) has no object, many accept an emendation to *timreynah*, 'will be bitter, obstinate' (Haller, Paton, Bardtke, *NAB;* but cf. R. Gordis, *JBL* 95 [1976], pp. 45ff. [= Moore, *Studies,* pp. 410ff.]). *NEB* improbably regards **this very day** as the object. The simplest solution is to supply the sign of the definite object (*'et*) before 'what they have heard' (*'ašer šāme'û*) and translate: 'the ladies . . . will say (or, are saying) what they have

heard, namely, the reply (*dābār*) of the queen'. **contempt** will come
from the wives' side, **wrath** from the husbands'; the Persian aristo-
crat Memucan cannot imagine anyone acting differently from the
king. **in plenty**; lit. 'enough', used ironically.

   **19. If it please the king**: a deferential courtly formula, found
frequently in Est. (3:9; 5:4, 8; etc.; also Ezr. 5:17; Neh. 2:5) and
also, in Aramaic, in the Elephantine papyri (*AP* 27.19, 21f.; 30.23;
*AD* 3.5). **the laws of the Persians and the Medes**: The word
for 'law' (*dāṭ*) is a Persian loanword properly meaning 'decree' or
'administrative decision'—which this is. **Persians** and **Medes**:
usually in this order, though the reverse is found in the phrase 'the
laws of the Medes and Persians' in Dan 6:8, 15. **so that it may not
be altered**: There is no extra-biblical attestation of the irrevocability
of Persian law mentioned in 8:8; Dan. 6:8, 12, 15—a feature that has
attracted exaggerated attention, since such irrevocability is entirely
predictable in a highly bureaucratised autocracy and escape clauses
could easily be inserted if likely to be required (cf. on Ezr. 4:21).
In any case, it is probable that the meaning here is that the decision
should be incorporated among official decisions so that it will be
strictly carried out ('*ābar* properly means 'become invalid' rather
than 'be altered'). **Vashti is to come no more before King Ahasuerus**: There is an irony in prescribing as her punishment what is
really her own decision (v. 12); Memucan assumes that not to appear
before the king is the worst possible fate that can befall Vashti, but
it is precisely the point of this episode that such need not be the
case. **Vashti** is already—in word—deposed; no longer is the title
'queen' used. **another who is better than she**: narrative foreshadowing of Esther. **better** will mean 'more obedient', so the reader
is alerted to any tendencies on Esther's part towards 'disobedience'
or conflict with the king. But *ṭôḇâ* can also mean 'more beautiful';
is it hinted that the loss of Vashti as object for display (v. 11) can
be more than adequately compensated for?

   **20.** Ahasuerus will do his empire a favour by doing a favour to
his own sex. **high and low**: the same phrase as in v. 4; it must be
satirically meant that the citizens of his empire who appear in all
their ranks at the beginning of the story to gaze at the imperial
magnificence are at the end shown up to be, in all their ranks,
equally at risk in the battle of the sexes. It is ironic also that the
news of Vashti's disobedience, which Memucan has conjectured will
spread as rumour (v. 17), will necessarily be given official credibility
by the decree designed to scotch its influence.

   **21. Memucan**, though mentioned last in v. 14, has spoken for
his fellow-princes, though they themselves now hear his proposal

for the first time. They naturally agree with him, because it is
obvious that he has said what the king wanted to hear.

**22. letters to all the provinces:** on the Persian government postal
system, see on Ezr. 4:8–16. Paton solemnly rehearses the names of
every known **script** and **language** in the empire, concluding that
scribes adept in these tongues could not conceivably have all been
available in the imperial chancery. Such a judgment is rash, and
misses the point of the evident hyperbole which is intended to
display the super-efficiency of the Persian administrative machine
to do everything—except ensure that a man be master in his own
house! **speak according to the language of his people:** The targums
and many Jewish commentators thought this meant that a husband
should not submit to using his wife's mother tongue, if that was
different from his own; the case is somewhat reminiscent of Neh.
13:23–24. But such a situation must have been comparatively rare.
*RV* refers the clause to the decree: 'and should publish it according
to the language of his people'; but this sense is improbable after a
clause giving the content of the decree. Gerleman, denying that the
previous clause means that every man should be master in his own
house, translates both clauses 'so that every chieftain should be
addressed in the speech of his people'; but such a phrase is
redundant, offers a forced meaning of *śōrēr bᵉbêtô*, 'master in his
house', and involves a revocalisation of *mᵉdabbēr*, 'speaking', to
*mᵉdubbar*, 'spoken to, addressed'. The most popular solution is to
read for *ûmᵉdabbēr kilᵉšôn 'ammô* ('and speaking according to the
tongue of his people') *ûmᵉdabbēr kol-šōweh 'immo* ('whatever suited
him'; so Moore)—which makes the best sense, though *šōweh* properly means 'appropriate'; or else *ûmadbîr kol-nāšāyw 'immô* ('and
keeping all his womenfolk in subjection'; following H. Junker,
*BZAW* 66 [1936], p. 173; similarly Bardtke, *NEB*)—which strains
the Hebrew. Alternatively, we could read *ûmᵉdubbār bilᵉšôn nō'am*,
'and be addressed civilly (lit. with a pleasant tongue)'; or else delete
the clause as a dittograph (*NAB*, following LXX) or transpose it to
precede 'that every man be master in his own house' (so *NIV*).

What cannot be mistaken in this narrative is the satirical movement from solemnity to pathos, from imperial pomp to the most
unprepossessing aspect of domestic life: the attempt of husbands to
shore up their 'authority'. The rabbis of the Talmud already
observed this humorous note in the story when they commented:
'What sort of decree that is sent unto us, that every man should
show himself ruler in his own house? Even the weaver is master in
his own house. So when the decree came to destroy Israel they took
it also as a joke' (TB *Meg.* 12b).

It would be interesting to know whether our author was aware of the traditions reported by Herodotus, that Atossa, Darius' wife, 'completely ruled him' (7.2–3), and that Xerxes was in his later years very much influenced by his wife Amestris (9.109–113).

## ESTHER BECOMES QUEEN
### 2:1–18

Of all the characters in the first chapter (sixteen persons are mentioned by name), only Ahasuerus survives into the second chapter. The prelude has obviously been narrated as an introductory sketch of his character, as well as to account for the vacancy that Esther will now fill. Here the narrative of the remainder of the book is set in motion by the suggestion of the king's pages; and two more of the four principal characters of the book are introduced: Mordecai and Esther.

The narrative of this episode is interrupted twice; once for a 'flashback' explaining the presence of Mordecai and Esther in Susa and their relationship to one another (vv. 5–7), and once for an account of the customs of the Persian royal harem (vv. 12–14)—which, like the cameos of 1:6–8, highlights the luxury and ostentation of the court. The narrative is split up by these two interruptions into three parts of roughly equal length: in vv. 1–4 a means of filling the vacancy is proposed, in vv. 8–11 Esther becomes a candidate, in vv. 15–18 Esther secures the position. Though the outcome is predictable, the very inevitability of the plot and its lack of suspense have an ingenuous charm that somewhat disguises the busy functionality of the narrative. For in this chapter several fundamental explanations have to be given—for the sake of subsequent events—of how it is possible for a commoner to become queen, of how a Jewish girl can be queen of Persia, of how it is Esther who is chosen by Ahasuerus, of how links can be maintained between Esther and the Jewish people.

**1. After these things:** Ahasuerus' regrets may have begun, as far as the narrative tells us, the morning after or as long as three years later; for it is four years after Vashti's deposition before Esther is installed as queen (v. 16), and the story requires only an interval of one year for Esther's preparation in the harem plus periods of indeterminate length while the maidens from the empire are assembled in Susa (v. 8) and while Esther waits for her turn (v. 15). Whether the interval is filled by Xerxes' absence on his expedition against the Greeks is a much discussed matter; see Introduction, III. **he remembered Vashti:** The sequel, the suggestion of his pages, hints not only that Ahasuerus voiced his memory (though *zākar* does not actually mean 'mentioned') but also that he felt some regrets at Vashti's dismissal. For it is **after** his wrath has **abated** (*śkk*, as of the flood in Gen. 8:1) that he remembers her **and what she had done and what had been decreed against her;** the narrator allows us to sense for ourselves the disproportion of her offence and her irrevocable punishment (1:19).

**2. the king's servants:** i.e. his personal attendants (*na'ar*, lit. 'young man, servant'; cf. Nehemiah's 'lads', Neh. 4:23). It is not clear that they are to be identified with the seven 'chamberlains' of 1:10. It is over-subtle to attribute their suggestion to a fear that their lives would be endangered should Vashti return to power (Paton), for it is not they who counselled her dismissal, and the narrative does not permit us to contemplate a revocation of the decree. **virgins:** Since Heb. *bᵉtûlâ* means only 'young woman of marriageable age' (see G. J. Wenham, '*Bᵉtûlāh*, "A Girl of Marriageable Age" ', *VT* 22 [1972], pp. 326–48; *TDOT*, II, pp. 338–43), there is no emphasis on virginity (though it is no doubt implied), and the phrase simply means 'beautiful girls'.

**3. officers . . . to gather all the beautiful young virgins:** The language is probably deliberately reminiscent of 1 Kg. 1:2–4, where a beautiful young girl is sought for the aged king David. The Talmud, noting that no 'officers' were appointed in 1 Kg., contrasts the two accounts: in Israel men brought their daughters gladly; in the Persian empire, officers had to be appointed to search, because fathers hid their daughters. **the harem,** lit. 'the house of the women', located by the 19th-century excavator M. A. Dieulafoy in the north-west corner of the palace (*REJ* [1888], p. 276), though the only remains at Susa date from a later period. **their ointments:** see on v. 12.

**4.** This plan for obtaining a new queen would be most likely to provide a commoner queen from one of the many non-Persian races inhabiting the 127 provinces of the empire (1:1). It is often said that according to Herodotus (3.84), the king could marry only a daughter of one of the seven noble Persian families (cf. on 1:14; and see also Introduction, III); if that were so, while the pages' plan may have been a satisfactory way of obtaining concubines, it could hardly have been employed to choose a queen. It is a dramatic necessity, of course; and it may be suggested that if a Persian king was so severely restricted in his choice of wife, it would have been a matter of common knowledge which would have prevented the very conception of the story of Esther. Most commentators find here the essential clue that the story as a whole is to be regarded as a fantasy, but if there was no legal barrier to a Jewish girl becoming a Persian queen, the question of the book's connection with history must be determined on other grounds. Presumably the reason why another of Ahasuerus' wives was not elevated to the throne in place of Vashti was that none of them had 'pleased' him. The narrative stresses how difficult it is to please a Persian king, and how easy to displease him.

The story of the search for a bride is obviously analogous to that of the *Thousand and One Nights*, where also only one girl (Scheherazade) can charm the king and so become queen, her father gaining in the process the post of vizier. See E. Cosquin, 'Le prologue-cadre des Mille et une Nuits. Les légendes perses et le Livre d'Esther', *RB* 18 (1909), pp. 7–49, 161–97. Such stories are found universally, both as folk-legends (Cinderella) and as historical tales (e.g. as reported by Marco Polo from China: *The Travels of Marco Polo* [Everyman edn, 1908, pp. 162–5]; and also in Byzantium: cf. Bardtke, pp. 295f.).

**5–6.** The narrative of the king's search for a queen is necessarily interrupted in order to introduce Esther; and before she is introduced, it must be explained how she comes to be **in Susa**—and hence the story of **Mordecai** must be given. **a Jew:** Of first importance for the narrative as a whole, and therefore mentioned first, is the Jewishness of Mordecai and Esther. **in Susa the capital,** or rather, in the acropolis of Susa (cf. 1:2). The implication is that he lived there, and that he was therefore some kind of Persian official (as the LXX addition says explicitly in A2). **Mordecai:** The name is a Hebrew form of the Babylonian Marduka, 'man of Marduk' (the city-god of Babylon); it is attested in an Aramaic letter of the fifth century BC (*AD* 20), in Persian treasury records (G. G. Cameron, *The Persepolis Treasury Tablets*, p. 84), and, most importantly, as the name of an accountant, a subordinate of the satrap of Babylon and Beyond the River *c.* 485 BC (A. Ungnad, 'Keilschriftliche Beiträge zum Buch Esra und Ester', *ZAW* 58 [1940–1], pp. 240–4 [= Moore, *Studies*, pp. 356–60]; and *AfO* 19 [1959f.], pp. 79–81). Ungnad's claim (*ZAW* 69 [1942f.], p. 29) that there are hardly likely to have been two officials at Susa with the same name—and that therefore we have a definite literary attestation of Mordecai—is open to doubt; it is however followed by S. H. Horn, 'Mordecai: A Historical Problem', *BibRes* 9 (1964), pp. 14–25, and by R. Gordis, *JBL* 100 (1981), p. 384. Another Mordecai is mentioned among the home-comers from Babylon in Ezr. 2:2; so, despite the evident Babylonian origin of the name, it is not offensively unJewish. Possibly Mordecai was a 'Gentile' name roughly equivalent to some Hebrew name (cf. on v. 7; Dan 1:7). Certainly, the supposition of Jensen and others that the story is mythical in origin, Mordecai being identified with Marduk and Esther with the goddess Ishtar, is today given no credence (see Introduction, V).

It is natural to read Mordecai's genealogy as containing the names of distant ancestors, especially because the Benjamite **Kish** was the father of Saul (1 Sam. 9:1) and a **Shimei** is known as a member of the phratry (*mišpāḥâ*) to which Saul's family belonged (2 Sam. 16:5); it would be highly appropriate that a man with such forebears should get the better of Haman, the Agagite, descendant of Saul's enemy Agag (1 Sam. 15; see further on Est. 3:1). Yet it is impossible for anyone to be descended both from the Kish and the Shimei of the books of Samuel. If Kish and Shimei are not his immediate ancestors, Mordecai himself is apparently made out to be one of those exiled in 597 BC (so *NEB*)—which would make him at least 120 years old at the time of our story—a rather improbable situation, not least because Esther his cousin could hardly then qualify as a good-looking girl. We may suppose either that the narrator is confused chronologically or that it is Kish who was the person exiled with Jeremiah. Against the former possibility is the improbability that the narrator was unaware of the striking memory that at the return from exile in the time of the first Persian king only the oldest men remembered the Solomonic temple (see on Ezr. 3:12). The latter possibility is indeed not the most natural interpretation of the Hebrew, but is by no means precluded.

**carried away with Jeconiah,** *or*, Jehoiachin: see 2 Kg. 24:10-16. The implication may be that Mordecai's family was among the Judean nobility.

**7. had brought up . . . adopted:** Adoption is unknown in Hebrew law, the nearest parallel to it in the *OT* being set in a foreign locale (Exod. 2:10). Jews of the diaspora may well have taken over the custom, which is well attested in Babylonian legal documents. On adoption, see S. I. Feigin, *JBL* 50 (1931), pp. 186-200; I. Mendelsohn, *IEJ* 9 (1959), pp. 180-3; J. van Seters, *JBL* 87 (1968), pp. 401-8.

**Hadassah . . . Esther:** As we have supposed for Mordecai (v. 5), his cousin also had a Gentile and a Jewish name, **Hadassah** being Heb. for 'myrtle' (on plant names as personal names, see Noth, *IP*, pp. 230f.), and **Esther**, probably a form of Ishtar, the name of a Babylonian goddess, less probably from Pers. *stâra*, 'star'. See also A. S. Yahuda, 'The Meaning of the name Esther', *JRAS* (1946), pp. 174-6 (= Moore, *Studies*, pp. 268-72). The link between this introduction to Mordecai and Esther and the surrounding narrative is held back till the last: it is because she is **beautiful and lovely,** and for no other reason, that she makes her appearance in the story. Only as events develop will we see her intelligence, resourcefulness and bravery.

**8.** Naturally, there has been an administrative decree (**edict,** *dāṯ*, as in 1:19) authorising the gathering of candidates. Plutarch tells us that Artaxerxes had 360 concubines, 'all women of the highest beauty' (*Artaxerxes* 27.2), though here of course it is not a quest for a concubine but a wife that is undertaken. **into the king's palace:** or more precisely, the 'house of the women' (v. 9), the harem. The narrator effortlessly forecloses any criticism of Mordecai; the three passive verbs, 'were heard' (*RSV*, **were proclaimed**), **were gathered** and **was taken**, portray an irresistible series of events. In the Greek additions to Esther, Esther affirms that she is in the palace only under constraint (C 26–27). It is unnecessary for the narrative that Esther should have been living in Susa, but Mordecai's presence in Susa is essential.

**9. the maiden pleased him:** To 'please' (*yāṭab*, 'be good') is the oil in the wheels of the Persian bureaucracy; cf. the phrase in 1:21; 2:4 (twice), and 'pleasing' (*ṭôb*, 'good') in 1:10, 11, 19; 2:2, 3, 7, 9). **won** (*nāśā'*) **his favour:** Bardtke points out that in Esther this phrase has a more active sense than the similar phrase 'found (*māṣā'*) favour'. Esther is a success, even before Ahasuerus sees her. **quickly provided her:** The period of twelve months' preparation could not be shortened, but it was Hegai's decision when her course of beauty treatment should begin. As 'a connoisseur in such matters' (Paton), a man who 'knew better than anyone else the king's taste in women' (Moore), Hegai discerns in Esther a likely successor to Vashti. **her ointments:** more correctly, 'her massage with ointments', according to the regimen of v. 12. **her portion of food:** delicacies (cf. Neh. 8:10, 12), some of them in this case being no doubt contrary to Jewish dietary law (though the addition in C 28 denies it); v. 10 elaborates this point especially. Esther's behaviour differs from that of Daniel and his friends (Dan. 1:8–15), and of Judith (Jdt. 12:1–2). Each of the candidates was apparently attended by **seven maids** (cf. the seven chamberlains of 1:10); that Esther's were **chosen** may mean that they were superior to the other girls' attendants; that they were **from the king's palace** probably means that they, like all the attendants, were maintained from the royal purse.

**10.** Why had Esther **not made known her people?** It cannot have excluded her from consideration as a potential queen, for Ahasuerus later accepts the revelation of her origins without comment (7:3). To conceal her background hardly 'required extraordinary adroitness' (Witton Davies), nor would Mordecai's daily enquiries have necessarily given the truth away (as Paton). Mordecai must simply have feared for Esther's sake the kind of anti-Jewish feeling he himself evoked in Haman (3:4–6). The suppression of information about her race has of course a dramatic function also: the truth will be revealed when it will make its most positive impact.

11. Some have argued that only if **Mordecai** were a eunuch could he have had access to news of Esther. But, on the one hand, we need not suppose that contact between the **harem** and the outside world was exceptionally difficult (cf. Otanes' continued contact with his daughter, Herodotus 3.68f.); and, on the other hand, the story does not assert that Mordecai saw or heard news of Esther every day, but only that he frequented the area in hope of gleaning information about her.

Several elements in the narrative are reminiscent of the Moses story: an adoptive child enters a foreign court, prospers there, but keeps its racial identity secret, while a relative watches carefully from a distance (see Gerleman, pp. 11–23). Whether the parallel is deliberate is hard to say, especially since many features of the Joseph story are also apparent (see L. A. Rosenthal, 'Die Josephsgeschichte, mit den Büchern Ester und Daniel verglichen', *ZAW* 15 [1895], pp. 278–84 [= Moore, *Studies*, pp. 277–83]; 'Nochmals der Vergleich Ester, Joseph, Daniel', 17 [1897], pp. 126–8; cf. P. Riessler, 'Zu Rosenthal's Aufsatz, Bd. XV, S. 278ff.', *ZAW* 16 [1896], p. 182; Berg, *Esther*, pp. 123–42).

12. The **turn** of each girl was probably a once in a lifetime chance to make an impression on the king. The **twelve months** course of **beautifying** is of course a ludicrously extended period, heightening yet again the extravagance and artificiality of the court. W. F. Albright supposed that the period was 'accompanied by the extensive use of fumigation [with aromatics], which would have both hygienic and therapeutic value' ('The Lachish Cosmetic Burner and Esther 2:2', in H. N. Bream, R. D. Heim, and C. A. Moore, *A Light unto My Path* [J. M. Myers Volume], pp. 25–32 [= Moore, *Studies*, pp. 361–8]); but the practice of impregnating the skin and hair with the fumes of burnt cosmetics is paralleled by customs of semi-nomadic Ethiopian tribeswomen of the nineteenth century AD, a culture rather distant from the court of ancient Persia.

13. **given whatever she desired:** by way of jewellery and clothes, presumably, which would remain her own possession. See further v. 15.

14. The **second harem** under the supervision of a different eunuch is obviously the house of the concubines as distinct from the harem of the girls undergoing their beauty treatment. **summoned by name:** One of the targums adds 'distinctly and in writing'—which well epitomises the atmosphere of the Persian court, and encourages us to regard the narrator as more than faintly satirical of the Persian bureaucracy and as relishing his own exaggerated depiction. On life in the oriental harem, see E. F. Weidner, 'Hof- und Harems-Erlasse

assyrischer Könige aus dem 2. Jahrtausend v. Chr.', *AfO* 17 (1956), pp. 257–93.

**15.** Esther's relationship to Mordecai is repeated because of its cardinal significance for the story. That **she asked for nothing except what Hegai . . . advised** is rich in subtlety: there is the modest appraisal of her own talents which creates a sense of import- ance in those who advise her; there is the quintessentially diaspora self-sufficiency of accepting no favours from Gentiles (cf. Dan. 1:15; Tob. 1:10–11); there is plain native cunning in distinguishing herself from her hundreds of competitors by deliberately dressing 'down' for the occasion and relying on natural charm—to say nothing of the impression she will make on the king by not taking the chance of enriching herself at the king's expense. As she had won the favour of the chief eunuch (v. 9), so now she wins the favour (*nāśā' ḥēn*) of all who see her before she departs for the king's apartments—a sure narrative token that there too she will win favour (v. 17).

**16.** The date is the December-January of 479–478, some four years after Vashti's deposition (1:3). In the interval, if the dates preserve historical reminiscence, Xerxes (Ahasuerus) has been two years involved in his unsuccessful war against Greece (see Introduc- tion, III.(ii).2). But the narrator cares nothing for that, and the **seventh year** and **tenth month** may well be symbolic notices of the successful completion of the search for a queen (Schildenberger, p. 66). Paton remarks, none too subtly, that 'at the rate of one a day for four years, there must have been 1,460 maidens on the waiting- list ahead of her'; and others suppose that we are meant to calculate that at least some 1,000 candidates had been examined (as in the *Thousand and One Nights*). A general impression is, however, what matters here: Esther cannot be the first candidate, for such a narra- tive requires the tension of expectation; but neither may the period of waiting be too extended, for the narrative has yet far to run.

**17.** There is a distinction between the **women** who were already members of the harem and the **virgins**, or rather, girls, who had been assembled to provide a queen for Ahasuerus. Esther's victory is narrated very briefly, yet formally. The **royal crown** that Vashti had declined to wear (1:11) now comes to rest on Esther's head.

**18.** The **banquet** given by the king **for** Esther is undoubtedly meant to contrast with the banquet given *by* Vashti (1:9). Ahasuerus thinks that he has now got himself a little woman who will be receptive and obedient. Accompanying the banquet was a 'rest' (*haʾnāḥâ*), more probably a holiday (*NEB, NAB*) than a **remission of taxes** (*RSV*), or a political amnesty, or a release of slaves, or exemption from military service—as variously argued. The fore- shadowing technique favoured by our author ensures that we will see here a parallel to the Jews' culminating banquet and 'rest' (*nōaḥ*) from their enemies (9:16, 17, 18, 22). The giving of royal **gifts** likewise picks up the theme of the special 'portions' that Esther has herself received (2:9) and points forward to the ritual of the giving of portions in 9:22 (cf. also Neh. 8:12).

MORDECAI SAVES THE KING'S LIFE

**2:19-23**

This episode has primarily a foreshadowing purpose: it prepares for the sequence of events in ch. 6. It is appended to the story of Esther's accession to the throne in order to remove it as far as possible from the occasion when it will become significant for the movement of the narrative. At the same time, it allows Mordecai, who has been introduced along with Esther in vv. 5–7, to step forward for a moment in his own right. The documentary character of the Esther narrative is, as Gerleman observes, preserved even in this condensed episode by notes of the time-setting and of the names of the conspirators.

**19.** A gathering of the maidens a **second time** (*šēnît*) is inexplicable, since once Esther had been chosen as queen no further maidens needed to be sought in that fashion (the quest in 2:2–3 is not for numerous concubines, but solely for a single queen). Of the many explanations offered, only two are plausible: (i) that *šēnît* is a misplaced marginal note to v. 20, observing that its contents had already been given in v. 10 (W. Rudolph, 'Textkritisches zum Estherbuch', *VT* 4 [1954], pp. 89–90); (ii) that *šēnît* means 'further', 'secondly' (as in 2 Sam. 16:19), introducing a second event that occurred at the time of the gathering of the maidens (Gerleman). The difficulty here is that Mordecai's information about the assassination attempt can only have been passed on after Esther had become queen (v. 22) and therefore not while the gathering of the maidens was taking place. *NAB* helps by translating 'From the time the virgins had been brought together, and while Mordecai was passing his time at the king's gate, Esther had not revealed . . . And during the time Mordecai spent at the king's gate . . .' *NAB* proffers the further suggestion (similarly Paton) that *šēnît* means 'to resume', a reference to the fact that in a longer form of the Esther story this episode had already been recounted at a place corresponding to A 12–15 of the Greek version. **at the king's gate:** While this may indicate only Mordecai's habit of resorting to the palace area to hear news of Esther (as v. 11), most modern opinion is that it suggests that he was or became some kind of palace official—which would explain more probably how he gained news of the planned assassination than if he were merely a casual lounger at the gate. LXX has throughout Esther and also in Dan. 2:49 'at the king's court', which may be a correct interpretation (not an inner-Greek corruption, as Moore thinks). See further, H. Wehr, 'Das "Tor des Königs" im Buche Esther und verwandte Ausdrücke', *Der Islam* 39 (1964), pp. 247–60; O. Loretz, 'Šʿr hmlk—"Das Tor des Königs" (Est 2,19)', *WO* 4 (1967), pp. 104–8; H. P. Rüger, *Bib.* 50 (1969), pp. 247–50; Xenophon, *Cyropaedeia* 8.1.6; Herodotus 3.120.

**20. her kindred or her people:** the reverse order from v. 10, for here it is her relationship to Mordecai, there her racial origin, that is important.

**21. eunuchs who guarded the threshold,** i.e. of the king's private apartments. According to one of the targums, their complaint was that since Esther had come to court they had been able to get no sleep at night. They form a further parallel with the Joseph story, corresponding to the pharaoh's butler and baker—the same word *qāṣap̄ is used of the king's anger in Gen. 41:10 as is used of the eunuchs' anger here. It is characteristic of the Esther narrative that quite minor characters are mentioned by name (cf. on 1:10); contrast the absence in the Joseph story of names of the pharaoh's courtiers, even though they play a much larger narrative role.* **Ahasuerus** himself died, according to Diodorus Siculus (11.69.1–2) and Ctesias, *Persika* 29), as a result of such a conspiracy; so also did Artaxerxes III Ochus in 338. To be **angry** is often used in the ancient Near East for political rebellion; in the Esther story anger lies just below the surface of the bland bureaucracy, and rage is an important motivation in the narrative as a whole (1:12; 3:5; 5:5; 7:7; cf. 1:18; 2:1; 7:10).

**22. Esther told the king:** The narrator will keep for another occasion (4:11), where it will create dramatic tension, an observation on the difficulty and danger of trying to communicate with the king. Here it is not to the purpose of the story; perhaps also we are meant to contrast Esther's easy access to the king in her honeymoon days with the coldness implied by 4:11*b* four years later (cf. 3:7). Gerleman sees in Mordecai's silence and obscurity contrasted with Esther's visibility a parallel to Moses ('no man of words') and Aaron (Exod. 4:10, 15f.).

**23. hanged on the gallows:** probably impaled on wooden stakes, *tālâ being used as in Ezr. 6:11 (q.v.).* Crucifixion was also used by the Persians; see A. Christensen, in *Handbuch der Altertumswissenschaft*, ed. W. Otto, III/1, 3, 3, 1 [1933], p. 273); for new evidence of (Roman) crucifixion, see J. F. Strange, *IDBS*, pp. 199f. The height of the 'wood' prepared by Haman in 5:14, 50 cubits (= 75 feet), is however often thought to imply death by hanging.

**recorded in the Book of the Chronicles:** The keeping of such records was no doubt inherited from the Babylonians (cf. on Ezr. 4:15; and see A. R. Millard, *Iraq* 26 [1964], pp. 34f.). Herodotus notes that at the battle of Salamis, 'whenever he saw one of his officers behaving with distinction, Xerxes would find out his name, and his secretaries wrote it down, together with his city and parentage' (8.90). Cf. also Herodotus 8.85, where a list of King's Benefactors is mentioned, and Diodorus Siculus 2.32. It is without parallel that such a deed should go unrewarded at the time; Herodotus several times mentions Persian kings' rewards for services rendered (3.139–41; 5.11; 9.107). But of course it is a dramatic necessity for Mordecai's reward to be postponed to ch. 6. The neglect of Mordecai will also contrast with the unexplained elevation of Haman that immediately follows.

HAMAN'S PROMOTION AND PLOT AGAINST THE JEWS

3:1–15

The last of the four principal characters of the book is here introduced, and with him the main action of the story can at last get under way. In this chapter two scenes unfold: the first in vv. 1–7, where a confrontation between Haman and Mordecai develops, the second in vv. 8–15, where a conspiracy between Haman and the king is hatched. In moving from the first scene to the second, Haman advances from being the enemy of Mordecai to becoming 'the enemy of the Jews' (v. 10), a title he will bear again once the Jews have the upper hand of him (8:1; 9:10, 24).

**1.** Why Ahasuerus should have **promoted** Haman above **all the princes** of 1:14 is of no consequence for the story, though the unaccountable promotion contrasts nicely with the inexplicable overlooking of Mordecai in the previous scene. The name of **Haman** and his father **Hammedatha** are no doubt Persian, though their meanings are debated. While **the Agagite** also was probably in its original form a Persian title or gentilic, it has obviously been shaped by our narrator to appear as the name of a race descended from Agag, the Amalekite foe of Saul (1 Sam. 15:8–33). This interpretation is at least as old as Josephus who represented ·Agagite' by 'Amalekite'. Especially if Mordecai is portrayed as a descendant of Saul's family (see on 2:5), but also because Agag appears in an oracle of Balaam (Num. 24:7) as an inveterate opponent of Israel, the name must have a symbolic value. See further on 9:7–10.

**2. did obeisance:** Herodotus likewise notes the practice of obeisance at the Persian court to kings and the highest nobility (1.134), though Greeks were adverse to the custom (7.136); see further

Feodora Prinzessen von Sachsen-Meiringen, 'Proskynesis in Iran', in F. Altheim, *Geschichte der Hunnen* (1960), pp. 125–66. Why **Mordecai did not bow down** is obscure; he tells the other courtiers rather cryptically it is because he is a Jew (v. 4), but Jews shared the oriental custom of prostration (e.g. 1 Sam. 24:8) which they did not regard as a breach of the first and second commandments (Brockington). The reason can only be that as a Jew he would not give honour to a representative of a race anciently hostile to his own. For the narrator this is understandable national pride—though he does not necessarily applaud it. Mordecai here is no exemplar of a 'live and let live' policy for the diaspora (cf. Introduction, IV), however much his cousin may have had to compromise and conform on the other side of the palace wall (the narrator of Daniel takes a much stricter line on diaspora life). Considering that the plot against the Jews, and the whole narrative action, arises from Mordecai's refusal to do obeisance, the narrator must be strongly concerned to defend freedom of conscience—for he makes no judgment upon Mordecai's behaviour, but simply presents it as the datum of the story yet to ensue.

**3–5. transgress the king's command:** Here Mordecai's natural pride is brought out into the open as civil disobedience, in contrast with his loyal behaviour in 2:21–23. There is a tension between outward and inward obedience, between genuine and uncritical loyalty to the state. That Mordecai should be badgered **day after day** (cf. the same phrase in the Joseph story, Gen. 39:10) by the **king's servants who were at the king's gate** suggests strongly that he was among their number (cf. on 2:19). **whether Mordecai's words would avail:** The issue is whether Jewishness can exempt one from obedience to the Persian laws. **they told Haman:** It is an interesting narrative trait that Mordecai's public defiance cannot be observed privately by Haman, but must be the subject of a public deposition.

**6.** Haman has studied his master well. As Vashti had discovered, any disobedience is a state matter and the only penalties an autocracy cares for are extreme ones. There is a logic in Haman's supposition that if Jewishness is the ground of Mordecai's non-compliance, all Jews are potential law-breakers. The novelistic thing to do would be to institute an empire-wide test of loyalty, but for our narrator that would be a half-measure uncharacteristic of the Persian state. He cannot resist, however, the satirical note as he says that very thing; Haman thought it 'beneath his dignity' (Paton) or **disdained to lay hands on Mordecai alone**.

**7.** The narrative does not require this sentence, and v. 8 could follow naturally on v. 6. Nor is there any further allusion in the story as a whole to the casting of lots until we reach 9:24–26. And even so it is never made explicit how precisely the casting of lots is to affect the Jewish people. For these reasons most commentators regard the verse as the intrusion of a liturgically minded editor; and the stilted style may also point to the author of 9:23–28 as the editor responsible. See further on 9:24–26.

The **first month** of the year, in the Babylonian nomenclature **Nisan** (March-April), was in Babylonian thought at least the time of the year for determining destinies. Why were lots, lit. **the lot**, or, to use the term borrowed from the Babylonians, **Pur**, cast? The most natural assumption is that it was to determine the most propitious day for the execution of Haman's plans. Since the set day for the pogrom was the thirteenth of the twelfth month, Adar (v. 13), we would expect that date to be mentioned here; and indeed LXX adds at the end of the verse 'so as to destroy in one day the people of Mordecai, and the lot fell on the fourteenth day of the month' (similarly Old Lat.)—the fourteenth being perhaps a trivial error for thirteenth under the influence of 9:17ff. This reading is followed by *NEB, NAB*. **day after day . . . month after month:** i.e. 'for the day and the month' (*JB*). The phrase cannot mean that lots were cast every day from the first to the twelfth month, for on the thirteenth of the first month the day had already been fixed (cf. vv. 12f.). The casting of lots, no doubt by an astrologer (a magus), is attested among the Persians by Herodotus (3.128) and Xenophon (*Cyropaedeia* 1.6.46; 4.5.55).

**8.** The elements of Haman's speech are similar to those of Memucan (1:16–20): first, the precise nature of the offence, then a proposed solution (introduced by 'if it please the king'), then a statement of the advantages to be gained. In both cases, the disproportion between the actual events (Vashti's refusal, Mordecai's refusal) and the interpretation of them (wrong to all princes and peoples; contrary to the national interest) is striking.

**Haman said to King Ahasuerus:** As in 2:22, access to the king presents no problem when nothing in the narrative hangs upon it. **a certain people:** Their name is suppressed now, to await Esther's revelation of her origins (though surprisingly the king does not appear to know that it is against the Jews that the slaughter is planned until ch. 8). The phrase (*'am-'eḥād*) perhaps carries the overtone of 'an insignificant people' (H. J. Flowers, *ExpT* 66 [1954–5], p. 273). The Jews were obviously not **scattered abroad** throughout **all the 127 provinces**—that is hyperbole—but Haman means to hint at the influence of an underground movement. **dispersed** may be not a repetition of 'scattered', but may signify Jewish separateness and exclusivism; **being different** has always been mistrusted. It is only a half-truth that **their laws** (more correctly, 'their customs', *dāṯêhem;* cf. on 1:8) **are different from those of every other people**, for though Jewish dress, food, speech and religion were peculiar to themselves, so were the habits of many of the citizens of the empire, and the Persians prided themselves on their tolerance toward ethnic groups. What is particularly injurious about Haman's speech is that he uses the same word (*dāṯ*) for Jewish custom and Persian law, and can give the appearance of reasonableness in sliding from 'their customs are different' to **they do not keep the king's laws** (a similar criticism of the Jews is made in Ezr. 4:14–15). A show of colour is lent to Haman's accusation by Mordecai's refusal of obeisance to Haman which 'the king had . . . commanded concerning him' (v. 2). In his assumption that all Jews would act like Mordecai we are reminded of Memucan's assumption that all wives would act like Vashti (1:17f.). The reader knows, however, that Haman's generalisation is only the cloak for irrational hatred of the Jewish people. The Targums give at this point a host of possible reasons for Haman's hostility, which interestingly reflect Jewish perception of themselves. **not for the king's profit**: lit. 'not appropriate (*šōweh;* cf. on 1:22) for the king'; *šōweh* appears to be the Heb. equivalent of Aram. *'ᵃrîḵ*, 'fitting, worthy of an Aryan' (cf. on Ezr. 4:14). An appeal to the king's dignity and sense of racial superiority, Haman knows, cannot be gainsaid. This is not the last time that Jewish and Aryan 'interests' will conflict.

**9.** The money is a bribe, or more correctly the *baksheesh* that still is given to oil the wheels of government and business the world over. See M. Vogelstein, 'Bakshish for Bagoas?', *JQR* 33 [1942f.], pp. 89–92. The enormous sum does not alert the king to the likelihood that anyone who wants something as badly as Haman does cannot be principally motivated by concern for the king's dignity. The irony is thick; and it is at Ahasuerus' expense. The sum of **ten thousand** (silver) **talents** is truly meaningful only when set beside the revenues of the empire (cf. also on Ezr. 2:68; 8:26f.). Herodotus tells us that under Darius the total income of the Persian empire was 14,560 Euboeic talents (3.95), though this figure probably represents only the satrapies' contribution to central government (cf. on Ezr. 7:21–24). Haman's offer is two-thirds of that annual income! Another offer of money to Ahasuerus (Xerxes) is narrated by Herodotus (7.28): Pythius of Lydia, reputedly the second richest man in the world, offered Xerxes 3,993,000 gold darics (74,000 lbs. or 33 tons), a sum nine times the size of Haman's gift (reckoning the ratio of the value of gold to silver at 13:1). In this story too Xerxes refused the gift. In our narrative there is no hint that Haman hoped to raise the sum from plundering the Jews (v. 13 may even suggest that the Jews' attackers would be entitled to the plunder). **the king's treasuries:** cf. on Ezr. 5:17; 6:1.

**10.** The king responds promptly and decisively to his courtier's suggestion (as at 1:21); there is almost no action in the whole book that he initiates, apart from ordering that the book of the chronicles be read to him (6:1). The **signet ring** gave Haman full royal authority. Connection with the Joseph story is close here (see Gen. 41:42). It is not the king but the narrator who bestows a name or title upon Haman, **the enemy of the Jews**; the ironic contrast with Gen. 41:45 is obvious. We are probably not meant to speculate whether by giving Haman his ring the king intends to distance himself from the Jewish pogrom, or whether the honour is a reward to Haman for his concern for the royal dignity and the security of the empire. Certainly it is only Haman, and not the king, who is denominated the 'enemy of the Jews', but the question may well be raised whether the king is any friend to his subject peoples if he can be so casual about their welfare (cf. also on 7:5).

**11.** It is debated whether **the money is given to you** is a polite refusal (as with Pythius) or is a hint of the beginning of a round of bargaining (cf. Gen. 23:7–18). More probably, the fact that both **the money** and **the people** are **given** to Haman means that both are at his disposal—which is a courtly form of accepting the money (Mordecai certainly believes that by the end of the conversation Haman had promised to pay the money, 4:7). With **as it seems good to you** the royal authority (cf. e.g. v. 9 'if it please [lit. is good to] the king') is fully vested in Haman.

**12.** The passive verbs, **summoned, written, sealed,** convey the impersonality and cold precision of the proceedings (Gerleman). The **secretaries** are here lowly correspondence scribes (cf. Herodotus 7.100; 8.90), not the senior officials like Shimshai (Ezr. 4:9). See further, T. N. D. Mettinger, *Solomon's State Officials* (1971), pp. 19ff. Those addressed are three classes of officials: **satraps,** *'aḥašdarpᵉnîm,* from Pers. *khshastrapan,* 'protector of the kingdom' (see also on Ezr. 8:36), **governors** *(paḥ̱ôt)* of provinces or cities within a satrapy (as was Nehemiah, Neh. 5:14), and **princes** *(śārîm)* **of all the peoples,** leaders of ethnic groups, feudal lords, tribal chieftains. **on the thirteenth day:** The number 13 was unlucky among Babylonians and Persians; here the day has the added significance that the *fourteenth* of the **first month** was the day of deliverance from Egypt, the Passover. The narrator is teasing us: will the thirteenth or the fourteenth be the truly symbolic day for the Jews? **to every province in its own script:** The formality of the language (cf. 1:22) conveys the deliberateness of this act of royal authority.

**13-14.** The **couriers** were no doubt mounted, but portrayal of their speedy travel is postponed to 8:10 where it will be more significant for the plot. Accounts of the highly organised Persian postal system are provided by Herodotus (8.98; cf. 5.14) and Xenophon (*Cyropaedia* 8.6.17). The three synonymous verbs, **destroy, slay, annihilate**, carry the resonance of legal language, and the comprehensiveness of the edict, **all Jews . . . in one day**, has the icy precision of a heartless bureaucratic machine. **and to plunder their goods** seems tacked on to the decree, but it is not necessarily an afterthought; it stands in this somewhat isolated position by way of contrast with the Jews' later refusal to take plunder from their enemies (9:10, 15f.), despite being allowed to do so (8:11).

It seems inexplicable why there should be such an interval, of eleven months, between the proclamation and execution of the decree. As Paton drily remarked, 'The massacre of St. Bartholomew would not have been a great success if the Huegenots had been informed a year beforehand.' The dramatic necessity of allowing time for the counter-measures of Esther cannot account for such a lengthy period. Bardtke is no doubt correct in seeing no problem for the narrative here: there is no possible escape from the Persian empire, which is effectively coterminous with the known world, and the delay of execution only prolongs the agony of the Jews. Public knowledge of the planned pogrom over nearly a year can only intensify anti-Jewish feeling in order to be **ready for that day**. See also Introduction, III.(i).3.

**15.** Four scenes are skilfully depicted, and the action comes suddenly to a halt on a final note of uncertainty. (i) The **couriers** depart **in haste**, not because the matter is urgent, but because it is royal business (cf. 1 Sam. 21:8). (ii) The edict is read aloud (cf. on Ezr. 1:1) in the acropolis (*RSV*, **capital**) of Susa to officials and troops. (iii) The **king and Haman** sit **down to drink** because for them the business is concluded. (iv) The **city of Susa**, as distinct from the acropolis, hears the news and is **perplexed** or 'confused' (as in Exod. 14:3), since for them the business has barely begun. **sat down to drink**: Perhaps this is to be illustrated by Herodotus' report (1.133) that any decision made by Persians when sober was reconsidered while drunk—and vice versa.

## MORDECAI'S COUNTER-MEASURES

### 4:1-17

The previous episode centred around Haman; this one focuses on Mordecai, 'the Jew', the counterpart of Haman, 'the enemy of the Jews'. Mordecai appears at the crucial points of beginning and end of the episode, and it is only in response to his suggestions that any hope of resistance to the decisions of ch. 3 can begin to be entertained. Though here for the first time in the narrative the Jewish people appear, the significant action remains in the hands of the four principal characters. After a brief scene (vv. 1–3) in which we see a public reaction to the court intrigue of ch. 3, the story reverts to private conversation, between Mordecai and Esther (vv. 4–17).

**1–2.** The scene needs no formal introduction (as in 2:1; 3:1), since the previous scene was not firmly closed off (3:15*b*). Mordecai **learned all that had been done** not only from the public proclamation but also from his contacts within the palace (cf. v. 7). The mourning customs that Mordecai follows, with **rent . . . clothes, sackcloth** and **ashes**, are also appropriate for the receipt of bad news (see E. Kutsch, ' "Trauerbräuche" und "Selbstminderungsriten" im AT', *ThSt* 78 [1965], p. 26; D. R. Hillers, 'A Convention in Hebrew Literature: The Reaction to Bad News', *ZAW* 77 [1965], pp. 86–90). For a description of similar rituals of grief among the Persians after the battle of Salamis, see Herodotus 8.99. It is oversubtle to imagine Mordecai grieving in self-reproach because he now sees what damage his refusal to bow down to Haman has done to the Jewish people (Wildeboer). His **bitter cry** is not a funereal lament, but the cry of protest by the unjustly treated, *za'ᵃqâ* (cf. on Neh. 5:1). LXX correctly interprets its purport by adding 'An innocent people is condemned to death' (on *zᵉᶜ'āqā*, see G. F. Hasel, *TDOT*, IV, pp. 112–22). The content of such a cry is conventionally *ḥāmās*, 'violence'—which certainly is what is intended by the royal decree. No formal or legal accusation of the king is made by Mordecai (as against Gerleman); it is rather a gesture of protest. It is for this reason that he goes to the square (v. 6) before **the king's gate**, for it is a protest against the king; it is only because of the rules of Persian etiquette, that **no one might enter the king's gate clothed with sackcloth**, that he does not attempt to take his protest to the king's presence. There is no external evidence of such a rule, though Herodotus (3.117) does describe peasants from a distant country standing before the palace gates crying out for water.

**3.** Though the verse breaks the connection between v. 2 and v. 4, it should not be removed to follow 3:15, as some think. Its function is to mirror the action of Mordecai with that of Jews throughout the empire. In addition to, and preceding, the customary rituals observed by Mordecai, is mentioned **fasting**, which is usually a religious ceremonial; although God's name is never mentioned in the book, the Jews are not depicted as living without religion. The Jewish people are not primary actors in the story; so their grief is depicted with abstract, impersonal nouns and an impersonal verb (**most of them lay in sackcloth and ashes** is lit. 'sackcloth and ashes were strewn [as a bed] for most of them'). Mordecai, by contrast, as a principal character acts and speaks vividly.

**4–17.** The remainder of the chapter contains three scenes of communication of Esther with Mordecai, each more developed than the former. In v. 4 no words are spoken, and the gift of clothes is rejected. In vv. 5–9 a messenger is sent by Esther to Mordecai, and a message, both oral and written, is sent from Mordecai to Esther—the words are not reported. In vv. 10–17, a longer scene still, there is a report of words from Esther, from Mordecai, and from Esther again. A movement from ignorance to understanding to decision is brilliantly portrayed by this technique of scenic development. Esther initiates each of the communications, and the episode ends with Mordecai 'obeying' Esther's 'commands', but real progress in the unfolding of the plot is created by Mordecai (his mourning garb, v. 4; his news of the king's decision, and his challenge to Esther to approach the king, vv. 7–8; and his argument that subdues Esther's resistance, vv. 13–14).

**4.** Her **maids and her eunuchs** obviously know of her connection with **Mordecai** (cf. 2:22)—which is more than the king knows. They do not necessarily know that she is Jewish. **her maids**: as in 2:9; **her eunuchs** are first mentioned here (but cf. 2:14). **sent garments**: so that he could enter the palace. The implication is that, dressed correctly, Mordecai could converse with Esther (in fact, in the story they never speak directly to one another); things may be different from 2:11 now that she is queen. Mordecai's refusal, expressed brusquely with $w^e l\bar{o}$ ' $qibb\bar{e}l$, 'but he received it not' ($AV/KJV$), is explained reasonably enough by Josephus as 'because the sad occasion that made him put it [the sackcloth] on had not yet ceased'.

**5.** For the second communication a particular messenger is named, **Hathach**, 'courier' (J. Scheftelowitz, $MGWJ$ 47 [1903], p. 315) or 'the good one' (H. S. Gehman, 'Notes on the Persian Words in Esther', $JBL$ 43 [1924], pp. 327 [= Moore, $Studies$, p. 241]), who will be accompanied in the third scene by other eunuchs (cf. 'they told', v. 12). **what this was**: the sackcloth.

**7.** Mordecai's account fastens on the vast **sum of money** involved as indicating the seriousness of the business. No doubt we are meant to see in his knowledge of **the exact sum** Mordecai's familiarity with palace affairs.

**8–9.** The written **copy** of the edict that Mordecai sends into the palace is a physical counterpart of the clothes that Esther has sent out; this token cannot be refused. With it goes not a request but a command ($\d{s}iwweh$, **charge**, $RSV$) which Mordecai can presume to

give as her guardian, and which the reader knows from 2:10 is likely
to be obeyed. Esther's obedience in 2:10 was precisely over the issue
of her ethnic identity; then it was to be concealed, now it must be
revealed. The Jews are now to be regarded as **her people**, not just
Mordecai's, as in vv. 1–3. **show . . . explain**: Is it suggested that
the edict was in Persian, which needed to be translated (into
Aramaic) for Esther's benefit?

10–12. This, the third and most dramatic of Esther's communications, is couched in direct speech. There seems a hint of mild
reproach in it: **all the king's servants know**—but you, Mordecai,
apparently do not. Esther's hesitancy in acceding to Mordecai's
'commandment' (v. 8) should not perhaps be regarded a sign of
cowardice: the crucial factor, which Mordecai cannot be expected
to know or even guess, is that at this time the queen happens not
to have been summoned by the king for more than thirty days. The
extra-biblical evidence concerning the **law**, or rather 'decree' ($d\bar{a}\underline{t}$)
to which Esther refers has been variously interpreted, but it is not
really unclear. Some supposed parallels quoted by many commentators from Herodotus (3.118, 140) describe peculiar situations and
neither confirm or deny the rule mentioned here. Herodotus 1.99,
often cited in this connection, concerns the *Mede* Deioces, not a
*Persian* king; and it is in any case self-evidently implausible that
'nobody was allowed to see the king', especially because it is also
reported that it was a particular disgrace for anyone to laugh or spit
in his presence. Herodotus (3.84) and Cornelius Nepos (*Conon* 3)
make it quite plain that the 'law' in question must have concerned
*unannounced* and *unauthorised* entry into the king's presence. The
possibility that Esther should request an audience with the
king—which would not expose her to any danger—remains unmentioned, partly for reasons of dramatic tension, but also no doubt
because there can have been no assurance that an audience would
have been granted, given that she is not in very good standing with
Ahasuerus. **sceptre**: for an illustration of Darius with his sceptre,
see *ANEP*, p. 463; on the etymology of *šarbîṭ*, see most recently J.
Sasson, *VT* 22 (1972), p. 111. **they told Mordecai**: Only Hathach
is mentioned in v. 10, but the other eunuchs must be included here
in v. 12, or else the plural is indefinite, viz. 'Mordecai was told'.

13–14. Mordecai's reply, likewise reported in direct speech, is
remarkably blunt; he does not beseech, he gives directions; he does
not treat her as a Persian queen, but still as his adoptive daughter.
His forthright **think not that in the king's palace you will escape**
is, indeed, not so much a threat or a reproach as a counterweight to
the mortal risk Esther will run if she approaches the king uninvited;
staying out of the king's presence is no less dangerous than entering

it—an ironic situation in the Persian court, but one which Vashti had already encountered in her own way. The decree is against all Jews (3:13). And even if the Jewish people are saved by some other means, Esther and her family, including Mordecai, will be punished (by God) for her failure to act. Mordecai's faith in God's faithfulness to his people is expressed in the memorable words **relief and deliverance will rise for the Jews from another quarter**, even though God is not expressly mentioned. Contrary to common opinion, it is not likely that **from another quarter** is an indirect way of referring to God (cf. the use of *māqôm*, 'place, quarter', in later Hebrew for 'God'; see A. Spanier, 'Die Gottesbezeichnungen *hammāqôm* und *haqqādôš bārûk hû'* in der frühtalmudischen Literatur', *MGWJ* 66 [1922], pp. 309–14); for deliverance through Esther and deliverance from God cannot be contrasted; and if 'place' means 'God', what does *'another* place' mean (P. R. Ackroyd, *ASTI* 5 [1966f.], pp. 81–4)? Nevertheless, no matter where deliverance comes from, God's providence will have been at work; other possible avenues for its operation are Jewish officials (of similar standing to Nehemiah) or an armed revolt by the Jews. The possibility (or more exactly, the hope) of a providential purpose in Esther's being on the throne at this moment is expressed by **who knows . . . ?** Cf. Jon. 3:9 for a similar 'who knows?' of hope (cf. also 'perhaps' in 1:6); the phrase signifies more than mere possibility. On the idea of the concealment *and* intervention of God here, see J. A. Loader, 'Esther as a Novel with Different Levels of Meaning' *ZAW* 90 (1978), pp. 417–21.

**15–17.** Esther's decisive conviction expresses itself in the imperatives **Go, gather**, a 'command' according to v. 17. Resolved to identify herself wholly with her people, she insists that they should share her preparations. The **fast** she prescribes is not the mourning fast they are already engaged in (v. 3)—and of which she knows (v. 4)—but the fasting that accompanies intercession to God (cf. Ezr. 8:21, 23; Neh. 1:4; 9:1); H. A. Brongers categorises this as a preparatory fast ('Fasting in Israel in Biblical and Post-Biblical Times', *OTS* 20 [1977], pp. 1–21). Absence of specifically religious words is of course characteristic of the book, but the religious significance is unmistakable. **all the Jews in Susa:** a considerable number, seeing that according to 9:15 they could later kill three hundred of their opponents. A fast **for three days** is unusually long (it was normally from morning to evening, Jg. 20:26; 2 Sam. 1:12) and that it should last **night** and **day** is exceptionally strict, only two fasts in later Jewish law being prescribed for a full 24 hours. The Heb. hardly means 'night **or** day', i.e. three 12-hour fasts (as Gordis). The two fasts of this episode (vv. 3, 16) contrast with the feasts which open and close the book (1:3, 5, 9; 2:18; 9:17f.). The

Targums correctly observe that no indication of time has been given since 3:12 where the thirteenth of the first month was mentioned. Our story-teller may well mean that the Jews fasted on Passover, the fourteenth day, despite the law of Exod. 12—so severe was their danger. **against the law**, lit. 'not according to the decree (*dāt*)'. The motif of obedience comes to the surface again; now, as never before, there has come about a conflict of loyalties, which will be resolved in favour of the Jewish people and against the Persian empire. The book of Esther, the least rigorous and most accommodating of the literature of diaspora Judaism, still maintains a line beyond which compromise with the governing authority cannot be sustained. Compromise (as over food laws, disguise of one's racial origins) has always been in the interests of survival; now it is survival itself that is at stake. **if I perish, I perish:** a similar formulation in the Joseph story (Gen. 43:14). It does not here signify resigned fatalism (Paton) but courageous determination.

ESTHER'S FIRST AUDIENCE

5:1–8

The narrative action at this point could almost be over. Esther could fail to have the royal sceptre extended to her; then she would be executed and the story of Esther would be ended. Alternatively, she could succeed in her mission, and—barring the difficulty of overturning a royal decree (which is handled successfully in ch. 8)—the Jewish people would be saved. What we have, however, is a retardation of the main plot throughout chs. 5–7; in a series of brilliant scenes the secondary plot of the conflict between Haman and Mordecai is thoroughly worked out in an almost surrealistic manner before the more soberly conceived main plot is resumed in ch. 8.

1. The scene is set before the action begins. In harmony with the faster flow of events, an indicator of proximate time is given, linking this episode with the previous one (cf. 5:9; 6:1, 14; 8:1; contrast 2:1, 16; 3:1, 7). **put on her royal robes:** Sackcloth could not be worn within the palace itself. The image of Mordecai's natural behaviour is being conjured up as a counterpart to Esther's unnatural, formal behaviour. Here royal clothes must correspond to royal **palace** and royal **throne**. The **inner court** was apparently adjacent both to **the king's palace** which contained the royal apartments and the throne room (*bêt hammalᵉkût*, 'house of kingship'; the term is used loosely in 2:16). *RSV* translates *bêt hammelek* (lit. 'king's house') by both 'king's palace' and 'king's hall', but the latter term is better reserved for the place where his throne stood.

The occasion must be a day of audience, for otherwise **the entrance** would not be open.

**2. she found favour:** the same phrase as in 2:15, 17, 'she won his favour'; her beauty must be the cause.

**3.** The title **Queen** both in the narrative (v. 2) and in the king's mouth conveys the formality of court etiquette and is a signal of the future success of the rightful queen's rightful request. The king's generous promise, **even to the half of my kingdom,** is an encouragement—but does not yet guarantee Esther's victory. This courtly formula (also in 5:6; 7:2; cf. 9:12) is not meant to be taken literally (cf. on 3:11). It would be bad form, not to say risky, to take advantage of the royal generosity, and Esther's apparently reckless throwing away of her opportunity ('psychologically most improbable', Paton) is not simply dramatically desirable but fully intelligible as the first exchange in a play of oriental courtesies. To be sure, the narrator is teasing us with the possibility that Esther may take the king at his word. Herodotus tells a story of Xerxes' being urged by a mistress to keep such a promise (9.109–111); cf. also Mk 6:23.

**4.** The **dinner** (*mišteh*, 'banquet') is, like the royal robes of v. 1, the Persian counterpart of the Jewish fasting. The irony is complex: while the Jews fast because of the king's decree that puts them in the power of Haman, their Jewish protectress at the Persian court prepares a feast for both the king and Haman. Why Haman is invited by Esther is a tantalising question for ancient and modern commentators alike. The Talmud tractate *Megillah* (15b) mentions twelve possible reasons, with the footnote that when Elijah was asked to adjudicate he decided in favour of all the reasons! There are obviously dramatic reasons why the downfall of Haman is best played out on stage and not simply determined in his absence. There may be also more prudentially pressing reasons, in that it is safest if Esther can witness with her own eyes the king's response to her plea and Haman's reaction. The narrator himself does not linger over the point, but he is likely to see aesthetic, dramatic and moral implications in a public humiliation of the enemy of the Jews—which the banquet scene will provide.

**5.** Haman is to be brought **quickly** only because all official business must be done in haste (cf. 3:15). But with the word the narrator begins to heighten the tension (see also the notes of haste in 6:10, 12, 14). **that we may do as Esther desires:** dramatic irony, for Esther's desire is for far more than a banquet.

**6. as they were drinking wine,** lit. 'at the banquet of wine', i.e. when the meal proper is over, and the king may be presumed to be relaxed (cf. 1:10).

7–8. The second postponement of her request is generally thought to serve solely the literary purpose of prolonging the suspense. That it certainly does, but there is a narrative reason for the postponement. Esther's first response has been to invite the king to a banquet (v. 4); her second response is to oblige the king in advance to **grant** her **petition** and **fulfil** her **request,** and to signify his obligation publicly by attending a second banquet with Haman. Unlike the first banquet, which she said she had already prepared, the second will be prepared only when the king has agreed—by his acceptance of the invitation—to meet the demand Esther will make. Esther has now given notice that she intends to take the king's generosity literally (contrary to etiquette), but makes it difficult for him to take his promise back: he would have to decline the invitation to the banquet—and what excuse could he give? By the end of her speech Esther has been able to represent what *she* wants as **what the king has said**; it has all been a delicate play of bargaining, while the object of the play has remained undisclosed.

## HAMAN'S PRIDE A THREAT TO MORDECAI

### 5:9–14

After the many formal scenes that have unfolded hitherto, this scene is surprisingly intimate and psychologically explicit. The reader does not expect to be given an entrée into the homelife of Haman; the narrator adroitly depicts the sinister in a familiar, domestic setting, and portrays a vain, volatile and—perhaps worst of all—unsubtle Haman. The farcical but black surrealism of ch. 1 is with us again; Haman at home, worsted by his inferior Mordecai, mirrors Ahasuerus in the palace, worsted by his inferior Vashti. Like Ahasuerus who must put every woman in the kingdom in her place in order to assert his own dignity, Haman must butcher the whole race of the Jews to conquer his own inferiority feeling.

9. We last met with such a contrast of mood at 3:15, when Haman had successfully concluded his business with the king. The contrast here, however, is not external, but within Haman's emotions. **Mordecai** being now **in the king's gate** must have put off his mourning garments (cf. 4:2); the three days' fast enjoined by Esther (4:16) is now presumably over (cf. on 5:1). Far from failing to bow down to Haman (3:2), Mordecai will now not even 'rise' in respect before him (cf. Job 29:7f.) nor even show any signs of fear. G. R. Driver's suggestion that $z\bar{a}^c$ means, not 'trembled' but 'deviated' (cf. Arab. $z\bar{a}ja$), i.e. moved aside for him (*VT* 4 [1954], p. 236 [= Moore, *Studies*, p. 398]) makes good sense, but the meaning is unattested. Mordecai's heightened disrespect for

Haman must reflect his growing confidence now that Esther has shouldered the Jewish cause. **filled with wrath:** Ahasuerus' temperament (1:12) is mirrored in his minister's.

**10.** Haman's 'restraint' does not produce an unnatural delay (as Paton); it matches his 'disdain' in 3:6 to lay hands on Mordecai alone. There it led to a far-reaching plot against the Jews; here it will lead to a concentrated plot against Mordecai's life. **sent and fetched,** i.e. for a banquet. The custom of sending slaves to escort guests to a banquet is implied (cf. Lk. 14:17).

**11–13.** Haman's speech, the centre-piece of this scene (cf. the use of direct speech in ch. 4), reaches its point only in v. 13. His family and friends do not need to be told of his **riches,** his **sons,** and his **promotions,** nor is his speech simple self-pity. It is an invitation for their advice. In Persian circles, it appears, everyone relies on advice (cf. 1:13–22; 2:2–4, 15; 3; 4; 6:6–10)—foolish, as often as not—, and no one seems capable of action without elaborate consultation. **his riches:** cf. 3:9. **his sons:** Among the Persians, says Herodotus (1.136), 'the chief proof of manliness is to be the father of a large family of boys'; Haman has ten (9:7f.). The queen's invitation means to him that he is not only esteemed politically but is regarded as a friend by king and queen. Their personal friendship is however swallowed up by the personal hate he feels for Mordecai; he is pathetic in his self-revelation that **all this does me no good.** Haman is a case-study in anger.

**14.** There must be many ways of disposing of Mordecai, but Haman's friends rightly understand that something more than his enemy's death is required to satisfy Haman. It must be public humiliation; **a gallows fifty cubits** (80 feet) **high** will be visible throughout Susa, even though planted in the courtyard of Haman's house (7:9). It is probably a pole on which the dead body is to be impaled (cf. on 2:23). And Mordecai's death must not be an act of private vengeance, but authorised by **the king.** Above all, the death must be arranged **in the morning,** so that Haman can **go merrily with the king to the dinner**—and, incidentally, so that, from the reader's point of view, it will be too late to expect any intervention by Esther at the banquet.

MORDECAI IS REWARDED BY THE KING

**6:1–14**

The momentum of the narrative has now become very pressing; Mordecai's fate cannot wait for a new day but must be decided in that same night in which the 'stake' has been prepared for him (5:14). Here there is no room for human initiatives such as have

been played out so adroitly by Esther in the previous scene. Now
everything must be providential—or rather coincidental (which is
the narrator's cipher for 'divinely arranged'). The king's sleeplessness, the finding of the passage about Mordecai, the fact that he
has not been suitably rewarded already, the arrival of Haman in
time to give his advice—all these key events are such pure chance
that the reader is compelled to see in them the divine providence.

**1–2. the king could not sleep:** lit. 'the king's sleep had fled'.
The motif of royal sleeplessness is used also in Dan. 6:9; 3 Esd.
3:3; cf. also Shakespeare, *Henry IV, Part II*, iii.1.4–31. The **book
of memorable deeds,** or rather simply 'the chronicle of daily events'
(*NEB*) is referred to in Ezr. 4:15; in Esther it has been mentioned
as the 'Book of the Chronicles' (2:23; *dibrê hayyāmîm*, as here) and
the attentive reader will know immediately how the story must
develop. **they were read:** The Heb. suggests a lengthy reading. The
passage about **Mordecai** seems only to have been reached (**found**
does not mean it was looked for purposely) at daybreak when Haman
was in the outer court (for the daybreak motif, cf. Dan. 6:19).

**3.** It is a remarkable coincidence that Mordecai's service should
not have already been rewarded, for Persian kings were famed for
their eagerness to reward well-wishers (Herodotus 3.138ff.; 5.11;
9.107; Thucydides 1.137f.; Xenophon, *Hellenica* 3.1.6). Herodotus
mentions a list of King's Benefactors, using the Persian word
*orosangai* (8.85).

**4–5.** As usual, advice has to be taken. It is the neatest irony of
all in the story that, when any courtier would have served the king's
purpose, it is **Haman** who must give advice on how Mordecai should
be honoured, and moreover, that he should be in the position to
give that advice only because he is early at the palace to get authorisation for Mordecai's execution. **the outer court:** Even Haman
cannot enter the king's presence without permission (4:11). That
only Haman is about is a hint that the hour is unconscionably early.
Haman also has missed some sleep.

**6.** The motif of 'misdirected speech' or 'conviction out of one's
own mouth' is also realised in the finely told parable of Nathan (2
Sam. 12:1–7) and the story of the wise woman of Tekoa (2 Sam.
14:1–17). But here there is the nice twist that both parties are
unaware of the implications of the speech. Is there also an irony in
the way the king unintentionally destroys Haman by keeping from
him the name of the man he wishes to honour, just as Haman had
intentionally kept from the king the name of the people he wished
to destroy (cf. Moore)? In any event, the king is not interested in
why Haman has been waiting to see him, and Haman is interested
in nothing but his own status (as in 5:11–13); **honour** is his life-

blood, and the thought of honour will divert him even from his plan against Mordecai.

**7–9.** Haman's response begins with an anacoluthon: 'The man whom the king delights to honour—let royal robes be brought . . .'. He is absent-mindedly savouring the king's phrase (as already 'to himself', v. 6; and twice in v. 9), and speaks before he has shaped his sentence. Dommershausen observes the absence of the courtly formula 'if it pleases the king', attributing it to Haman's preoccupation with his future honour; Striedl (p. 88) and Moore think it a sign of Haman's increasing self-confidence. **robes . . . which the king has worn:** Haman relishes intimacy with the king (cf. the giving of clothing in 1 Sam. 18:4); that is what is honour for him (and cf. on 5:11–13). Is it because the king senses that intimacy with royalty is Haman's ambition that he will accuse him of an attempted rape of Esther (7:8)? Plutarch recounts a story of a Persian king giving a robe to a man but forbidding him to wear it (*Artaxerxes* 5); the symbolism may be the same. **the horse which the king has ridden:** cf. 1 Kg. 1:33. The **royal crown** is set on the head of the horse. For an illustration of decoration on horses' heads as represented on the Apadana at Persepolis, see Moore, pl. 4; it is not clear that the decoration is a crown, however. The turbans on horses' heads depicted in Assyrian reliefs (W. Forman and R. D. Barnett, *Assyrische Palastreliefs*, Pls. 43, 59, 64, 83; G. Dalman, *Arbeit und Sitte*, v, p. 279) may not be royal insignia. We might translate 'a horse which the king has ridden when the royal diadem has been set on his head' (omitting the *waw* of *wa'ašer*); similarly Gerleman. The marks of honour have meaning principally for Haman; the populace may well not know that it is the king's robe or the king's horse, splendid though they may be. He seeks no wealth or official position; all he wants to be publicly known is that **the king delights to honour him.** The **open space** is in **the city,** where there will presumably be more people than in the acropolis (cf. on 1:2).

The resemblance of this scene to that of Joseph's elevation in Gen. 41:42–43 is plain (see also on 3:10), but the narrator deliberately deviates from the Joseph story in stressing that the clothing must be the king's own and not just 'fine linen', that the horse must be the king's own and not just harnessed to the 'second chariot', and that the proclamation must be that it is the king who is honouring Haman, not just the people (contrast 'Bow the knee' in Gen. 41:43).

**10.** The reversal of the fortunes of Haman and Mordecai is accomplished in a single sentence from the king. The narrator seems to have saved for this moment the information that Haman is not only prime minister but also one of the 'nobles' (*part<sup>e</sup>mîm,* as in

1:3), whom one would think to be the 'seven princes' noted by name in 1:14, but among whom Haman has not appeared. It is at this moment that Haman's ancestry will be most to his disadvantage: he happens to be the most available representative of 'the king's most noble princes' whom he himself had specified for the task (v. 9). Though the king does not realise it, the bitterest irony lies in his appellation of Mordecai: **the Jew**. The 'enemy of the Jews' (3:10) must punctiliously honour a Jew. The king cannot have learned that Mordecai was a Jew from the chronicles, for it was only after the conspiracy of 2:21–22 that Mordecai acknowledged his Jewishness in the court (3:4). The narrative must assume he has learned it from his 'servants' (v. 3). Contrary to common opinion, there is no contradiction between the king's honouring of the Jew Mordecai and the decree for the extermination of the Jews; for at this juncture the king still does not know that the people he has agreed should be wiped out are the Jews (their name is not mentioned in the conversation with Haman, 3:8–11, and the decree which specifies them is issued by Haman, not by the king personally, 3:12). Admittedly, the king must be the only person in the empire who is unaware of the details of the edict; but his ignorance may be regarded as one of the many meaningful coincidences of this episode.

**11.** We are not invited to consider Mordecai's reaction to this rather foolish ceremonial. In itself, it has no value for him, for he may well sink into oblivion again. Haman's plans may only be delayed, and the edict against the Jews still stands. It is only Esther's denunciation of Haman in ch. 7 that will lift the sentence from his people.

**12.** Another crisp and provocative contrast like those of 3:15 and 5:19 is presented. For **Mordecai** nothing has changed and he returns to his place at **the king's gate**. For **Haman** nothing has outwardly changed, but the symbolic value of events is evident to him and his associates. He is **mourning** for the loss of face he has suffered, and perhaps also for the approaching calamity he sees as inevitable. To have the **head covered** is a sign of mourning the dead (2 Sam. 15:30; Jer. 14:4), perhaps as an identification rite (cf. on Ezr. 9:3). *NEB*, 'with head uncovered', follows the rather unconvincing identification of *ḥāpâ*, 'cover', with an Arab. cognate; the argument is that normally the head was covered (Brockington). As the roles are reversed, Haman adopts Mordecai's garb while Mordecai is clothed in the garment Haman had coveted for himself. And Haman's covering his head is a foreshadowing of his final disappearance from sight, with his face covered (if that is what 7:8 means).

**13.** Haman's **wise men** must be his friends; the word is not to be emended (as *NEB*, *JB*) but understood as 'advisers' (*NAB*); he

is an eminent Persian, and so must have counsellors like the king's
(1:13), who can interpret the significance of events for him. Haman
hardly needs their interpretation, nevertheless. They cannot be
uncertain whether **Mordecai . . . is of the Jewish people,** since
Haman has already told them he is (5:13). There is in fact no
objective reason why Haman should fear the worst, but his friends
are convinced that Jews are invincible; **if** must mean 'since'. This
is a striking capitulation (Dommershausen), as much for its setting
in the plot as for its content. Could this be the advice that Haman
never sought when he set out to destroy the Jews? And could his
counsellors be voicing the narrator's belief in the predictions of the
fall of Amalek before Israel (Exod. 17:16; Num. 24:20; 1 Sam.
15:2f.; cf. 2 Sam 1:8f., 13–16)? If so, they speak on behalf not only
of the narrator but of diaspora Jewry generally.

14. The narrative draws quickly to its climax; the scenes of ch.
6 and ch. 7 are dissolved into one another by two narrative tech-
niques of compression. First, **while they were yet talking with him**
imposes the banquet scene of ch. 7 upon the domestic conversation
of 6:13 (for an effective parallel, see Job 1:16–18). Second, this
final sentence merges the two locations, speeding up the action by
breaking down the scenic divisions (similarly at Job 2:7). **brought
Haman in haste:** not as though he had forgotten the banquet or
was reluctant to go; we have here simply the conventions of royal
business requiring haste (cf. on 3:15) and of guests being escorted
by the servants of their hosts (cf. on 5:10).

### THE FALL OF HAMAN
### 7:1–10

The narrative here reaches its climax; though the fate of the Jews
remains undetermined, and will not in fact be settled until ch. 9,
the fall of their arch-enemy is firm evidence that they will ultimately
escape his design upon them. The three scenes presenting Haman
at court nicely reflect the movement of the narrative: in the first
(3:8–15) Haman initiates the conversation and achieves his purpose;
in the second (6:4–11; 5:5–6 assigns no independent action to
Haman) the king initiates the conversation and Haman is diverted
from his purpose; in the third (7:1–10), Haman is excluded from
the conversation and has his own purpose turned against him.
Though the narrative of this chapter is powerful, the characteris-
ation is slight; Haman's desperate appeal for his life and the king's
attempt, but evident inability, to handle his own anger are the only
interesting psychological depictions.

1. The **feast** must be imagined as taking place in the afternoon, since much is yet to happen on the same day (7:10–8:2).

2. **the second day:** i.e., the day of the second banquet. The king uses the same conventional language as in 5:6, with the exception that now he adds **Queen Esther** (as in 5:3), perhaps expressing his goodwill towards her. Throughout the scene (with only two exceptions, vv. 6, 8), the narrator refers to her as 'the queen' or 'Esther the queen'—which is never the case in the more intimate scene between her and Mordecai (ch. 4). Here she behaves regally, there as Mordecai's ward.

3. As queen she addresses the king with formal etiquette (as in 5:4), but also—as nowhere else in the book—addresses the king in the second person (**in your sight**). Formally, too, she repeats the king's language, **petition, request, given** (*RSV* 'granted' in v. 2). Esther has thoroughly assimilated Mordecai's arguments (4:13f.): **my life** and (the life of) **my people** are inseparably entwined. Paradoxically, in the moment when she pleads for her own safety she puts herself in greater danger by revealing her Jewishness. And in the moment when she is most obedient to Mordecai she first disobeys his one command—not to make known her people (2:20).

4. **we are sold:** She can hardly say that it is in fact the king who has sold them (see 3:9–11), and so must put it in the passive. She has been well primed by Mordecai, and knows both of the sum of money offered by Haman (see 4:7) and the exact terms of the edict prepared by Haman (**destroyed . . . slain . . . annihilated;** cf. 3:13). The reason why she would have kept her peace if the Jews' plight had simply been to be **sold merely as slaves**—a common enough occurrence (cf. Neh. 5:8)—is that such **affliction** would be **not to be compared with the loss to the king.** This can only mean it would be too trivial a matter to bother the king (on *nzq*, 'trouble, bother', see H. L. Ginsberg, *VTS* 16 [1967], p. 81; R. Gordis, *JBL* 95 [1976], pp. 55f. [= Moore, *Studies*, pp. 420f.]). *NEB* has 'would not be such as to injure the king's interests', but this does not adequately express the force of *šōweh*, 'appropriate, fitting' (cf. on 3:8). Older versions, translating *haṣṣār* as 'the enemy' rather than 'the distress', often have something like 'although the adversary [i.e. Haman] could not have compensated for the king's damage' (*RV*), viz. the damage the king would sustain if he were to lose income from the Jews' taxes!

5. In the double question there is a double irony: the first that it is the king who has 'sold' the Jews (Haman has 'bought' them); the second that, whether the culprit is the king in his fecklessness with his subjects or Haman in his genocidal design, both the conspirators are 'here'. The plot on the life of the king was foiled by one

Jew, Mordecai; the plot on the life of the queen by another Jew, Esther—the narrative has many such resonances. **would presume:** lit. 'has filled his heart' (similarly Ac. 5:3).

6. Esther's two-fold response corresponds to the king's question. 'Who?' is answered by **A foe and enemy!**, 'where?' by **This wicked Haman!** The banquet has turned out exactly as planned: Haman is both unmasked and outnumbered.

7. No narrative motivation for the king's withdrawal to the garden is offered, and even Haman's perception that **evil was determined against him by the king** will not explain it. Though the queen's life is threatened, the king can hardly punish Haman for a decree that has gone out in his own name (Brockington). What the king lacks at this juncture is the advice of courtiers that he has always been able to count upon; for the first time he has to make a decision for himself, and his withdrawal may be a sign of his incapacity to handle the situation. He certainly reaches no decision on the strength of Esther's revelation.

Haman's reaction is less cryptic. He has seen the king's **wrath** and knows what that means. In turning to Esther to plead for his life he creates delightful ironies which he has no time to savour. Here is Haman who that morning expected to slay the Jew who had not bowed before him, fallen to the ground before the Jewess to beg for his life. Here is Esther, one moment pleading for her own life, the next importuned by Haman for his. Here is Esther who recognises that her fate is identical with that of her people, and Haman, whose professed anxiety for the security of the empire (3:8) has been completely eclipsed by his own personal danger.

8. Whether in his anxiety Haman had fallen **on the couch** or only **beside** the couch of Esther is unclear from the Heb. *'al*; according to *NEB* he had 'flung himself across the couch', while *JB* sees him 'huddled across the couch'. Esther is obviously not sitting but reclining, in the Persian manner (Herodotus 9.80, 82). It is probable that Haman's approach was contrary to courtly etiquette; an Assyrian harem regulation decreed that 'if a courtier speaks with one of the women of the palace, he must not come closer to her than seven paces'. Admittedly, this particular regulation, cited by E. F. Weidner, *AfO* 17 (1956), p. 288, comes from the 11th century BC, but Weidner remarks that Persian ceremonial was heavily dependent upon Assyrian custom (p. 258). Though the reader of Esther cannot be presumed to know such details, the king's reaction to the scene is plain enough. He cannot easily have mistaken Haman's gesture as an attempted assault or rape, and his outraged cry **will he even assault the queen in my presence, in my own house?** is decidedly theatrical. In any event, it is Haman's

action that apparently makes the king's mind up for him. The male chauvinist knows how to act when he imagines his honour affronted. Esther does not protest at the king's misreading of the situation. Her silence is dubbed callous by some; but is it not true, in another sense, that Haman by his plot has indeed already 'assaulted' the queen in the king's own house? **they covered Haman's face:** Commentaries generally refer to a custom attested in Greece and Rome, though not in Persia, of covering the head of a person condemned to death (Livy 1.26.6, 11; Quintus Curtius, *History of Alexander* 6.8.22). But this is a covering of the **face**, and there has been no evident sentence passed on Haman. Rather than translate with *NEB*, 'Haman hid his face in despair' (reading *ḥuppû*), we should follow Gerleman's suggestion: 'Haman fell down in a dead faint' (in accord with the Arab. phrase *juniya* (or, *juniya 'alaihi*).

**9. Harbona:** one of the seven eunuchs in 1:10. His speech mirrors that of Haman's wife and friends at 5:14, and the subject is the same, the **gallows** or stake **fifty cubits high;** only the persons of the condemned have changed places. How Harbona knows of the 'gallows' is not at this moment stated; but Josephus (*Ant.* 11.260) no doubt represented the narrator's intention correctly: 'This he knew, because he had seen the gallows in the house of Haman when he was sent to summon him to the royal banquet, and . . . learned for what it was intended' (cf. 6:14). For a minor character, Harbona makes a uniquely positive contribution to the action; his intervention is necessary because Esther has had no means of knowing of Haman's plan against Mordecai. What he offers is a piece of unsolicited but welcome information, which is effectively another charge (note **moreover**) against Haman, this time as the enemy of a man **whose word saved the king** (2:21–23).

**10.** The last hanging on gallows, or rather, impalement on a stake, in the story was the fate of the conspirators against the king; the story neatly folds back upon itself by making this impalement that of the man who plots both against the queen and against the man who saved the king from the earlier conspiracy.

The **anger of the king,** which has persisted since v. 7, is now **abated.** Previously the king's anger had been a token of his irrationality (1:12); after it had abated (2:1) he seemed somewhat foolish. This is hardly the point here, though his outburst against Haman has in itself been quite ineffectual in counteracting the menace his decree still offers to Esther and the Jewish people (just as his rather whimsical exaltation of Mordecai in 6:10–11 has already been ineffectual). Even when his anger has abated he cannot quite see where his duty lies; beyond his perfunctory and rather pointless gift of the 'house' of Haman to Esther, it seems to be only at Esther's

prompting that the more significant gift of his signet ring is made
to Mordecai (8:2). It will again have to be Esther who takes the
initiative to safeguard herself and her people.

### HAMAN IS REPLACED AND HIS PLOT OVERTURNED
### 8:1–17

One knot—and that the principal one—remains to be untied: the
edict against the Jews still stands, and, being written in the king's
name and sealed with his ring (3:12), it is irreversible. The narrative
does not disclose the ingenious solution to the conundrum until the
last possible moment; and it will be Mordecai, not the king, who
devises the solution. First, however, the king's permission to seek
a reversal of his decree is required—a task that falls most naturally
to Esther.

**1.** Very formally, with titles for each personage, the narrative
recounts the king's dispositions: it is **King Ahasuerus** who gives to
**Queen Esther** the 'house' of **Haman, the enemy of the Jews**.
Haman's **house** includes all his property and probably also his
family. According to Josephus (*Ant.* 11.17) and one narrative of
Herodotus (3.128f.), the property of a traitor was confiscated by the
Persian state. **came before the king:** i.e. was given the status of
those officials who 'saw the king's face' (1:14). **what he was to her:**
how they were related.

**2.** The gift of the king's **signet ring** not only signifies that
Mordecai has now fully taken over Haman's position, but also
prepares for the effective use of that ring in vv. 8, 10. The ring is
the means of life or death for the Jews. **Esther set Mordecai over
the house of Haman:** Mordecai takes Haman's place both officially
and personally.

**3.** Esther's renewed appeal to the king is represented as occurring
on the same day as Haman's downfall and Mordecai's elevation.
Contrary to common opinion, the narrative does not describe a
second 'audience' with the king like that of 5:1–8. Esther is already
in the king's presence and has already been speaking to him (telling
him of her relationship to Mordecai, v. 2); now she speaks **again**
(lit. 'added to speak'). She is not risking her life as in ch. 5, for
there is no hint that she has come before the king unbidden; there
would be in any case no call to do so now that Mordecai as prime
minister has ready access to the king. It transpires in v. 7 that
Mordecai is present, but this is emphatically Esther's scene.
**fell at his feet:** not in an act of obeisance (for which the verbs
*kārāʿ* or *hištaḥᵃwâ* are used) but as a suppliant. In 7:8 it had been
Haman's turn to 'fall' (*nāpal*, as here) at *her* feet; but she begs not

for her own life but only for her people's (v. 4). The **tears** are the
first clear sign of emotion on Esther's part, who has seemed cool-
headed, not to say calculating, throughout the narrative. Her
weeping is a further sign that, despite the formality of vv. 1–2 and
the king's gesture with the sceptre in v. 4, this is an occasion as
informal as it is possible to be at the Persian court. Noticeably, it
is Esther and not the king who has the first word (contrast 5:3;
6:6).

**4. held out the golden sceptre:** There is no need to imagine that
the **sceptre** had only the significance it bears in 5:2; here it is a sign
of favour and permission or encouragement to 'rise' (v. 5).

**5.** The delicacy of her request—**to revoke** a royal decree—is
reflected in her prefacing it with four conditional clauses, the first
two being familiar as forms of courtly politeness (cf. 1:19; 5:4, 8;
7:3), the second two being new. **if the thing seem right:** The
adjective *kāšēr* is equivalent to *šōweh*, 'fitting', in 3:8; 5:13; 7:4; on
the face of it, it is highly improper to suggest that a decree signed
with the king's seal should be altered, let alone 'reversed' (*AV/KJV*).
The narrator can hardly mean us to believe (*contra* Bardtke) that
Esther is unaware of the irreversibility of the 'law of the Persians
and the Medes' (1:19). Esther cleverly puts as last of the
conditions—which have unobtrusively become reasons—her own
charm (**if . . . I be pleasing in his eyes**), which may reasonably be
expected to linger most efficaciously in the king's mind. Esther also
discreetly refers to the decree not as a royal production but as **letters
devised by Haman**.

**6.** Esther rests her case wholly upon her own feelings (**how can
I endure**), and in so doing unmistakably appeals to the king's
sympathy for her personally. Whatever reason there may be for
saving the Jews, in the end Esther makes it an issue of whether the
king is willing to spare her suffering or not. The rather detached
narrative can be psychologically penetrating when it chooses. **to see
the calamity that is coming:** borrowed from Gen. 44:34.

**7–8.** Mordecai is drawn into the king's reply because it is he who
will dictate the new decree (vv. 9f.). The king has been touched by
Esther's appeal, but his response is not wholly unambiguous. Most
commentators see his reference to giving Esther Haman's house and
to his disposing of Haman as his sign of his favourable disposition
toward the Jews, to which v. 8 adds a *carte blanche* permission to
write what they choose so long as it does not contravene any previous
decree. But it is not impossible that the king means that he has
already done all he is able to do (LXX suggests that his response is
a reproach), and that from now on the Jews must make their own
way, though they have his blessing to do anything that is not illegal.

It is hard to resist the impression that the king is washing his hands of the matter, just as in ch. 3 he had not really wanted to know any details of the people against whom the first odious decree was devised. The official reason for Haman's death has now become **because he would lay hands on the Jews,** though this is hardly how the narrative of ch. 7 reads. **for an edict . . . cannot be revoked:** The king is obliged to mention the fact because Esther's request (v. 5) ignored it. Probably the **for** gives as the reason why any future action must be left to the Jews the fact that the existing decree cannot be reversed. The king's logic is defective, however, for if there is no legal barrier to framing a countervailing decree there is no reason why he should not be the one to do so.

**9–14.** The language of this episode naturally mirrors that of 3:12–15, for the narrator has a liking for the ironies implicit in repetition with differing intention (cf., e.g., 6:6f.). The divergences are often significant.

**9.** The date is two months and ten days later than Haman's edict (3:12) and so in May/June; the seventy days between the threatened annihilation of the Jews and their release from danger will have struck a chord with every attentive post-exilic reader of the book: the seventy days are (are they not?) the seventy years of exile. The time that has elapsed has by no means been clearly consumed in the events of the intervening chapters; for no longer than four days appear to have passed between the conversation of Esther and Mordecai in ch. 4 and the present moment. Some interval may be supposed between 3:15 and 4:1, and between 3:3 and 3:4, as also between 8:8 and 8:9 (the vague phrase **at that time,** deviating from the strict temporal succession in the counterpart to those verses in 3:12, may be inserted precisely for the purpose of creating distance between the two verses). The narrator has obviously been torn between his attachment to the symbolic number seventy and his desire for a rapid progression of the narrative; the latter impulse has evidently predominated, but not to the extent of involving him in a contradiction. **concerning the Jews:** reading *'al,* 'concerning', for MT, *'el,* 'unto' (as *RV, NEB*). The MT reading is perhaps defensible as ranking the Jewish community before the highest officials of the Persian provincial government (Bardtke). **from India to Ethiopia, a hundred and twenty-seven provinces:** an addition to the contents of 3:12, based on 1:1; it stresses how widespread the Jewish dispersion is, no doubt hyperbolically. **also to the Jews in their own language:** a further addition; it is strictly otiose, since they are included in the previous phrases, but it is obviously a point to be emphasised.

**10. mounted couriers . . . the royal stud:** This whole phrase elaborates the single word 'couriers' in 3:13. Obviously the narrator has reserved this material for use in this place where the speed of the imperial post is of positive advantage to the Jewish people. It is less probable that the narrator thinks of a more rapid postal service employed by Mordecai to spread the countervailing decree more quickly (so Paton). **swift horses . . . royal stud:** two obscure words of Persian origin; Gerleman translates '[couriers] of the various post-stations'.

**11–12.** The decree issued in the king's name by Mordecai is an almost exact duplicate of Haman's letter in 3:13—only the objects of the decree of annihilation differ. There it was the Jews; here it is **any armed force . . . that might attack them.** Unlike the pogrom planned by Haman, the Jews' self-defence will not be racially motivated; and even though, as in Haman's decree, **plunder** is allowed to be taken, it is three times remarked in the subsequent chapter (9:10, 15, 16) that in fact the Jews took no plunder of their enemies. Modern readers are understandably squeamish about inclusion of **children and women** among the objects of permitted annihilation; it may be noted, however, that the phrase has its counterpart in Haman's decree, and that no word is spoken later of any actual slaughter of women and children (cf. 9:15f.). Possibly, in fact, we should translate 'that might attack them, their children or their women, and that might plunder their goods' (similarly R. Gordis, *JBL* 95 [1976], pp. 49–53 [= Moore, *Studies*, pp. 414–18]).

**13.** The decree authorising Jewish self-defence is, like that of 3:13f., proclaimed **to all peoples,** and not just to the Jews. There will be no element of surprise in the Jewish resistance, and the population of the empire will have to figure out as best it can the total effect of the two decrees that neither directly contradict nor cancel one another out.

**14.** A repetition of 3:13, with the addition of the reference to the couriers being **mounted on their swift horses** (as in v. 10). The decree of the Persian king permitting Jewish resistance to hostility from their neighbours and from the state has of course a significance beyond the horizon of the narrative: it becomes a scriptural authority for a robust self-assertion by diaspora Jewry.

**15.** We encounter the same chronological tension in the narrative as in v. 9: while the narrator would like to present a rapid sequence of events, as if **Mordecai went out from the presence of the king** immediately after the interview of vv. 7f., the notation of time in v. 9 interposes a considerable interval. In any case the abrupt and logically unmotivated mention of Mordecai's going out of the king's presence signals the intimacy with the king he now enjoys in Haman's place. So too do the **royal robes of blue** (or 'violet', *NEB*)

**and white**, the imperial colours we have met with in 1:6. (Joseph also has been clothed in white at his elevation, Gen. 41:42; for the use of purple as a colour of distinction, see also Dan. 5:7, 29; 1 Mac. 10:20, 62, 64; Lk. 16:19.) The **crown** (*$^a$teret*) is not the imperial crown (*keter*) we have encountered in 1:11; 2:17; and 6:8 (where it functions in Haman's fantasising); Mordecai wears the head-dress of a Persian noble, possibly no different from Haman's everyday attire, but for obvious dramatic reasons first described here. Herodotus tells of the bestowal by Xerxes of a gold crown upon a man who had saved him from a disaster (8.118). The symbolic values of clothing have already been called upon by the narrator (cf. 5:1); here Mordecai's clothing effects the permanent reversal of his wearing sackcloth in 4:1, a reversal anticipated by 6:11. The **city of Susa** that **shouted and rejoiced** cannot be solely the Jewish population, but the inhabitants as a whole who are represented as instinctively pro-Jewish (as also is implicit in 3:15, where 'the city' is in confusion because of the first edict from the palace; the size of the Jewish slaughter of their enemies in Susa, that occupies them for two days, comes as something of a surprise in 9:15). Can there be any doubt that the first edict is now effectively countermanded? Who in the empire, if Susa is anything to go by, will want to avail themselves of the first edict's permission to destroy the Jews? Mordecai's elevation is symbolically the elevation of the Jewish people, for whereas in 3:15 it was the issuance of the decree that threw the city into confusion, here it is apparently the sight of Mordecai clad in garments of honour that stimulates the city's rejoicing.

**16.** The four-fold expression, **light and gladness and joy and honour**, designedly mirrors the four-fold mourning, fasting, weeping and lamenting in 4:3. **light** as a metaphor for prosperity appears in Job 22:28; Ps. 27:1; 36:9; 97:11; etc.; but it is curious in this prose narrative. Perhaps it alludes to the illuminations that will be characteristic of the Purim festival (Ringgren). If **light** refers to the objective deliverance of the Jews, **gladness and joy** depicts their own consequent emotion, and **honour** the (objective) esteem in which they are now held (to be elaborated in v. 17*b*).

**17.** An unexpected, almost surrealist, note is added by the conclusion **And many from the peoples of the country declared themselves Jews**. The **peoples of the country** figure in Ezr. 9:2, 11 as 'the peoples of the land' (*'ammê hā'āreṣ*), i.e. of the land of Israel. Here they are the various nations of the Persian empire. Their conversion to Judaism cannot be represented as insincere, for there is still no advantage to be gained in being a Jew; the first decree still stands, and the second decree gives the Jews rights only against those who attack them. Their **fear** is not that they will suffer at the hands of the Jews, for they are safe if they are not enemies of the Jews. Their fear must be a religious awe such as falls upon the inhabitants of Canaan (Jos. 2:9) and Transjordan (Exod. 15:16) and Egypt (Ps. 105:38). This uninvited proselytism is presented by the narrator as the climax of the success story that has occupied the chapter; Ahasuerus' gift to Esther of the house of Haman has become a token of the gift of **many** of Ahasuerus' subjects to the Jewish people. Once again, the narrator speaks for post-exilic Jewry (not necessarily for the late Greek period, as some think); see further, M. H. Pope, 'Proselyte', *IDB*, III, pp. 921–31.

At this point the story of Esther might well have concluded. It would be a delightful irony, and one fully worthy of the Jewish sense of humour, if the resolution of the conflict between the two royal edicts had been left up in the air; a stalemate is perhaps in the end the best one can hope for, and it is certainly infinitely preferable to a defeat. It would be true also to diaspora life to represent the relations between the state and the Jewish people as unresolved tension, it never being wholly clear whether the state is ultimately protector or threat. And that the unseen hand of God should so conspicuously rescue the Jews from disaster that even Gentiles should discern where the divine favour lay and spontaneously convert to Judaism—what more fitting climax to the story of the rise of a Jewish girl to the Persian throne? If it were not for the evidently inferior narrative conception and execution of chs. 9–10, the foregoing suggestion would be whimsical. But many scholars have found secondary material in the sequel of the narrative, and in the remainder of this commentary notice will be taken of hints that the whole of these chapters form a secondary addition to an earlier tale of Esther that concluded with 8:17. A more developed argument that an earlier Esther story ended at this point is provided in my study, *The Esther Scroll. The Story of the Story* (1984).

### HOW ADAR 14–15 BECAME THE PURIM FESTIVAL

### 9:1–32

The function of this segment of the narrative is primarily to explain how the days following the thirteenth of Adar came to be celebrated as the festival of Purim. The foregoing narrative requires, if anything, a depiction of the resolution of the conflict between the two royal decrees; but this it conspicuously fails to provide. There is not a word to suggest that the enemies of the Jews actually put into operation the first edict against the Jews, nor that any Jew was killed or plundered on the fateful day. On the contrary, the Jews seem to take the initiative in killing (which was not intended by the second edict), and exact a fearful toll.

Even if we may leave aside the unsavoury morality of the story (and its surrealism certainly dampens down the horror), the narrative is quite simply clumsy—a trait we have not once detected in the preceding chapters. Among its awkwardnesses are the following: the motif of the king's generosity (vv. 12f.), the account of the variant days of observance of the festival (vv. 17–19), the repetition of the plot of the narrative (vv. 24–25), the confirmation of Mordecai's letter (vv. 29–32). Whether or not 8:17 constituted the ending of an earlier version of the story of Esther, it is tempting to suppose that the material that now occupies chs. 9 and 10 is of secondary origin and was composed by a narrator (or authors) of inferior artistry: (see further, D. J. A. Clines, *The Esther Scroll* [1984]).

The narrative contains these elements: (i) Jewish slaughter of their enemies throughout the empire and in Susa (vv. 1–10); (ii) Esther's interview with the king extending the period of permitted slaughter by one day (vv. 11–15); (iii) an explanation of the difference between Jews of the empire and Jews of Susa over the date of celebration of their victory (vv. 16–19); (iv) a letter sent by Mordecai to regulate the observance of future celebrations (vv. 20–28); (v) a second letter sent by Esther on the same subject (vv. 29–32).

## A CHANGE OF FORTUNE FOR THE JEWS
### 9:1–19

This narrative of the thwarting of the first royal decree concludes—and rather runs into the sands—with details of the observance of a commemorative festival in the author's own day, the name Purim being applied to the festival.

1. Nothing has been said of the interval of nearly nine months between the second decree of 8:8f., published on the twenty-third day of the third month and this fateful day, the thirteenth of the twelfth month (already announced at 3:13)—except that there has been a growing fear of the Jews in general (v. 2) and of Mordecai in particular (v. 3). More surprisingly, the narrator appears to know of (or at least, to acknowledge) only *one* royal **command and edict**. This means that whereas the tension in the preceding narrative has culminated in the promulgation of two irreversible but fundamentally contradictory decrees, in the narrative of this chapter only the decree authorising Jewish vengeance on their enemies (cf. 8:13) is taken into account. We may infer that from the Jewish perspective this second decree is the only one that matters, or—perhaps more

appropriately—that this chapter is the work of an author who did not appreciate the irony of the situation as it was left at the end of ch. 8.

It is surprising also that **the enemies of the Jews** should be regarding this as the day when they **hoped to get the mastery** (*šlṭ*) **over them** when in 3:13 it was a question, not of having mastery, but of destroying, annihilating and slaying (*šmd, hrg, 'bd*) all Jews—such destruction to be carried out not simply by their 'enemies' but by the whole populace including the imperial officials. Perhaps we are to think that the second decree has begun to erode the force of the first decree, so that the only citizens of the empire prepared to implement the first decree have classified themselves as 'enemies of the Jews', and authorised mass slaughter has become increasingly unrealistic as the Jewish strength has manifested itself. Alternatively, we may simply say that this narrative is out of harmony with chs. 1–8. Certainly in the question of who has **the mastery** the author shows his hand as a member of a subject race; for him it is all-important that the 'scattered people' (cf. 3:8) should have a powerful advocate at court (v. 4; 10:2f.), should do 'as they pleased' with their enemies (v. 5), and should find 'relief' (vv. 16, 22). This is the reversal of fortunes ('the situation was reversed', *NAB;* **changed,** *RSV*) that every subject longs for; the passive verb does not directly name God as the author of the change, but the coincidences that have brought it about are not to be traced to human devising.

**2.** The Jews gather to **lay hands on** (i.e. to kill, as in 2:21; 3:6; 6:2) their enemies whereas the decree had permitted them to gather and 'defend their lives' (8:11)—which is what the Jews elsewhere in the empire did (v. 16); in other respects this verse follows the wording of the decree very closely. Presumably **such as sought their hurt** are identical with 'any . . . that might attack them' (8:11), but here also there may be a significant variation: 'attack' is a physical act, 'seek the harm' may be solely volitional (cf. Num. 35:23; 1 Sam. 24:9; Ps. 71:13, 24). Either the narrator has no compunction about an aggressive interpretation of the decree (and indeed, if it really is a life and death matter the moral difference between attack and defence is reduced); or else we have in this chapter a narrator with a different perception from that of ch. 8. **no one could make a stand against them:** This is a miraculous state of affairs, since the Jews are envisaged in 3:12f. as expecting to have the force of the imperial army ranged against them. The reason given, that **the fear of them had fallen upon all peoples,** made some kind of sense as an explanation of mass proselytism in 8:17; here, however, it purports to explain why the opponents of the Jews were unable to defend themselves against Jewish attack; it does not carry a great deal of conviction. We must see in **the fear of them** a fear of their God (desacralised, perhaps, as Gerleman says, comparing Exod. 15:15f.).

**3-4.** The imperial decrees had required provincial authorities to massacre the Jews (3:12f.) and allowed the Jews (without official assistance) to defend themselves (8:11). It is clumsy of the narrator to have the authorities disobey the first decree when his purpose would be as well served to have the Jewish resistance entirely responsible (with unspoken divine assistance) for their own outstanding success. It is no explanation that **the fear of Mordecai had fallen upon them**, since Mordecai's function is now to defend the laws of the king rather than simply to assure the survival of his people. This narrative does not read as if there had been an unalterable decree of the Persians and Medes against the Jews. In this note of the co-operation of the imperial officials with the Jewish cause we are reminded of Esther's determination to 'go to the king, though it is against the law' (4:16); though in her case the illegality of the action has attention drawn to it, and we would have expected that, for dramatic reasons, the same would apply here.

**princes . . . satraps . . . governors . . . royal officials:** The order in 8:9 was satraps, governors, princes; there may be a hint that it is the leaders of ethnic groups (**princes**, *śārê hammᵉdînôt*) rather than the Persian officials (**satraps, governors**) who take the lead in assisting the Jews; for the terminology, cf. on 3:12. How they **helped** the Jews is left entirely vague, a narrative weakness.

**5.** The vagueness of this crucial episode further suggests an inferior narrative talent to that responsible for chs. 1-8. It is the dream of the diaspora community that the tables will be turned (*hāpak*, 'changed', v. 1) and that they for a change will be able to do 'as they please' (lit. 'according to their will [*rāṣôn*]'); contrast Ezr. 9:7, 9; Neh. 9:36f. To be able to do as one pleases is in Est. 1:8 a sign of imperial favour; Israel last enjoyed that privilege at the conquest of Canaan, so the diaspora mentality believes (Neh. 9:24) (*rāṣôn* in both passages).

**6.** Though the slaughter is not depicted, its effects are stated in detail. **five hundred** slain **in Susa the capital itself**, viz. the acropolis, must signify immense hostility against the Jews within the Persian bureaucracy, a situation we have been little prepared for in the notes of pro-Jewish sentiment at 3:15; 8:15, 17. In chs. 1-8, indeed, the plot against the Jews has been represented as due wholly to Haman's personal loss of face (though it may be thought that 3:2ff., presented an ambiguous picture of the attitude of the other courtiers).

**7-10.** The **ten sons of Haman**, each with a genuine enough
Persian name (see H. S. Gehman, *JBL* 43 [1924], pp. 327f. [=
Moore, *Studies*, pp. 241f.]), may be presumed to have perpetuated
their father's hostility, all the more so since they have been deprived
of their inheritance (8:1f.); yet no narrative motivation for the
slaughter of them is provided. **they laid no hand on the plunder**:
This thrice repeated assurance (also vv. 15, 16), despite specific
permission for plundering (8:11), may have an ethical motivation,
to cast the slaughter as essentially self-preservation with no intention
of self-aggrandisement (cf. the motivations in Gen. 14:22f.; and the
holy war renunciation of 'banned' goods in Jos. 7; Deut. 20:16ff.;
but contrast the equally acceptable motif of 'spoiling the
Egyptians'—cf. on Ezr. 1:4). More tempting is the possibility that
the Jews' behaviour against the sons of the Agagite (3:1) is
contrasted with that of Saul against Agag the Amalekite (1 Sam. 15);
there the consequences of taking the spoil proved quite disastrous. If
this is the explanation, it is strange that Haman is not here called 'the
Agagite'; can the narrator have missed the point of the (traditional?)
insistence on refusing to take spoil? It does not appear that the point
of contrast between the Saul and the Esther stories lies in the
matter of the devotion of potential spoils to the 'ban' of ceremonial
destruction (as W. McKane, 'A Note on Esther IX and I Samuel
XV', *JTS* 12 [1961], pp. 260-1 [= Moore, *Studies*, pp. 306-7]).

**11-15.** The extension of the decree for a further day seems
unnecessary on narrative grounds and its achievement is the most
awkward piece of narrative in the whole book. Gerleman's claim
that the narrative owes its existence only to the need to explain the
fact of a later two-day festival (vv. 18f.) is attractive. Everything is
contrary to narrative expectation, but without the surprise or irony
that generally signals intentional deviation from dramatic norms.
The king's astonishment upon hearing of the number of the slain
in the acropolis is reasonable enough, as is his extrapolation of
events to the rest of the empire. Why then should he invite a further
request from Esther, who is at the bottom of this massacre of the
king's subjects? And why is the king so desperate to please Esther
when she has not approached him with any request? Why also
does the king take, for the first time in the book, a significant
initiative—and that without any courtly advice? Why does Esther
request an extension of a day (she gives no reason)?

**11. those slain** does not include any Jews. It must be simply that
victory over their enemies makes the loss of their own compatriots
insignificant. It can hardly be envisaged that not a single Jewish life
is lost, though the narrative would allow us to think so. Any mention

of Jewish deaths may of course be unsuitable for the joyful festival
of Purim.

**12.** The formal machinery of 'the king's presence' (cf. 5:1f.;
6:4f.; 8:1, 15) is dispensed with—for what reason is hard to discern.
Here it is almost the quickly rattled Ahasuerus we earlier met in
1:13ff. who must turn this time to his queen for advice for his next
move. Have too many of his courtiers, fêted in 1:5, succumbed to
the Jewish attack? Despite the masterful language (**it shall be
granted you**), is he now effectively at Esther's mercy? Has she, like
her people, at last gained the upper hand?

**13.** Esther's request lacks narrative motivation. The decree
against the Jews applied only to the thirteenth of Adar, and the
decree allowing Jewish self-defence makes sense only against the
background of the first decree. If on the fourteenth the Jews suffer
any illegal attack they need no royal permission to defend themselves; royal permission for Jewish self-defence only became envisaged because there had been royal permission for the extermination
of the Jewish people. But if the author of this chapter reckons only
with one decree, which, far from simply allowing Jews to defend
their lives, gives Jews a free hand to deal with their opponents as
they will (vv. 1, 5), Esther's request is for a boon which will further
Jewish supremacy at the heart of the Persian empire. The king
would like the killing to stop, but he is powerless before the Jewish
'mastery' (*šlṭ*, v. 1)—and has he not himself been an 'enemy of the
Jews' (cf. on 3:10; 7:5)? The queen has it in her power to put a
stop to it, but the moment has not yet come. And as for the public
impalement (cf. on 2:23) of the bodies of the **ten sons of Haman**,
that needs royal permission for the same reason as the planned
impalement of Mordecai by Haman (5:14): it is not an act of private
or racial vengeance but an act of Persian legality.

**16.** The number slaughtered by the Jews holds no hidden moral
problem for the narrator; it is a token only of the vast size of the
Persian empire, the distribution of the Jewish population
throughout **the king's provinces**, and the evident anti-Semitism
infecting the empire. **got relief**: There is no celebration of blood-
letting here; as in vv. 18, 22, it is 'rest' (*nûaḥ*) that is valued (*nôaḥ*
is not to be emended to *niḥôm*, 'avenged themselves', as W.
Rudolph, *VT* 4 [1954], p. 90); 'rest' has been envisaged since the
time of Deuteronomy as an ideal state of affairs (Dt. 3:20; 12:9; cf.
*NIDNTT*, I, pp. 254ff.), and this is the ultimate dream of diaspora
Judaism—to be allowed to live in peace. Its literature shows it not
to crave confrontation but to negotiate for co-operation without
undue compromise. The rest brought about by Esther's successful
intercession with the king has been foreshadowed much earlier by

the 'rest', or holiday, throughout the empire proclaimed by Ahasuerus in celebration of Esther's accession to the throne (2:18).

**17–18.** This is an elaborate, not to say cumbersome, explanation
of the differing practice of celebrating the Jewish survival. **gathered**:
sc. 'to defend their lives' (as in v. 16).

**19.** The custom of celebration on **the fourteenth of Adar** takes
as its aetiology the story of the Jewish escape. This is not to say
that the whole narrative of the present book of Esther was composed
in order to explain an existing custom; it could be that the verse is
a gloss, accounting for a practice observed by country Jews in the
author's own time. The verse raises two difficulties of its own: (i)
Since the custom of **the Jews of the villages** is mentioned, why is
there no mention of the custom of the Jews of the cities? In Dt. 3:5
'villages' are contrasted with fortified cities. (Some codices of LXX
add: 'But those who dwell in the cities keep also the fifteenth of
Adar . . .'; we cannot tell if this preserves an original reading or
was inserted to supply an obvious deficiency.) (ii) This practice
conflicts with Mordecai's instruction in v. 21 that *both* the fourteenth
and the fifteenth are to be observed (vv. 20–22 may of course be
secondary to this verse). **send choice portions**: cf. on Neh. 8:10.

MORDECAI'S LETTER CONCERNING THE CELEBRATION
9:20–28

It is one thing to engage in celebration because the threat of extermination has been lifted; it is another to determine to repeat the
celebration annually. These verses outline three steps (Moore) by
which the deliverance of the Jews came to be commemorated in the
festival of Purim: (i) the letter of Mordecai enjoining observance of
the fourteenth and fifteenth of Adar (vv. 20–22); (ii) the Jews'
undertaking to follow Mordecai's instruction (vv. 23, 27–28); (iii) a
confirmatory letter from Esther and Mordecai (vv. 29–32). Many
believe that vv. 20–32 are an addition to the original book of Esther.
The proposal advanced here, that vv. 1–19 are also an addition, can
be extended by the suggestion that vv. 20–28 are secondary even to
vv. 1–19, in that vv. 20–22 give an alternative view of the matter
of v. 19 and vv. 24–25 recapitulate the story of the main narrative
of 2:1–9:14, in almost the style of a catechism (Bardtke). See further,
D. J. A. Clines, *The Esther Scroll*; for a different view, see B. W.
Jones, 'The So-called Appendix to the Book of Esther', *Semitics* 6
(1978), pp. 36–43.

**20. recorded these things**: probably not a reference to the
preceding narrative but to the letters about to be mentioned. As
distinct from the letter of Mordecai as the prime minister in 8:9 (cf.

3:12), this letter is not directed to the provincial officials but solely to **the Jews**; have we here a mark of a different conception of Mordecai's function from that portrayed in the main narrative? It is a matter of imperial concern, not only of Jewish interest, to know which days are officially public holidays for the Jewish populace (in the 'Passover Papyrus' from Elephantine, it is not the Jewish priests but the Persian governor of Egypt who is the first to be informed of regulations for the Jewish festival; *AP* 21), but here all is told from the point of view of Jewish national customs.

**21.** Resolution of the conflict over the two dates of celebration is secured by arranging that *both* days should be days of holiday. Is there a hint of the Persian principle for the resolution of official conflict (which we have seen in ch. 8), viz. both decrees must stand? Or have we simply the compromise of a Jewish academy bringing into harmony the practices of their co-religionists? In either case, what is implied is that, as soon as Mordecai heard that the fourteenth had seen celebrations throughout the empire whereas the Jews in Susa had not 'had relief' until the fifteenth, he solved the impending disagreement. Verse 19, on the contrary, has suggested that the celebration of the fourteenth had become a practice over many years.

**22. the month**: In agreement with a superficial reading of 3:7, it is the month Adar, and not explicitly the day, that was chosen by Pur, the lot; 3:7, however, though it specifies the month (see 3:13), implies that the day was also chosen by lot. **feasting . . . gladness . . . choice portions . . . gifts**: No religious ceremonies are prescribed; it is represented as a secular festival, in keeping with the explicitly non-religious atmosphere of the narrative. This remains the essential character of the festival in Judaism, the most significant addition to the customs 'enjoined' here being the reading of the roll (*megillâ*) of Esther. The Talmud tractate *Megillah* is in part devoted to questions concerning the correct procedure for that reading.

**23.** It hardly seems necessary to record Jewish agreement to Mordecai's instructions; it is important, however, if the instructions effect a reconciliation of differing established customs. The wording reeks of committee drafting: they agree to 'make customary' (*qibbēl*; cf. Moore) *both* what **they** have decided themselves (which was to differ from one another, **as they had begun**) *and* what **Mordecai** has **written to them** (which was to agree with one another).

**24–25.** This summary of the plot is needless for the narrative of the book as a whole; it finds a place here presumably because it is envisaged as part of the letter of Mordecai (v. 20). Verse 23 has indeed appeared to conclude the notice of Mordecai's letter by expressing Jewish response to it, but it is not unreasonable to present

as the reason for the response material conceived of as belonging to
the letter. In fact, this summary may well have an origin independent even of the secondary material of this chapter; but it functions
as the necessary information which Jews throughout the empire
should know in order to appreciate the full significance of the
festival. From their standpoint, all that has happened is that there
has been a royal decree permitting them to defend themselves
against their enemies (ch. 9 does not seem to acknowledge the earlier
royal decree for the extermination of the Jews); they have defended
themselves successfully and have naturally determined to celebrate
the occasion. What they do not know, and what Mordecai must
therefore tell them, is of the events in Susa that lay behind the
fateful thirteenth of Adar.

**24.** Though the narrator missed the opportunity to mention
Haman's ancestry on the previous occasion he referred to him (see
on vv. 7–10), here, for his final appearance in the narrative, Haman
wears his full symbolic nomenclature: he is **the Agagite**, the inveterate foe of Israel (cf. on 3:1), and now—for the first time—**the
enemy of all the Jews**; previously he has been just 'the enemy of
the Jews' (3:10; 8:1; 9:10, 24). '*All* the Jews' (vv. 20, 30), will
therefore celebrate deliverance from his plot. **to crush and destroy**:
not the usual triple phrase ('to destroy, to slay, and to annihilate',
as in 3:13 and 8:11)—perhaps a further sign of the difference in
authorship between the body of the narrative and this supplement.
There may also be a play on the assonance between 'Haman' (*hāmān*)
and 'to crush them' (*hummām*).

**25. When Esther came before the king**: The Heb. does not
mention Esther, and it is preferable to understand *bᵉḇōʾāh* as 'when
it (*sc.* the plot, Heb. *maḥšāḇâ*) came' (similarly *RV*, *NEB*). This
narrator evidently does not give the same prominence to Esther as
did the narrator of chs. 1–8. The narrative of chs. 1–8 or 1:1–9:19
likewise knows nothing of **orders in writing** that Haman should be
executed; even the decree authorising the impalement of Haman's
sons nine months after Haman's death (9:14) is not explicitly said
to be a written one. These differences do not necessarily presuppose
the existence of a variant story of Esther (as Lebram, *VT* 22 [1972],
pp. 214ff. [= Moore, *Studies*, pp. 211ff.]); they may result from
the crystallisation of the narrative around three poles: Haman's plot,
the king's intervention, and the death of the Jews' enemies (cf.
Bardtke). Alternatively, some have thought that 'with the letter'
('*im-hassēp̄er*) could mean 'despite the letter' originally written in his
name commanding the execution of all Jews (3:12) (so Gerleman,
following Haupt, *AJSL* 24 [1907–8], pp. 170f. [= Moore, *Studies*,
pp. 74f.]); but the difficulty is that the nature of 'the' letter in

question cannot easily be inferred from this compressed account and in any case '*im*, 'with', can hardly mean 'despite' (Neh. 5:18 is no real parallel).

**26.** Why is the festival called **Purim**, 'lots', when in the story only one Pur, 'lot', has been cast (3:7)? In English we say 'cast lots' in the plural, but the plural is relatively rare in Heb. (*gôrāl*, 'lot', is generally singular). It may be because the festival occupies *two* days; the number of the noun *pûr* could have become assimilated to the number of *yāmîm hā'ēleh*, 'these days'. But, although the author of this addition to the story is no master of subtlety, it is hard to resist the possibility that the name Purim is intended by the author to signify the *double* chance that created the story and the festival in celebration of it: the chance that determined disaster for the Jews and the 'chance' that provided for their deliverance, a 'chance' which was in reality a divine providence. See further, for a similar interpretation, A. D. Cohen, ' "*Hu ha-goral*" ["that is, the lot"]: The Religious Significance of Esther', *Judaism* 23 (1974), pp. 87–94 (= Moore, *Studies*, pp. 122–9). Whether such is an historical explanation of the origin of the name Purim is a different matter; see further, Introduction, V.

The celebration of Purim is regarded by the author of this addition as primarily the result of a *community* decision (contrast vv. 29–32). Mordecai's **letter**, by which must be meant the 'letters' of v. 20 and not the book of Esther itself, was indispensable for its information on the background of the attack on the Jews, and carried the authority of the Persian prime minister; but it seems primarily because of what the Jews **had faced in this matter** and because of what **had befallen them** that they collectively **ordained** and **took it upon themselves** to celebrate the events of Purim (v. 27). This would probably be more close to the historical origins of any celebration of relief from imminent disaster, as the narrative of vv. 17f., representing a spontaneous celebration, suggests.

**27–28.** The commemoration of Purim is by this addition to the book transformed into a binding obligation upon all Jews for all times; though the Persians cannot overcome the Jews by force of arms their concept of unalterable law has here (ironically) gained the mastery in Jewish society: the festival will be observed **without fail**, by Jews of all generations and all who may come to call themselves Jews. **all who joined them**: The custom of proselytism (cf. Isa. 56:3, 6) is presupposed by the author of this addition; in the main narrative a different term is used for those who 'declared themselves Jews' (8:17), though they too must be regarded as proselytes. **keep these two days**: As in v. 21, we have a variation from the narrative of 9:1–19, where it appeared that country Jews in the

writer's time kept only the fourteenth and Jews of Susa only the
fifteenth as the Purim festival. The exhaustive formality of the
language may be explained as necessary for the authorisation of a
new festival not prescribed in the Pentateuch.

## ESTHER'S LETTER CONCERNING PURIM
### 9:29–32

This paragraph seems somewhat superfluous, and has the air of an
alternative account of the institution of Purim—in which Esther
rather than Mordecai plays the chief part. It is not necessary to
follow J. C. H. Lebram in distinguishing in the book as a whole
between an 'Esther' source (as in 7:1–4) and a 'Mordecai' source
(as in 7:7–10) to make the distinction here (see his 'Purimfest und
Estherbuch', *VT* 22 [1972], pp. 208–22 [= Moore, *Studies*, pp.
205–19]; similarly Bardtke, pp. 248–52). Secondary—or even
tertiary—though this paragraph may be, it has itself undergone
several redactional alterations (e.g. the references to Mordecai,
which seem not to be original, and the description of this as the
'second' letter about Purim in v. 29). On the complex process which
has produced this most problematic passage in the whole book,
see S. E. Loewenstamm, 'Esther 9:29–32: The Genesis of a Late
Addition', *HUCA* 42 (1971), pp. 117–24 [= Moore, *Studies*, pp.
227–34]).

**29.** Esther's authority and the consequent obligatoriness of the
observance are heavily stressed. She is **Queen** Esther (as contrasted
with Mordecai who is simply **the Jew**). She is named (unlike
Mordecai) with her patronymic as **daughter of Abihail** (is the
meaning of Abihail, 'my father is strength', meant to carry some
resonance? Certainly it links her back into the Jewish people despite
her status as a *Persian* queen). She **gave full written authority,** or
'wrote the whole valid deed' (Loewenstamm, *HUCA* 42 [1971], pp.
119f. [= Moore, *Studies*, pp. 229f.]), or, as conventionally translated, 'with all authority' (for a recent defence of this view, see
Berg, *Esther*, p. 54 n. 49)—whether to the Jewish people directly or
'to Mordecai' in the first place (as Brockington and *NEB*, emending
*ûmordᵒḵay* to *lᵉmordᵒḵay*). The verb 'wrote' (*wattiḵtôḇ*) is in the
feminine singular, which makes it likely that reference to Mordecai
is a secondary addition (on the grammatical point, cf. on Neh. 8:9).
Her letter which is itself **the second letter about Purim** can hardly
have been written **confirming** itself. Rather than delete 'this second'
(*hazzōʾṯ haššēnîṯ*) as a corruption (W. Rudolph, *VT* 4 [1954], p. 90),
or as a gloss (Gerleman), we could translate 'Esther wrote with
full authority this second letter about Purim in order to make its

observance obligatory' (though this reading is not in accord with the Masoretic punctuation).

**30. Letters were sent**: The Heb. has 'and he sent', which should probably be regarded as an impersonal verb ('and one sent', 'and there were sent'). Appropriately to Esther's royal status, her letter is sent not simply **to all the Jews** who were in all the provinces of the king (as v. 20), but equally **to the hundred and twenty-seven provinces'**; the celebration of Purim will be a matter of concern for imperial authorities everywhere (cf. on v. 20). **words of peace and truth**: probably not a reference to the tone of the letter as 'neither hostile nor imperious' (Moore), nor the initial salutations of the letter, viz. 'greetings of peace and truth' (Bardtke; Gordis, *JBL* 95 [1976], pp. 57f. [= Moore, *Studies*, pp. 422f.]). The letter itself is not in fact reported, but only a brief description of its contents; it would be strange to report only its opening words, and in any case 'truth' is not attested as part of a salutation formula. Comparison with 10:3, where Mordecai speaks 'peace' (*šālôm*) to his people in the sense of 'pleasantly', suggests rather that Esther's letter was pleasant but authoritative (cf. Gerleman). A quite different interpretation by *NAB* views the whole verse as referring to Mordecai's earlier letter as 'documents of peace and security'.

**31.** Here, unlike v. 29, it is **Queen Esther** that appears to be a secondary insertion, since the clause must refer to *Mordecai's* letter earlier recounted (vv. 20ff.). Esther's letter makes mention implicitly of the question of the correct dates for the observance of Purim (**at their appointed seasons**), but, more importantly, goes beyond Mordecai's letter in linking the celebration of Purim with the cycle of **fasts and their lamenting**. This will mean at least that, though Purim is a joyful festival at which mourning rites are out of place, 'the traditional fasting and lamentations serve to remind Israel of the background of Purim and provide the proper context for the season of joy' (B. S. Childs, *Introduction to the Old Testament as Scripture*, [1979] p. 604). But it is probable also that the practice of fasting prior to Purim is envisaged as already developed by the Jewish community (**as they had laid down for themselves**) and needing not Esther's instituting but her blessing. We know for certain that at least since the ninth century AD the thirteenth of Adar (the day chosen by Haman for the pogrom) has been observed as a fast. This fasting will recall 4:3 (cf. v. 16), where there was national fasting 'wherever the king's command and his decree came' for the extermination of the Jews; relief from that prior occasion of fasting through the promulgation of another royal decree does not do away with the memory of national danger—which remains a fact of Jewish existence. Esther's letter enshrines the principle that 'he

who forgets the past is doomed to repeat it' (Santayana). The juxtaposition of a solemn ritual and a riotous festival at which revellers
are exhorted by the Talmud to 'drink wine until you can no longer
distinguish between "Blessed be Mordecai" and "Cursed be
Haman"' (TB *Meg.* 7b) picks up the ambivalence of feasting and
fasting in ch. 4, and of feasting and danger in ch. 1 and ch. 7 (cf.
also 3:15*b*). See also Berg, pp. 37ff.

**32.** This summary of the significance of Esther's letter as set
forth in vv. 29–31 could well serve as a conclusion to the whole
book. Esther's **command** (*ma'ᵃmar*) is identical with her letter. The
only time previously in the book when anyone transgressed a royal
*ma'ᵃmar* is at 1:15 where Vashti's disobedience to the king brought
about her expulsion from the court; may the implication be similar
here? The decree in the form of a letter was **recorded in writing**
(lit. 'written in the book'), not (as some think) in *this* book of Esther
but in some official record like 'the Book of the Chronicles' (2:23;
6:1; 10:2). The emphasis upon writing (vv. 26, 27, 32) does suggest
that the festival of Purim is to be 'regulated by the carefully recorded
events of the oppression and deliverance' (B. S. Childs, *Introduction
to the Old Testament as Scripture*, p. 604); but equally it is being
stressed that regulation of the Jewish cult is a proper concern of
Persian officialdom.

### A FOOTNOTE ABOUT MORDECAI

### 10:1–3

This paragraph, like 9:20–28 and 9:29–32, is strictly unnecessary
for the purposes of the narrative, and may well be yet another
secondary addition. The style is very stilted with a conventional
formula referring to the record of the 'acts of Mordecai'; we may
presume that some editor was unhappy with the prominence given
to Esther by a book ending with 9:32, and decided to bring Mordecai
back into the limelight for the closing verses. What we have here
results from the same tendency as caused Purim to be known, at
least in the first century BC, as 'Mordecai's day' (2 Mac. 15:36). The
opposite tendency, to see Esther as the primary actor, obviously
prevailed, since the book is known by her name.

Secondary though these verses may be, they nevertheless link
well with themes of the preceding narrative, so much so that D.
Daube could argue that they belonged to the original narrative ('The
Last Chapter of Esther', *JQR* 37 [1946f.], pp. 139–47).

**1.** The book has begun with a depiction of Ahasuerus' imperial
power, and will conclude on the same note, with a reference to his
authority over **the land and the coastlands** (lit. 'islands') **of the**

**sea**. The latter phrase is found elsewhere in Isa. 11:11 and 24:15, where it indicates the furthest extent of the dispersion of Israel; perhaps the royal authority is viewed here primarily as encompassing the whole Jewish people 'scattered abroad and dispersed among all the peoples in all the provinces' (3:8). But the author may have particularly in mind the westernmost reaches of the Persian empire, viz. the coasts of Asia Minor and the islands of the Aegean, as far, as Herodotus puts it, as 'the islands and the inhabitants of Europe as far as Thessaly' (3.96).

Why should Ahasuerus be said here to lay **tribute** on his empire? D. Daube made the ingenious suggestion that this was Mordecai's plan for raising the 10,000 talents (3:9) lost by the failure of Haman's plan against the Jews. But 3:9ff., if it does not rather depict a polite refusal of the money, assumes that Haman would have already paid the money in exchange for permission to issue the decree, and in any case the king had already confiscated Haman's property (8:1). More probably the power to exact taxes is simply indicative of Ahasuerus' authority and resultant wealth, a theme with which the book opened (1:1, 4: 'reigned', 'showed the riches of his royal glory'). If *mas*, 'tribute', here means not a money-tax, but a 'forced labour', as it does elsewhere, the author may be thinking of Solomon's use of the *mas* as a symbol of his power (1 Kg. 4:6; 5:13; 9:15, 21). See further, I. Mendelsohn, *Slavery in the Ancient Near East;* T. N. D. Mettinger, *Solomonic State Officials*, pp. 128ff.; J. Harmatta, 'Das Problem der Sklaverei im altpersichen Reich', *Neue Beiträge zur Geschichte des Alten Welt I* (1964), pp. 3–11.

**2.** A new element has entered the depiction of Ahasuerus' **power and might** since it was first portrayed in ch. 1: it is now not the might possessed by Ahasuerus alone, but might that is delegated to Mordecai, who as grand vizier is 'the real ruler of the Persian empire' (Paton). We have the impression that the king's power is mentioned here primarily to invest Mordecai with the greatest possible dignity. **full**, or 'exact', **account**: the same word (*pārāšat*) as in 4:7, where the 'exact' sum of money promised by Haman is reported to Esther; G. R. Driver is probably correct in seeing this as a 'decree of greatness', i.e. a 'patent of nobility' (*VT* 4 [1954], pp. 237f. [= Moore, *Studies*, pp. 399f.]).

**the Book of the Chronicles of the kings of Media and Persia** is reminiscent of the sources referred to in Kings and Chronicles (e.g. 'the book of the acts of Solomon', 1 Kg. 11:41); it may be that our author has no personal knowledge of such a book and its contents but very reasonably assumes that Persian kings must be just as particular as Israelite kings in recording events of their reign and the official titles of their leading courtiers (such as **the full account**

of the high honour of Mordecai); the formula **are they not written in . . .** is clearly an imitation from earlier Biblical historiography. No doubt the same book as is referred to in 2:23 as 'the book of the acts of the days' and in 6:1 as 'the book of memorable deeds, the acts of the days' is in mind.

**3.** Mordecai's position as **next in rank** to the king is designedly reminiscent of Joseph in the second chariot of Egypt (Gen. 41:43) and perhaps also of Jonathan as 'second' to David (1 Sam. 23:17). The title 'the second' is attested as a standard Persian term (cf. H. Volkmann, 'Der Zweite nach dem König', *Philologus* 92 [1937f.], pp. 285–316). But mere achievement of high office by Mordecai **the Jew** is not sufficient explanation for the regard in which his people held him; even what he **had done** for his nation is not enough: it is what he continued to do for them (**sought** and **spoke** are present participles in the Heb.). Mordecai, who has entered the story as a person of little power (he is perhaps a minor official; cf. on 2:5–6), a Jew, an exile, a foster-father whose child is taken into the royal harem (2:5–8), concludes the story as a figure who wields Persian authority in support of his kinsmen. To have such a friend at court, like that Pethahiah b. Meshezabel who was 'at the king's hand in all matters concerning the people' (Neh. 11:24), must have been the dream of every Jew whether of Palestine or of the diaspora. The closing words of the book admirably express 'both the possibility of a rewarding and creative life in a foreign court and in the same moment of the possibility of service and devoted loyalty to one's people and religious identity' (W. L. Humphreys, *JBL* 92 [1973], p. 216).

# INDEX OF AUTHORS

Abel, F.-M., 220, 221
Ackroyd, P. R., 12, 25, 43, 64, 65, 75, 117, 122, 188, 302
Aharoni, Y., 50, 150, 220
Ahituv, S., 54
Ahlemann, F., 6, 7, 18, 187
Albrektson, B., 87
Albright, W. F., 6, 10, 12, 13, 20, 22, 44, 221, 226, 289
Allrik, H. L., 45, 48
Alt, A., 44, 52, 65, 171, 220
Andersen, F. I., 39, 48, 67, 84
Anderson, B. W., 256
Andrews, D. K., 37
Avigad, N., 146
Avi-Yonah, M., 119, 146, 150, 202, 220, 233

Badè, W. F., 172
Bardtke, H., 254, 255, 266, 267, 270, 278, 279, 281, 283, 286, 288, 298, 315, 316, 325, 327, 329, 330
Barnett, R. D., 308
Baron, S. W., 168
Barth, C., 160
Bartlett, J. R., 57
Batten, L. W., 5, 21, 46, 81, 137, 171, 186
Baynes, N. H., 68
Beebe, H. K., 188
Bentzen, A., 10
Berg, S. B., 267, 269, 274, 281, 289, 329, 331
Bewer, J. A., 42, 60, 176
Bickerman, E., 34, 36, 37, 39, 79, 92
Billerbeck, P., 185
Bimson, J. J., 51
Blenkinsopp, J., 56
Boecker, H. J., 148
Boer, P. A. H. de, 142
Bottéro, J., 42, 169

Bowman, R. A., 8, 11, 16, 19, 20, 21, 66, 79, 90, 91, 131, 182, 239
Brandenstein, W., 105
Braun, R. L., 26
Bright, J., 13, 20, 22, 44, 63, 103, 160, 176, 225
Brockington, L. H., 50, 70, 137, 168, 294, 309, 312, 329
Brongers, H. A., 302
Brown, J. P., 68
Browne, L. E., 8, 110
Bruce, F. F., 13, 23
Brunet, A.-M., 26, 27
Burrows, M., 149
Buss, M. J., 56

Callaway, J. A., 51
Cameron, G. G., 77, 81, 90, 275, 286
Caquot, A., 28
Cazelles, H., 20, 21, 105, 266
Charles, R. H., 66
Cheyne, T. K., 23
Childs, B. S., 256, 262, 330, 331
Christensen, A., 292
Clines, D. J. A., 10, 35, 81, 183, 204, 252, 267, 319, 320, 325
Coats, G. W., 38
Cody, A., 54, 185
Coggins, R. J., 59, 73, 75, 81
Cohen, A. D., 264, 328
Cohen, B., 167
Cook, H. J., 252
Corkill, N. L., 154
Cosquin, E., 266, 286
Crenshaw, J. L., 270
Cross, F. M., 3, 9, 17, 18, 24, 128, 145, 220, 225, 248

da Deliceto, G., 137
Dahood, M., 71
Dalman, G., 308
d'Alviella, G., 230

Danby, H., 58
Daube, D., 331, 332
Delekat, L., 175
de Ward, E. F., 190
Dieulafoy, M. A., 285
Dommershausen, W., 267, 277, 308, 310
Driver, G. R., 38, 40, 80, 178, 244, 305, 332
Duchesne-Guillemin, J., 278, 279
Dunand, R., 20, 88
Dupont-Sommer, A., 104

Eichrodt, W., 29, 229
Eilers, W., 79
Eissfeldt, O., 5, 7, 8, 21, 45, 103, 126, 182, 255, 256, 280
Eliade, M., 230
Ellenbogen, M., 42
Ellis, R. S., 88, 123, 159
Emerton, J. A., 21, 22, 23, 24, 225
Erbt, W., 5, 7
Ewald, H., 41

Falk, Z. W., 106
Feigin, S. I., 287
Fensham, F. C., 196
Fernández, A., 124
Finkel, J., 254
Fitzmyer, J. A., 86
Flowers, H. J., 295
Fohrer, G., 5, 8, 13, 76, 94, 126
Forman, W., 308
Forster, W., 142
Fraine, J. de, 17
Freedman, D. N., 25
Frost, S. B., 70
Frye, R. M., 103
Fustel de Coulanges, N., 142

Gadd, C. J., 37
Galling, K., 21, 36, 42, 44, 60, 61, 65, 79, 85, 88, 91
Gan, M., 267
Gaster, T. H., 265
Gehman, H. S., 261, 278, 279, 300, 323
Gelin, A., 11

Gelston, A., 67
Gerleman, G., 264, 267, 276, 278, 283, 291, 292, 297, 299, 308, 313, 317, 322, 323, 327, 329, 330
Gertner, M., 185
Ghirshman, R., 275, 277
Gilkey, C. W., 73
Ginsberg, H. L., 39, 311
Glueck, M., 70
Godley, A. D., 256
Goldingay, J., 25
Goldman, M. D., 39
Gordis, R., 177, 256, 257, 258, 260, 268, 271, 281, 286, 311, 317, 330
Granild, S., 10
Gray, J., 49, 144
Grintz, J. M., 51
Grohman, E. D., 51
Grosheide, H. H., 17

Haller, M., 5, 281
Hallevy, R., 65
Hallock, R. T., 90
Haran, M., 56, 239, 241
Harmatta, J., 332
Harrison, R. K., 10
Hasel, G. F., 123, 299
Haupt, P., 277, 278, 327
Held, M., 164
Heltzer, M., 276
Herzfeld, E., 79
Hillers, D. R., 299
Hinz, W., 36
Hölscher, G., 44
Holladay, W. L., 139
Hoonacker, A. van, 101
Horn, S. H., 286
Hoschander, J., 256, 258, 260
Hruby, K., 184
Humbert, P., 120
Humphreys, W. L., 267, 270, 271, 333

Imschoot, P. van, 195
In der Smitten, W. T., 6, 10, 122, 130

Jacoby, F., 142, 143
Janssen, E., 63
Japhet, S., 10
Jastrow, M., 121
Jellicoe, S., 23
Jensen, P., 265, 286
Jepsen, A., 17
Jeremias, J., 58
Johnson, A. R., 70
Johnson, M. D., 58
Jones, B. W., 325
Jones, D. R., 63
Joüon, P., 129
Junker, H., 283

Kahan, A., 172
Kapelrud, A. S., 6, 68, 122
Katzenstein, H. J., 99
Kaupel, H., 124
Kegel, M., 187
Kellermann, U., 5, 6, 7, 14, 17,
    19, 20, 24, 45, 64, 85, 102, 103,
    140, 145, 148, 149, 179, 182,
    189, 212, 219, 224, 240
Kent, R. G., 36, 68, 80, 84, 94,
    102, 174, 276
Kenyon, K., 145, 146, 147, 150,
    155, 156, 159, 179, 230
Kitchen, K. A., 13, 171
Klein, R. W., 46
Koehler, L., 57
König, F. S., 276, 277
Kopf, L., 168
Kraeling, E. G., 78, 89, 144
Kugler, F. X., 95, 101
Kutsch, E., 299

Labuschagne, C. J., 193
Landau, Y. H., 35
Larsson, G., 35
Lebram, J. C. H., 266, 327, 329
Lefèvre, A., 22
Legrain, L., 37
Legrand, Ph.-E., 258
Lehmann, M. R., 127
Levin, S., 185
Levine, B. A., 56
Lewis, C. S., 160

Lewy, J., 263, 265
Liebermann, S., 239
Liebreich, L. J., 193
Lipiński, E., 190
Livingston, D., 51
Loader, J. A., 269, 270, 302
Loewe, R., 171
Loewenstamm, S. E., 253, 329
Lohfink, N., 121
Loretz, O., 292
Lusseau, H., 6, 23

McCown, J. J., 145
McDaniel, T. F., 141
McKane, W., 323
Maier, J., 59
Malamat, A., 50, 58, 70, 79, 128,
    129
Martin, R. A., 253
Mayrhofer, M., 105
Mazar, B., 48, 145, 229
Meinhold, A., 267
Mendelsohn, I., 153, 287, 332
Mettinger, T. N. D., 297, 332
Meyer, E., 18, 102, 182
Mezzacasa, F., 188
Michaud, H., 124
Milgrom, J., 126
Milik, J., 202
Millard, A. R., 70, 261, 279, 293
Miller, C. H., 269
Moor, J. C. de, 75
Moore, C. A., 252, 253, 260, 270,
    276, 278, 279, 281, 283, 288,
    292, 307, 308, 325, 326, 330
Moran, W. L., 70
Morgenstern, J., 76, 188
Moscati, S., 243
Mosis, R., 27
Motyer, J. A., 59
Mowinckel, S., 4, 22, 45, 103, 183
Myers, J. M., 11, 23, 39, 55, 71,
    80, 94, 124, 137, 140, 162, 168,
    256

Naumann, R., 86
Newsome, J. D., 27
Nicholson, E. W., 75

Nober, P., 105, 106
Noordtzij, A., 27
North, R., 25, 26, 118, 130, 173, 174, 190
Noth, M., 6, 8, 13, 17, 36, 45, 46, 47, 51, 57, 63, 109, 125, 131, 287
Nyberg, H. S., 80

Oesterley, W. O. E., 6, 182
Olmstead, A. T., 84, 105, 141, 164, 167, 169, 275
Oppenheim, A. L., 276
Orr, A., 35

Paton, L. B., 253, 255, 256, 257, 260, 261, 265, 275, 279, 281, 283, 285, 288, 290, 291, 294, 298, 303, 304, 317, 332
Pavlovský, V., 10, 20, 23, 78, 113
Payne, D. F., 25
Pelaia, M. B., 41
Pelzl, B., 112
Petersen, D. L., 69
Pfeiffer, R. H., 6, 7, 26
Pillet, M., 277
Ploeg, J. van der, 147
Plöger, O., 24, 28, 122, 192
Pohlmann, K.-F., 3
Pope, M. H., 127, 129, 319
Porten, B., 17, 18, 22, 37, 73, 76, 78, 85, 91, 104, 120, 127, 130, 133, 136, 166, 169, 207, 212, 216, 247
Porter, J. R., 18, 108
Purvis, J. D., 14

Rabin, C., 42
Rabinowitz, I., 148
Rad, G. von, 5, 27, 145, 182, 192
Radday, Y. T., 269
Rahlfs, A., 107
Rainey, A. F., 17, 21, 77, 79, 84
Rast, W. E., 24
Rehm, M., 17
Riessler, P., 289
Rinaldi, G., 102
Ringgren, H., 265, 267, 318

Ritter, H. W., 279
Robertson, E., 59
Robinson, T. H., 6
Rose, M., 57
Rosenthal, F., 77
Rosenthal, L. A., 267, 289
Rost, L., 36, 92
Rowley, H. H., 13, 17, 18, 20, 21, 145
Rudolph, W., 5, 6, 7, 11, 12, 13, 19, 20, 23, 25, 28, 42, 43, 44, 45, 46, 52, 55, 60, 61, 63, 74, 76, 80, 82, 102, 108, 149, 162, 163, 180, 182, 186, 187, 191, 193, 199, 200, 201, 215, 226, 229, 231, 238, 291, 324, 329
Rüger, H.-P., 292
Rundgren, F., 93, 106
Ryle, H. E., 41

Sachsen-Meiringen, F. von, 294
Saley, R. J., 24, 136
Santayana, G., 331
Sasson, J., 301
Saydon, P.-P., 11
Schaeder, H. H., 99, 102, 182
Scheftelowitz, J., 300
Schiemann, R., 173
Schildenberger, J. B., 290
Schmidt, E. F., 90
Schneider, H., 8, 46, 82, 132, 163
Sellin, E., 5
Selms, A. van, 17, 19, 20
Semler, J. S., 256
Simons, J., 51, 52, 155
Skinner, J., 129
Smith, S., 80, 86
Snaith, N. H., 11, 21, 70, 124
Spanier, A., 302
Speiser, E. A., 56, 123
Steck, O. H., 197
Stiehl, R., 278
Stinespring, W. F., 27
Strange, J. F., 292
Striedl, H., 269, 308
Swete, H. B., 2

Tallqvist, K. L., 41

Talmon, S., 17, 18, 75, 170, 219, 270, 271
Thiele, E. R., 137
Thompson, R. J., 209
Thomson, H. C., 86, 175
Torrey, C. C., 5, 6, 7, 8, 11, 44, 92, 254
Tromp, N., 42
Tuland, C. G., 88, 233

Ungnad, A., 286
Ussishkin, D., 155

Van Beek, G. W., 239
Van Seters, J., 287
Vaux, R. de, 36, 40, 48, 56, 75, 90, 94, 105, 110, 166, 183, 209, 229
Vermes, G., 237
Vogelstein, M., 296
Volkmann, H., 333
Vos, C. J., 183
Vriezen, T. C., 29, 57, 91

Wehr, H., 292
Weiden, W. A. van der, 237
Weidner, E. F., 41, 140, 279, 289, 312
Weill, R., 155

Weinberg, J. P., 40
Weingreen, J., 206
Weiser, A., 12, 188
Wellhausen, J., 8, 23, 67, 103, 182
Wenham, G. J., 285
Whitley, C. F., 35
Wildeboer, G., 299
Williamson, H. G. M., 3, 10, 27, 39, 202
Wilson, R. D., 34, 36, 226
Winter, P., 202
Wiseman, D. J., 35, 40, 113
Witton Davies, T., 247, 278, 288
Wolf, C. U., 128
Wright, G. E., 88, 220
Wright, G. R. H., 91
Wright, J. S., 10, 17, 21, 88, 258
Würthwein, E., 75

Yahuda, A. S., 287
Yamauchi, E. M., 275
Yaure, L., 237
Yeivin, S., 155

Zevit, Z., 145
Zimmern, H., 140, 265

# GENERAL INDEX

Abar-nahara, *see* Beyond the River
adoption, 287
Aeschylus, 274
Agagite, 293, 323
Ahasuerus, *see* Xerxes I
Amestris, 258–9
anger, 167, 292, 313
Antiochus III, 257
*Aramaic Documents* (ed. G. R. Driver), 78, 81, 82, 87, 106, 143, 282, 286
*Aramaic Papyri* (ed. A. E. Cowley), 8, 13, 18, 36, 37, 45, 49, 58, 78, 79, 81, 85, 86, 87, 89, 91, 93, 127, 128, 133, 144, 145, 151, 168, 174, 201, 207, 219, 238, 240, 282
archives, 81, 90
Artaxerxes I, 12, 15–16, 77, 136
Artaxerxes II, 24, 136
Ashurbanipal, 79
Athanasius, 255
Athenaeus, 277
Augustine, 255

Babylon, 89
*baksheesh*, 296
ban, 129
banquet, 275–8, 304, 311
Barrakab, 94
Benjamin, towns of, 221–2
Beyond the River, 46, 77, 79, 84, 143, 275
Booths, Festival of, 186–8

Cambyses, 240
Carthage, council of, 255
census, 177–9
Chronicles, 307, 332
Cicero, 257
circumambulation, 230
city-building, 142
Cornelius Nepos, 301

covenant, 126, 200
Ctesias, 142, 258, 276, 292
cubit, 91
Cyrus II (the Great), 14, 34–9

daric, 61
Darius I, 15, 258
Darius II, 82
David, 26–9
debt, 165–70
dedication, 95, 227–33
defence, 163–4
Diodorus Siculus, 144, 292, 293

Ecbatana, 90
edicts, 36, 90–4, 101–6, 297, 317, 320
Ephiphanius, 255
Esarhaddon, 73, 75
eunuch, 140, 279, 292
Eusebius, 2
Ezra memoirs, 6–8, 106

family, extended, 39, 108, 130
fasting, 111, 121, 302, 330
father's house, *see* family, extended
first fruits, 208
foreigners, 189, 236–8; *see also* marriage
foundations, 69, 71, 80, 88

generation, 13
Geshem, 147–8, 174
God, 30–31, 94, 98, 186, 268–71, 302

Haggai, 83
harem, 285, 288–90, 312
Hebrew (language), 247
Herodotus, 78, 86, 91, 94, 97, 103, 104, 142, 164, 257, 258, 259, 260, 261, 274, 275, 276, 277,

278, 280, 281, 289, 292, 293,
295, 296, 298, 299, 301, 304,
306, 307, 312, 314, 318, 332
high priests, 99, 224–5
Hilary, 255
Hippo, council of, 255
holiness, 111, 112, 113
Horace, 277

impalement, 94, 292, 306, 313
incense, 239
interpretation, Biblical, 204–11

Jerome, 2
Jerusalem, area, 179
Jerusalem, population, 211–2
John Hyrcanus, 143
Josephus, 35, 37, 104, 121, 143,
151, 164, 176, 206, 207, 212,
225, 248, 278, 281, 300, 313, 314
Judah, towns of, 50–1, 220–1

lament, 162, 168, 299, 330
law, Jewish, 181–6, 204
law, Persian, 81–2, 282, 296, 301,
303, 315–7, 328
laymen, 48–53, 68, 203–4, 213–5
Lebanon, 68, 143
legitimacy, 25–6, 58
letters, 78, 174, 325–31
Levites, 54–6, 109, 184–5, 202–3,
217, 224, 226–7, 228–9, 231–2,
234–5, 241–2
Livy, 313
Luther, M., 4, 255

Macrobius, 278
magi, 280
marginal notes, 42, 43, 102, 291
marriage, 116–8, 205, 245–8
Melito, 2, 255
messianism, 27–8, 85
mina, 61
'misdirected speech', 307
Mithridates VI Pontus, 257
money, 171, 296
mourning, 120–1, 137, 190, 299,
309

music, 70, 230

Nebuchadrezzar, 40, 87
Nehemiah memoirs, 4–5, 136
Nethinim, 56
new year's day, 183
'novel', 256–7
numbers, 41–2, 45, 60

oath, 127, 247
Origen, 2

'palaver', 128
Passover, 96
penitence, 189–99
Pentateuch, 100, 182
'people(s) of the land', 75, 119, 318
Philo, 237
phratry, 48, 287
Plutarch, 278, 288, 308
Polo, Marco, 286
post, Persian, 298, 316–7
prayer, 121–5, 137–40, 142, 160–1,
174, 192–9
priests, 53–4, 108, 201–2, 215–6,
223–6, 231, 234–5
'prime produce', 209, 210
protest, see lament
provinces, 275, 316
purification, 229–30, 238–40
Purim, 263–6, 295, 325–31

Quintus Curtius, 313

retribution, 122–4
Rhabanus Maurus, 255

sabbath, 95, 205–6, 242–5
sabbatical year, 206
sacrifice, 63, 66–7, 91, 93, 131,
207–8, 233
salt, 80–1, 104
Samarians, 72–76, 158–65
Samaritans, 25
Sanballat, 144, 159
Sargon, 73
satrapies, 259
scribe, 78, 85, 99, 297

scroll, 90
Shakespeare, W., 307
shame, 122
Sheshbazzar, 40–1, 88–9
slavery, 56, 167
'Solomon's servants', 57
Strabo, 109, 277
Susa, 137, 275
synergism, 271
synoecism, 179, 211–2

Tattenai, 84–5
taxation, 105, 167, 170, 207, 290, 332
temple, 29, 37, 68–72, 83–4, 88, 91, 175
temple vessels, 42, 112–3
Thucydides, 307
tithes, 209, 241–2

Tobiah, 145, 177, 238–40

Unleavened Bread, 97
Urim and Thummim, 59

walls, 80, 86, 92, 124, 136, 149–58, 159, 176, 230–3
wisdom, 270
worship, 63–7, 69–71, 96–7, 181–6, 233

Xenophon, 89, 97, 103, 140, 275, 277, 281, 292, 295, 298, 307

Xerxes I, 76, 258, 260–1, 274–5

Zechariah, 83
Zerubbabel, 64–5, 84, 89
Zoroastrianism, 36